THE GENESIS OF NOTO

An Eighteenth-Century Sicilian City

Stephen Tobriner

THE GENESIS OF NOTO

An Eighteenth-Century Sicilian City

STEPHEN TOBRINER

A. Zwemmer Ltd

Published by A. Zwemmer Ltd, 26 Litchfield Street, London WC2

Designed by Charlton/Szyszkowski
Printed in Great Britain by BAS Printers Limited,
Over Wallop, Hampshire

British Library Cataloguing in Publication Data
Tobriner, Stephen
The Genesis of Noto—(Studies in Architecture; vol. 21).
1. Architecture, Baroque—Italy—Noto
2. Noto, Italy—Buildings
I. Title II. Series
720'.9458'14 NA1121.N67

ISBN 0-302-00543-9

Contents

	Acknowledgements	page 9
	Introduction	11
	Abbreviations	15
	List of Illustrations	16
	List of Figures	18
	List of Maps	18
Part I	**Politics and Planning of Urban Recovery**	
Chapter 1	Noto Antica on the Eve of the Disaster	20
Chapter 2	Disaster and a Decision: A New Site for Noto	25
	The Viceregal Government faces the Disaster	27
	Home Rule in Noto after the Earthquake	28
	The Viceregal Government intervenes	28
	An Indictment of Medieval Cities	29
	The Abandonment of Noto Antica	31
	Criteria for Selection of a New Site	32
	Sites Selected for New Noto	33
	The Chosen Site: The Pianazzo on the Feudo of the Meti	36
	Spanish Policies and the Selection	40
Chapter 3	Disenchantment and Dissent: the New City challenged	43
	A Forced Move	43
	Ad Hoc Planning on the Slope of the Meti	44
	Unhealthy Conditions and Plague on the Slope of the Meti	45
	Transfer of the Lowermost Institutions to the Summit	46
	The City grows on the Slope	46
	Dissension after Five Years on the Site: A Vote to settle or abandon the Meti	47
	The Upper-Class Position	48
	The Lower-Class Position	49
	Further Manoeuvres support Return to Noto Antica	49
	The Opposition is Heard	50
	A Compromise: Two Cities	51
	The Giudice Ruling: An End to Disagreement	51
Part II	**The Growth of Eighteenth-Century Noto**	
Chapter 4	An Uncertain Genesis: A Plan for New Noto	54
	Reconstructed History of Noto's Plan: The Early Stages	54
	S. Nicolò—SS. Crocifisso Axis	56
	The Existence of Two Grids	56
	Two Grids indicate Two Separate Settlements	57
	The Plan *circa* 1712	58
	Genesis of the Plan	60
	The New City in 1712	65

Chapter 5 An Eighteenth-Century City: Noto in the 1750s 66
Evidence for Reconstructing Noto *circa* 1750 66
Noto: An Open City 71
Noto's Roads and Boundaries 72
Noto's Dual Internal Organization 73
Street Names 75
The Corso Sequence 76
The Corso: The Beginning 79
Piano of S. Francesco 81
The Corso continues 86
The Main Piazza 87
The Corso between the Main Piazza and Piazza S. Domenico 93
Piazza S. Domenico 94
The Corso ends 97
The Corso and the Open Spaces as Outdoor Rooms 97
The Summit 100
Influences on the Plan of Noto and its Position in European Urbanism 102

Part III Architecture and the Eighteenth-Century City

Chapter 6 Building Types and Life in Eighteenth-Century Noto 110
Religious Architecture and the City 110
Plans of Religious Houses and Churches 113
Upper- and Middle-Class Housing 114
Netinese Palaces 117
Lower-Class Houses 119
Social Status in Building: Differentiating Huts from Palaces 122
An Emphasis on Exteriors 123
Chapter 7 A Netinese Style 124
Orders on Palaces and Religious Houses 124
Ornamental Motifs and Conservative Façades 125
Noto's Church Façades 131
A Fusion of Styles 132
One Building—Several Architects 137
The Appearance of Stylistic Unity 140

Part IV The Eighteenth-Century Architects

Chapter 8 Rosario Gagliardi (1698?–1761?) 142
Gagliardi Rediscovered 143
Gagliardi's Treatise 144
Gagliardi in Noto 152
S. Maria dell'Arco 153
The Monastery of S. Chiara and its Church 159
The Church of the Convent of S. Domenico 164
Gagliardi Fragments: SS. Crocifisso and S. Nicolò 168
Gagliardi and the Belfry Façades of SS. Salvatore and S. Carlo 169
Rosario Gagliardi the Architect 170
Chapter 9 Sinatra and Labisi: Interpreters of an Idiom 172
Vincenzo Sinatra (active 1730–67) 172
Noto's City Hall 173
An Elusive Personality 179

Sinatra defined by the House of the Crociferi Fathers 180
Sinatra's Style 181
Paolo Labisi (1720?–1798?) 181
Labisi begins the House of the Crociferi Fathers 184
S. Camillo, Church of the Crociferi Fathers, and the High Baroque 190
Influence of Christian Wolff on the Design of S. Camillo and the House of the Crociferi Fathers 191
Problems with the House of the Crociferi Fathers 195
Labisi's Treatise 196
S. Agata: More Frustration for Labisi 197
Labisi and Noto's Architecture 198

Part V The Eighteenth-Century City Endures

Chapter 10 Noto Frozen in Time 200
Conclusion 203

Notes 205
Documents and Appendices 225
Bibliography 245
Index 249

To my Father

Acknowledgements

The late Lorenzo Gori-Montanelli, then my instructor at the Stanford University campus in Florence, first suggested I visit Sicily in 1964. I returned in 1967 and lived in Sicily in 1969 and 1970, completing my PhD dissertation on Noto for the Department of Fine Arts of Harvard University in 1971. After several visits to Sicily during the 1970s the draft of the present book was completed. Since my first trip to Sicily I have accumulated many debts, only a few of which can be enumerated here.

During my visits to Noto over the years I was aided by numerous townspeople. Among them Dr Carlo Schembari, former mayor of Noto, and Giuseppe Fortuna, former secretary of the Comune of Noto, deserve special thanks. Dr Gioacchino Santocono-Russo, the Head Librarian of the library of the Comune of Noto, helped me obtain rare books and generously allowed me to borrow others. Bruno Ragonese, former assistant librarian and one of the leaders in the campaign to preserve Noto Antica, has been a constant friend over the years, who never tired of sharing his insights about the fauna and flora of Noto's territory. Luigi Di Blasi and Francesco Genovesi oriented me to the state of research on Netinese architecture, and helped by their great interest in Noto's architectural heritage, and by their assistance in the Archivio di Stato of Syracuse. Dr. Corrado Gallo and Gaetano Passarello helped in clearing up problems in the interpretation of the history of Noto. Father Vincenzo Caruso and the nuns who lived in S. Chiara in the early 1970s were good enough to let me enter and measure the cloister. The Marchese di Castelluccio and the Impellizzeris let me into their homes. Antonietta, Anna and Maria Francesca Messina let me copy valuable photographs and recounted much about nineteenth-century and early twentieth-century Noto. Nella and Enzo Mazzone and Piero and Silvanna were loyal friends. Hundreds of Netinese who knew me simply as *l'americano* helped me from day to day by describing life in Noto and letting me into their homes.

Without the help of the staffs of the archives in Syracuse, Palermo, Naples, and Simancas, Spain, this work could never have been written. I owe special thanks to Dr Giuseppe Leonardi, the former Director of the Archivio di Stato in Syracuse, who was extremely helpful during my first months in the archives.

In Syracuse, Guiseppe Mazza generously let me study his Gagliardi documents. Friends in Palermo, Prof Maria Accascina and Prof Maria Giuffrè, offered hospitality and useful advice. In Catania, Prof Giuseppe Giarrizzo generously offered assistance and suggestions. I am also indebted to Prof Paul Hofer who kindly showed me his preliminary maps of Noto which in 1969 he was preparing for an extensive work on Noto and other cities in south-eastern Sicily.

During the period I was writing my dissertation on Noto at Harvard I was aided by the late Prof John McAndrew who gave me all his books on Sicily and tried to prepare me for what to expect working there. Prof. George Kubler spent hours discussing my project and never failed to give excellent advice. Prof Peter Weiler, at that time a graduate student in history, waded through the problems of organizing the bewildering history of Netinese events with me. I am particularly grateful to Prof James Ackerman, whose humour, encouragement and humanity helped me through my year in Noto, and my education at Harvard.

This book could never have been written without the generous Travelling Fellowships awarded by Harvard University and the support of the University of

California through a Humanities Institute Summer Grant in 1972 and a Humanities Research Fellowship in 1973.

Throughout the time that I was preparing this book, Anthony Blunt patiently suggested changes in the drafts. My colleague at Berkeley, Prof Spiro Kostof, gave me the incentive to complete my work. My wife, Frances, helped in editing the manuscript and continually clarifying my ideas. I am indebted to Diana Lorentz for typing the manuscript, to Bernie Stein, of Swatt and Stein architects, and Marjie Spiegelman for the graphics, to James Hong and Barrie Rokeach for printing my photographs, to Paolo Polledri for checking the Italian and to Richard T. Smith for transcribing the Spanish.

Professor Emeritus Walter Horn of the University of California and William McClung of the University of California Press helped arrange this joint publication with A. Zwemmer Ltd. Mr Desmond Zwemmer deserves thanks for his help and patience.

I am also indebted to Liliane Dufour, who, in 1979, when this book was in press, sent me a book she jointly published with Bernard Huet and Henri Raymond, *Urbanistique et société baroques* (Institut d'études et de recherches en architecture et urbanisme, 1977). Three documents the authors present were germane to Noto's story, for the most part supporting the hypotheses presented in this book. I altered several pages in Chapter 4 to reflect the new information provided by the most important document and have mentioned others in the footnotes.

Last, I would like to thank my father, Mathew O. Tobriner, Associate Justice of the Supreme Court of California, to whom this book is dedicated. His views on the relationships between art and society and our trips together to the towns of California inspired me to study cities, and to write this book.

Introduction

The city of Noto (altitude: 159 metres; population: 23,551) lies on the eastern slopes of the Hyblaean mountains 5.5 kilometres from the Ionian Sea in south-eastern Sicily.[1] Noto can be reached by car by driving 32 kilometres south-west of the ancient city of Syracuse along a road which laces its way through luxurious orange, olive, and almond groves. Few people stop at the little city on their swift journeys around the island, bound for the Greek temples of Agrigento, or the ancient wall of Gela. It has neither first-class restaurants nor hotels to tempt the passing tourist to stay for a while to examine its treasures.*

Yet Noto is undoubtedly one of the most beautiful and best preserved eighteenth-century cities in Europe. In the 1920s, Sacheverell and Osbert Sitwell, adventurers in a then little-frequented Sicily, came upon sleeping Noto. They praised the quality of its exuberant architecture and the amazing excellence of its plan.[2] Since the Sitwells' visit a long line of European artists, architects, and scholars have visited the city, each bestowing upon it some special praise. Michelangelo Antonioni chose Noto for the setting of a sequence in his 1959 classic *L'Avventura*, in which he places his hero and heroine on the belfry of one of Noto's churches, and has them examine the magnificent scene below.[3] John J. Ide, in an article entitled *Noto, the Perfect Baroque City* (1958), quoted one enthusiastic visitor:

> Noto is one of the most beautifully-built towns in Europe and this remote little place comes out in the memory like Würzburg or Nymphenburg as one of the finest achievements of the age which produced Mozart and Tiepolo.[4]

Noto owes its present appearance to a catastrophe which struck south-eastern Sicily in the last decade of the seventeenth century: on 11 January 1693, in a series of violent shocks, an earthquake destroyed more than forty cities, killing thousands. The rebuilding of these cities constituted one of the largest urbanistic undertakings of the eighteenth century. Present-day Noto was one of these cities, built in the eighteenth century to replace the ruined old city, Noto Antica. The citizens of Noto addressed themselves to the problems which all the earthquake-ravaged cities of eighteenth-century Sicily faced, and which will face the present inhabitants of earthquake-prone urban centres from Messina to Tokyo to San Francisco with every major shift of the earth's continental plates: where, after the inevitable disaster, should a city be rebuilt? How should it be designed to avoid future disasters? Noto's re-creation suggests what factions of a population might take control of the rebuilding operations, and offers one example of what the outcome of rebuilding might be. It is at once a unique case of rebuilding, and a clue to possible conditions occurring elsewhere after a seismic disaster.

But how did Noto as it was reconstructed achieve the singular beauty acclaimed by visitors? The eighteenth-century city which rose after the destruction of Noto Antica was on the outer boundaries of Europe, ruled by Spain; yet its architecture is highly sophisticated and arranged on an Italian plan although Spain was the dominant political force on Sicily and south-eastern Italy. What factors account for Noto's cultural independence from Spain? How were styles transmitted to Noto and why were they adopted? And, even more puzzling, who designed Noto's city plan and constructed its buildings?

*This situation will soon change with the opening of a new hotel just outside Noto.

The questions that Noto poses for me as an architectural historian are primarily those related to its form. This book is concerned with the physical history of the city. But I see the physical history as a manifestation of the economic, political, and social life of Noto. The composition of this book is based on the idea that a city can be explored from different points of view and with various methodologies without sacrificing a unified exposition. In the case of Noto an urbanistic history alone or an architectural history alone would yield only fragmentary results. By combining architecture and urbanism I attempt to uncover the 'urban culture' of Noto – how its buildings and plan worked in the context of the society which created them. I have tailored the methodology I used to the kind of objects under investigation. I have used formal analyses of given façades (a very conservative method) coupled with a discussion of building types (a less traditional method in American architectural history). I also have combined strictly urban history in the first part of the book with strictly biographical histories of the architects at the end of the book. I have analysed 'high architecture' but I also have tried to examine the architecture of the lower classes, so called 'vernacular architecture'.

This eclectic methodological approach is suited to Noto, a city in which both the quality of the architecture and the plan distinguish it from its neighbours. Using these methodologies has enabled me to contribute to an understanding of both the city plan as it evolved and the people responsible for city buildings. I do not see the analysis of the architects as an addendum to an urban history but an integral part of it. I am only sorry that the documents at my disposal were not complete enough to delineate more about the people – both patrons and architects – who assumed crucial roles in the creation of Noto.

It may be helpful to see this book in the context of other studies of urban centres in the seventeenth and eighteenth centuries. There are other authors whose methodologies have been similar to mine. Of the few monographs on seventeenth- and eighteenth-century cities published in the last decades I think mine resembles most closely the approach of André Corboz in his book on Carouge (*Invention de Carouge 1772–1792*, Lausanne, 1968). Corboz's work is a model of detailed scholarship which I can only hope to emulate, but our approaches are similar. Corboz's approach combines architectural and urban history. He presents the political, economic, and social issues as well as the architectural and planning problems. In addition, within the confines of his study (1772–1792) Corboz gives a feeling of the city as an organically changing form: planning solutions change with styles and urban dilemmas, and the ideal is often at odds with the practical. He shows the city as it evolves, what Vance calls the 'morphogenesis' of a city.[5] In describing the evolution of Carouge, Corboz was able to isolate and analyse the contribution of each architect in turn, something I can not do in Noto because of the lack of firm documentation.

Noto, unlike Carouge which developed continuously in one place, was constructed anew in a different location after its destruction in 1693. In that respect I see my book as a companion volume to Jose-Augusto França's excellent *Lisboa pombalina* ... (1965) which investigates the rebuilding of Lisbon after the 1755 earthquake. My book follows the same general 'before and after' format that França used in his analysis of the city, and attempts to link political, economic, and aesthetic issues with the establishment of the new town as França did for Lisbon.

Augusto Cavallari-Murat's *Forma Urbana ed Architettura nella Torino Barocca* exemplifies what my book does not do. This enormous work, certainly the most exhaustive study yet produced on a seventeenth- and eighteenth-century city, is a collaborative work which minutely analyses Turin building by building, quarter by quarter. The outcome is a complex and fascinating map and a series of articles full of relevant if obscure detail. A tremendous amount of data emerges but, because of the format and detail, major themes are obscured. The city becomes so multifaceted as to be difficult to comprehend. For me Cavallari-Murat's method was impossible to implement: one person cannot hope to study even a small city in such detail alone. Likewise, while the book is extremely useful to the specialist, it seems to have lost the balance between scholarly detail and general concepts which I think makes interesting reading.

The present book is an overview of Noto's architecture and plan with an in-depth analysis of particular themes and issues rather than a uniform, minute house-to-house survey. I was not a member of a team, and my work both suffered and gained from the fact. I could not cover as many issues or visit as many crucial buildings or archives, but on the other hand I was free to propose hypotheses and to follow them to their conclusions. Further, not being an Italian may not have been a disadvantage, because being outside the society helped me to see Noto in a broader context. Using a wide range of methods both for the on-site evaluation of buildings and for work in the archives I thought I could solve some of the mysteries of Noto. My goal in publishing this book is to make the urbanism and architecture of Noto available to urbanists, historians and architects, and, although the subject is esoteric, I wanted this book to be readable enough to entice non-specialists to use it.

One of the reasons I was attracted to a study of Noto in 1968 was the paucity of scholarly research on both the architecture and urbanism of Sicily. The standard handbook for seventeenth- and eighteenth-century Italian architecture and urbanism, Rudolf Wittkower's *Art and Architecture in Italy 1600–1750* (1965), barely mentioned the architecture of Sicily. E. A. Gutkind's *International History of City Development* (1969) while including Sicilian cities did not analyse the urban recovery of south-eastern Sicily after the 1693 earthquake. The only up-to-date introduction to the architecture of eighteenth-century Sicily was Anthony Blunt's *Sicilian Baroque* (1968). While major books had been written about areas close to Palermo like Piano dei Colli and Bagheria, south-eastern Sicily had been neglected. When books like G. Gangi's *Il Barocco nella Sicilia orientale* (1964) did appear they were visual surveys rather than documented studies. Few Sicilian scholars had concentrated on south-eastern Sicily and those that did, like G. Agnello, did not delve deeply enough into the archives to satisfy my curiosity about the rebuilding process. Even Salvatore Boscarino's urban history of Catania, *Vicende urbanistiche di Catania* (1966), which is an extremely informative assembly of new information about Catania's plan, did not offer new insight into the first crucial years after the earthquake of 1693. Boscarino relied instead upon the documents unearthed by F. Fischera in his *G. B. Vaccarini e l'architettura del Settecento in Sicilia* (1934) but went no further.

The only scholar who seemed to be carefully re-examining earthquake cities was Maria Giuffrè whose *Utopie urbane nella Sicilia del '700* (1966) and *Miti e realtà dell'urbanistica siciliana* (1969) set new standards for innovative and scholarly research in Sicilian urban studies. Giuffrè's careful analysis of post-earthquake cities was extremely interesting because she considered the town plans to be manifestations of Sicily's political situation. Her use of footnotes and bibliographical references was a refreshing change from the usual practice of visual surveys without scholarly machinery behind conclusions. She carries on some of the perceptive work which E. Caracciolo started in his *La Ricostruzione della Val di Noto* (1964) but never completed.

When I began my studies on Noto the most valuable source was the scholarship of Corrado Gallo, a political historian living in Palermo who had written a series of articles on the reconstruction of the city. In 1968 the most comprehensive book on Netinese architecture was Nicolo Pisani's *Noto—Barocco e opera d'arte* (1960). Full of enthusiasm, attributions and the first documents to be published, Pisani's work formed the basis for later scholarship on Noto.

Gioacchino Santocono Russo's *Precisazioni sull'architettura barocca di Noto* (1968) filled some of the gaps in Pisani's account and brought the discussion of Netinese sources up to date. Aside from Santocono's article, several descriptive articles based largely on Pisani's work form the body of published material on Noto. Among the most prominent are J. J. Ide's *Noto—the Perfect Baroque City* ... (1958) and Françoise Popelier's *Noto ville baroque de Sicile* ... (1962). Both articles discuss architecture and urbanism but mainly repeat earlier information about Noto. Among the most perceptive essays on Noto was Stefano Bottari's contribution to *Sicilia, Guida d'Italia* (1968) and his fascinating *Contributi alla conoscenza dell'architettura del'700 in Sicilia* ... (1955), in which he attributes new buildings to Rosario Gagliardi. From a totally different viewpoint Gaetano Passarello's *Guida della Città di Noto* (1962) was also a valuable source. Its author, a local antiquarian, has collected interesting and for the most part reliable information about the history of the city, its institutions and its buildings.

Two studies published since 1969 have added considerably to the recent scholarship on Noto. The most significant is Luigi Di Blasi's and Francesco Genovesi's *Rosario Gagliardi, Architetto dell'Ingegnosa Città di Noto* (1972). Di Blasi and Genovesi published drawings attributed to Rosario Gagliardi along with an admirable collection of documents on Gagliardi's life. This book, published privately by amateur historians, is the most valuable yet published on Netinese architecture.

The second recent book published on Noto is Cleofo G. Canale's *Noto—La Struttura Continua della Città Tardo Barocca* (1976). I would like to draw a few distinctions between Canale's work and my own, and thereby avoid running commentary in the footnotes.

Canale's book ostensibly covers the same material as mine does but in fact Canale does not carefully describe Noto nor tell its story in a coordinated manner. The informative material reproduced in the plates and the potentially intriguing maps remain mute without the commentary to explain them. The documents that Canale published were culled by Lucia Cugno, whose work formed the basis for Bottari's attributions in his *La Giara* article; these are interesting but again are left unexplained and unimplemented. The text, plates, maps, and documents do not work together to explain the city to the reader.

Canale does not expose his deductive process of thought about this complex city to us. His main thesis, that Noto was a showplace for the aristocracy and clergy, is to my mind correct, but he goes no further into the actual creation or functioning of the city nor does he discuss individual buildings in the context of his thesis. It would have been a shame had the critical dialogue about what happened in Noto stopped with his book.

I see my own work as another step in the investigation of Noto. Though more methodical than Canale's treatment, it too will be subjected to criticism and evaluation. Professor Paul Hofer's anticipated publication will open yet other aspects of Noto's territory to study. Noto and south-eastern Sicily warrant these investigations—in this forgotten outpost of Europe remarkable cities were built which have outstanding churches, monasteries and palaces. The book which follows is my attempt to do justice to the complex urban and architectural history of Noto, 'the perfect Baroque city'.

Abbreviations

AdSN	Archivio di Stato, Naples
AdSP	Archivio di Stato, Palermo
AdSS	Archivio di Stato, Syracuse
ACMdN	Archivio, Chiesa Madre di Noto
ACMdS	Archivio, Chiesa Madre di Siracusa
AGdS	Archivo General de Simancas
Amico	Amico, V. *Dizionario topografico della Sicilia.* 2 vols. Translated by Di Marzo. Palermo, 1856.
Canale	Canale, C. G. *Noto – La struttura continua della città tardo-barocca.* Palermo, 1976.
Di Blasi	Di Blasi, L. and Genovesi, F. *Rosario Gagliardi, Architetto dell'ingegnosa Città di Noto*, Catania, 1972.
D.S.	Documents Section
Gallo, 1964	Gallo, C. 'Noto agli albori della sua rinascita dopo il terremoto del 1693'. *Archivio Storico Siciliano*, XIII, 1964, 1–125.
Gallo, 1966	'Problemi ed aspetti della ricostruzione a Noto e nella Sicilia orientale dopo il terremoto del 1693'. *Archivio Storico Siciliano*, XV, 1966, 89–190.
Gallo, 1967	'Noto dopo il terremoto del 1693, l'acquedotto di Coffitella ed il debito Starabba'. *Archivio Storico Siracusano*, XIII, 1967, 33–64.
Gallo, 1968	'Vicende della ricostruzione di Noto dopo il terremoto del 1693 (1697–1700)'. *Archivio Storico Siciliano*, XVIII, 1968, 1–47.
Gallo, 1970	'Dall'inutile referendum del 1698 circa il sito della riedificanda città di Noto alla definitiva decisione del Cardinale Giudice'. *Archivio Storico Siciliano*, XIX, 1970, 3–111.
Gallo, 1975	'Il terremoto del 1693 e l'opera di governo del vicario generale Duca di Camastra'. *Archivio Storico Siciliano*, IV, 1975, 3–21.
Giuffrè, 1966	Giuffrè, M. 'Utopie urbane nella Sicilia del '700'. *Quaderno dell'Istituto di Elementi di Architettura e Rilievo dei Monumenti della Facoltà di Architettura di Palermo*, nos 8–9, December 1966, 41–75.
Giuffrè, 1969	*Miti e realtà dell'urbanistica siciliana.* Palermo, 1969.
Littara, 1593	Littara, V. *De Rebus Netinis.* Palermo, 1593.
Littara, 1970	*Storia di Noto Antica dalle origini al 1593 (De Rebus Netinis).* Translated by F. Balsamo, Rome, 1970.
Tortora, 1891	Tortora, F. *Breve notizia della città di Noto prima e dopo il terremoto del 1693.* Editor C. Bonfiglio Piccione. Noto, 1891.
Tortora, 1972	*Breve notizia della città di Noto* . . . Editor F. Balsamo. Noto, 1972.

List of Illustrations

1 Aerial photograph of the site of Noto Antica today. (Photo: Istituto Geografico Militare, Florence.)

2 Engraved view of Noto Antica copied from a lost original. Mid-eighteenth century? Present location unknown. (Photo: *Atti e Memorie*, Istituto per lo studio e la valorizzazione di Noto Antica, Noto, 1972, Anno III, cap. IX.)

3 Panorama of Noto Antica from the west, 1887. Museo Comunale di Noto.

4 Noto Antica seen from the west today.

5 An eighteenth-century map of the feudo of the Falconara with a list of property owners and boundaries. (AdSN, Archivio Pignatelli-Avola, Scaffo IV, no. 3944, 1369–1695 Pianta. no. 190. Photo: AdSN.)

6 The church of the abandoned hermitage of Madonna della Marina.

7 Present-day Noto seen from the roof of Madonna della Marina.

8 A view south towards the coast from the feudo of Busulmone, a proposed site for the new Noto.

9 An aerial photograph of the feudo of the Meti today. (Photo: Istituto Geografico Militare, Florence.)

10 An anonymous eighteenth-century map illustrating the old and new cities of Noto and Avola as well as the territory between them. (AdSN, Archivio Pignatelli-Avola, Scaffo IV, no. 3944, 1369–1695, last page. Photo: AdSN.)

11 Aerial photograph of Avola (M. Giuffrè, 'Utopie urbane nella Sicilia del '700,' *Quaderno dell'Istituto di Elementi di Architettura e Rilievo dei Monumenti della Facoltà di Architettura di Palermo*, n. 8–9, Dec., 1966, p. 57.)

12 Plan of Avola. In V. Amico, *Lexicon Topographicum Siculum*, Palermo, 1757, II.

13 Plan of Avola indicating how its piazzas and churches are balanced on either side of the main piazza.

14 Land Fortress, P. Cataneo (P. Cataneo, *I quattro primi libri di architettura di Pietro Cataneo senese*, Venice, 1554, Libro Primo, p. 20).

15 City on the Sea, P. Cataneo (P. Cataneo, *I quattro primi libri di architettura di Pietro Cataneo senese*, Venice, 1554, Libro Primo, p. 24).

16 Ideal city, V. Scamozzi (V. Scamozzi, *Dell'Idea dell' architettura universale*, parte prima, Libro secondo, cap. XX, p. 166).

17 Veduta of Noto, P. Labisi, *ca.* 1750–60. In collection of the Biblioteca Comunale di Noto.

18 Veduta of Noto, P. Labisi, *ca.* 1750–60. Detail of inscription. In collection of the Biblioteca Comunale di Noto.

19 Veduta of Noto, P. Labisi, ca.1750–60. Detail of Noto's streets. In collection of the Biblioteca Comunale di Noto.

20 Aerial view of Noto from the south.

21 Aerial view of Noto from the south with the buildings bearing the same numbers they do on Labisi's veduta.

22 Noto as seen from a low hill to the south on the old road to Pachino.

23 Map of the city of Noto in its territory, V. Sinatra, 1764. In the collection of the Biblioteca Comunale di Noto.

24 The boundaries of eighteenth-century Noto.

25 Vico Nea, Noto.

26 Ronco Masaniello, Noto.

27 Piazza Taranto today.

28 Aerial view looking west down the Corso.

29 Viale Marconi and the Villa looking west toward the Corso and the arch of Ferdinand II.

30 The arch of Ferdinand II from the east.

31 Piano of S. Francesco. Partial view.

32 Piano of S. Francesco. Eastern approach.

33 Piano of S. Francesco. Western approach.

34 Veduta of Noto, P. Labisi, *ca.* 1750–60. Detail of Piano of S. Francesco. In Collection of the Biblioteca Comunale di Noto.

35 Aerial photograph of the Piano of S. Francesco.

36 SS. Salvatore. Joining of the two blocks of the eastern façade.

37 The Corso between the Piano of S. Francesco and the main piazza.

38 The monastery of S. Chiara isolated on a nineteenth-century basement.

39 Fountain high on the side of SS. Salvatore.

40 Veduta of Noto, P. Labisi, *ca.* 1750–60. Main piazza. In collection of the Biblioteca Comunale di Noto.

41 Aerial photograph of the main piazza from the east.

42 The main piazza seen from the east with the city hall on the left.

43 The main piazza seen from the east with the church of S. Nicolò and the staircase in front of it.

44 Main piazza with trees. Early twentieth century. (Photo: collection of Di Giorgio, Noto)

45 An aerial photograph of the main piazza from the north.

46 Hercules Fountain seen from the south in its present position in Villetta Ercole on Piazza S. Domenico.

47 The façade of S. Carlo and the Jesuit college on the Corso between the main piazza and Piazza S. Domenico.

48 An early twentieth-century view of Piazza S. Domenico. (Photo: Birelli, collection of Messina family, Noto)

49 An early twentieth-century view of Piazza S. Domenico. (Photo: Birelli, collection of Messina family, Noto.)

50 Veduta of P. Labisi, *ca.* 1750–60. Detail of Piazza S. Domenico. In collection of the Biblioteca Comunale di Noto.

51 The façade of S. Domenico seen from the west.

52 The façade of S. Domenico seen from the east.

53a Map of Piazza S. Domenico drawn by P. Labisi, 1749. In collection of the Biblioteca Comunale di Noto.

53b Anonymous map of Piazza S. Domenico, mid-eighteenth century. In collection of Francesco Genovesi, Noto.

54a S. Girolamo, the church of the monastery of Montevergine seen from Via Nicolaci.

54b S. Maria del Carmine, church of the convent of the Carmelites as seen from Via Ducezio.

55 The northern façade of the Casa del Refugio with nineteenth-century basement.

56 The Piano of SS. Crocifisso seen from the south.

57 Demolition on Via Sallicano showing the bedrock out of which the first storey of the demolished house in the centre was carved. (Photo: 1972)

58 Plan of Nuevo Baztán, Spain, by J. B. de Churriguera. (L. Torres Balbas, et al., *Resumen historico del urbanismo,* Madrid, 1954.)

59a Plan of Nochistlan. (F. del Paso y Troncoso, ed., *Papeles de Nueva España*, Madrid, 1905–6.)

59b Plan of S. Fernando de Béxar (San Antonio), Texas, *ca.* 1730 (Olin Library, Cornell University, Ithaca, New York.)

60a City of Catania prior to the 1693 earthquake. (G. Braun and F. Hogenberg, *Civitates Orbis Terrarum*, V. 1598.)

60b City of Catania after the 1693 earthquake as it looked in the eighteenth century. (A. Leanti, *Lo stato presente della Sicilia*, Palermo, 1761.)

61 St. Petersburg Plan (unexecuted), J. B. A. Leblond, 1717. (I. A. Egorov, *The Architectural Planning of St. Petersburg*, Ohio, 1969, fig. 4.)

62 Aerial view of Nancy. Place Stanislas and the Place de la Carrière. Design of E. Héré de Corny, 1752. (Photo: Jules Richard, Paris.)

63 Dwelling, Via Roma.

64 Dwelling, Via Grimaldi.

65 Vico Trigona looking north with lower-class dwelling in the centre of the photograph.

66 S. Croce, Lecce. Upper part of the façade. (Photo: M. di Puolo, C. Bestetti, Edizioni d'Arte, Milan, Rome.)

67 Façade of Palazzo del Barone Massa, Catania, begun 1694. (Photo: Tim Benton.)

68 Minutes of Joseph Capodicasa, ASS, 1729–1730, R-1. First page illustrating Sicilian penchant for fanciful ornament which includes both abstract embellishments and realistic faces.

69 Nicolaci palace balconies.

70 Nicolaci palace. Façade.

71 Nicolaci palace. Portal.

72 Copy of Vignola's Ionic order with griffin frieze. Volume of drawings in the Mazza collection, Syracuse.

73 Landolina palace (S. Alfano). Façade.

74 Landolina palace (S. Alfano). Ground plan. Nineteenth century. Collection of Francesco Genovesi.

75 Landolina palace (S. Alfano). First floor. Nineteenth century. Collection of Francesco Genovesi.

76 Oratory of S. Filippo Neri. Façade.

77 Impellizzeri palace (S. Giacomo). Façade.

78 Convent of S. Francesco. Courtyard.

79 Convent of S. Maria del Carmine. Dormitory portal.

80 Jesuit College. Eastern courtyard looking north-west.

81 Astuto palace, Façade from the west on Via Cavour.

82 Bishop's palace. Luigi Cassone, 12 April 1853 (AdSP. Inventario 6A, Ministro e Real Secretaria di Stato presso il Luogotenente Generale in Sicilia. Ripartimento lavori pubblici, piante topografiche, progetti etc., no. 82 Photo: AdSP.)

83 Bishop's Palace. First floor. Drawn by Luigi Cassone, 12 April 1853 (AdSP. Inventario 6A, Ministro e Real Secretaria di Stato presso il Luogotenente Generale in Sicilia. Ripartimento lavori pubblici, piante topografiche, progetti, etc., no. 82 Photo: AdSP)

84 Bishop's palace in foreground, Trigona palace in the background. As seen from the upper terrace of the city hall.

85 Trigona palace (Cannicarao). Main portal on northern side of building facing Via Cavour.

86 S. Maria del Carmine. Nave.

87 S. Maria del Carmine, Detail of nave decorations.

88 S. Carlo Borromeo. Nave.

89 S. Carlo Borromeo. Detail of nave decoration.

90 Convent of S. Francesco di Paola. Façade from south.

91 S. Agata. Façade.

92 S. Maria di Gesù. Façade.

93 S. Nicolò. Western side. Five-lobed window surround.

94 S. Nicolò. Western side.

95 S. Nicolò. Cornice on western side.

96 S. Nicolò. Façade.

97 Frontispiece, treatise by R. Gagliardi, Mazza Collection, Syracuse.

98 Ground plan for pentagonal church, Study A, treatise by R. Gagliardi, Mazza Collection, Syracuse.

99 Pentagonal temple. S. Serlio, *Tutte l'opere d'architettura et prospetiva*, Venice, 1619, p. 205 v.

100 Section F, treatise by R. Gagliardi, Mazza Collection, Syracuse.

101 Section E, treatise by R. Gagliardi, Mazza Collection, Syracuse.

102 Section H, treatise by R. Gagliardi, Mazza Collection, Syracuse.

103 Ground plan F, treatise by R. Gagliardi, Mazza Collection, Syracuse.

104 Ground plan E, treatise by R. Gagliardi, Mazza Collection, Syracuse.

105 Elevation F, treatise by R. Gagliardi, Mazza Collection, Syracuse (L. Di Blasi-F. Genovesi, *Rosario Gagliardi*, Catania, 1972, tav. 10).

106 S. Agata, Catania, G. B. Vaccarini. (Photo: Tim Benton.)

107 Elevation E, treatise by R. Gagliardi, Mazza Collection, Syracuse (L. Di Blasi-F. Genovesi, *Rosario Gagliardi*, Catania, 1972, tav. 9).

108 Façade study L, treatise by R. Gagliardi, Mazza Collection, Syracuse (L. Di Blasi-F. Genovesi, *Rosario Gagliardi*, Catania, 1972, tav. 14).

109 Façade study K, treatise by R. Gagliardi, Mazza Collection, Syracuse (L. Di Blasi-F. Genovesi, *Rosario Gagliardi*, Catania, 1972, tav. 5).

110 Façade Study, R. Gagliardi, Di Blasi Collection, Noto (L. Di Blasi-F. Genovesi, *Rosario Gagliardi*, Catania, 1972, p. 88).

111 S. Giorgio, Ragusa. Façade. Designed by R. Gagliardi.

112 S. Giorgio, Ragusa. Façade elevation. R. Gagliardi. Drawing in church sacristy.

113 S. Giorgio, Ragusa. Plan. R. Gagliardi. Drawing in church sacristy

114 S. Giorgio, Ragusa. Longitudinal section. R. Gagliardi.

115 S. Giorgio, Ragusa. Elevation of side. R. Gagliardi.

116 Plan of the abolished monastery of S. Maria dell'Arco with modifications. Drawn by the Ingegnere Direttore, Innocenzo Alì. AdSP Inventario 6A. Ministro e Real Secretaria di Stato presso il Luogotenente Generale in Sicilia. Ripartimento lavori pubblici, piante topografiche, progetti . . ., no. 124.

117 Façade of S. Maria dell'Arco. Looking north on Via Speciale.

118 Exterior doorway and main courtyard, S. Maria dell'Arco.

119 S. Maria dell'Arco. Façade.

120 S. Maria dell'Arco. Façade.

121 S. Maria dell'Arco. South door of church.

122 S. Maria dell'Arco. North door of church.

123 S. Maria dell'Arco. Interior of church.

124 S. Chiara. Plan of foundations by R. Gagliardi. Collection of the Biblioteca Comunale di Noto.

125 S. Chiara. Plan of first floor by R. Gagliardi. Collection of the Biblioteca Comunale di Noto.

126 S. Chiara. Plan of second floor by R. Gagliardi. Collection of the Biblioteca Comunale di Noto.

127 S. Chiara. Exterior from the north-west.

128 S. Chiara. Exterior from the south-west showing door originally opening onto the main piazza.

129 S. Chiara. Pilaster capital.

130 S. Chiara. Interior.

131 S. Domenico. Façade.

132 Façade study G. Treatise by R. Gagliardi, Di Blasi Collection, Noto (L. Di Blasi-F Genovesi. *Rosario Gagliardi*, Catania, 1972, tav. 13).

133 Section study G. Treatise by R. Gagliardi, Di Blasi Collection, Noto (L. Di Blasi-F. Genovesi, *Rosario Gagliardi*, Catania, 1972, tav. 38).

134 Plan study G. Treatise by R. Gagliardi, Di Blasi Collection, Noto (L. Di Blasi-F Genovesi, *Rosario Gagliardi*, Catania, 1972, tav. 37).

135 S. Domenico. Interior of nave from altar.

136 S. Domenico. Arcade and clerestory window.

137 S. Domenico. Chancel.

138 SS. Crocifisso. Façade.

139 Tower of old monastery of SS. Salvatore.

140 Tower of the church of S. Carlo Borromeo. Detail.

141 City hall from the steps of S. Nicolò.

142 Nineteenth-century elevation for the city hall project. Francesco Cassone, 16 November 1880. Biblioteca Comunale di Noto.

143 Late nineteenth-century photograph of the city hall. Mauceri Collection, Noto.

144 Léon Dufourny, *Notes rapportées d'un voyage en Sicile fait par lui en 1789*, MS Cabinet des Estampes, Bibliothèque Nationale, Paris, Ub. 236, Vol. 1, n.p.

145 Amalienburg, Nymphenburg.

146 Mon Repos, Ludwigsburg, Stuttgart, designed by La Guépière (P. du Colombier, *L'Architecture française en Allemagne au XVIIIe siècle*, Paris, 1956, II, pl. 19).

147 Sanssouci, Potsdam. Garden façade.

148 Sanssouci, Potsdam. Sketch of proposed ground plan drawn by Frederick II, 1744 (G. Pilze, *Sanssouci*, Dresden, 1954, p. 30).

149 Villa Falconara. Northern façade.

150 Château de la Masson, Montpellier. J. Giral, 1723 (A. Joubin, *Montpellier aux XVIIe et XVIIIe siècles*, Paris, 1912, p. 75).

151a Pilaster, garden of Landolina palace (S. Alfano).

151b S. Girolamo, the church of the monastery of Montevergine.

152 House of the Crociferi. Western façade from north.

153 House of the Crociferi. Western façade from south.

154 House of the Crociferi. Northern façade.

155 House of the Crociferi. Southern façade.

156 House of the Crociferi. Atrium.

157 House of the Crociferi. Main stairway.

158 House of the Crociferi. Stairway landing.

159 House of the Crociferi. Refectory.

160 House of the Crociferi. Plan of first floor by P. Labisi. Biblioteca Comunale di Noto, 1750.

161 House of the Crociferi. Plan of second floor by P. Labisi. Biblioteca Comunale di Noto, 1750.

162 House of the Crociferi. Dormitory as seen from the west, by P. Labisi. Biblioteca Comunale di Noto, 1750.

163 House of the Crociferi. Design of dormitory as seen from the north. P. Labisi. Biblioteca Comunale di Noto, 1750.

164 House of the Crociferi. Southern façade elevation. P. Labisi. Biblioteca Comunale di Noto, 1750.

165 House of the Crociferi. Longitudinal section through southern portion of dormitory and church. P. Labisi. Biblioteca Comunale di Noto, 1750.

166 House of the Crociferi. Longitudinal sections through dormitory. P. Labisi. Biblioteca Comunale di Noto, 1750.

167 House of the Crociferi. Design of the church of S. Camillo. P. Labisi. Biblioteca Comunale di Noto, 1750.

168 House of the Crociferi. Design of the church of S. Camillo with description and approval of the project. P. Labisi. Biblioteca Comunale di Noto, 1750.

169 Plan for study C, treatise by R. Gagliardi, Mazza Collection, Syracuse.

170 Plan for oval church, treatise by R. Gagliardi, Mazza Collection, Syracuse.

171 Doric order. C. Wolff, *Elementa Meteseos Universe*, IV, 1746, Ta. 4. MS Biblioteca Comunale di Noto.

172 Elevation of building. C. Wolff, *Elementa Meteseos Universe*, IV, 1746, Ta. 17. MS Biblioteca Comunale di Noto.

173 Aperture designs. Drawn by P. Labisi in C. Wolff, *Elementa Meteseos Universe*, IV, 1746, unnumbered plate. MS Biblioteca Comunale di Noto.

174 Nineteenth-century stereopticon photograph looking north on Via Rocco Pirri. Mazza Collection, Syracuse.

175 S. Agata, Interior.

176 The main piazza of Noto. Late nineteenth-century photograph taken before alterations completed. Collection of Mauceri, Noto.

177 The main piazza from the top of the city hall looking north-east.

List of Figures

1 Plan of the city of Ragusa. Page 31
2 Plan of Montevago. Page 55
3 Vico Trigona in the modern city of Noto. Page 121
4 Reconstruction of the Piano of S. Francesco before the lowering of the Corso in the 19th century. Page 84
5 Former monastery of S. Chiara. First floor. Page 161
6 Former monastery of S. Chiara. Second floor. Page 161
7 City Hall. Basement. Page 173
8 City Hall. First floor. Page 173

List of Maps

1 Map of Sicily indicating cities wholly or partially destroyed in the 1693 earthquake. Page 26
2 Map of Sicily. Detail of inset in Map 1. Page 30
3 The Meti. Contour map reconstructing the appearance of the two grids from the buildings on the site, *ca.* 1694. Page 44
4 Noto's north-south axis. Page 57
5 Reconstruction of Noto in 1712. Page 59
6 Noto's symmetrical plan. Italia's plan for balancing Noto's piazzas. Page 62
7 Noto's churches and religious houses. Page 111
8 Noto's palaces. Page 115

Part I
Politics and Planning of Urban Recovery

Chapter 1 Noto Antica on the eve of the disaster

For millenia Sicilians lived in the city of Noto Antica before it was so utterly destroyed by the earthquake of 1693. The people's attachment to the site on the summit of Monte Alveria survived even the destruction of the city itself. Not only did the Netinese resist leaving the site of their city in 1693, but their allegiance to it endures today, nearly two hundred and ninety years later. The present Institute for the Study and Utilization of Noto Antica after a long crusade is beginning to achieve its goal, the recognition of the site of Noto Antica as a national landmark.[1]

When the people were wrenched from Noto Antica in 1693 and transferred to Noto Nuova essential features of life in the old city were transferred with them. Although many of the 1693 population perished, the old city succumbed to ruin, and the new city of Noto Nuova rose on a virgin site, the institutional and social organization of the city remained largely intact. The change of place, population, and image did not alter the social hierarchy which controlled civic life: the aristocrats who owned vast tracts of land still built enormous palaces that dominated the town; the clergy still controlled large financial resources which insured the proliferation of churches, monasteries, and convents in the new town, most bearing the same names and having the same affiliations as they did in the old city. The essence remained the same although the image changed. The sketch of Noto Antica

1 Aerial photograph of the site of Noto Antica today.

which follows establishes a vantage point from which to view the evolution of Noto Nuova.

On the eve of the earthquake Noto Antica was one of a number of small, handsome, relatively anonymous cities existing in late seventeenth-century Sicily. Mention of Noto in contemporary Sicilian histories of the eighteenth century, or in present-day histories of Sicily, is rare.[2] Although it was once the administrative headquarters for its province, the Val di Noto (Map 1), by the late seventeenth century Noto's political importance was eclipsed by Syracuse, head of the Diocese for the south-eastern portion of the island.[3] Noto ranked behind regional seaports like Syracuse and Trapani in economic vitality, political power, and military might. Syracuse was in turn less important than larger, more populous cities like Catania, Messina, and Palermo.

In 1693 Noto Antica occupied the entire summit of a heart-shaped outcrop called Monte Alveria which stood in the foothills of the Hyblaean mountains of south-eastern Sicily (Pls 1–4). Aside from a small neck of land at the northern extremity of the site, Monte Alveria's steep slopes and precipitous cliffs isolated it from the surrounding hills. Below it flowed the headwaters of the Asinaro River which transformed the deep ravines and narrow valleys along its banks into rich farmlands. Monte Alveria enjoyed a cooler climate than that of the coast, while being relatively near the rich coastal plain and the sea.

The rugged and highly defensible site had been occupied for thousands of years.[4] First a late Bronze Age settlement, occupied by a Sicilian people called Sikels, Noto Antica was ruled in succession by Greeks, Romans, Byzantines, Moslems, Normans, Germans, Frenchmen and Spaniards. To Renaissance Netinese historians Noto was the capital of the legendary Sikel king Ducetius; it was from Noto, they surmise, that the Sikels, the native Sicilians, fought off the Greek settlers from Syracuse.[5] When the town finally fell to the Syracusan conquerors, they called it Neas or

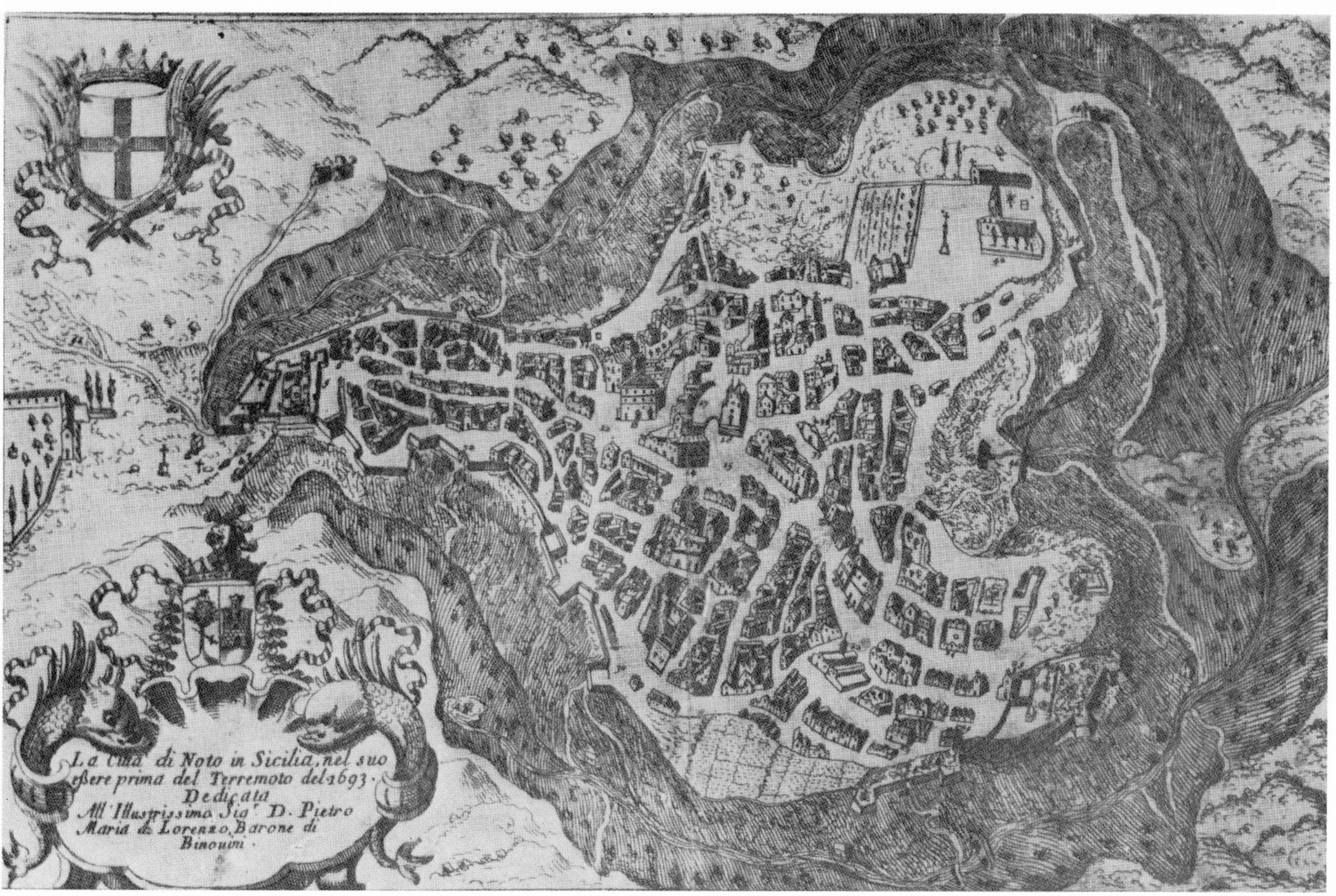

2 Engraved view of Noto Antica copied from a lost original. Mid-eighteenth century? Present location unknown.

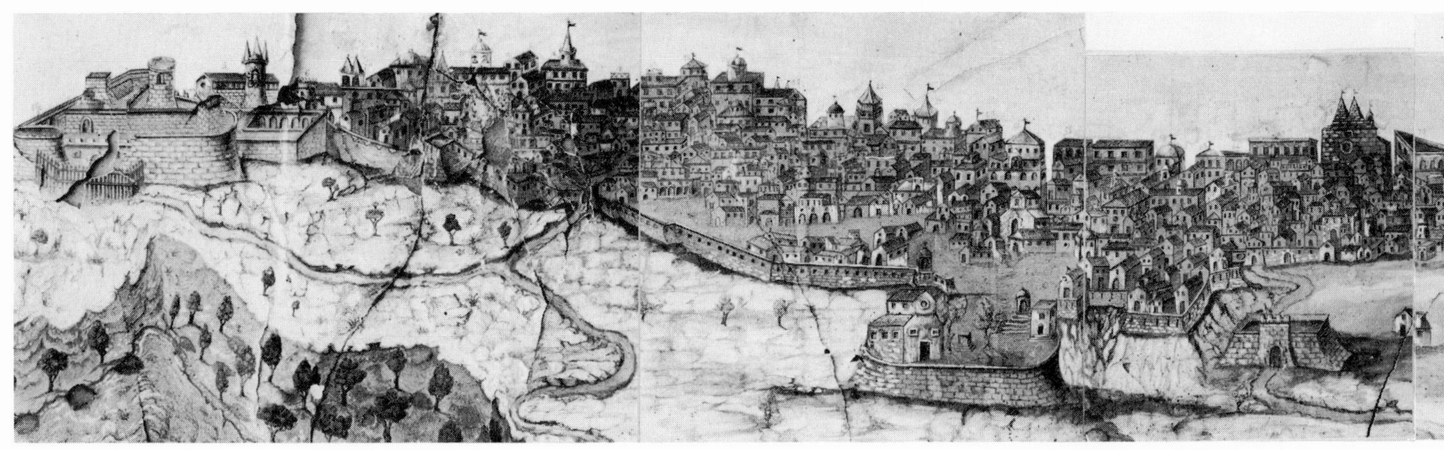

3 Panorama of Noto Antica from the west, 1887. Museo Comunale di Noto.

4 Noto Antica seen from the west today. Ruins of the fortress are at the extreme left of the photo.

Neathon. Under Rome it became Netum, and under the Moslems, Noto. Local historians explain that the Arabs called the city Noto because the word meant 'eminent place' in Arabic.[6] The Arabs divided Sicily into three administrative districts, one of which they called the Valley of Noto after the city.[7] In spite of the application of its name to a third of the island, the city never played a crucial role in the history of Sicily.

Although Noto was not as important as neighbouring centres like Catania and Syracuse it was a powerful city judging from its numerous aristocracy and large territory.[8] The city, with a population of about 12,000 in 1693, boasted 56 churches, 19 monasteries and convents; because religious institutions were usually supported by land grants and donations from the local aristocracy the large number of churches and religious houses indicates Noto was a prosperous city.[9] It also possessed a passable if not modern system of fortifications which had been used in 1674 to suppress the rebellion in Messina.[10]

Although Noto probably did not engage in heavy export traffic, its major products, herbs, citrus fruit, grapes, sugar cane, olives, rice, wheat, wool, and silk, could probably be traded within Sicily.[11] The economy of the whole Mediterranean basin was in decline by the late seventeenth century so the chances of Noto trading heavily outside Sicily seem rather remote, especially since it lacked a port.[12] Certainly sugar cane was no longer profitably grown in Sicily and the wool trade couldn't have been too good considering French and English competition. Wheat and rice were easy to store and in constant demand throughout Europe but efficient transportation and an organized exporting procedure may have been lacking. Wheat was stored in magazines by the sea, and when needed was transferred to waiting ships by means of small lighters. Since we know that it was difficult to ship wheat from Palermo because of high taxes, Moslem raids, and the lack of a Sicilian merchant fleet, export from Noto was probably even more difficult. In spite of a sizeable artisan population, Noto, like other Sicilian cities, lacked the kind of commercial creativity that spurred the growth of the great cities of northern Italy. Instead the real basis of the city's wealth lay in its citizens' ownership of land and water rights more than in

commercial activity. The city depended upon traditional agricultural methods to produce revenue from its numerous fiefs. Within this territory, which was extensive for a city of Noto's size (see Map 1), rich and fertile soil abounded. In addition, the coast of Capo Passero with its fishing industry was also within Noto's territory.

In 1630 Noto had a population perhaps as numerous as 26,000 but a recurrence of the plague which decimated seventeenth-century Europe reduced Noto's population to 12,000 just before the earthquake.[13] Even in the early part of the century Noto was not a large city as compared with Lisbon (pop. 73,000) or Florence (pop. 64,428).[14] But it was a reasonable size for a Sicilian city: Noto's population was nearly the same as that of nearby Syracuse; and Catania, one of the most powerful cities in south-eastern Sicily, had a mid-century population of 11,340 after the plague.[15]

The most accurate depiction of Noto Antica is an engraved view of the city, drawn sometimes after the earthquake but based on a pre-1693 original which is now lost (Pl. 2).[16] The engraved view of Noto Antica illustrates the city girdled by its curtain walls and guarded by a major fortification to the north on the neck of land joining Monte Alveria to the nearby hills, the city's weakest defensive position.

Noto's medieval street pattern followed the contours of the site. Its two major piazzas, S. Venera and Piazza Maggiore, are positioned in the centre of the city at the confluence of the two lobes of the heart-shaped mountain. A third important open space, the Piano of SS. Crocifisso, opened to the south of the northern fortifications. Noto's main street, Via Piana, ran from the northern fortress through Piano of SS. Crocifisso to Piazza S. Venera and Piazza Maggiore.[17] The main administrative buildings of the city—S. Nicolò (the Chiesa Madre) and the Magistrate's palace—were located on the Piazza Maggiore.[18] The two most important religious institutions, the churches of SS. Crocifisso and S. Nicolò, where the city's colleges of canons resided, were linked by Via Piana along a north-south axis.[19] The fortress at the northern gate of the city was garrisoned and controlled by the Spanish administration which also may have coordinated the defensive network of the entire city.

Although at least one city square had been enlarged since the 1400s, on the eve of its destruction Noto's plan had been little touched by the revolution of post-medieval urbanism.[20] Instead Noto's overall plan was in accord with organic geomorphic medieval plans common to Europe.[21] It is similar to plans of many Italian hill-towns which grew within the confines of protective walls on the summits of mountains and plateaux. Towns like Assisi, Todi and Orvieto, just to mention a few, all have geomorphic plans which conform to the nature of the terrain and strategically-located piazzas on which the civil and ecclesiastical institutions of the city stand. In smaller hill-towns like Coreglia in the province of Lucca, Colle Val d'Elsa in the province of Siena, and Fosdinovo in the province of Massa e Carrara, the same general principles that govern Noto's town plan were in practice:[22] the towns all straddle the summits of hills and are guarded by fortresses which occupy the highest ground. The main street of each town, like Noto's, runs along the ridge of the mountain or hill on which the city is built, connecting the main gate and the castle to the more important civil and ecclesiastical centres.

While the appearance of individual buildings within the city is difficult to surmise, most of the architecture seems to date from the Middle Ages and the Early Renaissance. Surviving visual documents present conflicting evidence about single structures but seem to agree on the general appearance of the city.[23] One such document is a panorama of Noto Antica as seen from the west copied in 1887 from a prior version (Pl. 3). Most of the buildings depicted in the panorama seem plausible enough in the context of Noto's history. The dome of the Alagona palace is in keeping with what we know about Moslem domes in Sicily.[24] The arcades which can be seen throughout the city were common through Europe from the early Middle Ages to the Renaissance. Many of the larger palaces, monasteries, and convents have wide façades with evenly-spaced registers of rectangular windows, which probably indicates that they were constructed after the fourteenth century. Many incorporate medieval towers, perhaps for defence or prestige, which may have been derived from Italian prototypes. Top-floor arcades, on the other hand, indicate possible Spanish influence.[25] Several palaces and religious houses bear oval windows on their façades which identify them as sixteenth- or seventeenth-century buildings.

The only documented seventeenth-century building in Noto Antica is the college of the Jesuits, planned by the well-known seventeenth-century Sicilian architect, Natale Masuccio of Trapani.[26] Although the building may not have been constructed by Masuccio himself, his presence in Noto Antica shows that seventeenth-century architectural styles had definitely reached Noto Antica. The remains of a carved keystone with boisterous sculptural decoration in the ruins of Noto Antica further indicates that Masuccio's brand of inventive Michelangelesque sculptural decorations may have penetrated the city. It is important to bear in mind, however, that Masuccio's mixture of Late Renaissance ornament with Early Renaissance volumetric simplicity survived in Sicily a hundred years after such experimentation had run its course in mainland Italy. By the time the earthquake struck, the great masters of the Baroque in Rome, Cortona, Bernini, and Borromini were dead. Stylistically Noto Antica and Sicily as a whole were far behind the latest architectural styles flourishing in the rest of Europe.

On the eve of 9 January 1693, Noto Antica stood on Monte Alveria as a patchwork of various eras, its buildings, fortifications and plan recording the long history of its occupation of a single site. It was a city in harmony with its geographical position, with riches from its vast territory, a royal fortress, and a healthy site. It would never be the same again. For on 9 January and 11 January 1693 the city would be shaken, destroyed, and forced to undergo a painful metamorphosis.

Chapter 2 Disaster and a Decision: A New Site for Noto

The present-day city of Noto stands seven kilometres from the ruins of the abandoned city of Noto Antica, destroyed so completely by the earthquake of 1693. Noto is a 'new town' built from scratch on the location it now occupies.[1] This chapter will first consider how unusual it is to move a city, even after complete destruction, and then explore the reasons for the transfer of the entire city to a new site. It is possible to understand such a move and the new site selection by looking at planning practices, scientific beliefs, and political policies of the 1690s as they affected Noto specifically.

Noto's transfer runs directly counter to the usual trend which is to rebuild a city where it has fallen. Although scorched by fire, shaken by earthquakes, or devastated by wars, cities are most often rebuilt on their original sites. Even cities that stand on the most hazardous ground – like San Francisco, California, or Managua in Nicaragua – are rarely abandoned.[2] Messina, a port town on the eastern coast of Sicily, was totally destroyed by earthquakes in 1783 and 1908, only to be rebuilt in the same place each time.[3] Catania, a Sicilian city lying at the foot of Mt Etna, was ruined at least three times by earthquakes or spectacular eruptions, but rose again on the same location.[4] After the most frightening and best publicized disaster of the eighteenth century, the Lisbon earthquake of 1755, plans to rebuild elsewhere were swiftly dismissed and the city arose in the same place.[5] In modern times citizens have quickly rebuilt Tokyo, Anchorage, and numerous Californian towns in spite of the knowledge that future earthquakes were inevitable. Hiroshima was hurriedly resettled, although the effects of radiation on its soil were totally unknown.[6]

The earthquake which destroyed Noto came in two major shocks. An eyewitness records the second shock which struck Noto on Sunday morning, 11 January 1693:

> Then came an earthquake so horrible and ghastly that the soil undulated like the waves of a stormy sea, and the mountains danced as if drunk, and the city collapsed in one miserable moment killing more than a thousand people.[7]

This terrible earthquake gravely damaged more than forty other cities in south-eastern Sicily (Map 1).[8] Its destruction reached from Messina in eastern Sicily across the island to Palermo in north-western Sicily. A report sent to the Spanish government from the offices of the Viceroy in Messina gives a notion of the scope of the disaster:

> On the 9th, at 2:45 a.m. Italian time, the first tremor took place, which lasted a long Credo. No damage was noted in Messina, but the second one came about on the 11th of the same month at 4:30 a.m. It lasted a quarter of an hour and caused great grief as no house or palace remained undamaged and many fell to the ground. The dead, which have been counted, so far number forty-three, but because everyone is in such a sorry state we have been unable to discover others. The processions and harsh penitences which have been made are without equal in the world. And there have been many public confessions . . . The coastal area is broken up in several places . . . No one dares walk in the streets . . . The after-shocks still continue but they are very light. At the least trembling one anticipates a quake, so great is the state of fear we are all in.

As to the extent of the damage, the report cites forty cities destroyed.

> All these cities, towns and manors are levelled without even the foundations showing. The city of Catania is like the palm of your hand, except for the seaward walls. Its ruins have buried more than sixteen souls, and in this city, as in the others that are lost, one hears underground the cries of persons calling for mercy and aid . . . From Palermo there are reports via letters that the quakes threw down many palaces and houses in that city, but that the rest have remained standing . . . All the inhabitants of the said city find themselves scattered throughout the fields, and the houses and palaces that remain standing are being buttressed with haste.[9]

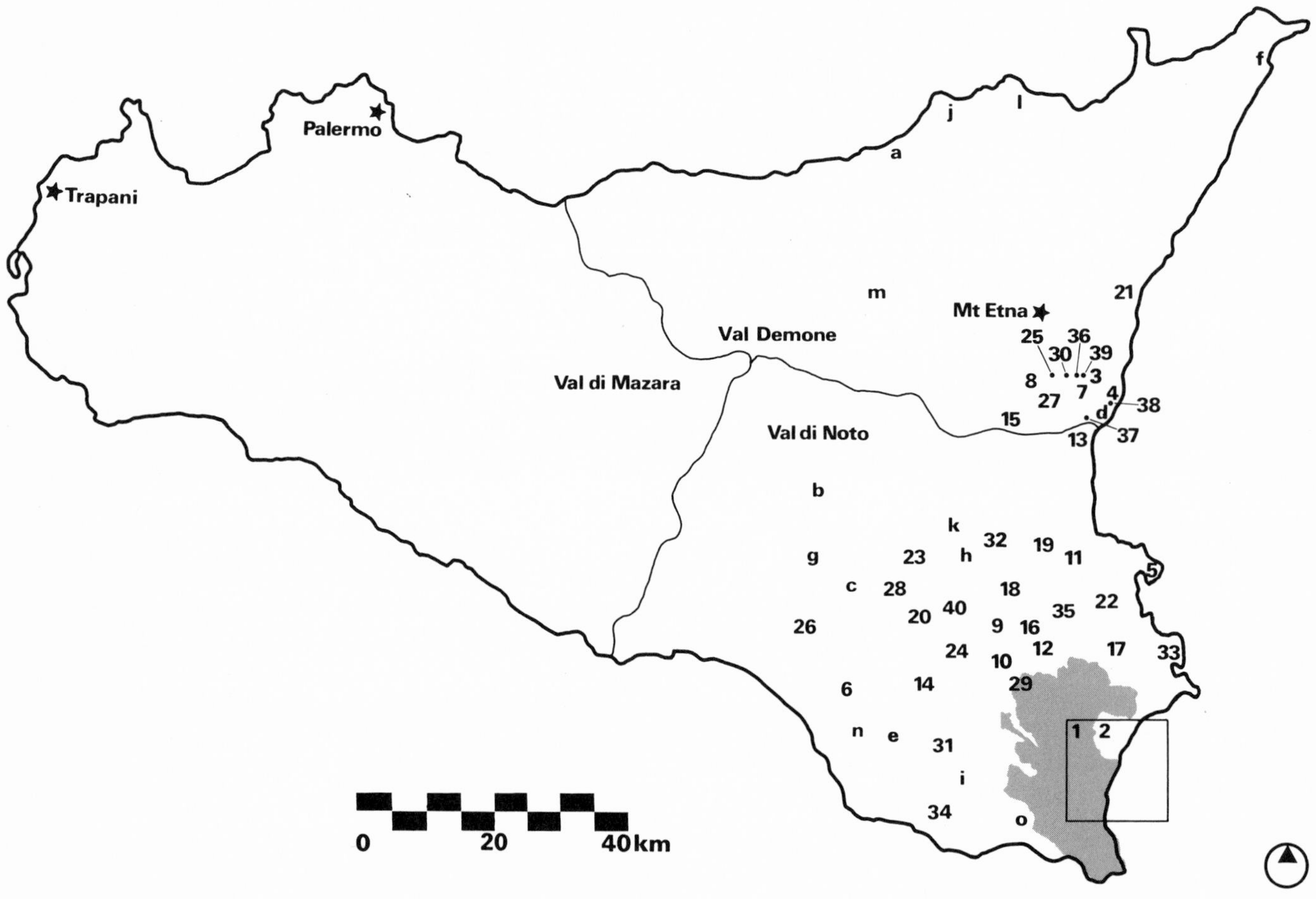

Map 1 Map of Sicily. Letters indicate cities partially destroyed in the 1693 earthquake. Numbers indicate cities which were largely or wholly destroyed by the earthquake. The darkened area represents the territory of Noto as it may have looked before modern losses. The present territory can be visualized by subtracting the finger-like extensions on the west side of the territory and the area on the cape (called Capo Passero) to the south. (The territorial outline is based on a map published in an article by E. Bresc.

Aci S. Antonio (3)
Aci S. Filippo (4)
S. Agata (a)
Aidone (b)
Augusta (5)
Avola Vecchia (2)
Biscari (6)
Bonacorsi (7)
Borello or Stella Aragona (8)
Buccheri (9)
Buscemi (10)
Caltagirone (c)
Carlentini (11)
Castel d' Aci (d)
Cassaro (12)
Catania (13)
Chiaramonte (14)
Comiso (e)
Fenicia Moncada (15)
Ferla (16)
Floridia (17)
Francofonte (18)
Lentini (19)
Licodia (20)
Mascali (21)
Massa Nunziata (27)
Melilli (22)
Messina (f)
S. Michele (g)
Militello (h)
Mineo (23)
Modica (i)
Monterosso (24)
Naso (j)
Nicolasi (25)
Niscemi (26)
Noto Antica (1)
Occhiolà (Grammichele) (28)
Palagonia (k)
Palazzolo (29)
Patti (l)
Pedara (30)
Ragusa (31)
Scordia (32)
Scicle (34)
Sortino (35)
Spaccafurno (Ispica) (o)
Syracuse (33)
Tre Castagne (36)
Tremestieri (37)
Trezza (38)
Troina (m)
Via Grande (39)
Vittoria (n)
Vizzini (40)

The Viceregal Government faces the Disaster

The extent of the earthquake damage suffered by Sicilian cities forced the Spanish government to implement recovery policies to halt the deteriorating economic and political situation. Spain already faced grave economic problems.[10] Its trade with the New World steadily dwindled as the importation of silver gradually ceased. Mismanagement of the agrarian sector forced peasants to leave the countryside causing a steady shrinkage of the population and the diminution of arable land. Spain's blunders at home had been perpetuated on its Sicilian kingdom. One of the crisis areas was agriculture. Sicily developed a monoculture of wheat in the sixteenth century based on a simple two-course crop rotation which by the seventeenth century had begun to have ruinous results. Lands were deforested to make way for more fields which led to unalterable erosion. In the market place inept administration and profiteering often led to crises when so much grain was exported that there were acute shortages on the island. Even before the earthquake struck the Spanish rulers of Sicily had faced a series of internal revolts and economic disasters in that country. In 1647, a bread shortage caused revolt to flare in Palermo.[11] In 1674, Palermo's rich rival, Messina, tried to revolt against the Spanish Hapsburgs by inviting Louis XIV to claim the city.[12] After three years of fighting Messina was finally subdued, but then was financially ruined by government reprisals to the extent that the richest and most venturesome trading city of Sicily would never regain its position. Also in the 1670s, popular riots spread to Catania and other cities, and disorder reigned throughout the countryside as mobs, who had obtained weapons during the Messina war, resorted to brigandage. Occurring just after this previous disorder, the earthquake damage only accentuated the despair of the populace and their rulers. The result was that people in individual cities did not come to each other's aid. Rather, looting occurred and anarchy reigned until the central government intervened.[13]

In January 1693, the Viceroy of Sicily, the Duke of Uzeda, tried to organize a central administration to meet the earthquake disaster. He appointed two special juntas or councils to help direct relief efforts, decide monetary policy, and interpret the dispatches from officials in the field.[14] One junta was composed of secular nobles and dealt with civil problems. The other junta, composed of aristocratic church officials, considered ecclesiastical matters. The Viceroy directed these juntas to meet every Tuesday and Thursday in Palermo until the problems caused by the earthquake were solved.

Sharing emergency power with the juntas were originally two Vicars General, individuals appointed by the Viceroy as his personal lieutenants who were to supervise recovery efforts.[15] One was to be assigned to each of the two administrative provinces of Sicily (Val di Noto and Val Demone) whose towns had been destroyed by the earthquake. By appointing the Vicars General himself and giving them extraordinary *ad hoc* powers, the Viceroy side-stepped the tangle of baronial privileges and the confusing array of largely atrophied governmental bodies that composed Sicily's government.[16] Uzeda's first appointments were Giuseppe Lanza, the Duke of Camastra, as the Vicar General of the Val Demone, and the Prince of Aragona as the Vicar General of the Val di Noto. However, within two weeks of his appointment an attack of gout forced the Prince to resign, and the Viceroy then gave this assignment also to the Duke of Camastra.[17] The Duke, with powers in every way similar to those of the Viceroy, therefore assumed a crucial role in the reconstruction of Sicilian cities, and became the most important single figure in shaping Noto's future.

Camastra came to his task as an already experienced administrator.[18] He had proven himself an able public servant and ambitious politician during the latter part of the seventeenth century. In the 1660s he served as a Captain of the Armed Cavalry of the Kingdom of Sicily. In the 1680s he served in the prestigious office of the Captain of Justice of Palermo. He later became a Pretore, the highest judicial officer of Palermo. During the rebellion of Messina, he raised a troop of Italian infantry to put down the rebels, and, for his services, a noble council recommended that he receive the coveted Key to the Bedchamber of the Hapsburg king in 1682.

To help Camastra in directing the reconstruction of the damaged cities, other administrators were sent to south-eastern Sicily. One of these was Don Giuseppe Asmundo, a member of the Great Court of the Kingdom and a powerful aristocrat from Catania.[19] Yet another administrator sent to south-eastern Sicily was the Flemish military engineer, Colonel Don Carlos von Grunemburg.[20] Grunemburg was the Royal Engineer of the King of Spain, responsible for planning and building the huge polygonal citadel (begun 1681) which was erected to guard Messina after its unsuccessful rebellion in 1674. This knowledgeable engineer, a specialist in fortification, must have been what we might call the city planner of the recovery team.

Home Rule in Noto after the Earthquake

Camastra, Asmundo and Grunemburg began their work of reconstruction with Catania, south-eastern Sicily's largest city Camastra, arrived in Noto on 24 February 1693.[21] Until late February Noto was left to find its own solutions, administered by its Captain of Justice, Antonino Impellizzeri, and by its senators.

Noto established its first city headquarters outside the ruined town's northern gate. Impellizzeri stated later that he chose the site because wood, masonry, and even water were all available in the ruins of Noto.[22] And on 15 February, a town council composed of the city's senators met outside the walls (Pl. 2, to the left of no. 3).[23] They decided that the city of Noto should be rebuilt where the ruins stood. In addition to affirming that wells still flowed in the city, and building materials were plentiful, they cited the strategic importance of Noto Antica, adding that a major part of the city's walls still stood. Furthermore, they stated that the 'ancients' who were wiser than they had chosen the place, which proved its merits. Satisfied that their reasons were justified by practical considerations and community tradition, the Netinese dispatched a communiqué to the Tribunal of the Royal Patrimony affirming that the city would be rebuilt on its old location.

Shortly after it was decided to remain on the old site, however, the question was debated once again perhaps during Camastra's first visit from 24 February to 8 March.[24] Doubts about the practicability of rebuilding on the old site came to a head in this meeting, which was open to the community at large, and it nullified the judgement of the first council by opting to move the city. Several new locations for the city came into the discussion but none enjoyed universal support.

Thus, when the Duke of Camastra returned to Noto in April 1693, he found the populace at an impasse as to where the city was to be rebuilt. If the people of Noto had been agreed in choosing one location, they would have presented at least a strong mandate to the government, but internal dissension called for an external mediator to settle the indecision of the people and their leaders. So, by default, the fate of Noto was largely decided not by the Netinese but by the chief administrator of the territory, Giuseppe Lanza, the Duke of Camastra.

The Viceregal Government intervenes

Just how arbitrarily Camastra acted in his role as governmental mediator is unclear from documentary evidence.[25] The historically-recognized account of the transfer of the city, written by Padre Filippo Tortora in 1712, portrays Camastra as a simple administrator who tried to resettle the city as a majority of the population wanted it. But two other chroniclers, Antonino Impellizzeri, in an account written in 1698 and addressed to the government, and an anonymous chronicler, in a detailed history of Noto written in 1727, disagree with Tortora. Impellizzeri sees Camastra as an outright dictator who transferred Noto by manipulating a city council to vote for the move. And the anonymous chronicler mentions that Camastra returned to Palermo from Noto 'with little honour', suggesting that Camastra's actions in Noto were questionable in character.[26] Each of these three historians of Noto has a bias: Tortora wanted to justify the site, endorsed by the clergy, on which the city finally rose in the eighteenth century, and probably wanted to silence old controversies. Impellizzeri had a vendetta against Camastra and Asmundo, who had taken him to court for alleged irregularities concerning confiscation of property after the earthquake (despite his zeal for keeping down looting, it was suspected that Impellizzeri may have also appropriated goods for himself).[27] Impellizzeri was also vehemently against the transfer of the city, so his account, written as an appeal to the Viceroy, was probably slanted. The anonymous chronicler seems to have had no other motive than to give an alternative to Tortora's version of the events following the 1693 earthquake. Both the anonymous chronicler and Impellizzeri seem a shade closer to the seamy side of the political events than Tortora.

Despite their differences, however, all three historians agree on the major events and decisions. According to all three, the Duke of Camastra, who came to Noto in April, called his own council. Tortora mentions that the Duke had already voiced his opinion that the new city should be rebuilt on the ruins of the old, but that, because some citizens did not want to remain on the site, he was swayed to consider alternatives.[28] Impellizzeri, however, implies that the council itself was far from legitimate, stating that Camastra gathered a few nobles and some other people together in 'the name of the public and the church', and then 'baptized' those assembled a 'council'.[29]

Tortora and the anonymous chronicler record, in their fashion, how the members of Camastra's council voted.[30] 'Some' wanted to remain on the site of Noto Antica; 'many' wanted to rebuild the city ten kilometres away from Noto Antica, on the shores of a shallow bay guarded by the Vendicari tower on Capo Passero. 'Many' were in favour of the plain of Madonna della Marina, near the present site of the city but closer to the coast. 'Others' were partial to the plain of Rumanello in the feudo of Busulmone, still in the mountains but closer to the sea than Noto Antica. 'Not a few' wanted to move to the feudo of Falconara, a rich, tree-covered, relatively flat site in the basin of the Asinaro River near the coast. Tortora mentions that the hermitage of S. Giovanni detto la Lardia, on a narrow ridge just to the north of the present city of Noto, and the Stampace tower, closer to the coast near the ruins of the Greek city of Helorus, were both suggested. At the end, the anonymous chronicler comments mournfully, 'the remainder of those present selected a place at the end of the feudo of the Meti where they finally decided it [the city] should be; what an unhappy selection'. Tortora concludes less negatively but similarly casts a shadow on the choice by mentioning Camastra's reservations:

> And finally the group that wanted the feudo of the Meti prevailed. The Duke of Camastra, considering the site, only liked the summit of a hill, which today we call the Pianazzo, where he said the city should be rebuilt.[31]

An Indictment of Medieval Cities

The story as told by these Netinese documents does not include sufficient reasons for abandoning the old medieval city nor any indication of why the new site on the Meti was chosen. Only by inference, from documents explaining the actions of other cities, can Noto's transfer and new site be explained. Of the forty ruined cities in Sicily, only a handful were transferred: Noto, Avola, Grammichele (formerly Occhiolà), Ferla, Sortino, Ispica, Buscemi, and Ragusa.[32] Documents from Avola, which was moved, and Catania, which was not, indicate that the abandonment of Noto Antica was probably due to dangers inherent in its medieval plan and rugged site.

Avola lies four kilometres south-east of present-day Noto and, like Noto, Avola was transferred from a high mountain summit (Map 2, no. 10) to the coastal plain (Map 2, no. 11) after the earthquake of 1693. According to communiqués to the King, the locals themselves did not want to rebuild Avola in the same location, 'because of the risk of a new disaster, the place being mountainous . . .'.[33] The King, in a dispatch to his Viceroy, explains that the major problem is the old city plan itself:

Map 2 Map of Sicily. Detail of inset in Map 1. South-eastern Sicily showing the old and new positions of Avola and Noto and the proposed locations for the new Noto.

1 Noto Antica
2 Pianura of Cugno di Vasco
3 Feudo of Busulmone
4 S. Giovanni detto Lardia
5 Feudo of the Meti with the present city of Noto
6 Hermitage of Madonna della Marina
7 Feudo of the Falconara
8 Stampace tower
9 Vendicari tower
10 Avola Vecchia (Avola before 1693)
11 Present site of Avola

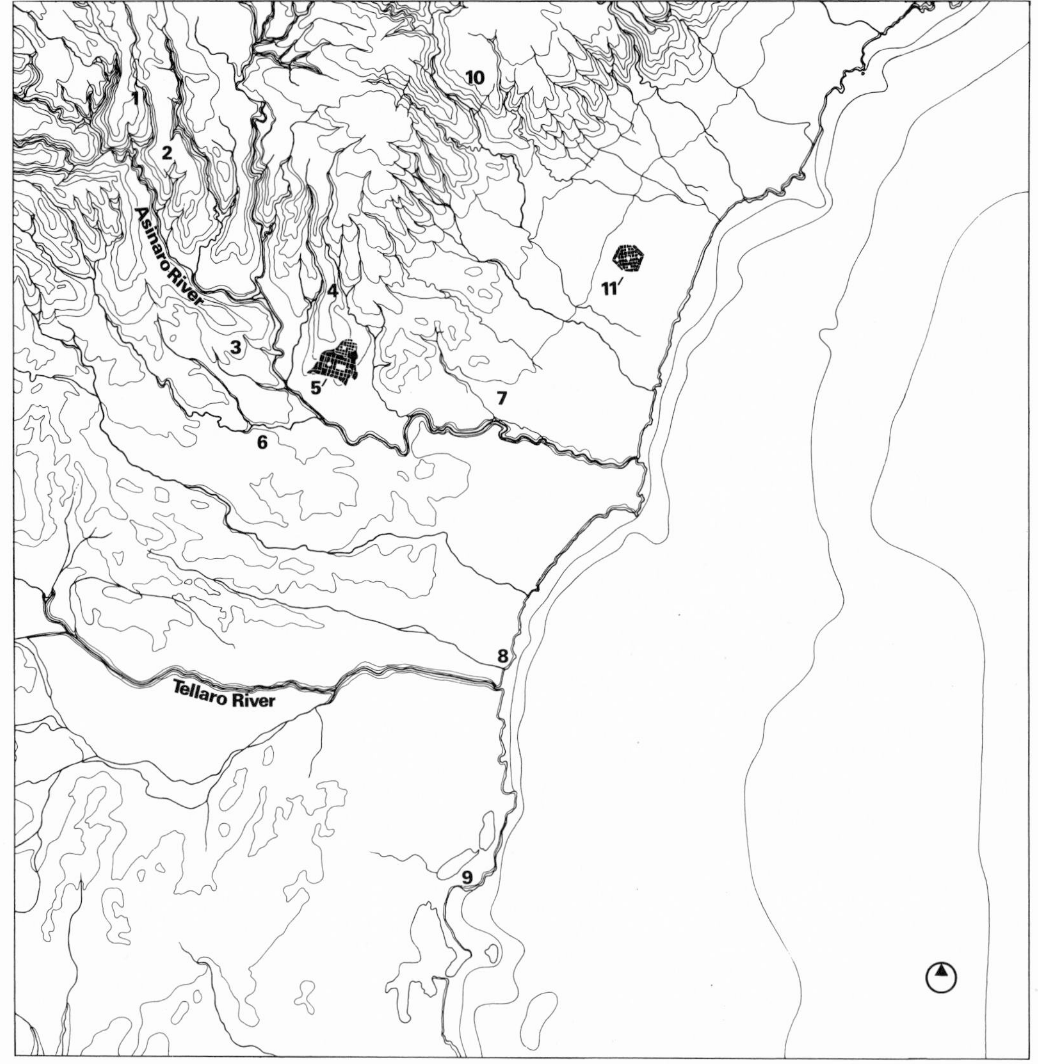

> Rebuilding on the old site was not abandoned willingly, but because of real necessity – both for the hillside being broken up and for the narrowness of the site and its streets. The houses are also constructed in a very dangerous way, one above the other, so that with the least tremor one house would pull all the others down with it, as was learned in the last earthquake when the most damage was occasioned by the poor arrangement of the city on the site. To this is added the great expense which would be necessary to make the location suitable for rebuilding since the heaps of rubble cannot be removed.[34]

In the council of Catania, its citizens refused to abandon the site of their ruined city, citing its fine air, its vicinity to the sea, and its strong walls which still stood after the earthquake.[35] They mention that to leave such a fortified location would have been 'crazy'. However, the Catania council clearly connected their existing narrow medieval streets with loss of life and property. They recognized the fact that Catania would fall prey to future earthquakes and, while rebuilding on the same site, planned for future tremors. Catania's new streets were to be very wide to provide extra space for moving through them after future earthquakes. Also, to make them safer, streets were to be straight and at right angles to one another (furthermore it was felt that such streets would be more beautiful, because they would conform to the 'rules of architecture'). The council further observed that, if owners could in some way be able to remain near their property after an earthquake, looters would be discouraged. They envisioned the piazzas as safe camping areas within the city, offering a refuge for nearby property owners who could be close enough to their possessions to guard them. Wide streets running from one piazza to another would assure communication throughout a ruined city. Thus, the Catania council, in its forward-looking preparations for a probable earthquake, legislated against organic medieval planning and constricted streets.

Transfers of other cities confirm these conclusions. The apparent reason for the transfers of Ispica, Buscemi, Sortino, Grammichele and Ragusa seems to have been a quest for more level, more accessible sites. Ispica, for example, was previously located on the slopes of tortuous valley walls; Ragusa clung to massive outcroppings. The new cities were refounded on flatter, more easily approached sites. Ispica was transferred from its narrow valley to the expansive summit of a nearby hill, Grammichele to a flat summit, and Ragusa, Buscemi, and Sortino to nearby sloping hillsides. Ragusa's present-day plan incorporates the geomorphic plan of the old city which was never abandoned, and the flatter geometric plan of the new city (Fig. 1.)

Fig. 1 Plan of the city of Ragusa. The smaller grid on the extreme left is modern, the coarser grid around the church in the centre of the city is the new city settled after the earthquake of 1693. The organic, medieval pre-earthquake city is on the right.

Almost three hundred years after the earthquake of 1693, accessibility and level siting were still the main criteria which decided where cities should be rebuilt in Sicily. In 1968, western Sicily fell prey to a strong quake which destroyed many of its towns. One of the towns which was almost completely obliterated was Gibellina, a medieval hill-town. In 1973 the survivors of the earthquake were still living in a temporary settlement some kilometres distant from Gibellina. A new town, as yet unbuilt, had been planned for a level site on the plains, closer to the highway and a railway siding. Even the temporary settlement was erected in a more accessible location than the old.[36]

The Abandonment of Noto Antica

Existing views which illustrate pre-earthquake Noto show a tightly-packed medieval city with meandering streets which would have been just as inaccessible as Ragusa's or as vulnerable to earthquakes as Avola's. Like the Avolese, the Netinese may have seen medieval building practices as a potential hazard, and it is possible that the Netinese too saw the narrow streets of Noto Antica and its hilly site as an irredeemable liability in an earthquake. They may have concluded that the site could not support the kind of level geometricized plan and organized development that safety from earthquakes demanded.

Condemnation of Noto's medieval character may have overruled the virtues of rebuilding on Noto's old site, which, as Impellizzeri pointed out, had flowing wells, operable mills, and partially standing walls. Besides being impregnable, the site was healthy and rich in agricultural resources and grazing land. It was situated on a road leading inland, and was a commercial centre for the Val di Noto. Because of these characteristics, the move from the old city was contested by many citizens. Yet, although hidden political motives may have played a part, the logic of the transfer of Noto in light of the above examples of other cities cannot be denied.

In addition, the very character of the disturbances recorded at the site of Noto Antica was interpreted as a bad omen of future disasters according to seventeenth-century scientific knowledge.[37] Witnesses heard a wind under the ground just before the earthquake which was interpreted as meaning the ground was not firm. Engineers who visited the site after the earthquake mentioned that part of the hill-top actually broke away from the rest of the rocky hill on which the old city stood. The earthquake omens and the very real seismic activity at Noto Antica added to the strong arguments for abandoning the old location.

If we assume that safety, accessibility, and level siting may have decided the second council against rebuilding Noto Antica on the same site, we still have no indication of why the Meti was chosen and the many other sites vetoed. The only method available for answering this question is again to measure the suggested sites for the new Noto against what other Sicilian cities considered favourable site conditions. The best set of criteria to use are those of Noto's neighbour, Avola (Map 2, old city no. 10, new city no. 11).

Criteria for Selection of a New Site

Communiqués from the new city of Avola (Map 2, no. 11) define the favourable attributes of its site.[38] The communiqués were written to the King of Spain and to the Viceroy by Avolese who were defending the choice of the new site of the city against the Viceregal juntas who felt the site was too close to the sea to be safe. The communiqués therefore extol the virtues of Avola with enthusiasm, firmly emphasising every possible advantage, so that the King would not order the transfer of the new city. The most important of the communiqués reads as follows:

> By order of the Prince of Santa Flavia, the Councillor, brother Angelo Italia, master of the Jesuit order, was invited to the city to select the best site with the most salubrious air for the re-edification of the new city. Conferring over the location, and carefully assessing the entire territory of Avola, he found nothing superior to the feudo owned by the University of Avola called Mutubini in which he laid out the new city in the form which was transmitted to the Viceroy. A mile distant from the sea lies an extremely beautiful and very large plain which extends more than forty miles to the north and thirty miles to the east. The area can be traversed by carriage. Through the middle of the city flow the waters of the fountain called Miranda. . . . And because the site of the city is in the middle of the Contrado of Modica Road—the passage to the good part of the cities of the Val di Noto—Your Viceregal Eminence can't imagine the admiration of the site given by all those that pass. Many of the Cavalieri from nearby cities come to enjoy the beautiful view [of the city] which is a marvel to everyone and provokes the envy of the neighbouring territories and cities . . . . Many fosses [earthworks] have been made around the site for defence . . . but because the beaches of Avola are all full of rocks . . . it is difficult for the Corsairs to disembark. In fact for decades no one can remember the Corsairs disembarking. . . . Some ministers have stated their desire to move the new city of Avola to another location farther away from the Sea because of fears of contraband. But this fear really doesn't apply to Avola's situation: for many years Avola's grain and wine magazines were located near the beaches, but as the ministers would confess there have never been any incidents of stealing. In fact, stealing was much easier to accomplish before, because now the magazines for wine and grain have to be built near the new city, and thus in view of everyone. They'll all be afraid, and it will be impossible for those who want to steal. . . . If Avola is built on the site designated by brother Italia it will be a great service to His Majesty and there will be less occasion for fraud.[39]

Using the foregoing defence of Avola, we can abstract the following good qualities of its site and disposition:

1 The site was chosen by a qualified authority who assessed a wide range of alternatives and selected the best possible location.
2 The site was within the territory of Avola.
3 The site was near the coast on a flat and fertile plain on a major road.
4 The site had its own fresh water supply, which ran two mills (mentioned in another communiqué).[40]
5 Given the nature of the coast, no costly walls were necessary; even if attacked the city could be defended from earthworks.
6 The site had salubrious air. By this the communiqué means that according to the standards of the Roman author Vitruvius the air of the site was not pestiferous. Vitruvius counsels his readers on choosing the most healthy kind of site:

> Now this will be high and free from clouds and hoar frost, and with an aspect neither hot nor cold but temperate. Besides, in this way a marshy neighbourhood shall be avoided. For when the morning breezes come with the rising sun to a town, and clouds rising from these shall be conjoined, and with their blast shall sprinkle on the bodies of the inhabitants the poisoned breaths of marsh animals, they will make the site pestilential.[41]

As a crude map of the area shows, Avola stands on a flat fertile plain near the banks of the Asinaro River (Pl. 10).[42] Although no marsh as such is close by, the Asinaro River basin is sometimes alive with mosquitoes, which are probably the poison breaths to which Vitruvius refers.[43] The site is also very hot in summer. Yet it seems to have passed the salubrious air test with flying colours.

Sites Selected for New Noto

With the rationale for the placement of Avola in mind it is easier to assess the townspeople's suggestions for Noto's new site. Map 2 (nos 2–9) illustrates the eight proposed locations for the new Noto. These fall into three groups: mountain, coast, and coastal plain. Seven of the sites are closer to the coast than Noto Antica (no. 1) was, indicating a tendency to favour the coastal plain over the inland mountains, probably due to the fear of resettling the city on land which would be as treacherous in earthquakes as Noto Antica's site was. Likewise, as Avola's resettlement demonstrates, coastal positions with traversable fertile, flat territory were preferred to isolated mountain positions.

Two sites, suggested by those who still pined for mountain locations, were understandably voted down. One suggested site was Cugno di Vasco (no. 2), a finger-like ridge on the eastern flank of Monte Alveria, on which Noto Antica stood. Aside from being free of ruins, Cugno di Vasco suffered the same deficiences as Noto Antica. About six kilometres south of Cugno di Vasco stood the hermitage of S. Giovanni detto la Lardia (no. 4). Although closer to the coast, the hermitage straddled a spur of mountains, and these steep slopes made the area around the hermitage unsatisfactory, although the final site for the city, the Pianazzo on the Meti, is just one half kilometre away.

In order to seize the greatest economic benefit from the move, citizens suggested that Noto try to develop harbour sites. One group voting in Camastra's council wanted to rebuild Noto next to the medieval tower of Vendicari on Capo Passero (no. 9). The medieval tower, armed with two bronze cannons, was manned by the Knights of Malta, who supplied their island fortress from magazines nearby.[44] A large expanse of salt flats lies near the tower, which overlooks a beautiful beach. With dredging, the site could yield an adequate harbour for small ships. To aid the Netinese, Raimondo Parillos, the Grand Master of Malta, offered to construct a harbour near the grain magazines.[45] However, the citizens of the powerful city of

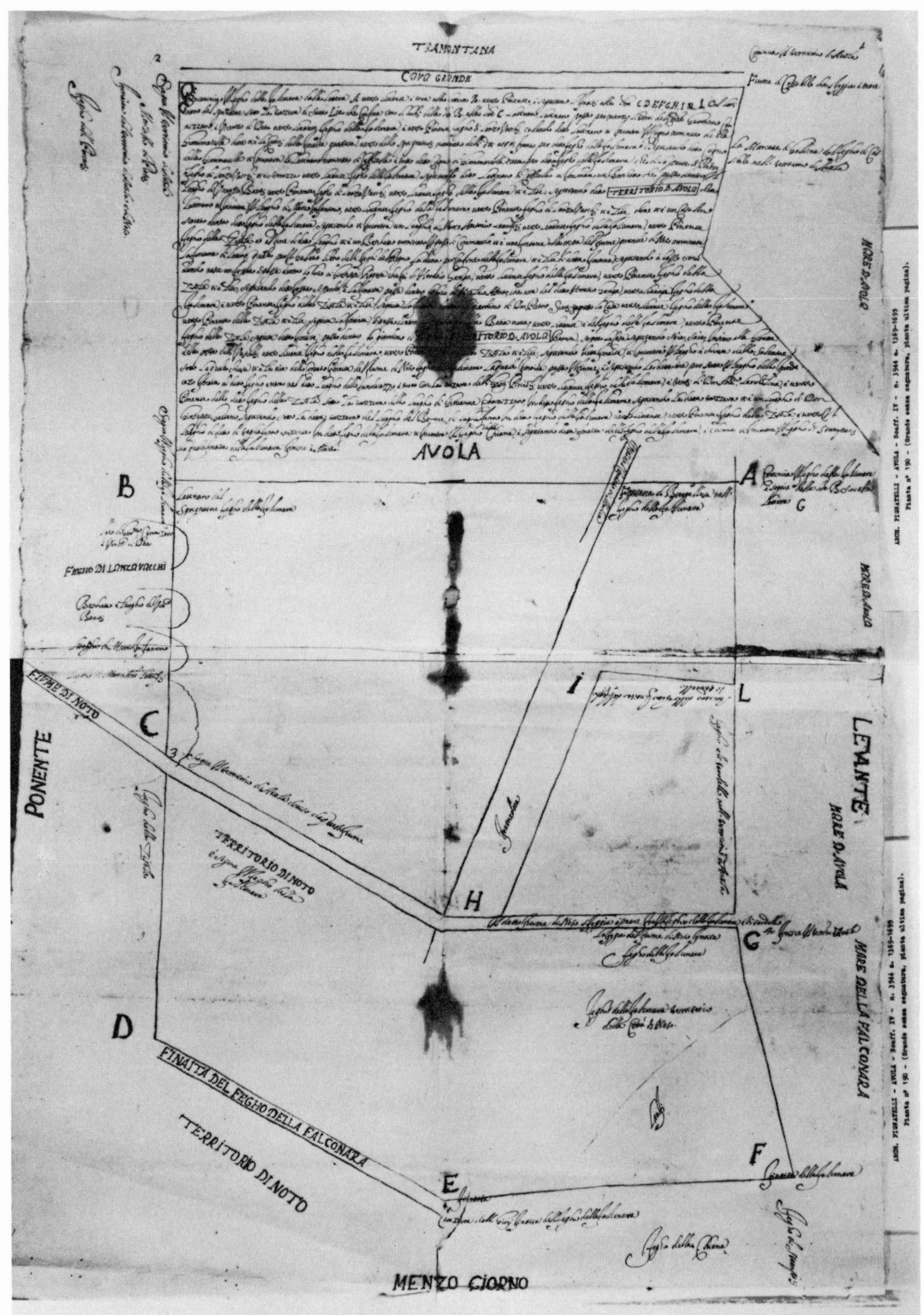

5 An eighteenth-century map of the feudo of the Falconara with a list of property owners and boundaries. The position of the Asinaro River shows how extensive the feudo of the Falconara was. Letters CC mark the river bed in the direction of Noto on the left and of the sea on the right.

Syracuse, which lies about 40 kilometres north-east of Noto, began to fear that a new harbour town might challenge their supremacy as a port. The Syracusans argued bitterly and lobbied well against Noto's new harbour site, defeating Noto's initiative.[46]

A second coastal site (no. 8), this one on a bluff overlooking the Stampace tower, built in 1315, was suggested.[47] Near the tower stood the ruins of the Greek city of Helorus. The Netinese looked upon Helorus with great pride, probably because the ancient ruins demonstrated Noto's link with the glories of classical antiquity.[48] Although the site offered little commercial advantage, it would at least have been closer to the rich plains of Noto's territory than the old city was. The agricultural workers of Noto could have been much closer to the most productive land in the

6 The church of the abandoned hermitage of Madonna della Marina.

territory, and perhaps increased occupation might have helped crop production in the area. The danger of the Stampace tower site was that it was close enough to the sea to be raided, yet did not compensate for that risk by providing the city with a harbour, and the Viceregal junta, which had attacked the new site of Avola for being so close to the sea, would never have approved of the establishment of Noto near the Stampace tower.

Rejecting the mountains and blocked in their efforts to move the city to the coast, the Netinese considered four sites along the coastal plain between the mountains and the coast. One of these was the feudo of the Falconara (no. 7) lying four and a half kilometres north-east of the Stampace tower on the banks of the Asinaro River.*[49] The feudo has extraordinarily rich soil which today supports luxurious almond and olive groves (for map of feudo see Pl. 5). The sites available within the feudo would have had all the attributes that Avola had. But half of this very favourable location was owned by the city of Avola, and the feudo was in fact within two kilometres of Avola's new location, and these factors effectively blocked any move to the Falconara feudo.

Another site between the mountains and the coast was the area around the hermitage of Madonna della Marina (no. 6).[50] The plain of Madonna della Marina is about five kilometres away from the shoreline on a slight rise, just one and a half kilometres distant from the Feudo of the Falconara. The ruins of the hermitage stand today among groves of olive trees on a gentle hill in what appears to be a very satisfactory location for a city (Pls 6–7). The area catches breezes, has a fair water supply, and lies on the Avola–Modica road. It does not have a good view of the coastline, however, and might thus have been subject to surprise attacks.

Further inland than Madonna della Marina, at the foot of the Hyblaean

*Throughout the text the name Asinaro is used to describe the river which passes beneath Noto Antica and runs past Noto Nuova to the sea. Officially the river changes its name to Fiume di Noto between the new city and the sea.

7 Present-day Noto seen from the roof of Madonna della Marina.

8 A view south towards the coast from the fuedo of Busulmone, a proposed site for the new Noto.

mountains, lies the territory of the feudo of Busulmone (no. 3), owned by the Sortino family of Noto. The feudo as a whole is very hilly, with several narrow fingers of land extending to the south-east (Pl. 8). On one of these is the plain of Rumanello suggested as a site for the city.[51] It commands sweeping views of the coast and plains. Though access to the feudo is more difficult than that to Madonna della Marina, it has a better defensive position because of its distance from the coast and its higher elevation.

The Chosen Site: The Pianazzo on the Feudo of the Meti

The fourth site on the coastal plain, and that which was finally selected for the new Noto, was the *Pianazzo* (large plain; in local dialect, *chianazzu*) of the feudo of the Meti at the extreme north-eastern portion of Noto's administrative territory.[52] The feudo of the Meti (no. 5) lies to the north-east of Madonna della Marina, to the south-east of the feudo of Busulmone, on the north-western border of the feudo of Falconara, five kilometres from the coast and seven kilometres from old Noto. The hill on which the existing city is built rises just to the north of the Asinaro River,

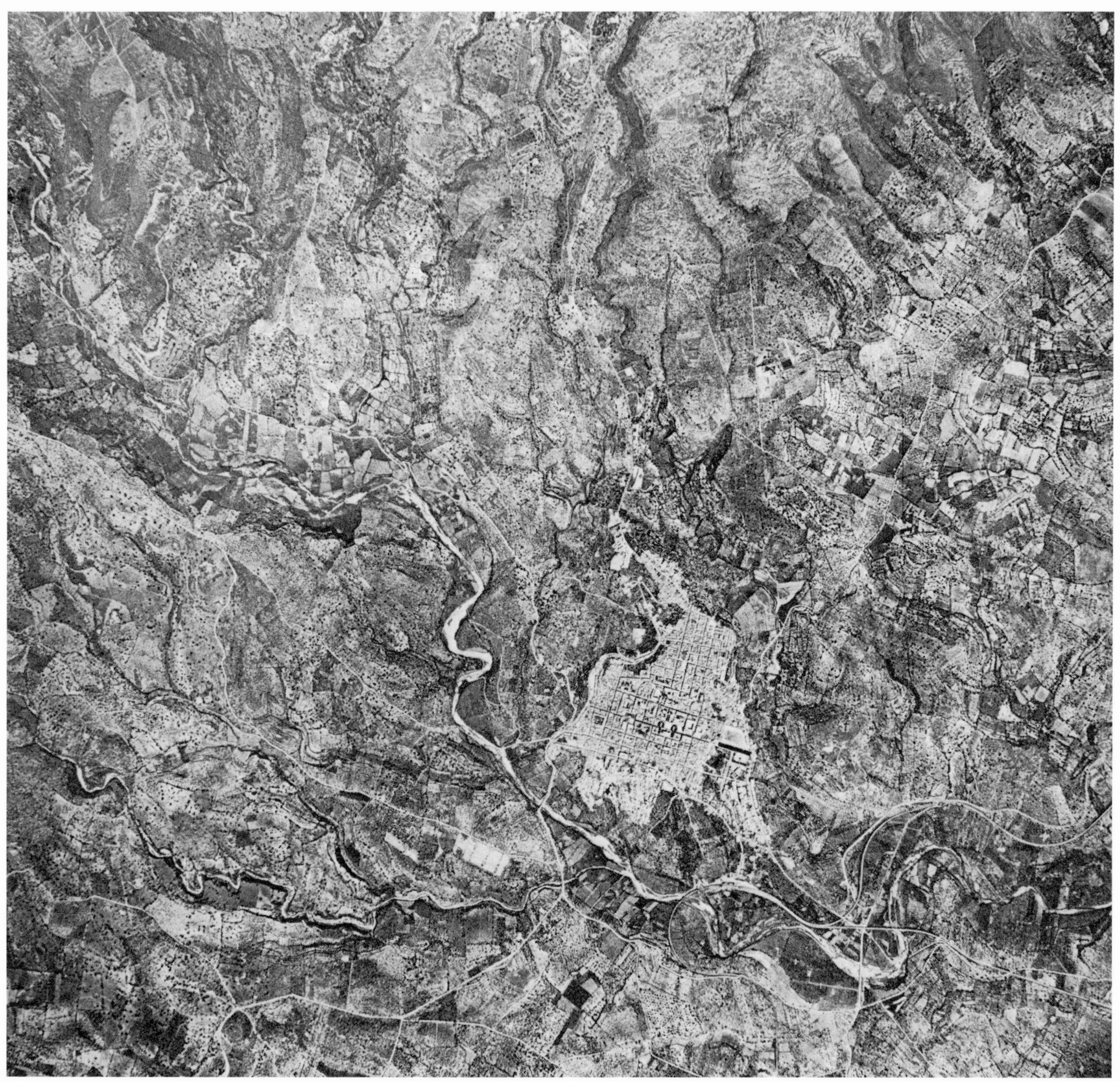

9 An aerial photograph of the feudo of the Meti today with the city in the centre and the Asinaro River snaking towards the sea.

which also flowed below the old city (Pl. 9). The Duke of Camastra consented to the choice of the Meti on the condition that the city would be erected only on the Pianazzo, the large plain at the summit of the hill, and not on the slopes below it (Map 3).[53]

The Pianazzo shares many of the virtues of the feudo of Busulmone, just across the Asinaro River. Both overlook the road into the interior which follows the deep valley of the Asinaro. Both offer fine positions from which defenders could view the sea, the coastal plains, and the mountains to the north. Both are high enough to catch the breezes above the hot plains, yet close enough to the coastal road and the sea to benefit from trade.

The Pianazzo is isolated from the surrounding countryside, yet is flat enough to accommodate the layout of a small city (but not a large one). The summit could be fortified on all sides: on the north and east cliffs separate it from the plain below; steep slopes drop away to the west; on the southern side, a drop of about sixteen metres separates it from the slopes of the Meti, which gently descend to the northern bank of the Asinaro River.[54] The river itself provides a secondary defensive boundary for the city. The only level approach to the Pianazzo is a ridge which connects the north-west corner to the mountain chain on which the hermitage of San Giovanni detto la Lardia stands.

The advantages of the Pianazzo on the Meti were the following:

1 A defensive position with good views of attackers and natural defensive barriers.
2 Cooler weather than the plains, with some distance from malarial mosquitoes.
3 Near the fertile plains, yet far enough from the coast to discourage surprise attacks.
4 Adjacent to the road leading into the interior and close to its junction with the coastal road.
5 Water enough for the mills of the city *if* channelled properly; enough potable water *if* aqueduct constructed.

To these obvious advantages, another more subtle one must be added: the Pianazzo is reminiscent in shape of the summit of Monte Alveria, on which the old city of Noto stood. Its similarity may have made the nostalgic remembrances of the old city more easily transferable to the new. In any case, choosing the site on the Meti was certainly understandable in the context of the choices available and the criteria for a good site suggested by the Avola communiqués.

Nevertheless, the Pianazzo had its disadvantages. Although the site itself was level, the approach was very arduous, somewhat limiting its accessibility. But the most damning qualities of the new site were its lack of immediately available water and its insufficient area. The former drawback could be remedied by an aqueduct, but the latter meant that Noto could not be planned as a level walled city entirely on the Pianazzo, but necessarily had to occupy the slope of the Meti. Unfortunately, officials realized the small size of the Pianazzo and the insufficient water supply too late to change their selection. They may have based their population calculations on the small number of citizens who gathered in the temporary quarters of Noto after the earthquake and thereby underestimated the area the new city required; only when more people began to return to Noto may the inadequacies of the site have become noticeable.

One of the most puzzling drawbacks to the site on the Meti was that it was owned by the city of Avola. A crude undated map of the territory of Avola in the Pignatelli Archives illustrates Noto Antica and Noto Nuova in the early 1700s (Pl. 10).[55] Around the symbolic representation of Noto Nuova, an encircling legend reads:

> The new city of Noto situated in the feudo of the Meti which is the property of the Seigneurs [?] of the State of Avola and from them conceded to the secretariat for a perpetual annual rent.[56]

The secretariat referred to on the map may have been the office of one of the King's secretaries. Camastra may have appealed directly to the King to order the Avolese to rent the site to Noto. Although no corroborating document has been found, there is no doubt that the city of Noto rented the Meti, probably from Avola.

At the time of the earthquake the Pignatelli family, who held the Dukedom of Terranova, owned Avola.[57] According to the city architect of Noto Nuova, Paolo Labisi, writing in the early 1770s, Noto's senate paid a yearly rent to Baron Melchiore Sirugo of Avola.[58] The Baron of Avola acquired the formal title of Baron of the Meti and Santa Domenica in 1790.[59] The only other piece of evidence for the ownership of Noto Nuova in the hundred years after the earthquake is Noto's tax account in the 1740s, which lists the city of Noto paying money to its 'Padrone'.[60] However, although Noto enlarged its territory by renting the new site from a succession of non-Netinese nobles, jurisdiction over the land was retained by the city of Noto because Noto was a fief of the King of Spain and had the right to govern

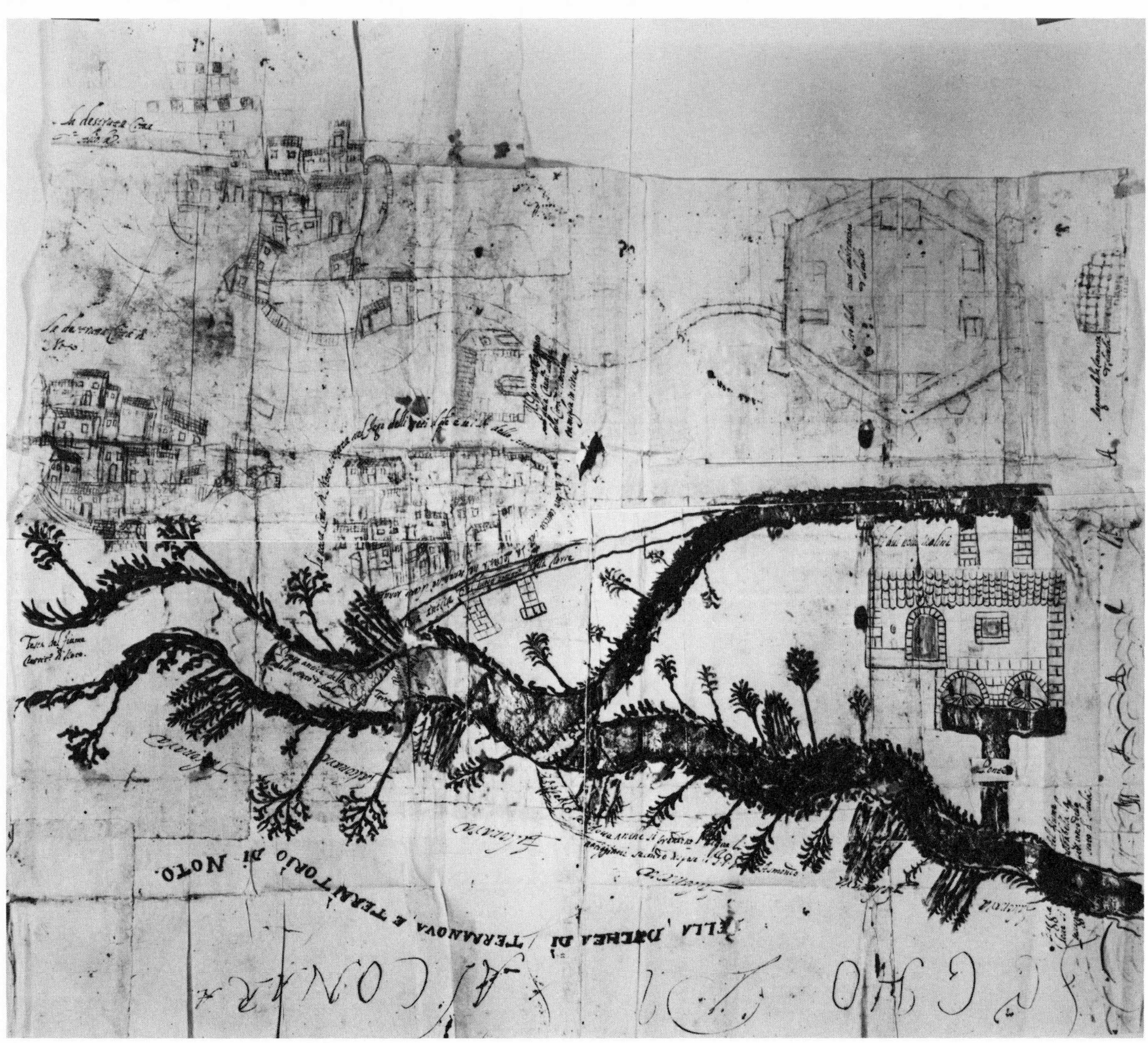

10 An anonymous eighteenth-century map illustrating the old and new cities of Noto and Avola as well as the territory between them. The interior of the island (west) would be on the left side of the map, the seashore on the right. The old city of Avola (La destrutta città) appears in the upper left and the new city is represented as a hexagon in the upper right. Below and to the left of the destroyed city of Avola is Noto Antica (La destrutta città di Noto). To the right of Noto Antica is the new location of Noto. Around its perimeter is the inscription discussed in the text. The mills (molini) under contention appear in the lower right. The artist includes notations of landmarks and even notes the interior plan of Avola's storage magazines on the shore (upper right).

its own affairs, albeit with allegiance to the King and his ministers.[61]

Given Noto's immense territory, why did the city have to rent land for its new site from an outsider? The answer to this puzzling question is still not clear, but perhaps it lies in the nature of land-ownership within the Netinese territories. Noto's nobles owned land in the mountains and on the coastal plains. Many of them had intermarried and thus established common interests, yet they were often rent apart by bloody feuds.[62] While one man might gain from the foundation of a city on his territory, the others might stand to lose, or at best remain the same. Again, part of the deadlock in the councils may have been caused by aristocrats and church officials recommending the use of the land that they or their allies owned. Perhaps in order to limit the gain of any citizen from the selection, a completely outside rented parcel of land was chosen. The Meti may have represented a kind of no-man's-land. Perhaps, too, the authorities genuinely believed that the site of the Meti was the best around, and that it would serve the city well while quieting the feuding nobles. Finally, it is even possible that the Duke of Camastra was trying to weaken Noto in favour of Avola: Giuseppe Asmundo's relatives, the strong Landolina family who had taken part in suggesting the site, made a petition to settle in the new Avola, completely deserting Noto.[63]

Spanish Policies and the Selection

There is one other factor that may have played its part in the selection of the site for the new city: the unstated economic and military policies of the Spanish crown. The Spanish had valid reasons for wanting Noto rebuilt closer to the coast. The fortress of Noto Antica, while superbly located, was a patchwork of bastions, towers, and curtain walls which could never have withstood a concentrated bombardment, and would have been judged obsolete by a military engineer favouring the unified designs of seventeenth-century fortifications in Europe. Therefore the strategic value of Noto Antica in the eyes of the Spanish may have been lessened. To rebuild the fortress, not only as it had been but improved as the Netinese would have demanded, would have cost a great deal, and the government was already faced with the prospect of rebuilding more than forty towns. During this same period, repairs on the main coastal fortresses of south-eastern Sicily – Augusta and Syracuse – were proceeding slowly, which indicates Spain's inability to support such enterprises.[64] And of course, in Sicily, Spain was definitely losing significant revenue because it was not receiving taxes from many stricken cities, including Noto. The crown could avoid the cost of rebuilding Noto's fortress by removing the city from its old site and putting it in a location where it would need no fortifications. Thus the new site could not be on the coast, because the sea was definitely unsafe; it could, however, be some kilometres removed from the sea, but nowhere near the old site, lest the people get nostalgic about their status as a former fortified town.

It is also probable that the Spanish wanted to defend both Noto and Avola, the town to the north-east of it, by making only one of them a fortress. If Avola were a fortress and if it were near Noto, then both cities could be protected for the price of one set of walls. The new site of Avola was just four kilometres north-east of the Meti and only one kilometre or so away from the sea. The plan for the new city of Avola was hexagonal (Pls 11 and 12), seemingly modelled on sixteenth-century prototypes of fortified cities. The streets were laid out not radially (as in the case of the famous Venetian fort of Palmanova), but in a grid plan, which resembles the admixture of grids and polygonal figures that Cataneo and Scamozzi represent in their treatises.[65] This plan was dictated not only by aesthetics, but by defence, a necessity since Avola was built so close to the shore. Thus the plan is not as irrelevant and old-fashioned as it might seem; even modern military engineers like the Frenchman Vauban were still designing grid-planned, polygonal cities and fortresses which were the descendants of Cataneo's sixteenth-century designs.[66]

Avola is illustrated by V. M. Amico in his *Lexicon Topographicum Siculum* (Palermo, 1757) as a fortified town (Pl. 12).[67] But the walls and bastions which are illustrated in the view do not seem convincing: they lack dimensions and possess not one gateway. In the text in which the author describes the city, he comments that its outer bastions are not yet complete, which explains their schematic character on the view.[68] What is certain from Avola's position, plan, and the evidence that fortifications were under construction, however, is that the city was meant to be fortified.

No such evidence of fortification is present at Noto, as we shall see. In fact, the citizens complained of a complete lack of protection, due to the scarcity of soldiers and the absence of a wall surrounding the city.[69] Thus, Avola seems to have been intended as a fortress from its inception, while Noto was not, and we might therefore hypothesize that Noto was positioned close to Avola in order to be protected from Moslem raiders by sea and robbers by land. In this manner, the crown cut its expenses by more than half. Avola was a baronial city so the crown may have been exempted from the expense of erecting its fortifications while these same low-lying bastions could nevertheless serve the purpose of Spain by protecting Noto. In addition, the crown saved the prodigious cost of clearing the roads to old Avola and old Noto.

There is a second reason why the Spanish may have preferred moving Noto to the Meti. Because of dwindling resources and the continuing danger of the French

11 Aerial photograph of Avola.

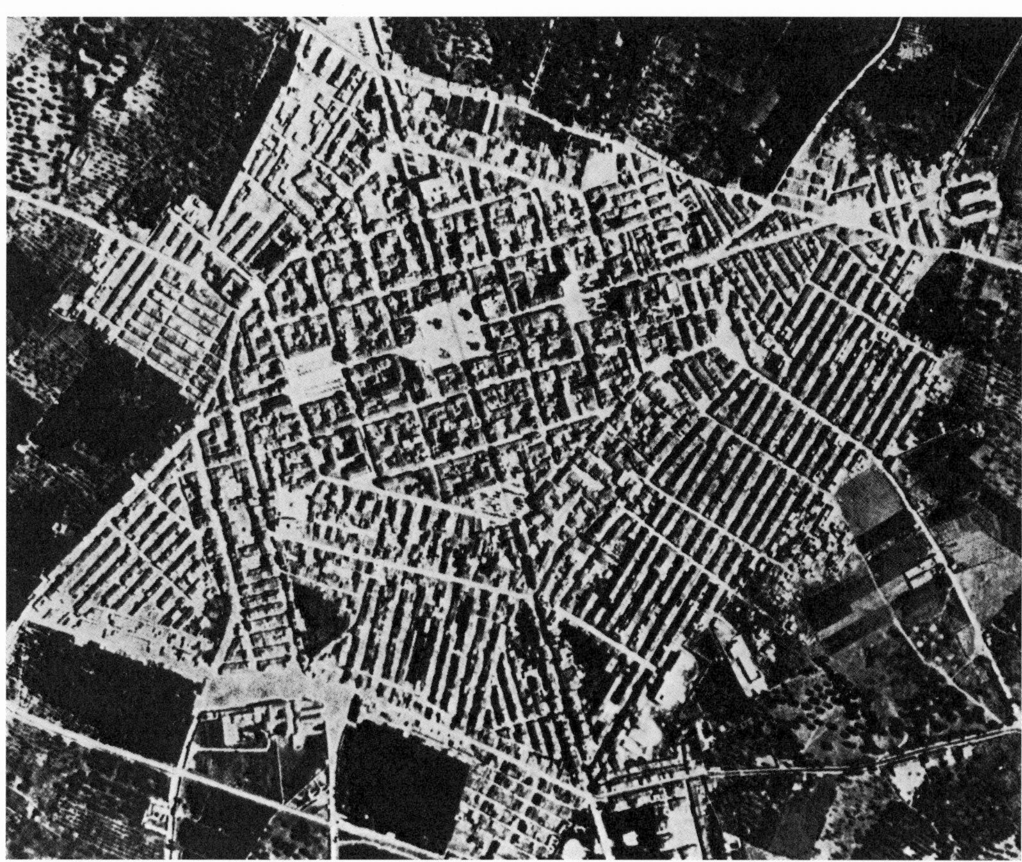

12 Plan of Avola.

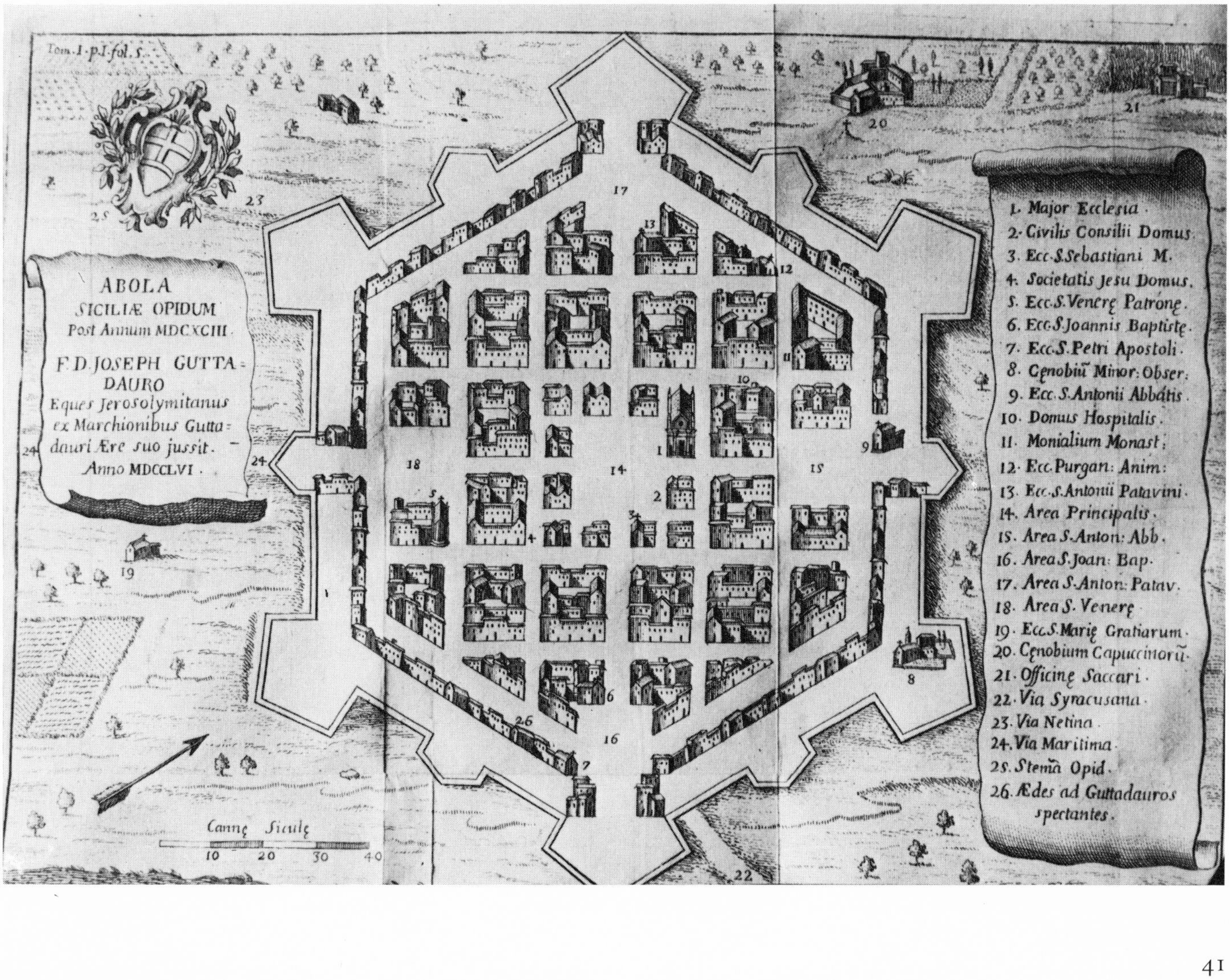

capacity to mount a Mediterranean naval attack, the Spanish were probably forced to place their faith in coastal defences at the expense of inland fortifications. Even if military advisers believed Noto's fortress was important insurance for the rear flank of Syracuse, they still had to think first of primary lines of defence, and certainly Noto could not be included in these. So the abandonment of both old Noto and old Avola would not only have saved money, but would probably have fitted nicely into an overall strategic policy which had phased out old inland forts.

Finally, by moving Noto, the Spanish authorities could both provide security for the tenuous road system which linked the parts of the island,[70] and bring workers to rich farmland. The transfer of the city brought a flow of people to the coastal plain, thereby encouraging commerce and agriculture. Both the Sicilians and the Spaniards used new cities in just such a manner. For centuries, Sicilian nobles created new cities to provide themselves with lucrative and prestigious fiefs, and often offered inducements to draw townspeople and farmers onto their lands.[71] Similarly, the Spanish monarchy directed the foundation and population of a string of cities along the important Cordoba–Madrid road in the eighteenth century to bring farmers to the deserted central plateau of Spain and to keep the vital communication route free from brigandage.[72]

Given the situation of Noto after the earthquake of 1693, its transfer to the Meti seems generally wise and understandable. Noto Antica was no longer judged a good building site, being outmoded by new concepts about where and how cities should be built. Isolated medieval cities with tortuous streets were being replaced by accessible flat geometrical cities. The Netinese, who saw their neighbours trying to establish new cities according to these standards, reluctantly agreed to leave the site of Noto Antica. It is true that the Netinese had to sacrifice their fortress but given the lack of money to repair it and rebuild the city, they had no other choice. The Netinese could see commercial advantages in moving toward the sea and the plains which may have compensated in their eyes for the defensive position and traditional associations which they had to leave behind. And the Pianazzo on the Meti was the perfect compromise site—between the mountains and the coast, on a promontory but flat, removed from the plain but not far. It met the criteria for a good building site: healthy air, available water, flatness, fertility, and natural defensive position on a hill. Finally, the transfer and refounding of Noto dove-tailed well with the policies of Spain, which wanted to cut costs by not rebuilding Noto Antica's fort, to populate the coast, and quickly to re-establish the city so that it could once again pay badly-needed taxes.

Chapter 3 Disenchantment and Dissent: the New City challenged

Both the people of Noto and the Viceregal emissaries, for their own interests, wanted a quick and decisive resolution to the problem of where to rebuild Noto. There were many sound reasons to support Camastra's decision to transfer Noto to the Pianazzo of the Meti. But the speed of Camastra's decision, the disorganization of Noto's scattered population, and an intransigence that characterized Noto's internal affairs jeopardized the rebuilding of Noto Nuova. The internal conflicts, described in this chapter, threatened the future of Noto on the Meti for nine years, from 1693 to 1702, and are an extended comment on the initial decision to transfer the city.

Two continuing struggles were responsible for this prolonged period of transition. The first and major rift was within the population itself. The upper class, clergy and aristocracy, wanted to remain on the new location while a majority of the lower class, artisans and agricultural workers, wanted to return to Noto Antica. The second rift was between the Netinese settlers and their Viceregal advisers. Within the Meti, the city could have been raised on one of two locations, the Pianazzo (hereafter called the summit) or the slope of the Meti (hereafter, the slope); the settlers endorsed the slope, the Viceregal advisers favoured the summit. These struggles will be described in detail because the social and political background of the founding of Noto Nuova is fundamental to understanding the building which resulted.

A Forced Move

Because the Netinese were not unanimous in their endorsement of re-siting on the feudo of the Meti, government authorities had to prod them to leave the old site of Noto Antica. The Duke of Camastra, perhaps foreseeing oncoming complications, wisely left at this point, leaving the deteriorating situation to Judge Giuseppe Asmundo, Commissary General, who implemented the evacuation of the old site.[1] The evacuation was initiated in May and continued through June 1693. In early May, Asmundo wrote a dispatch to the Viceroy in which he relates establishing the new city on the Meti with a 'spirit of not returning to the ruins'.[2] It was probably Asmundo who arranged a sacred procession of clergy which brought the most precious relic of the city, the arc of S. Corrado, patron saint of Noto, to the new site in summer 1693. City senators in togas welcomed the arc and sheltered it in a temporary hut on the slope of the Meti, thus investing the Meti with the ceremonial dignity of the old city.[3] Some of the people, perhaps most of the people, still did not want to build the city on the Meti. Impellizzeri probably overstates his argument when he writes that 'everyone uniformly did not want to leave . . . Noto Antica',[4] but no doubt dissension was widespread. The anonymous chronicler and Impellizzeri concur that the citizens were forced to move to the new site.[5]

If the Netinese were forced to vacate Noto Antica against their wishes, it would not be a unique situation in the annals of Spanish urban practice. In 1773, an earthquake destroyed the prosperous royal city of Santiago, Guatemala.[6] The Captain General representing the Spanish government decided to vacate the site in favour of a new location, giving the new city the name of New Guatemala. (The ruins came to be known as Old- or Antigua-Guatemala.) After a similar disaster in 1717, the citizens of Santiago had decided to rebuild on the same site, and there is no reason to presume that they would not have rebuilt the old city again in the same

Map 3 The Meti. Contour map reconstructing the appearance of the two grids from the buildings on the site, *ca.* 1694.
A First settlement
B Bed of Coffitella; the aqueduct intake is north of this point outside the map.
C Bed of the Asinaro River

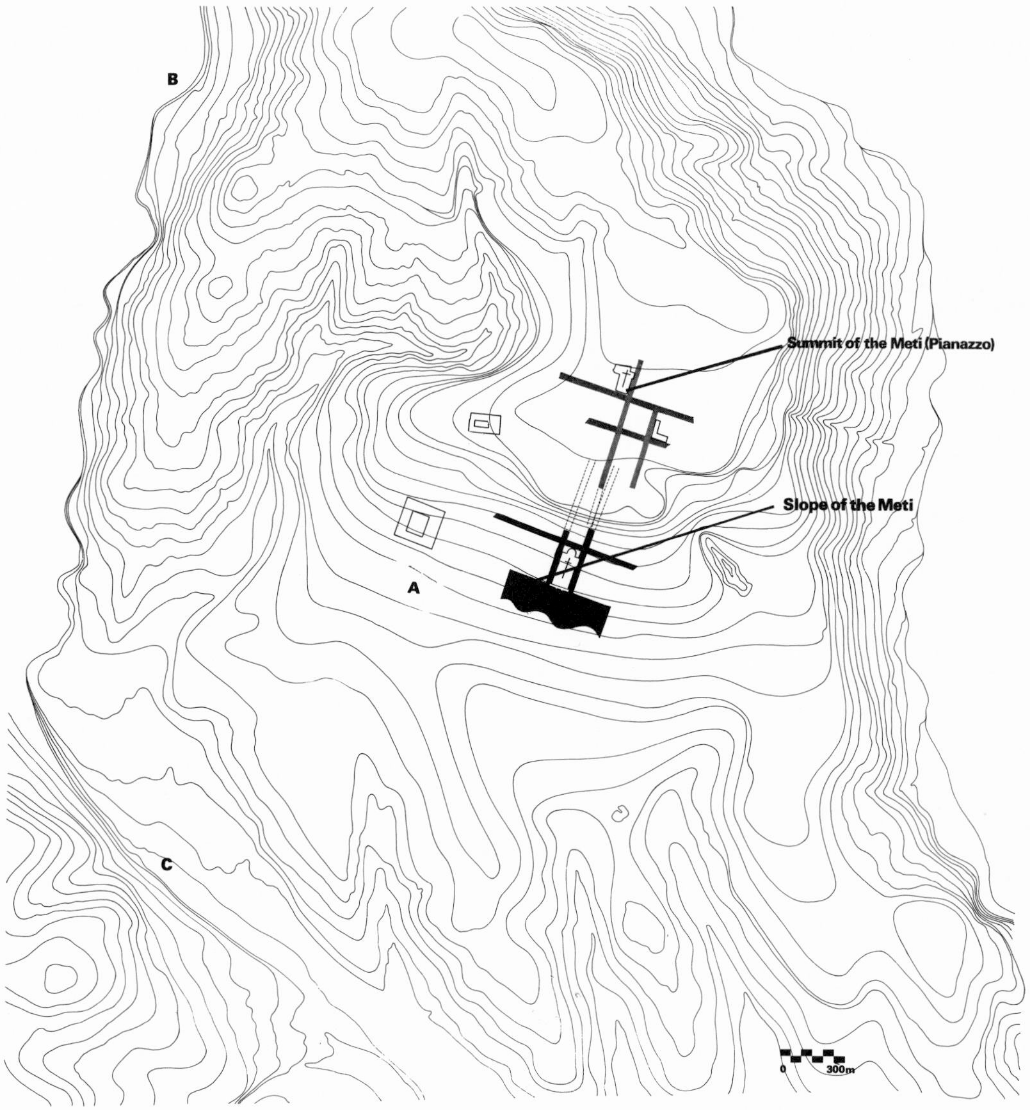

location after the earthquake of 1773. Yet in spite of the Archbishop's opposition and the city council's decision to rebuild on the same site, the Captain General commanded that the city be moved and that all surviving buildings be stripped and demolished.

Ad Hoc Planning on the Slope of the Meti

The leaders directing Noto's transfer and reconstruction were not as decisive as Guatemala's Captain General. Their vacillation and ineptitude are recorded in Noto's plan. Once Asmundo had assembled a portion of Noto's population on the Meti, he began to encounter problems in making them settle on the summit, the site insisted upon by Camastra because it was both healthy and defensible. Asmundo's first error was to allow the sacred procession from the old site to the new to deposit the arc of S. Corrado on the slope of the Meti instead of the summit (Map 3, letter A). By condoning a temporary resting place for the arc on the slope, Asmundo tacitly endorsed the establishment of Noto's ceremonial centre outside the summit. Asmundo may well have conceded to wishes of evacuees who may have felt the approach to the summit was too steep, and the summit itself too high and lacking in water.

Early in June, the King's secretary dispatched orders to Asmundo urging him to apply himself with fervour to the construction of Noto on the Meti.[7] Exactly where the city was to be built on the Meti is unspecified in these orders. But the secretary advises that the nobles – who evidently balked at settling on the site – should be encouraged to build their temporary dwellings on the Meti and thereby encourage others to do so.[8] He further advises that fences be constructed around religious houses to avert scandals which were rampant following the earthquake.[9] A Chiesa Madre was to be built, for the spiritual good of the city, and a city jail erected for the incarceration of the numerous thieves who roamed the countryside; mills were to be built for grain production, and an aqueduct.[10]

The secretary seemed concerned that some dissatisfied nobles might join forces with those commoners who refused to establish themselves on the new site. But by the end of June, six hundred huts were occupied on the new site, and the dissenting nobles had been persuaded to settle the Meti, serving as a good example for the commoners.[11]

Unhealthy Conditions and Plague on the Slope of the Meti

In July 1693, an epidemic struck the population. The anonymous chronicler and other observers, biased and unbiased, ascribe the cause of the epidemic to the rigours of transferring the city and to the poor qualities of the air on the new site. The chronicler recounts, for example, that the citizens:

> . . . having made the passage from that light and healthy air [of the old site] to this heavy and pestiferous atmosphere, in addition to those miseries – the loss of goods and relatives, the necessity of food and clothing – these miserable citizens were assaulted by the universal death, which it seemed everyone caught.[12]

Detractors of the Meti and even an unbiased team of royal investigators condemned the air on the new site as heavy, pestiferous, and unhealthy.[13] In the summer, the whole Meti, like most of the coast of Sicily, becomes extraordinarily hot and humid. An added disadvantage may have been malarial mosquitoes breeding on the plains and infecting the site.[14] The slope of the Meti, where the population lived in 1693, might have been slightly hotter and more humid than the summit, and somewhat closer to the mosquitoes. Certainly, if compared with the temperature of the old site in the summer, particularly the crispness of its evening air, the climate of the Meti would be judged less healthy.

The move to the site itself may have triggered diseases which were previously insignificant. As early as April, when most of the population had not yet moved to the Meti, sworn witnesses informed the Viceroy that people were suffering from diseases. The Viceroy asked Camastra to investigate. Camastra sent him sworn statements from physicians who said that no more than five persons had died of known diseases between 19 April and 22 May.[15] These deaths appear to have been a warning that went unheeded.

Although the initial move to the site began in May, people were still arriving in June, when the summer temperatures on the Meti begin to rise. There was some water on the site but not enough. The crucial Coffitella aqueduct was still under construction.[16] Site preparation and planning were haphazard at best because Asmundo and Camastra had misjudged the difficulty of laying out a city on the Meti. It isn't hard to imagine the population trying to establish itself on the new site in the blistering summer heat, exhausted and without shelter. The unhealthiness of the slope and the diseases that were threatening, combined with disastrous planning on the part of Asmundo and Camastra, precipitated an epidemic of the plague which killed as many as 3,000 of Noto's citizens, understandably dampening enthusiasm for the new site.[17] Many of those who survived the plague lost confidence in Noto and left the city, reducing its population from the pre-earthquake total of 12,000 to a meagre 4,000.

Transfer of the Lowermost Institutions to the Summit

In 1694, after the epidemic had subsided, Camastra returned to Noto only to find his orders for the placement of the city had been countermanded. Although Camastra had ordered the city to be erected on the summit, Asmundo had let the people remain on the slope, on which they were beginning to build permanent constructions. When Camastra found that people had been building on the slope of the Meti, he ordered them to move their huts up to the summit, which he had designated as the site for the city. In addition, when he found that the church of SS. Crocifisso and convents of S. Francesco di Paola and S. Maria di Gesù were being built low on the slope, he had their foundations transferred to the summit (Map 4). According to the anonymous chronicler, these three buildings were transferred to the summit because the air on the slope was 'heavy and unhealthy owing to the vicinity of the Asinaro River'. Yet the whole population was not moved from the slope, Padre Tortora explains, because of the hardships that the Netinese had already suffered. Assailed by protests, Camastra let S. Nicolò, the Chiesa Madre, remain on the slope. In the end, because the summit was too small to accommodate the entire city, and because it lacked easy access to water, a majority of the population settled permanently on the slope of the Meti.[18]

The City grows on the Slope

Asmundo, who had from the first permitted settlement on the slope, seems by November 1694 to have incorporated it into what he calls the 'design' of the city. The nature of this early plan for Noto will be examined more fully in Chapter 4, but for now it is important to see how the slope and summit were united into a single city. In his report to the Viceroy, Asmundo is still ambiguous about the slope, although he seems to include it in his idea of the 'site of the city':

> . . . but the principal difficulty is that none wants to transfer to the higher site of the Pianazzo which is the better and more assured one as much for the site of the city as for its good air; and one finds many people outside the site of the city settling in miserable huts . . . and these people have to be brought into the site of design [sic], . . . within a few days . . . I have transported a good part of the people [to the site].[19]

In the same communiqué, Asmundo asserted hopefully that the number of houses on the site, including the slope and the summit, grew from day to day.

Part of the reason for the growth of the city is explained by an ordinance promulgated in 1693 to make sure that people settled in Noto Nuova.[20] The ordinance declared that the university or senate of the town had the right to distribute land to anyone who needed it, upon approval of the architect or civil engineer of the city. If the person to whom the land was consigned did not built on it, he lost it. Obviously, to secure land in the new city, the people had to start building on it.

Ordinances designed to attract settlers were common in Europe from the Middle Ages to the eighteenth century.[21] Building plots that had become vacant were offered to those who were ready and able to build; subsidies and tax exemptions were often granted, and building materials supplied, or their transportation subsidized. Sometimes construction itself was partially paid for by the ruler. Protection was guaranteed. In Noto's case, the inducement was free or cheap land, which if not taken and occupied would fall to others.

Another reason for the building activity was that the church became anxious to establish its religious houses on the new site, in order to stop the scandals.[22] On 18 August 1693, the concern over possible scandals was communicated to Asmundo. These scandals ran the gamut from talking to outsiders to at least one case of sexual relations between a nun and a soldier. Later, in 1694, detailed instructions from the Bishop of Syracuse explain that the nuns in particular must be cloistered. Cloisters made of planks several metres high were to screen the nuns from the rest of the population, and a supervised *parlatorio* (visiting area) with grating was to separate them from their visitors.

The ecclesiastical community could well afford to build in Noto.[23] The church was collecting revenues for its proposed constructions and other expenses by charging an ecclesiastical tax on all the sacraments performed in Noto. Religious houses and churches stricken during the earthquake had special dispensation from the government and religious leaders to coin their gold and silver at the Palermo mint. They received money from Rome as well as assistance from the Spanish crown. In fact, the ecclesiastical junta in Palermo was well funded and able to spend vast sums on building projects while the secular junta complained it lacked money to repair even the primary forts of Sicily.

Dissension after Five Years on the Site: A Vote to settle or abandon the Meti

Even as the city grew, indecision and internal dissent jeopardized its existence. While Asmundo directed the layout and dispensed property, a group which had not consented to move Noto to the Meti in the first place became more vocal. The group was apparently led by Don Antonino Impellizzeri, the Marchese of Campo Reale and Noto's Captain of Justice, who ruled the city for a short time after the earthquake from a temporary site on the edge of Noto Antica. Thus, in spite of elaborate settlement operations continuing on the Meti, this group continued to lobby for a return to Noto Antica.

Outcries from these dissidents continued for years, and finally led the Viceroy, in October 1698, to request the Netinese to hold a vote which was to decide once and for all the site of the city.[24] Probably in hope of ending dissonance, the mandate was given to all male citizens of Noto instead of to a select group of nobles and ecclesiastics. It is possible, too, that the four senators governing Noto were themselves deadlocked, and the voting was one way to uncover the wishes of the people through direct participatory democracy. Because there was as yet no city hall, the referendum took place for several days in the present Piazza XVI Maggio, hereafter referred to by its original name, Piazza S. Domenico (see Map 6, letter A).

At the end of the referendum, the notaries tallied 747 votes, 266 in favour of the new site on the Meti, 481 in favour of the old site of Noto Antica.[25] The preponderance of votes favouring a return to the old city came from the lowest classes of the population. Small landowners and day labourers, identifying themselves as *uomini di çampagna* (farmers) or *popoli minuti* (working-class people) voted 249 to 44 to return to the old site.[26] A majority of the workers and artisans also endorsed the old site.[27] But the clergy, nobles, doctors, lawyers, notaries and pharmacists voted as a solid block for the new site.[28]

The aristocracy and clergy generally wrote after their names on the ballot that they wanted to remain on the new site because the Duke of Camastra said they should and the Viceroy approved his choice. In other words, they were unwilling to contradict the wishes of their superiors. It is doubtful that their loyalty stemmed from a sense of moral obligation to the Duke or the Viceroy; it was most likely motivated by the fear of reprisals from these powerful figures. Their vote may thus indicate that 'they knew their place' in relation to the central government of Sicily.

As opposed to the aristocrats and clergy who endorsed the Meti, Don Antonino Impellizzeri expressed the view of the majority of the lower classes in a long and critical commentary on Noto which he appended to his ballot.[29] According to Impellizzeri, conditions in Noto Nuova from 1693 to 1698 were extraordinarily poor. The population lacked everything: there was no profit from commerce, no cheese, no meat, no oil, no fruit, and no rice. Furthermore, the water supplied by the Coffitella aqueduct was not sufficient, and because the aqueduct was made of soft stones, the water came full of mud and small rocks. So murky was the water, claims Impellizzeri, that the people suffered from it. He accuses an unnamed 'gentleman' of having his water supply brought in from outside. In addition, the city was impossible to police, because of its awkward position, and was impossible to protect, because it was too close to the coast. He contrasted the new city with the old, explaining that Noto Antica had the advantage of the trade of the mountains and was protected by walls and bastions which completely surrounded it. The old city had guarded Syracuse from the rear, and had served against the 1674 insurrection of Messina. It had been strong and rich because of its mountain position.

It is impossible to discern all of Impellizzeri's motives for urging return to Noto Antica. Probably his concern was honourable but there are suggestions that private considerations may also have been involved. Impellizzeri's negative commentary on the conditions in the city may have been the outcome of a vendetta against Asmundo and Camastra, who had initiated the move to the Meti in the first place and who had brought Impellizzeri to trial for misconduct after the earthquake.[30] Impellizzeri not only may have been trying to discredit these outsiders, but may have been after an old rival within Noto itself: the strong Landolina family of Noto (some of whom had moved to Avola after the earthquake) was evidently related to the Asmundos of Catania.[31] It was a Landolina who may have been responsible for selecting the site on the Meti in the first place.[32] Impellizzeri could have been engaged in a feud with the Landolinas, or perhaps he saw them profiting financially from the position of the new city because it was close to the land they owned.

The Upper-Class Position[33]

Considering Noto's situation, the split in the population along class lines is understandable. The clergy and aristocracy had funds to invest in building, whereas the lower classes did not. Both the church and the individual nobles may have welcomed an opportunity to invest in land and buildings during the late seventeenth century – a period of economic depression and political uncertainty.[34] By the mere act of erecting a temporary structure, they claimed land on the Meti according to a 1693 proclamation.[35] They could then erect a building, rent its rooms, or use it as a storehouse, which in time of economic depression is a wise investment. They also may have understood that Noto's only hope for survival was as a magnet for provincial society. If it could not be a port like Syracuse, and if inland cities suffered from transportation difficulties, then at least it could be closer to the coast, and at the same time attempt to re-establish its reputation as a provincial centre.

Since the upper classes of Noto's society had overseers inspecting their fields and supervising workers, there was no need for them to be near the fiefs they possessed. They were free to settle anywhere they chose. Freed from the necessity of remaining in a given location and, while aware of economic conditions, free to invest where they wanted, the upper classes could consider the prestige of Noto as a provincial centre. A new location would give them more freedom to build in the style they wanted, enabling each one to present a façade in accordance with his place in society.

Medieval fortress cities perched on mountains were no longer in fashion. Seventeenth-century gardens required ample space, streets were more pleasing if straight and flat, squares more perfect if they spread over extensive tracts of land. All these features required a flatter site than Noto Antica's. Seventeenth- and eighteenth-century fortresses likewise were generally built on sloping but not mountainous terrain. Even someone unconcerned with the military aspects of a city's existence would have been aware of the aesthetic results of sprawling outworks, horns, and glacis which surrounded many contemporary European cities, symbolizing power and prestige.

The site on the Meti could not have been considered flat by any means, yet its slope was certainly more gentle than that of rugged Noto Antica, and it faced a beautiful view of the coast instead of the wild canyons of the old site. The site was also easily visible from the sea, and thus would have been seen by sea-going travellers, as well as those passing by it on the overland coastal route. Perhaps by choosing a new site, the aristocracy demonstrated their wish to build the new city as an urbane eighteenth-century centre. By opting for a new site, they had the opportunity to rebuild Noto from scratch in the style that they thought it required, on a site more conducive to seventeenth- and eighteenth-century aesthetic standards. Far from being averse to such a worldly perspective, the clergy may have welcomed it as an opportunity to enshrine the city, with its cult of S. Corrado, as a beautiful pilgrimage centre.

The aristocrats and clergy were also probably very much aware that the kind of city they had in mind would not only be more aesthetically pleasing, but likewise safer. Geometrical layouts, vast piazzas, and flat sites were all considered safer in earthquakes; since the new city suffered many small tremors on the new site, building in a manner to combat the danger of another 1693 catastrophe must have been a high priority among the educated population.

Likewise, given the fair-to-good possibilities of the successful establishment of a city on the Meti, the upper classes may have considered a return to Noto Antica impractical. Removing the city again would have further weakened it both psychologically and financially. Everyone would have had to start again, bearing the financial burden of building a road to Noto Antica, clearing a site, transporting material, and re-erecting what was begun on the Meti. Migration from the city had been a staggering task; returning to the old site would have endangered its ecclesiastical institutions and wealthy citizens by encouraging some of their number to leave Noto forever.

The Lower-Class Position

The lower classes, on the other hand, had far more to lose by the transfer of Noto to the Meti. From the beginning they may have been opposed to such a move, and the conditions on the new site only strengthened their opposition. Even a few of those who voted against returning to Noto Antica note that they would have wanted to rebuild there had they had the funds; but since they had spent so much on the Meti they could not move. The main reason the *uomini di campagna* voted so strongly against the new site may have been the distance they had to walk to their fields. The usual pattern in medieval settlements was that the tenant farmers or day labourers worked on fields close to the outskirts of the city; they could therefore walk to their small gardens and return to the city at night, a preference of Sicilians even today. By moving the city, the authorities destroyed the economic livelihood of these people by taking them away from the land they had cultivated for generations. Certainly they could enter into new agreements with landowers near the site of the new city but the soil they had cleared and cultivated and the small holdings they may have accumulated were now valueless.

For the small landowner living in a typical Sicilian terrace-house, it would have been easier to rebuild from the rubble on Noto Antica than to buy material or transport it to the Meti. Even the erection of a structure on the new site to secure land was probably impossible for some of them. Likewise, the artisans, merchants and workers probably had established markets and supply sources which would have been disrupted by the move. In addition to the very real economic considerations, the lower classes may well have felt more of an emotional tie to the ruined site of their city.

Further Manoeuvres support Return to Noto Antica

In response to the 1698 referendum vote, the Viceroy, now the Duke of Veraguas (Uzeda left office in 1696), sent members of the Tribunal of the Royal Patrimony to the town to resolve the situation. Camastra had resigned his office in 1695 so members of the Tribunal, in conjunction with the Bishop of Syracuse, Asdrubale Termini, were to decide Noto's fate. The members of the Tribunal considered the petitions sent to them, the report of the engineer, Giuseppe Formenti, and Termini's suggestions, and decided that 'the transfer of the city to the new site of the Meti was not well thought out'. They concluded:

> The Tribunal which represents the Viceroy His Excellency and the best service to His Majesty and the utility of His Reign rules that these citizens return to inhabit the old city, and that they leave the place where one finds them presently.[36]

The members of the Tribunal decided to move the city back to Noto Antica for the following reasons:

1 Because the Bishop of Syracuse said the site of Noto Antica was admirable and well-suited for the construction of a secure fortress.
2 The engineer and the ministers who had visited the old site praised its healthy air, its breezes, and its abundance of water.
3 They further said that it was a high place, and had fortifications which were inaccessible in many areas and therefore secure from attack. The fort itself could have been repaired for 4,000 *scudi* (presumably not an unreasonable sum).
4 The city could have been not only strong, but positioned in the centre of its territory. Below its walls, twenty-three mills could have been working.

In contrast to the favourable conditions in the old city, the site of the new city had little to recommend it. The air was not healthy because of its vicinity to stagnant water. It was without ventilation from the north, and therefore became too hot. They judged it a poor defensive position, easily subjected to invasions of enemies from the sea. It could not guard against contagious diseases since it was open to the sea and without walls. But to fortify and enclose the new site with walls would cost too much money. The ministers further argued that the old city acted as a protective outpost for Syracuse and Augusta in time of war. If the site were abandoned, then it might be used by the enemy to launch an attack against nearby fortresses. The old city was a backbone for the defence of south-eastern Sicily, but 'one couldn't hope for such service from a city open like a village [like the new city] without any means of defence'. The road leading to Noto Antica could have been cleared as others had been, and the churches and streets could have been built from municipal taxes since the crown had suspended royal taxes. They wrote optimistically about their endorsement of Noto Antica:

> Said city you will see shortly populated by all those who have left it because of the inconvenience of the new site to become vassals of nearby Barons. Those people for love of their patria will return to their old home.[37]

The Opposition is Heard

The ministers' decision, however, by no means settled the problem. The people who had invested in building on the new site, particularly the ecclesiastical institutions, were not in a position to be able to return to the old. So the disagreement between the two factions dragged on without solution. As the anonymous chronicler says, Termini left the city in more confusion than he found it.[38] For example, Don Corrado Bellofiore, the powerful head parish priest of Noto, in 1669 wrote a letter to the Viceroy protesting against the removal of the city from the new site.[39] As Bellofiore explained, the order of the Tribunal was 'the cause of the greatest sadness' and the effect was 'a great curse on all the poor citizens of the city who haven't done anything wrong'. The people of Noto suffered from a 'great curse of God because of the ruins wrought by the earthquake'; they made the journey to the new city, and:

> . . . to have to leave these constructions, to make another transfer, and there once again begin to build – and all this not because of any fault of the poor and ever-faithful vassals of the King our Master to whom they have always been faithful – is very painful . . . .

The people were poor, said Bellofiore, but the sacristans were more so because they were going without their patrimony. These ecclesiastics lived on the alms collected at mass. Bellofiore spoke both for himself and for his religious colleagues when he said:

> . . . if the order is executed to transport the city to the other location, the population won't be able to go, the ecclesiastics don't have the power to go, the convents of religious people can't possibly go, so each will move to the Baronial territories, and that will be ultimate ruin and the destruction of this city.

A Compromise: Two Cities

In the hope of appeasing both sides by compromise, the Tribunal of the Royal Patrimony in 1700 endorsed both the old and the new.

> . . . Everyone of the citizens is left perfectly free to continue to live in the old ruined site of the city just as those who have begun construction on said new site have permission to finish their constructions. . . .[40]

This equivocal ruling must have raised the inevitable question of which of the two cities would be the 'real' Noto and have the privileges that such a position implied.

In Ragusa, one of the other Sicilian cities destroyed by the earthquake of 1693, one group of people decided to remain on the rugged crag of Ragusa Ibla and rebuild the city; another group decided to move to a gradually sloping plain which overlooks the ridge leading to the old city, calling the new city Ragusa Nuova (Fig. 1).[41] Neither of the two groups gave in, so two cities were established, divided by a gate and presumably walls. The clergy decided to remain in the old city, as can be seen by the large number of churches and religious houses in Ragusa Ibla. Indeed, judging from the buildings, Ragusa Ibla was the important city during the early eighteenth century while Ragusa Nuova only came into its own in the late eighteenth and nineteenth centuries. When the two cities were rising after the earthquake, the Viceregal government sought to curb the fierce antagonism between them by forbidding citizens to use the words 'New' and 'Old'. But even today, the two cities, although united, still retain their separate identities.

However, in the case of Noto, the decision of the court to endorse two cities had a paradoxical effect, triggering a land rush in Noto Nuova. Perhaps the lower classes realized that they could not exist without the protection and commerce fostered by the church and the aristocracy; and perhaps the aristocrats who had only reluctantly settled in the new city now felt assured that the other members of the aristocracy and clergy had by their influence and physical presence once and for all established the new town on the Meti.

Noto Nuova began to come to life again. Tommaso Impellizzeri (not to be confused with Antonino), in an act probably representative of many of Noto's citizens, petitioned the King in 1701 to let him build on the site in the piazza of the new city which was originally assigned to him, saying that he had not built before because the site of the city had not been established, but that now he was prepared to do so.[42] Several gentlemen from the summit in the meantime petitioned to build an access road to the upper part of the city which could accommodate carriages.[43] Religious institutions began fighting with one another for the most commanding sites in the new city. The monastery of Montevergine fought the monastery of Santa Agata for the right to erect a suitable belvedere on their property so that they would be free from the gaze of the populace, yet able to see processions.[44]

The Giudice Ruling: An End to Disagreement

In Noto's protracted struggle, some of the people did not succumb to the influence of the clergy and the aristocracy, and continued to complain to Madrid. As the anonymous chronicler says: 'The miserable citizens advanced their requests with repeated anger, principally to the court of Madrid. . .'.[45]

In 1702, the Court of Madrid ordered the Viceroy Cardinal Giudice together with the Governor of Messina, Ferdinando Acagna, the Prince of Niscemi, and several engineers to assess the situation. The joint report issued to the King states that:

> . . . the site of the New City in the afore-mentioned area of the Meti is not of poor quality as its detractors claim; I examined this site which is on a hill exposed to wind and very advanced in buildings, churches, convents of friars and nuns, seminaries and regular houses all very good and with excellent plans.[46]

Obviously the reference to the Meti's moderate climate and good ventilation was an attempt on the part of the members of Giudice's party to dispel the claims that the site was unhealthy. The findings of this report contradict the description of the site's climate given by earlier witnesses because Giudice's group visited the Meti in October and November, its coolest months. Giudice may have known that they were seeing the city at a time when it was more healthy than in the summer months, yet he did not take this fact into consideration in his report. Most likely, he was more concerned that the city be established than with where it was established. The buildings under construction in the new city must have been powerful arguments against transporting it back to the site of Noto Antica. Most of the buildings Giudice mentions are ecclesiastical institutions, a fact which graphically illustrates that the church had already invested too much in the site to leave it.

As opposed to this building going on in Noto Nuova on the Meti, Noto Antica, note the reporters, was practically empty, in spite of its fine air and good water.

> We say to the Viceroy His Excellency that the site of the old city is to be found on a hill with very healthy air. One sees nothing there but the ruins from the earthquake except for two very small forts made by a shoemaker and two brothers that live there. . . .

It is not at all surprising that the site was so completely abandoned. According to the anonymous chronicler, the commoners had settled in Noto Antica and the aristocrats on the Meti. The commoners had little money available to finance buildings of any scale, and besides by 1702 many of them had probably followed the aristocrats and clergy to the Meti in search of employment.

The anonymous chronicler quotes Giudice as saying, 'the buildings have decided the feud.'[47] Unable to settle the fate of their city by themselves, the Netinese were forced to accept the ruling that quieted ten years of bitter internal struggle:

> Therefore we [Cardinal Giudice's commission] order that in conformity with the foregoing communication and the reasons expressed therein the feuds and controversies among the citizens of this city over the selection of the site for it must be put in perpetual silence. . . . We stipulate that the true and antique city of Noto shall be and must be for all time the one that is built on the site of the Meti.[48]

The fate of Noto was sealed. Because of Noto's inability to govern itself, the Spanish Viceregal government once and for all legislated that the site of Noto Nuova was the only true Noto. Thus Noto's two major conflicts were ended. The Netinese as a whole, upper and lower classes, had influenced the plan of their city by settling on the slope of the Meti rather than on the summit as directed by the Viceregal advisers. However, Noto's transfer from Noto Antica to the Meti was clearly a triumph of the upper classes just as one might have expected. It was they, the clergy and the aristocracy, who would pay for the rebuilding of the new city and direct the architectural realization of their hopes for the future Noto.

Part II
The Growth of Eighteenth-Century Noto

Chapter 4 An Uncertain Genesis: A Plan for New Noto

Even as embattled factions quarrelled over the fate of Noto, its plan materialized on the Meti. By 1712, ten years after Spain silenced all disputes within the city, the major features of Noto's plan were probably set. Yet only a few scraps of evidence indicate how the new city looked initially. This chapter attempts to fill the gap between the inception of the city in 1693 and Tortora's description of it in 1712 with a reconstructed history of Noto on the Meti derived from fragmentary information in written documents, a single visual document, and later depictions of the city.

A reconstruction of Noto Nuova's early history must take into account some of the most difficult and intriguing problems of Noto's plan. Why, for example, are the grids on the summit and the slope of the Meti unco-ordinated? On the other hand, what can explain the geometrical consistency and regularity of the positioning of the main squares on the slope of the Meti?

To answer these questions we will re-examine events discussed in the previous chapter, using them as evidence for the physical growth of the city. Let us return to the year 1693, and follow the activity which was occurring on the Meti. Using a modern contour map of the city, we will follow, as closely as possibly, the settlement of the Meti and the evolution of Noto's city plan.

A Reconstructed History of Noto's Plan: The Early Stages

The survivors of the earthquake, presumably compelled by Asmundo, made their way from the ruins of Noto Antica to the Meti. They approached the Meti from the south-west and continued until they stopped on the slope, either on the northern side of the Piazza S. Domenico (Map 3, letter A), or on the site of S. Nicolò, the Chiesa Madre (Map 4, no. 6). In one of these two places they set up a hut to shelter the arc of S. Corrado, the most precious relic of their city. The slope of the Meti was thus endorsed for settlement, against the wishes of the Duke of Camastra who had endorsed only the summit as the site of the city.

Two settlements composed of huts made of palms and branches developed: one occupied the area just to the south of the Piazza S. Domenico (Letter A) on what is now the southernmost boundary of the city near Piazza Calatafimi; the other, perhaps under pressure from Asmundo, occupied the northernmost part of the summit known as Cozzo della Fiera.[1]

Neither of these settlements fared well during that first year. The lower one, being too close to the malarial plain and without the proper water supply, succumbed to the epidemic which spread throughout the city killing many of those who had escaped the earthquake. After the epidemic had decimated the people, a fire started in the settlement on the summit. Because of strong winds and lack of water, the fire spread quickly through the temporary settlement. According to Tortora and the anonymous chronicler, it was only because the populace carried the arc of S. Corrado to the scene of the blaze that it was finally controlled, through the saint's miraculous intervention.[2]

Yet in spite of these setbacks, the foundations of some of Noto's most prominent buildings had already been laid by 1694. It seems unlikely that these buildings, which included the churches of SS. Crocifisso and S. Nicolò, were built in random locations.[3] The land had to be allotted in an orderly fashion; this means that even as early as 1693 there must have been a plan which stipulated how the site was to be subdivided. We know that the Senate of Noto in 1693 gained the power to dispense

Fig. 2 Plan of Montevago. Typical of the seventeenth-century city plans found in Sicily.

land to those who needed it.[4] Camastra and Asmundo, as later claims prove, likewise dispensed land. For example, in a complaint to the Viceroy years later the Dominicans, defending the right of their convent to privacy, mention that the land was given to them by Asmundo and Camastra, presumably in 1693.[5] Don Tommaso Impellizzeri, trying in 1702 to retrieve his right to build on a lot, states that Camastra conceded the area to him.[6] Any plan would have insured that the relevant religious institutions and private individuals received proper portions of land in the new city. Certainly the plan must have been in existence by 1694, because Asmundo at that time mentions his attempts to bring settlers into the 'design' of the city.[7]

If a plan was in fact in existence in 1693, what did it look like? Given the nature of the present city of Noto it is safe to say that the plan was based on a grid pattern. With few exceptions, the grid had been used throughout the seventeenth century in Sicily as a means for laying out new towns. Towns like Montevago, founded in 1640, had simple grid plans with a single large open space in the centre (Fig. 2).[8] And this time-honoured and relatively simple means for organizing open spaces and streets was used often in the rebuilding of Sicilian towns after the earthquake of 1693.

The major features of the grid plan begin to come into focus in several documents which record the Duke of Camastra's disapproval of the plan of the city. When Camastra returned to find the populace settling on the slope of the Meti rather than the summit, he ordered that several buildings, including S. Nicolò, be moved from the slope to the summit. The citizens' outcry over moving S. Nicolò stopped him from changing its location. As far as we know it remained exactly where it can be seen today. The Duke had better luck with the other religious buildings: he was able to transfer the church of SS. Crocifisso and the Convents of S. Francesco di Paola and S. Maria di Gesù from the slope to the summit. And if we assume that the institutions occupied then the same lots that they do today, it is clear that the church of SS. Crocifisso and the convent of S. Francesco di Paola are aligned on the same co-ordinates, indicating a guiding grid plan.

S. Nicolò—SS. Crocifisso Axis

There is a further indication of a ruling grid pattern. As Map 3 demonstrates, S. Nicolò and SS. Crocifisso are definitely aligned. SS. Crocifisso was the second most important church in the city; its placement helps to establish, at least on paper, the backbone for the two-level plan by connecting the 'centre' of the summit with the 'centre' of the Meti as a whole. It seems logical to suppose that the Duke of Camastra chose the new position that SS. Crocifisso was to occupy. By placing it on the summit, Camastra may have been trying to give that area the prestige that might encourage people to settle there. In addition, Camastra may have been aware of the iconographical link he was establishing with the positions the two churches had in Noto Antica before the earthquake. In Noto Antica, the church of SS. Crocifisso occupied a northerly position, while the S. Nicolò was situated at the other end of the Via Piana in the centre of town in a more southerly position. The churches in Noto Antica were the foci of two different quarters. The position of SS. Crocifisso may have been planned in alignment with S. Nicolò to recall the earlier relationship between the two structures, and so to popularize the summit as a kind of substitute for the narrow ridge on the northern side of the old city.

The SS. Crocifisso–S. Nicolò axis became the administrative backbone for Noto in the eighteenth century, and actually remains so today (Map 4). In 1693, the royal jail was erected, most likely on the same location it occupied in the mid-eighteenth century, on the southern edge of the summit between the two churches.[9] Just cater-cornered to the jail was the Monte di Pietà, the municipal pawn shop.[10] And following the same axis, below S. Nicolò, the city hall was built. The configuration of secondary church, Monte di Pietà, jail-castle, main church, city hall, suggests that the eighteenth-century planners adhered to the primacy of the axis. In the nineteenth and twentieth centuries, the axis was reinforced still further by additional buildings: the state penitentiary, the city clock tower, the main city hospital, and the Bishop's office.[11]

The Existence of Two Grids

Although the SS. Crocifisso–S. Nicolò axis binds together the two levels of Noto when seen in plan, the different orientations of the buildings reveal two separate grids. Map 3 illustrates that two of the religious buildings on the summit, while following the general north–south orientation of S. Nicolò, deviate from its exact orientation by about seven degrees. This discrepancy between the two orientations indicates that even in the first months of Noto's existence, two separate grids – one for the summit and one for the slope – existed. The same two grids are still visible today.

The grid on the summit, which must have been carefully specified by the Duke of Camastra, is oriented approximately 17 degrees east of due north.[12] The grid divides the summit very neatly into blocks (Map 4). The orientation of the grid is certainly logical enough. Its north-south streets ran towards the sea on a south-westerly angle, making the best of whatever breezes came from the coast. The streets and buildings within the grid would have fitted neatly into the ground allotted for the plan and used the natural boundaries of the summit to their best advantage.

The north-south streets of the summit grid, which could have been continued down the slope grid, perhaps by using steps, stop abruptly at the steepest ground separating the two parts of the city. With the exception of the central street on the summit which is approximately continued by the street below leading to S. Nicolò, none of the north-south streets of the summit is aligned with the north-south streets of the slope. The block sizes on the summit are smaller than those on the slope, and the slope grid is oriented in a more easterly direction.

The slope grid seems to have been conceived to fit most conveniently into the incline of the site. The Meti falls away toward the Asinaro on an axis of about 20 degrees east of due north. The logical placement of east-west streets was along the contour of the hill, running from 20 degrees north of west to 20 degrees south of east. Given the east-west co-ordinates, the north-south streets would have to run from 20 degrees east of north to 20 degrees west of south. This orientation, combined with the larger block sizes of the slope grid, produces a visual schism in Noto's plan.

Two Grids indicate Two Separate Settlements

Architects of the late seventeenth century did not lack the technology to solve the problems of lining up the grids. With the development of the compass and other aids, surveying in the late seventeenth or early eighteenth century had become quite accurate. Guarino Guarini in his *Architettura Civile*, published in 1737 but written during the seventeenth century, gives an account of the basic methods of compass traverse, triangulation, and levelling, all of which were well known in the late seventeenth century.[13] These same techniques in fact form the basis for our modern surveying.

It seems improbable that the Netinese intended the two grids to be misaligned. Vitruvius recommends that streets be oriented differently in order to deflect the wind, but the streets of Noto do not differ enough in orientation to affect climatic conditions between the upper and lower grids.[14] Aesthetically, the misalignment seems out of keeping with either sixteenth- or seventeenth-century practice, which prescribed that the plans of cities should be as symmetrical as possible.[15]

One hypothesis which might explain the misalignment is that Asmundo bungled the surveying, orienting the two grids in slightly different directions. Asmundo mentions his amateur survey to the Viceroy in a dispatch of 1693, saying that he himself measured terrain and designed streets because of the lack of trained staff.[16]

Map 4 Noto's north-south axis with the major community buildings constructed along it. Also indicated are the present day names of Noto's streets.
1 SS. Crocifisso
2 Monte di Pietà
3 S. Agata, now Trigona Hospital
4 Town clock
5 Jail
6 S. Nicolò
7 Bishop's palace
8 City Hall
9 S. Maria dell'Arco (first Bishop's palace)

However, a more compelling explanation might be that Asmundo, following the expressed command of Camastra, laid out the city on the summit of the Meti before people came to the site. Only after the people had settled on the slope was he forced to consider a grid for lower Noto. Thus he made the mistake of laying out one part of the city without considering the contours of the other, which he subsequently had to pull into the city plan. The slope called for east-west streets oriented along its contours; Asmundo had little choice but to lay out the lower grid in the most convenient manner possible, even if it did not align precisely with the previously laid-out summit grid.

The Plan *circa* 1712

From 1693 to 1712 a few documents begin to record the growth of the city and thereby to give some notion of the positions and chronology of Noto's streets and open spaces. An important visual document of this period with which to correlate the archival notices and Tortora's account of the city in 1712 is a map drawn by Giuseppe Formenti who assessed Noto's new site for the Termini commission in 1699.[17] By combining the scant visual and written information a reconstruction of early Noto can be accomplished.

As early as 1694 we know piazzas existed on the slope of the Meti because Asmundo mentions them in a communiqué. He writes that the unfinished aqueduct will bring water to the two piazzas in the city, but without naming them.[18] We know the piazzas were on the slope because Asmundo mentions in a later communiqué that he established three fountains on the slope (perhaps the third was located on a piazza too) but was unable to bring water to the Pianazzo because it was too high.[19] Therefore, neither of the piazzas he refers to was the open space in front of SS. Crocifisso on the Pianazzo, and there must instead have been open spaces in the lower part of the city. One of the piazzas existing in 1694 must have been Piazza S. Domenico in front of the Dominican church which was the site of the vote to decide the location of the new city in 1698. The second piazza was probably the one in front of S. Nicolò, since it was low enough to be served by the Coffitella aqueduct which Asmundo is undoubtedly discussing in the document.

The positions of the religious houses established in the early years of Noto's existence help to delineate the sizes of the blocks around the piazzas and to add to the early picture of Noto. By 1702 thirteen religious houses were erected in the new city.[20] By 1704 the third open space along the Corso, the Piano of S. Francesco, had been laid out, and by 1712 Piazza S. Domenico was the town market.[21]

A likely approximation of the plan of the city around 1712 is presented in Map 5. The map is a correlation of the written documents and a modified version of Formenti's map which has been superimposed over the existing city of Noto.

The city in 1712 looked very much like the present city because streets and block sizes were similar and the four major open areas, the Piano of SS. Crocifisso, the main piazza, the Piazza of S. Domenico and the Piano of S. Francesco were all in existence. The boundaries of Piazza S. Domenico (Map 5, a), perhaps the first piazza established on the slope, were identical to those of the present piazza.[22] Although the shapes of the other open spaces have changed, the spatial relationship established among them seems to have remained a constant throughout the history of Noto.

Across town from the unchanging Piazza S. Domenico was the Piano of S. Francesco, which had a far less stable history. As Map 5 indicates, the piano is far less regular in outline than Piazza S. Domenico and much smaller. It may have had the same eastern and northern boundaries that it does today, but its southern boundary may have been south of the Corso as indicated by the dotted line and letter d'. The piano, definitely in existence in 1704, when Tortora mentions that a statue of the Madonna (Map 5, no. 6) was erected upon it, may have been planned as early as the 1690s. Formenti's map illustrates only a small open space (Map 5, d') with the area between the convent (no. 5) and the Corso (approximately south to no. 6) apparently ready for development, and not to be preserved as an open area.[23] But by

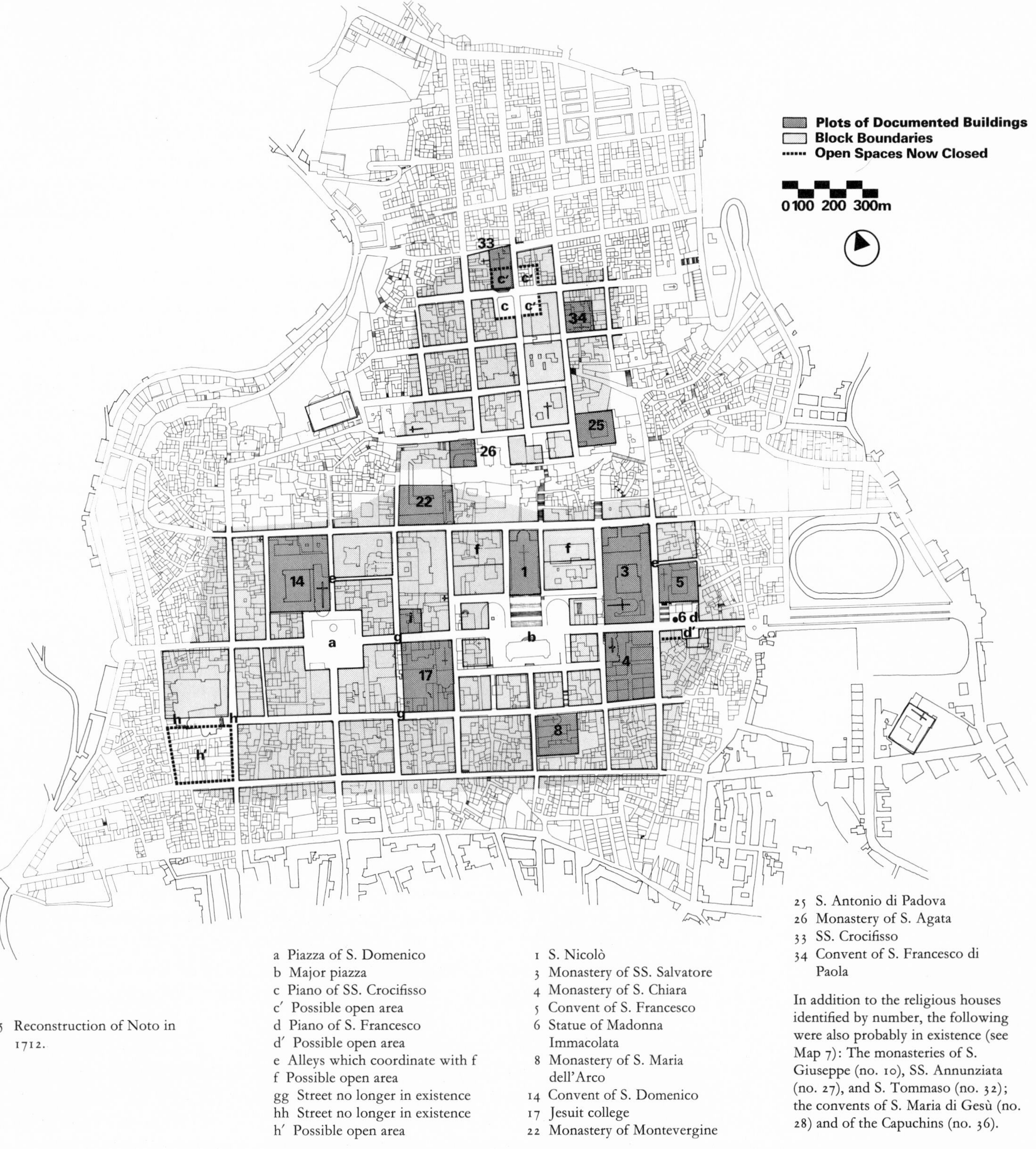

Map 5 Reconstruction of Noto in 1712.

a Piazza of S. Domenico
b Major piazza
c Piano of SS. Crocifisso
c′ Possible open area
d Piano of S. Francesco
d′ Possible open area
e Alleys which coordinate with f
f Possible open area
gg Street no longer in existence
hh Street no longer in existence
h′ Possible open area

1 S. Nicolò
3 Monastery of SS. Salvatore
4 Monastery of S. Chiara
5 Convent of S. Francesco
6 Statue of Madonna Immacolata
8 Monastery of S. Maria dell'Arco
14 Convent of S. Domenico
17 Jesuit college
22 Monastery of Montevergine
25 S. Antonio di Padova
26 Monastery of S. Agata
33 SS. Crocifisso
34 Convent of S. Francesco di Paola

In addition to the religious houses identified by number, the following were also probably in existence (see Map 7): The monasteries of S. Giuseppe (no. 10), SS. Annunziata (no. 27), and S. Tommaso (no. 32); the convents of S. Maria di Gesù (no. 28) and of the Capuchins (no. 36).

1704, less than five years later, the status of the piano had evidently risen again. It is possible that the initial idea of the piano was endorsed, with the 'L' shaped building just to the east of d' conforming to its boundaries. Later the piano was potentially rejected and the buildings north of the dotted line erected, and then reinstated, with the area between the southern wall of the convent and the Corso left open.

The balance established by Piazza S. Domenico and the Piano of S. Francesco would have been as compelling a force in the 1712 plan of the city as it is today and was probably seen as an organizing element from the plan's earliest inception. Although the piano is far smaller in area than S. Domenico, its arrangement is similar, with a church and convent on the north. How appropriate it is that the position of the Franciscan church and convent is exactly across town from the position of its rival, the Dominican church and convent.

The main piazza (letter b) in front of S. Nicolò (no. 1) looked not unlike it does today, but was planned to be far more regular as the map indicates. The two square blocks which flank the present city hall south of the Corso were to have been echoed by similar blocks on the north side of the Corso. Therefore, according to Formenti, the south, east and west sides of the piazza would have been each composed of two square blocks smaller than any others in the plan. The north-eastern and north-western blocks were never fully occupied and in fact abandoned by the mid-eighteenth century. Beyond these small blocks the demarcation of the larger grid is assured by the tax records of the Landolina-Rau family which record a palace, in the form of a series of mud huts, which was located on the Corso just west of the piazza (letter i).[24] The religious houses flanking the piazza also help to define the main piazza. To the south-east, the early foundation of S. Chiara (no. 4) and, to the north-east, the existence of SS. Salvatore define the larger blocks of the grid. Formenti illustrates only the northern portion of the buildings of SS. Salvatore, but the monastery had probably already laid claim to the whole block on which it was located.[25] The entire block to the south-west of the piazza was occupied by the Jesuit college (no. 17), the seminary, and the temporary Jesuit church. It is unclear whether the small blocks on the south-east and south-west sides of the piazza were planned when the coordinated positions of the Jesuit College (no. 17) and S. Chiara (no. 4) were selected.[26] The Jesuit college church of S. Carlo and the church of S. Chiara are so symmetrically ordered in relation to the church of S. Nicolò that the smaller blocks appear almost as afterthoughts.

Like the main piazza, the piano in front of the church of SS. Crocifisso looked far more regular in 1712 than it does today. According to Formenti the piano was a smaller version of Piazza S. Domenico, comprising the area marked c and c' on Map 5. The piano in 1712 probably still retained the form of a perfect closed-cornered square with streets diverging from the middle of each side. Given the evidence of the Formenti map and the surviving alleys within the present day city such a form certainly could have existed. Formenti illustrates the temporary church of SS. Crocifisso on the north-eastern side of the square, possibly with its façade facing east. It is entirely possible, but difficult to prove, that the original church of SS. Crocifisso partly survives in the Landolina chapel which projects west from the symmetrical transept of the church today as shown on Maps 5 and 7. If Formenti's depiction is accurate, the necessary enlargement of the church destroyed the configuration of the square by encroaching upon it as early as 1715 when the present church was begun.[27]

Over the years encroachment by religious houses and churches that needed more space closed both streets and open spaces in the city, in some cases destroying the clarity of the plan, as in the transformation of the Piano of SS. Crocifisso. In other cases, streets like the extension of Via Rocco Pirri (letters g–g), were closed by religious houses.[28] Via Ducezio (letters h–h) which once led to an unnamed open space (letter h') in the south-western part of the city was closed when the church of S. Maria del Carmine was built on it, and the unnamed open space disappeared. The private Nicolaci family church of S. Elia on Via Nicolaci, just south of the palace itself, likewise blocked off a whole street when it was built in the nineteenth century.[29]

Genesis of the Plan

Who was the author of this plan? It may have been a cumulative effort on the part of many individuals. Asmundo obviously laid out part of the city; he measured it himself, as we saw earlier. But was he the master planner? Tortora mentions that an aristocrat named Giovan Battista Landolina Salonia who died in the epidemic of 1693 was the 'principale disignatore' of the city.[30] 'Principale disignatore' could mean the principal designator of the site of the city, or designer of its plan, and exactly which of these two roles Landolina played is impossible to say. If Landolina

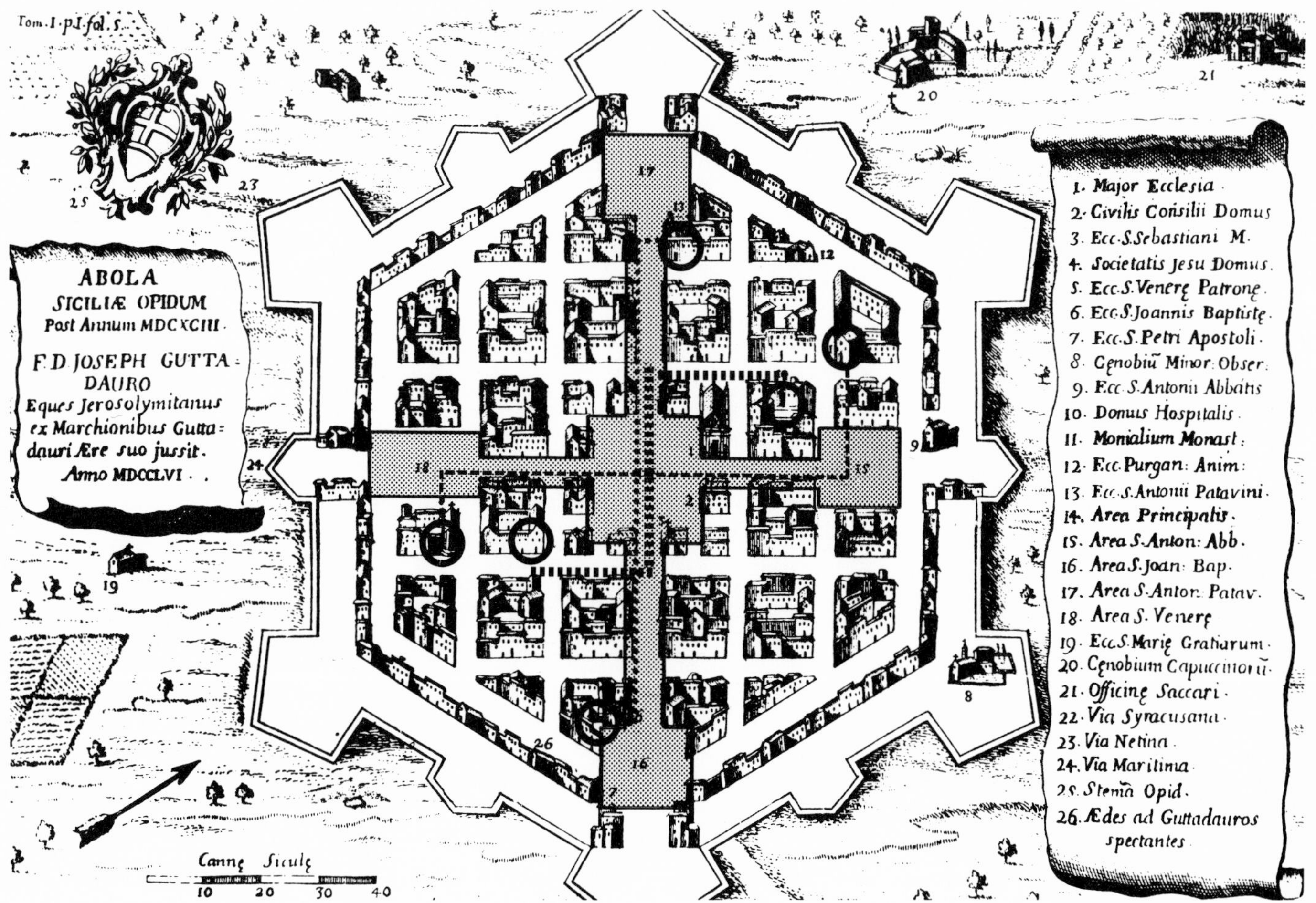

13 Plan of Avola indicating how its piazzas and churches are balanced on either side of the main piazza.

were an amateur mathematician or architect he certainly had the capability of plotting the whole plan.

There is yet another possibility, one which deserves serious consideration. Noto's anonymous chronicler mentions a Jesuit named Fra Italia, who

> took the design from a book of city plans, [and] had the streets designed with more order and symmetry.[31]

According to the anonymous chronicler, Fra Italia came to Noto 'when the commoners and the plebs finally quietened down . . .'; this suggests that he came in 1702, when the controversy over the new site began to abate. Documents in fact indicate that the anonymous chronicler's account is accurate: Asmundo credits a Jesuit engineer, Fra Angelo Italia, with drawing the plans for Noto. However, Asmundo's account, written some years after the fact, clouds rather than clarifies, Italia's contribution.[32] According to Asmundo, Italia first selected the slope as a appropriate site and began to plan the city. But this selection was obviously not endorsed by Asmundo who may have had Italia also design a city for the Pianazzo. Italia may have left the designs with Asmundo and returned to the nearby city of Avola where he was working. After the slope began to outgrow the Pianazzo in population he may have returned to the city to align the two grids. It is possible that he may have visited Noto any number of times between 1693 and 1700, consulting with those laying out the city.

Fra Angelo Italia was the author of the striking hexagonal plan of Avola which he laid out himself in 1693.[33] Italia had been trained in Palermo and had worked in Palma di Montechiaro, Licata, and Catania. He worked in south-eastern Sicily until the turn of the century, when he returned to Palermo where he died in 1700.

Map 6 Noto's symmetrical plan. Italia's plan for balancing Noto's piazzas.

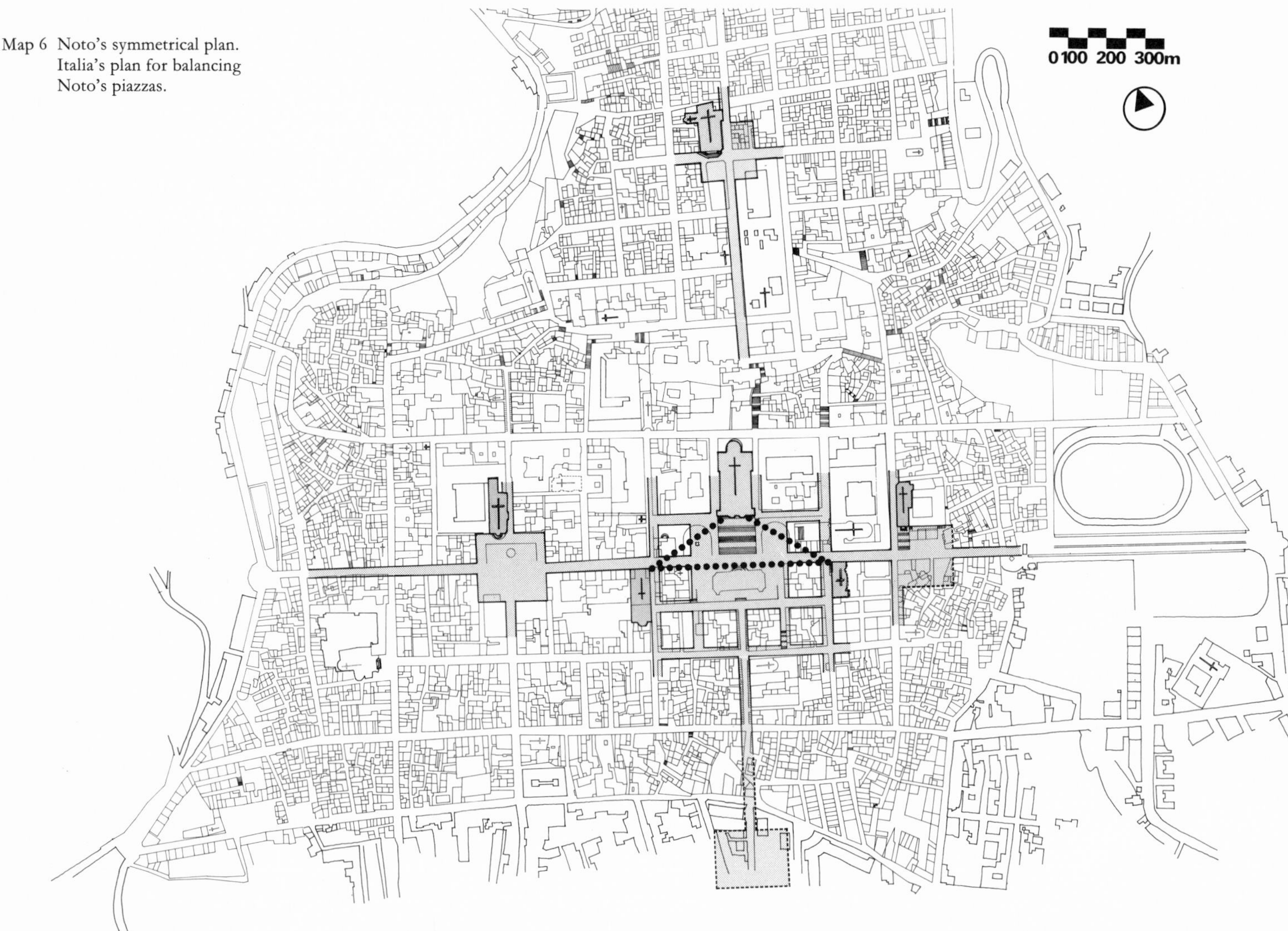

Italia's plan for Avola and Noto's plan are closely related, which indicates that Italia may very well have had a forming influence on the city of Noto. From his work in Avola it is easy to see that Fra Italia was captivated by Renaissance symmetry: the hexagonal plan of Avola is a paradigm of Renaissance order in a town plan, even to the point that the locations of the churches 'balance' one another, as in Pl. 13. The same kind of balance and order can be seen in Noto's plan: as Map 6 illustrates, the four main piazzas of Noto form an inverted 'T' with the Piano of SS. Crocifisso at its base. Piazza S. Domenico and the Piano of S. Francesco were intended to balance one another, but perhaps because the eastern part of the Meti was too steep, the piano was never laid out as such; it is also possible that an earlier, larger piano was later absorbed into the city. In either case, the piano is the remnant of an attempt to balance the east-west axis as the north-south axis is balanced by SS. Crocifisso and S. Nicolò. Both in aerial photographs and in experiencing the city on the ground, one is conscious of the three open spaces along the main street.

Just as they are in Avola's plan, the ecclesiastical institutions in Noto are carefully arranged (Maps 6 and 7). First, all the churches and religious houses seem to be distributed more or less evenly throughout the city. A diamond pattern continued from the main piazza throughout the city fairly accurately plots the positions of religious buildings at its converging points. Each of the major piazzas has a single church at its northernmost point. The three original churches on the main piazza form a perfect isosceles triangle with its apex at the S. Nicolò. Balance, symmetry and overall order, while not as apparent in Noto's plan as they are in Avola's, are nevertheless present.

What 'book of city plans' might Italia have used if the anonymous chronicler is correct? The most famous exponent of organizing a total plan through the

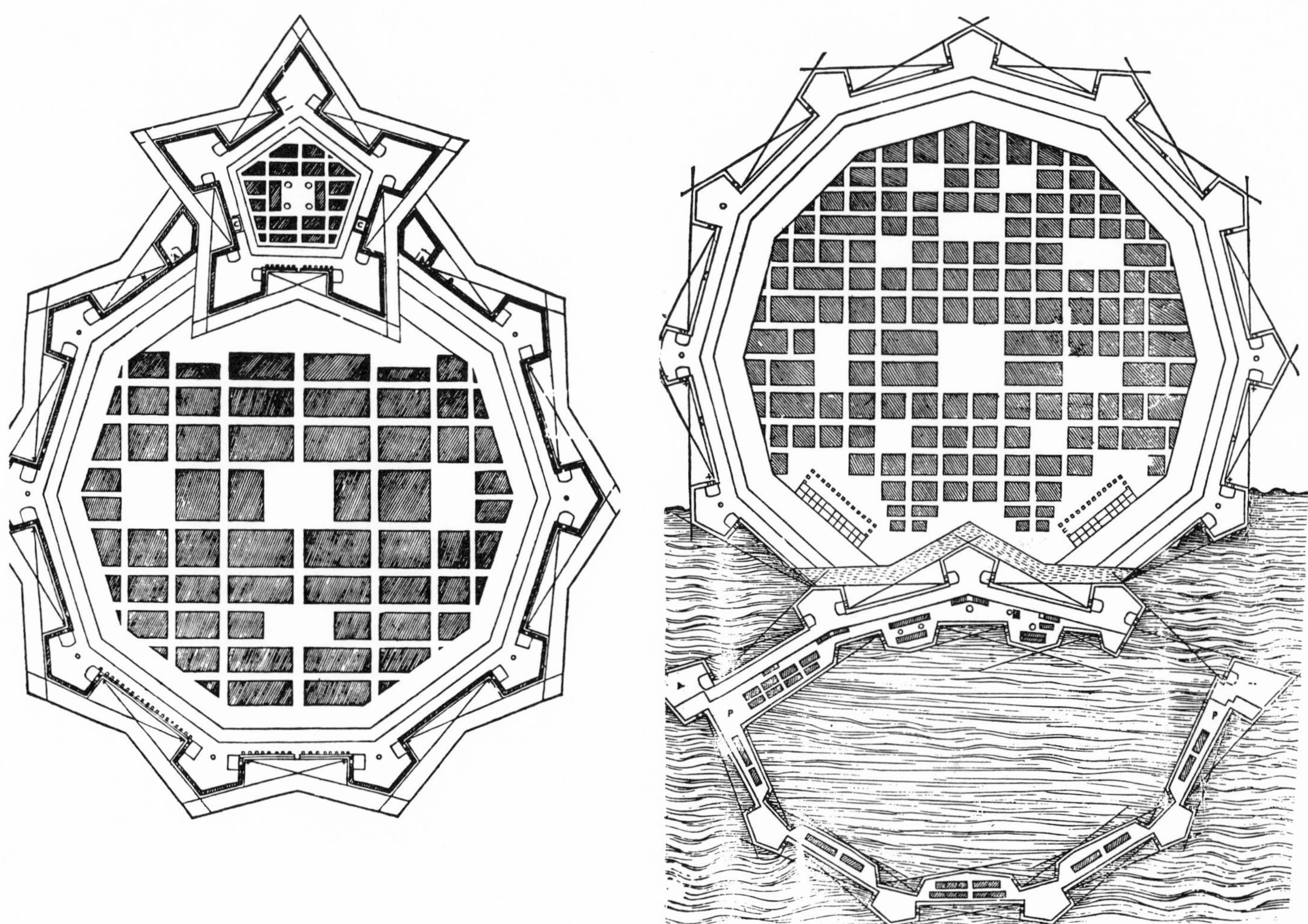

14 Land Fortress, P. Cataneo.

15 City on the Sea, P. Cataneo.

placement of symmetrical satellite piazzas around a central core was the widely read Italian theorist Pietro Cataneo, whose influential *I quattro primi libri di architettura* published in 1554 was an important sourcebook for later architects.[34] Cataneo presents several designs based on polygons, in which he plays on variations in the positions of the piazzas within the city walls and the placement of the citadel which guards the city itself (Pl. 14). He is always, even when simulating a casual arrangement, setting up an overall symmetry which unites the secondary open spaces within the city (Pl. 15). That is, by using the central piazza as his focus, he builds up a balanced pattern of piazzas on each side of it. The open spaces and the grid are conceived of as a complete harmonious design within the geometrical framework of the walls. They retain their symmetry in spite of Cataneo's modulation of the grid and altering of block and piazza sizes on either side of the main piazza. The unity, in fact, is not preserved by the grid but by the relationship between the open spaces: these are for the most part positioned on axes which run through the centre of the plan at right angles and divide it into four separate sectors. By keeping his piazzas near these axes, which cut through the diameter of the whole city, Cataneo produces the unified effect.

Closer still to the appearance of Noto is Vincenzo Scamozzi's ideal city, which is published in his *Dell'Idea dell'architettura universale* (1615).[35] In Scamozzi's city (Pl. 16), the central piazza is balanced by four satellite spaces. Exactly the same principle is used in Noto, but total symmetry is lacking because the Piano of S. Francesco either was never completed or was possibly changed. In addition, the Duke's moratorium on building on the lower part of the Meti precluded balancing the northernmost Piano of SS. Crocifisso with a corresponding southern piazza.

Noto's plan, placement of religious buildings, and division of functions establish

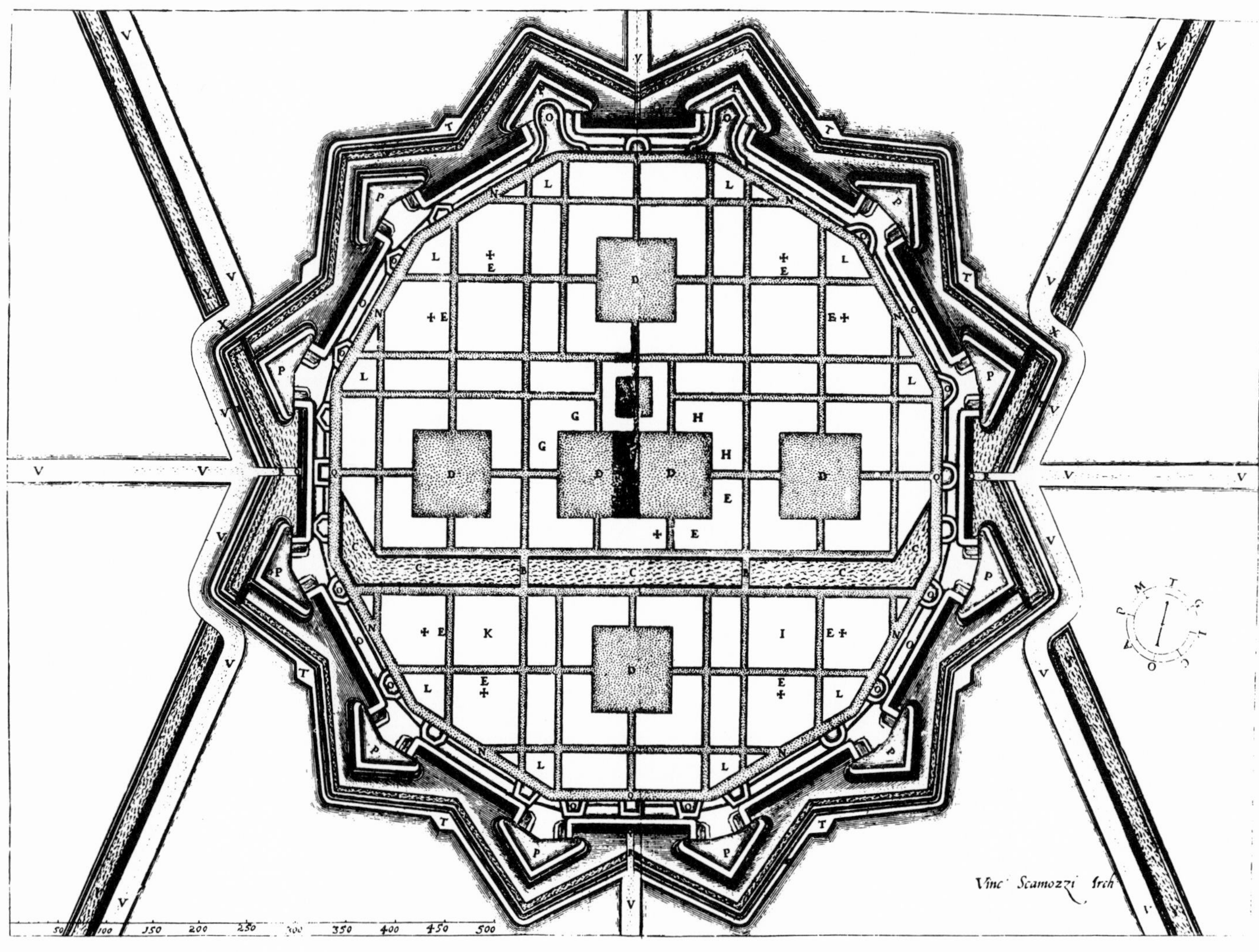

16 Ideal City, V. Scamozzi.

it in the tradition of Scamozzi. Scamozzi specifies that the central piazza should at its most prominent location contain the prince's palace (north of Piazza D–D), isolated from the buildings around it for reasons both of defence and majesty. Around the aristocratic main piazza, the important headquarters of the church and administrative offices are located. The function of market-places is relegated to the satellite piazzas. Churches are methodically placed around the town to appear symmetrical in plan, though their combined asesthetic effect could hardly have been appreciated at ground level.

In Noto's main piazza S. Nicolò takes the place of Scamozzi's prince's palace, being built as an isolated block. But following Scamozzi, the central piazza is reserved for the principal city church, the government functions, and the palaces of aristocrats. Piazza S. Domenico to the west was originally the city market-place, segregated from the church and government functions just as in Scamozzi's plan. Likewise, following Scamozzi who counselled a close relationship between the prince's palace, the courts of justice, and the jail, Noto's jail was located just to the north of S. Nicolò, not far from the main piazza in the centre of town.

Italia was certainly a major figure in the regularization of Noto's plan according to Italian principles, but later architects and engineers may have altered his scheme as early as 1712. Italia may have seen the intellectual balancing of churches throughout the city as a wise programme, fitting well into Italian Renaissance tradition and the needs of the clergy, but he may have missed the purely visual implications of his decision. In his Avola plan there is a singular lack of dramatic church siting. If in fact the church of SS. Crocifisso in Noto originally turned its side to the piano of SS. Crocifisso as I suggested, then Italia did not accentuate the forcefulness of the tie he had established between S. Nicolò and SS. Crocifisso. The later turning of the façade of SS. Crocifisso towards the south and the visual emphasis on the southern façades of the other churches of Noto add a quality to Noto that may not have derived from Italia. But certainly Italia seems to have established the spatial rudiments for the elaborations which would follow.

The New City in 1712

In practical terms the new plan of the city on the Meti, in spite of the efforts of Asmundo and Fra Italia, was far from satisfactory. The city was extremely difficult to defend because of its two-level development. It was also too large for a complete set of walls, and because it had no walls, it was open to roaming bandits; the citizens wrote time and time again to ask the government for assistance. The ground on which the slope grid was built was unstable, causing more than a hundred years of continual maintenance because the streets were often washed out during the rainy season.

The new city did have the advantage of being more spacious than the old, being built in the modern style of its day with relatively straight streets and the rudiments of a grid plan. However, while elements of unity are apparent in the plan, the overall effect of Noto's scheme remains loose. The indecision about whether to settle on the summit or the slope created two settlements, and the physical conditions of the site precluded complete unity and encouraged *ad hoc* solutions. Asmundo's inept surveying, as well as his administrative blunders, seem to have assured the city both a place on the awkward slope of the Meti and a very uneven grid.

Nevertheless, it would seem that in spite of the disadvantages of the site the aristocracy and the clergy got what they wanted: a city plan which was more modern and efficient than Noto Antica. They probably would have preferred an even more geometrically perfect plan, like Avola's. But ironically, the first devastating years that Noto's population spent on the site made their mark on the city plan, saving it from the boring predictability of a plan like Avola's. It is the imperfection of the plan, forced on it by the site and by its history, that gives Noto the visual excitement that makes it so different from other post-earthquake centres.

Chapter 5 An Eighteenth-Century City: Noto in the 1750s

By the late 1740s and early 1750s Noto was finally on its way to recovery—a period of brilliant rebirth. Noto's population had climbed slowly after the city's stabilization on the Meti in 1702. In 1712 the population was 6,600, still only about half of the pre-earthquake population of Noto Antica: of 87 noblemen who had lived in Noto Antica, only 44 resided in Noto Nuova; of 600 artisans who had worked in Noto Antica, only a pitiful 200 remained in Noto Nuova.[1] But by 1748 the population had risen to 10,083, including more than 125 noblemen, and although no documentation exists for a rise in the artisan population, surely such a rise did take place judging from the number of people involved in building trades.[2]

Imagine the city on the Meti growing denser every year as newcomers, attracted by offers of land, began to settle in the city.[3] At first, shortly after 1702, the city would have had a temporary quality, with some stone constructions being erected but timber predominating.[4] Mule-train after mule-train would be seen moving slowly up the valley of the Asinaro, to the ruins of Noto Antica. Empty when they left Noto Nuova, these mule-trains would return laden with stones from the ruins of Noto Antica to be reused on the site of the Meti.[5] Religious houses like S. Chiara were already in construction. Around such monumental buildings fragments of stone ornaments from Noto Antica were assembled, waiting to be set in place when the construction reached the proper point.[6] Beside the monumental stone buildings, crude stone huts with thick walls began to rise.

As time went on and permanent structures were built, the temporary buildings that had served as headquarters for the religious institutions were demolished. But for the first decade of the eighteenth century buildings were kept sturdy and low, usually not exceeding a single storey.[7] Probably not a single major building in the city was complete. But great plans were certainly afoot. Perhaps, as the survival of the city seemed more secure, the size of buildings, such as the church of SS. Crocifisso, was increased far more than Fra Italia would have expected.

In the second and third decades of the eighteenth-century monumental building began in earnest, with vaults of churches being completed and façades raised several stories high. But even in this period of growth and presumably of optimism, Noto was dealt another blow. The city, filled with newly completed buildings, was rocked by yet another major earthquake in 1727.[8] As people ran into the squares of the city, the façade of the church of S. Francesco, the vault of the church of S. Agata and the cross on the new church of SS. Trinità all fell in.[9] But earthquakes or not, the city continued to rise, if very slowly.

Evidence for Reconstructing Noto *circa* 1750

By the mid-eighteenth century several visual documents give a more complete idea of Noto's appearance. In the 1750s a veduta of Noto, the only one surviving from the eighteenth century, illustrates what the city looked like from afar.[10] Sometime around 1750 Paolo Labisi, a Netinese architect, climbed up a hill to the south of Noto and sketched a veduta, a combination bird's eye view and street map of the city (Pl. 17).[11]

In 1764 Vincenzo Sinatra, another Netinese architect, drew a map of the territory of Noto (Pl. 23), which can be used in conjunction with the Labisi veduta to delineate the boundaries of eighteenth-century Noto. The purpose of the Sinatra map, as the legend states, is to show the extent of malaria-free land within the city's

17 Veduta of Noto, P. Labisi, *circa* 1750–60.

territory.[12] Sinatra suggests the interior plan of Noto only summarily, with an ideograph, but he does take care in representing the boundaries of the city and labelling them.

Two other documents which bear on the reconstruction of eighteenth-century Noto are also maps, one dated 1749 and signed by Paolo Labisi (Pl. 53a), the other anonymous and undated (Pl. 53b).[13] Both maps represent the property lines of the blocks around Piazza S. Domenico and are therefore invaluable for reconstructing the interior portions of the city.

Used together the maps and veduta yield a fairly accurate picture of the city in the 1750s, some forty years after the main elements of the plan were initially laid out. In the rest of this chapter I will use these documents to compare the Noto of the 1750s with the city as it stands today, to illustrate what has changed since the eighteenth century and what remains. After thus establishing the appearance of Noto, I will discuss the sources of its appearance and its place in the context of European urbanism.

Looking at the city from the south (Pl. 21), we see that present-day Noto still looks very much as Labisi portrayed it. Encroachments of modern buildings, particularly around the periphery, are readily apparent, of course, but the basic arrangement of the grid and the placement of the major buildings in the city are nearly the same as they appear in the veduta. We can prove this by checking the positions of the major buildings which are identified by number on the veduta with the corresponding buildings identified by the same numbers on a modern aerial photograph. The correspondence between the street patterns can be seen by a simple comparison of the present streets (Pl. 20) with the streets represented in the veduta (Pl. 19) drawn 220 years earlier (see Map 4).

In the veduta, as in the aerial photograph, the grid in the lower part of the city is composed of five major east-west streets, the southernmost of which is Via Roma. While the other four are relatively straight, Via Roma is not. So the lower grid is mainly established by the four straight streets, which from north to south are Via Cavour, Corso Vittorio Emanuele, Via Ducezio, and Via Aurispa. The major streets running north-south, at 90° angles to the east-west streets, are part of a grid which today begins with Via Ruggero and Via Galilei on the west and ends with Via Zanardelli and Via Dogali on the east. Thus the purest part of the grid consists of the streets within the boundaries of Via Cavour on the north, Via Aurispa on the south, Via Ruggero and Via Galilei on the west, and Via Zanardelli and Via Dogali on the east. Going either north, south, east, or west outside these borders, the grid begins to disintegrate.

The boundaries of this inner grid enclose most of Noto's important civil and ecclesiastical buildings and define the central core of the city. Within them lie the

19 View of Noto, P. Labisi, *circa* 1750–60. Detail of Noto's streets.

city's two major piazzas, Piazza S. Domenico and the main piazza, both of which, as we shall see, have been greatly altered since the veduta was drawn. Adjacent to the eastern boundary of the inner grid, at the intersection of Corso Vittorio Emanuele and Via Dogali, is a third open space, the Piano of S. Francesco (no. 6). These three open spaces all occur along the Corso, the main street of the city.

The unnamed large open space in the south-western part of the city in 1699 and presumably in 1712 is no longer visible in the veduta. Houses have encroached upon it and the church of S. Maria del Carmine partially blocks access to it from Via Ducezio. This open space, probably a temporary gathering place early in the city's history on the Meti, was not a part of Italia's scheme and did not survive.

Noto's main piazza, called Piano di Chiesa Madre e Casa Senatoria in the eighteenth century, is today an aggregate of five spaces: the area around the city hall itself called Piazza Municipio, the areas on north-east and north-west sides of the upper parts of the steps of S. Nicolò, and the two horseshoe-shaped spaces on the north of the Corso adjacent to the lower parts of the steps of S. Nicolò.[14] In the veduta the main piazza has not yet been divided, appearing instead as a single open space called Area Majoris Ecclesiae (letter B). Piazza S.Dominico, identified as the Area Principalis (letter A) in the veduta, is balanced by the much smaller Piano of S. Francesco (Pl. 24, letter D; Pl. 21, no 6) on the other side of the main piazza. Thus, although the main piazza is not in the centre of the pure grid, the two other open spaces help to balance it and make the whole arrangement appear symmetrical.

This symmetrical arrangement in the core of the lower city is reinforced in aerial

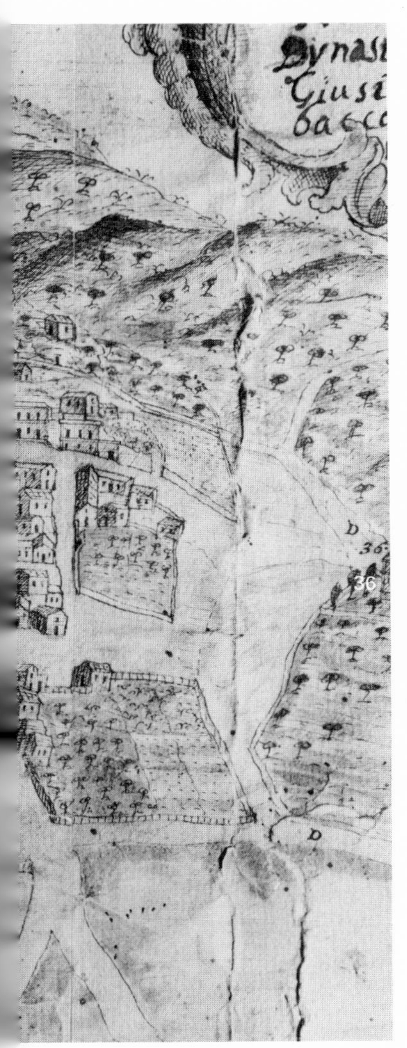

18 Veduta of Noto, P. Labisi, *circa* 1750–60. Detail of inscription. The inscription, originally dedicating the veduta to Jacobo (Giacomo) Nicolaci, who died in 1760, was later altered by Francsó (Franzo) Nicolaci in 1783 so that it could include the title of Prince of Villadorata which the family had acquired in the meantime. Rewriting the lower half of the inscription obscured Paolo Labisi's name, which however still can be seen underneath the present script.

20 Aerial view of Noto from the south.

photographs and the veduta by the Piano of SS. Crocifisso (letter C) in the upper city (Pl. 20). This open space unifies the lower and upper cities, despite the disparity of orientation and the discontinuity of the grid which stops at the steep gradient of the south side of the summit. Since the piano is aligned with the main piazza, it forms a north-south axis which runs through the city; this axis is marked by the façades of S. Nicolò and SS. Crocifisso. This north-south axis is in turn complemented by the symmetrical arrangement of the two piazzas on either side of the main piazza.

Although the veduta represents relationships between monuments and street locations accurately, as we have seen, it is not particularly trustworthy for the appearance of individual monuments. For example, the veduta gives one the impression that every building in Noto was totally completed in the 1750s. But dates on the buildings themselves as well as documents tell us that many of the buildings that Labisi shows completed were still under construction: the house of the Crociferi fathers (no. 15), shown on the veduta (Pl. 19), was just barely begun in the 1750s;[15] the church of the convent was not finished until the 1790s, and then it was built in a different form.[16] The façade of S. Nicolò (no. 1) shown completed in the veduta, had hardly reached the first entablature.[17] Likewise, there are some mistakes in the depiction of buildings which would have been completed by 1750. The church of S. Maria del Carmine (no. 22) has a fictitious dome and crossing.[18] Labisi turns the boatlike roof of the church of the monastery of S. Chiara (no. 4) into a dome.[19] Labisi has also used a little artistic licence to extend the cloisters of the religious houses to

21 Aerial view of Noto from the south with the buildings bearing the same numbers they do on Labisi's veduta.

the maximum limits of their properties although they probably never reached such dimensions. The southern and eastern tiers of rooms attached to the monastery of S. Chiara were never built.[20] It is doubtful that the southernmost extension of the Jesuit College (no. 17) was ever built.[21] In order to show his own design of the house of the Crociferi fathers (no. 15) to its best advantage, Labisi left out a half block of buildings that were definitely in front of it.[22]

Noto: An Open City

Documents prove that Labisi's view of Noto as an open city without fortifications or city gates is correct. Most major European cities built in eighteenth-century Europe fairly bristle with aggressive, low-lying bastions and escarpments. From Noto's beginnings on the Meti, citizens complained that the city could not be secured without fortifications but their requests were periodically refused by the central government.[23] Walls were sought both to regulate traffic within the city and to protect it from bandits – the very same tasks they would have performed in the Middle Ages. One reason Noto was not fortified is that the two-level site of the city was impossible to secure. Even the most advantageous site for a fortification, the edge of the summit between S. Agata and S. Nicolò, was a poor defensive position for the entire city. It was in this location that a small jail, called the castle, was erected in the earliest occupation of the Meti.[24] While the royal jail does command a sweeping view of the lower city and the coastline, a fortification in its location could never have controlled the city's boundaries or fought off an attacker. Any potential

22 Noto as seen from a low hill to the south on the old road to Pachino.

enemy with strong artillery could have shelled the lower part of the city from the hills of Avola to the east. The densely built-up lower city would have hindered artillery manoeuvrability and tactical flexibility. Thus the character of eighteenth-century Noto was that of an urbane city without protection placed, as if on natural grandstands, looking towards the sea.

Noto's Roads and Boundaries

Noto's lifelines to the rest of Sicily were its roads which struck out from the city to the north, east, south, and west.[25] Noto's roads were an exception to the general rule in Sicily because they could actually accommodate carriages. Eighteenth-century diarists universally deplored the road conditions in Sicily.[26] So insecure was overland communication because of the poor roads, that most people travelled by boat in spite of the ever-present danger of pirates. But the road system in Noto's immediate vicinity was surprisingly good. The French tourist Dufourny who came to Noto in 1789 praises the road from Pachino to Noto for its width, which could accommodate three carriages passing at once, and the anonymous chronicler mentions that carriages could be driven down another road to the sea.[27]

Labisi and Sinatra do not agree on the exact number of roads which led out of Noto, but they are in accord as to the direction of the main arteries (cf. Pls 17, 23, 9). One road left the city from the northern part of the summit and led to the hermitage of San Giovanni detto la Lardia and probably Noto Antica. This would have been the road to the interior which must have closely followed the course that the modern road in the same location does today. On the south-eastern edge of the city a road which led both to the coast and to the cities of Avola and Syracuse can be seen on the veduta as well as on the map. The course of this road was probably almost identical to that of the present road which leads from Noto to Syracuse. On the south side of the city Labisi illustrates three separate roads which ran in the direction of Capo Passero, and whose paths can still be seen today in spite of the fact that they are no longer in use.[28] From the westernmost of these roads, across the Asinaro River, Labisi must have sketched the preliminary studies for his veduta, as can be seen from a comparison of a photograph (Pl. 22) taken from that point with the veduta itself (Pl. 19). As to the roads which left from the southwestern part of the city, Labisi and Sinatra are in disagreement. In general, the road in both cases seems to have led to Ispica and Modica. The only question is whether one of these roads, as Labisi seems to indicate, also followed the banks of the Asinaro to Noto Antica and the interior or not.

The boundaries of Noto, where the city met the country, have changed radically since 1750. In order to return the boundaries of the city to their eighteenth-century state as illustrated in the veduta, we have to subtract all of Noto's more modern districts (Pl. 24). The entire district of high-rise apartments along Via Napoli and the road to Syracuse on the south-east, and the development of small houses and Noto's only skyscraper below Via Roma to the south are manifestations of post-war growth which must be subtracted from Noto's older core. Likewise, the fringe of houses around the summit and the northern road to the hermitage of San Giovanni detto la Lardia, built for the most part in the twentieth century, must be removed. The hill

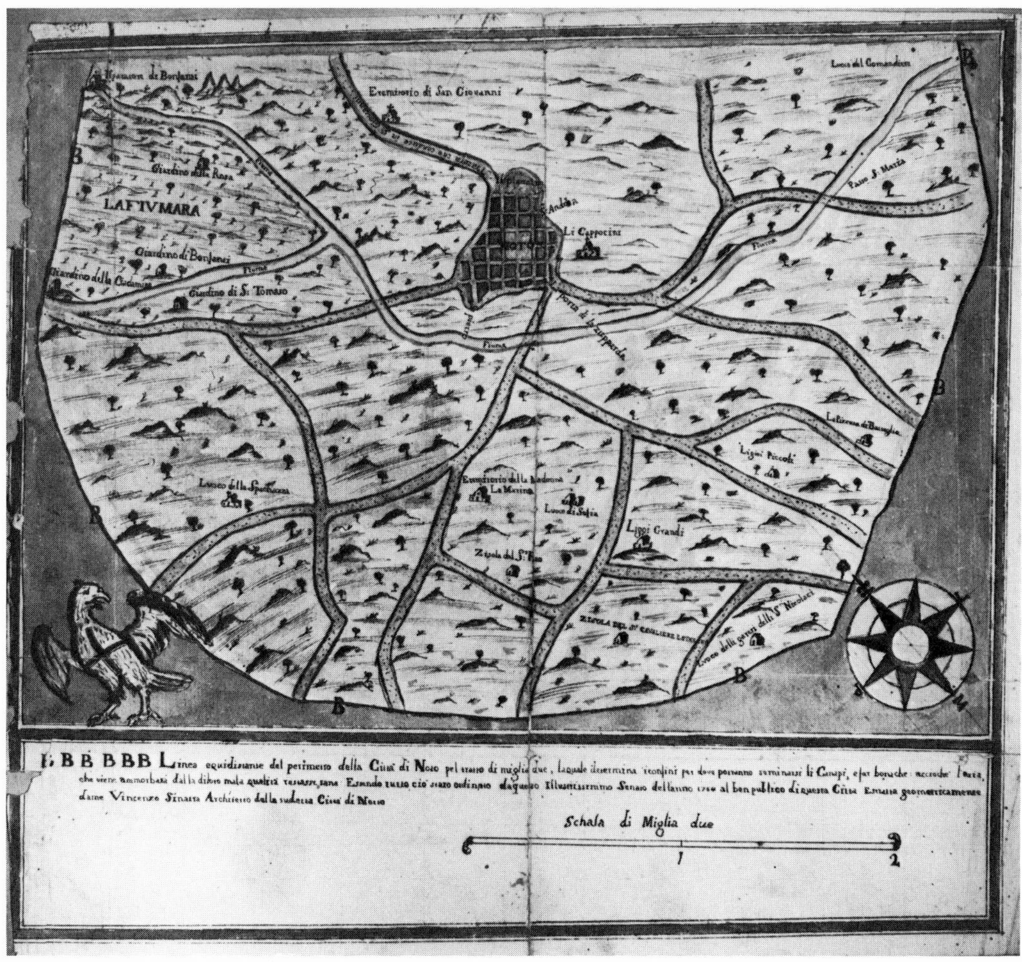

23 Map of the city of Noto in its territory, V. Sinatra, 1764.

on which the Capuchin convent stands is joined to the main part of the city by an artificial hill on which the Villa, Noto's civic garden and its main south-east approach, now lie; this must also be removed.[29] If we further subtract Noto's railway, the bridge over the Asinaro River to the south-west, the football field and the park, its boundaries would look similar to those of the veduta.

Noto's Dual Internal Organization

The veduta portrays only the geometrical side of Noto's plan but actually throughout the city, even within the inner grid, Noto has two faces: an exterior organization according to the geometry of the grid, and within that grid a more organic medieval settlement pattern. Although buildings fronting on the summit and slope grids follow the general orientation of the streets, buildings on the interior of the city blocks form more random patterns (Pls 20, 21). The post-Renaissance grid system dictates the co-ordinates for palaces, churches, monasteries and convents; lower-class dwellings in the interior of the blocks tend to follow the contour of the terrain. The grid, which was presumably designed as a framework for dividing lots within the city, only arranges façades neatly along the streets. Toward the perimeter of the city, the grid entirely disintegrates into a more medieval free-for-all siting, unplanned 'organic' or 'geomorphic' streets and alleys.[30]

Thus Noto divides itself into two cities: post-Renaissance and medieval. The first is the public façade of ceremonial Noto, the second the private environment of lower-class people living in the city (Pls 25–26). Narrow, twisting medieval streets, so unsafe in earthquakes, were exactly what the authorities were trying to avoid by moving the city. Medieval streets were in any case out of style and therefore undesirable for style-conscious Netinese to adopt. However, left to their own resources, the citizens of Noto returned to the urban tradition of their beloved Noto Antica.[31] After generations of living in the medieval streets and non-geometricized

24 The boundaries of eighteenth-century Noto. The area outside the circle represents the post eighteenth-century additions.
Letter A: Piazza S. Domenico
B: Main Piazza
C: Piano del SS. Crocifisso
D: Piano of S. Francesco.

plots of Noto Antica, they seem to have settled the Meti in the same ancient pattern. In a small way, the people who could not return to Noto Antica recreated it on the Meti.

Although plots around the central part of the upper and lower grids were carefully measured, as Labisi's plan of Piazza S. Domenico (Pl. 53) proves, plots within the blocks further away from the main streets become more random. These blocks are honeycombed with winding alleys which give access to the small buildings in their interiors (Fig. 3). Because of population pressures, land within the large blocks may have been sublet to small householders, bit by bit, without previous planning. Small winding alleys (Pls 25 and 65) were created to reach these inner spaces. This situation probably occurred in a planned city like Noto because individual plots seem to have been designed to accept large palaces and ecclesiastical buildings rather than modest dwellings.

In the development of each block, the exterior plots were probably taken first, leaving a hollow core inside the block, as the blocks on the lower right in the Labisi veduta illustrate (Pl. 19). Gardens developed within these inner cores, but were gradually replaced by houses when new settlers came to the city.[32] Houses must have spread back into the interior of the blocks along the alleys, which originated from gaps between the street-front houses. Originally many of these back alleys actually led from one side of the block to another, but with time the alleys were blocked and became small interior courtyards. Where the Renaissance grid breaks down, in the

25 Vico Nea, Noto.

core of the blocks, on the perimeter of the city, or on the steep slopes, the character of Noto becomes that of an intimate Medieval hilltown laced with alleys and stairways that exclude vehicular traffic and introduce a smaller scale than that of the monumental centre of the city.

Street Names

The names of both the more medieval streets and alleys and the straighter post-Renaissance streets of the city have all been changed since the 1750s. After the unification of Italy (*ca.* 1870) all of Noto's street names were changed as were those of other cities throughout Italy. Today Noto's streets bear the names of local heroes, heroes of the revolution, or dates of national importance.[33] But in the eighteenth century the main streets were often known by the churches which faced them. Thus Via Cavour was Strada di Montevergine, after the monastery which faced it (Pl. 17, no. 22), Via Ducezio was Strada del Carmine after the convent (no. 12) at its western terminus, Via Aurispa was Strada della Rotunda (no. 37), and so on.[34]

Noto's main street, the Corso Vittorio Emanuele, had a special name, the Cassaro.[35] 'Cassaro' is an Arab word meaning 'main street which leads to the fort'; the main street of Palermo is, for example, designated the Cassaro.[36] Although Noto had no fort the name was probably used just because it was the name of the famous street in Palermo. There were no street numbers in Noto in the eighteenth century.[37] Documents recording locations in Noto first list the street and then the names of the people or buildings that can be found on either side of the given location.[38]

26 Ronco Masaniello, Noto.

The Corso Sequence

The centre of Noto must be experienced and analysed sequentially in order to be understood. I will first describe a portion of the city as it looks today, then establish which features were added in the nineteenth century, and last, reconstruct the city as it was in the eighteenth century, commenting upon the features that have survived.

As we shall see, Noto was planned to be viewed from east to west. Only from this direction can the buildings in the main open spaces of the city be seen to their best advantage. The traveller who comes to Noto from Syracuse gets a controlled view of the city which was definitely calculated to play up its impressive character. So it is natural that this investigation should run from east to west following the Corso, just as the Netinese intended. The emphasis on the east as the entrance, which is present today and is also apparent in the veduta, might be due to the fact that the way to Syracuse and Catania, the two largest and most influential cities in south-eastern Sicily, was in that direction, or it might be, as Lévi-Strauss suggests, due to some unknown instinct that makes man build cities from east to west.[39]

Thanks to nineteenth-century improvements, the eastern approach to the city does not look at all as it did in the eighteenth century. One approaches Noto today from behind (to the east of) the convent of the Cappuccini and up a long tree-lined boulevard called Viale Marconi (Pl. 28). The park around it (called the 'Villa'), and the triumphal arch on its western side, are all products of the nineteenth century. Previously this area had been a deep gully, fill for which was probably provided

27 Piazza Taranto today.

from the operations which were being carried out to lower Noto's streets and thus make them more even. Evidence of this project will be seen later, but for now it is only important to note that this pleasant avenue leading into the city is wholly a nineteenth-century creation (Pl. 29).[40] The flower garden aspect, and the tunnel-like progression of the avenue under the attractive overhanging trees was not only absent from eighteenth-century Noto, but was foreign to the Sicilians' concept of the city.

French visitors coming to Italy and Sicily in the eighteenth century were amazed to find that the Italians were not accustomed to putting trees along the sides of their larger streets.[41] To the French this lack of shade in such a hot climate was just short of barbaric. The French traveller Denon noted that there were no promenades, in the French sense of the word, in the major Sicilian cities. However, the Sicilian nobility preferred to take to its carriages instead of walking. Perhaps for this reason no trees or landscaping were necessary. In Sicily the trend towards public gardens did not begin until the late eighteenth century, in Palermo, and arrived in Noto in the late nineteenth century in the form of the 'villa', or public garden.[42]

In the eighteenth century the approach to the city was more dramatic than it is today due to the discontinuity between the core of the city and its outskirts. One entered Noto from the south-west side of the convent of the Cappuccini and continued through the outskirts of town, either up the gully to the entrance to the

29 Viale Marconi and the Villa looking west toward the Corso and the arch of Ferdinand II.

main street, or down the gully, to the south-eastern part of Noto, to what is now Piazza Taranto (Pl. 27).[43] The Piazza Taranto is a forgotten part of the present city; as it is depicted on the veduta (Pl. 19) it opened out onto the approach to Noto from Syracuse and thus may have been a market-place on the edge of the city. If the city had been entered by walking up from the piazza toward the main street, the pleasurable shock of arriving at so noble a thoroughfare lined with impressive buildings would have been great indeed. If, on the other hand, the city were entered along the main street, it would have been necessary to climb up the steep slope of the gully before perceiving the entire length of the Corso. In either case, the effect would have been somewhat analogous to Bernini's Piazza of St. Peter's before Mussolini carved Viale della Conciliazione through the Borgo. Today this quality, surprise at suddenly finding oneself in a beautiful street at the top of the hill, has given way to the late Baroque and nineteenth-century feelings of spatial continuity and long vistas.

The Corso: The Beginning

A triumphal arch (Pl. 30) marks the entrance to the city proper and the beginning of the Corso. Because in the eighteenth century the city lacked gates, Noto's city fathers decided to erect this triumphal arch for the 1838 visit of Ferdinand II at the west end of the Villa.[44]

In the eighteenth century the Corso was probably unpaved: in the winter rainwater flowing down the north-south streets above turned it into a highway of mud; in the summer the dust was a nuisance. In the 1790s Bernardo Maria Labisi, Noto's city engineer, proposed that the whole street be levelled off.[45] Lower areas were to be filled and higher ones removed to make the street more serviceable. He proposed that sewers be installed under the street and a 'chain' of stones be laid along it to support the wheels of vehicular traffic. But Bernardo's plan was not implemented; mud and dust, in winter and summer, persisted until the late nineteenth century.

28 Aerial view looking west down the Corso.
At the bottom centre of the photograph is the Villa with Viale Marconi connecting the road to Syracuse (bottom left-hand corner) with the Corso, which begins behind (that is west of) the triumphal arch. To the left of the arch (south) is a modern open-air cinema. To the left of the cinema at the edge of the photograph is Piazza Taranto (Pl. 27). South of the Villa (left of the three buses in the bottom left-hand side) is the location of the Capuchin convent. On the very bottom is a nineteenth-century reinforcing wall and below it a World War II pillbox.

Finally, in the late nineteenth century, one hundred years later, a solution was devised.[46] All the streets were lowered until they hit bedrock, making them more stable, and, because they were then even more pleasing to the eye by nineteenth-century standards. All east-west streets on the slope of the Meti and all north-south streets on the summit were made as straight as possible. Also, sewers were carved under the streets to eliminate the drainage problem which had troubled the city from its inception.

30 The arch of Ferdinand II from the east.

Although the purpose of the widespread excavations was to reinforce streets throughout the city, this radical shifting of levels endangered many older buildings; some had to be faced with artificial masonry bases to shield the exposed soil on which they stood from the elements. A few streets could not be levelled, and in such cases the Netinese made them appear as level as possible. On the Corso, for example, the incline from the arch of Ferdinand II to S. Chiara was modified by lowering the street opposite S. Chiara by more than two metres and filling the gully to the east of the arch; while the incline was still relatively steep, it was at least more level throughout than was the original road bed.[47]

No evidence of the lowering of the streets can be seen in the first two blocks of the Corso because façades of the buildings which flank it were built in the nineteenth and twentieth centuries (Pl. 31). In general, these buildings preserve the feeling of the two-storey buildings in the same location on the north side of the street in the eighteenth-century veduta. They retain the two-storey elevations, and the sample corner pilasters, sometimes raised on pedestals, that can be seen in the veduta.

The width of the Corso is about 9.5 metres from one façade to the other. [48] This is slightly less than the minimum requirement for Catania's secondary streets (about

31 Piano of S. Francesco. Partial view.

11.4 metres).[49] The relative narrowness of the Corso illustrates that the stipulations made in the Catania council after the earthquake may not have been identical to those made in other cities. The narrowness of the Corso, combined with the two- and three-storey façades which flank it, sets up a very intimate scale which is carried throughout the city. In comparison to Catania's streets, Noto's streets would not be as safe during an earthquake; but on the other hand they are certainly more attractive because of their smaller scale, and help to block the hot sun during the summer much more effectively than those of Catania.

Piano of S. Francesco

About fifty metres from the Arch of Ferdinand II, travelling west on the Corso, a small open space becomes partially visible. As the traveller proceeds, he comes upon this open space, seemingly designed to be viewed from the east where he is standing (cf. eastern (Pl. 32) and western (Pl. 33) approaches to the piano). Three monumental buildings, the former monasteries of S. Chiara (Map 5, no. 4) and SS. Salvatore (no. 3), and former convent of S. Francesco (no. 5), are all concentrated at the intersection of the present Via Zanardelli, Via Dogali, and the Corso. The façades of the monastery block of SS. Salvatore and the church of S. Francesco

34 Veduta of Noto, P. Labisi, *ca.* 1750–60. Detail of Piano of S. Francesco.

all'Immacolata, both on the north-western corner, form the visual focus for the open space, which is called the Piano of S. Francesco.

When the present view of the Piano of S. Francesco (Pl. 32) is compared with Labisi's veduta (Pl. 34), the extent to which the piano was changed in the nineteenth century becomes apparent (cf. Fig. 4). It was originally much steeper from north to south and much larger than it now appears. The embankment and side stairways in front of the convent on the veduta marked the northern limit of the piano; the steps of the church of S. Francesco did not extend as far down as they do today; the shops below the embankment were not present.[50] With the lowering of the street in 1897, the two flights of steps closest to the street were added; their risers differ from those of the flight closest to the church, which mark the old ground level.[51] That ground level can be seen by looking behind the walls of the shops, where the old embankment is still preserved. The original street level can be judged from the height of the bases of the corner pedestal of the monastery of S. Chiara, added after the street was lowered; both are about two metres high, which means that the street was about two metres higher than it is today. Also in the late 1890s, the statue of the Madonna Immacolata, which originally stood in the centre of the street (Map 5 no. 6), was moved to a platform on the top of the shops.[52] The statue of the Madonna, which was erected in the piano in 1704 in wood and subsequently copied in stone, was an important part of the whole ensemble. In the eighteenth century it would have been encountered dramatically in the street; today it stands out of harm's way, far above the street.

Part of the beauty and drama of the modern piano derives from the height of the façades on its northern perimeter. That height is accentuated by several important changes which seem to have been made after the veduta was drawn. Foremost among these is a change which occurred in the façade of the monastery of SS. Salvatore, which must have been redesigned in the eighteenth century. For example,

33 Piano of S. Francesco. Western approach.

32 Piano of S. Francesco. Eastern approach.

Fig. 4 Reconstruction of the Piano of S. Francesco before the lowering of the Corso in the nineteenth century. The buildings in this drawing are illustrated as they appear today but the level of the piano, the stairs on the north side, and the position of the statue of Madonna Immacolata are represented as they probably appeared in the eighteenth century. Compare this figure with Pl. 32.

35 Aerial photograph of the Piano of S. Francesco.

the tower which plays such a prominent part in the effect of the modern piano (Pl. 36) does not appear in the veduta, nor does the separation between the lower block of the monastery, which flanks the piano itself, and the upper block along the uppermost portion of Via Dogali. The upper block in fact does not appear at all. The lower block of the monastery appears on the veduta as being three storeys high; as it exists today it has lost its third storey and has gained a basement from the lowering of the street. Although the veduta illustrates the Corso façade as being three storeys high it depicts only the uppermost storey facing Via Cavour to the north, because of the steepness of the hillside on which the monastery stands. The veduta's version of the monastery's appearance conflicts with the present situation in which there is a break between the two blocks, with the upper one having two full storeys on its northernmost part. Finally, the two blocks do not join together smoothly, indicating that no such combination was intended in the first place. The metopes on

36 SS. Salvatore. Joining of the two blocks of the eastern façade.

the cornices are not the same, and the ornaments around their apertures have completely different characters. The lower block has tighter, more constrained decoration whereas the upper has not only the Borrominesque sweep of the tower itself, but Roman Rococo window surrounds which are not in tune with the lower block. Some attempt was made to link the blocks by the addition of an ornamental arcade on top of the second storey of the lower one, but this combination does not work too effectively. Thus we might hypothesize that the upper block was built after the veduta was drawn.

The other changes in the piano which accentuate the height of the northern perimeter were caused by the lowering of the Corso itself in the nineteenth century. The stepped effect produced by the shops, the ramps, the stairs themselves, present the juxtaposition of levels and angles which culminates in the façades on the north-western side of the piano. All these details, which were added during the nineteenth century, accentuate the stage-like quality of the piano. It is not a space to be traversed but to be experienced from below. Looking at it from an angle, as one does approaching from the east, adds to its excitement and theatrical quality.

In the eighteenth century the Baroque character of the piano would have been much less apparent than it is today; the piano was a sloping simple rectangle. The spatial relationships between the Corso on the south, and the front door of the church of S. Francesco on the north would have been much smoother and more understandable; the space more usable, because it was not chopped up by the stairs and terraces; and the effect less cluttered. However, the statue of the Madonna, which was then standing directly in the roadway of the Corso, would have given the street more drama on its own level than it has today.

The Corso Continues

Proceeding up the Corso one finds oneself again hemmed in on both sides by buildings (Pl. 37). The former monastery of S. Chiara stands to the south and the former monastery of SS. Salvatore to the north. The basements of both buildings, added after the lowering of the street, are carved out of bedrock and disguised with masonry. The dormitory and church of S. Chiara (Pl. 38) have both been irreparably changed because their main entrances are raised above the street and rendered useless (as is the fountain (Pl. 39), now high in the air, on the wall of SS. Salvatore). Nevertheless, these two buildings still perform the function of pincers, squeezing off the enlarged space of the Piano of S. Francesco into a street again, before allowing entrance into the main piazza of the city.

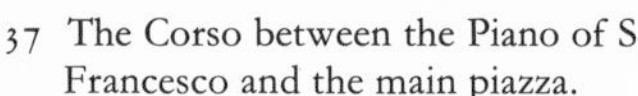

37 The Corso between the Piano of S. Francesco and the main piazza.

38 The monastery of S. Chiara isolated on a nineteenth-century basement.

39 Fountain high on the side of SS. Salvatore.

The Main Piazza

The main piazza of the city is almost impossible to perceive as a whole. This effect results largely from nineteenth-century alterations. In the veduta (Pl. 40) the piazza appears as a large open space dominated by the Chiesa Madre, S. Nicolò (since elevated to cathedral status in 1844). The space as it appears on the veduta can be envisaged as a 'T' with a stubby stem, and a long and narrow crown with a depth-to-length ratio of 1:5. The central axis of this space, between the city hall and the S. Nicolò, was emphasized by a monument, probably an obelisk, on either side of which were fountains. The small blocks planned for the north-eastern and north-western angles of the piazza in the early 1700s do not appear on Labisi's veduta, indicating that in the instance of the main piazza, open space was expanded, rather than contracted through encroachments as in the rest of the city.

The expansive organization of the main piazza was altered in the nineteenth century, fragmenting the mid-eighteenth-century whole.

As I mentioned in Chapter 5, the piazza is now divided by the stairs of S. Nicolò

40 Veduta of Noto, P. Labisi, *ca.* 1750–60. Main piazza.

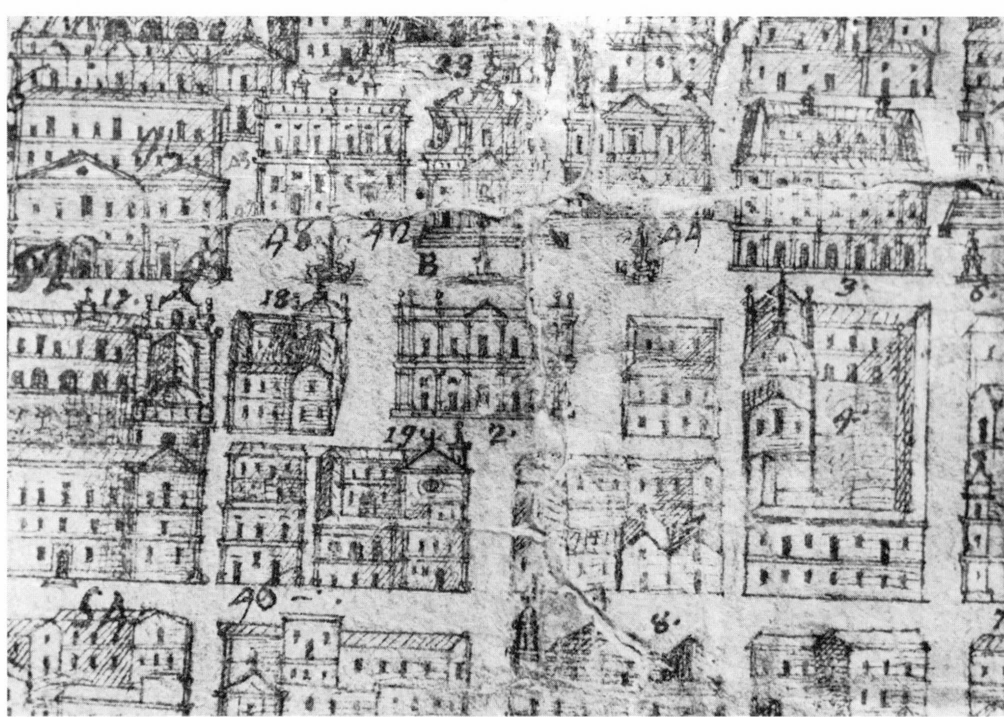

41 Aerial photograph of the main piazza from the east.

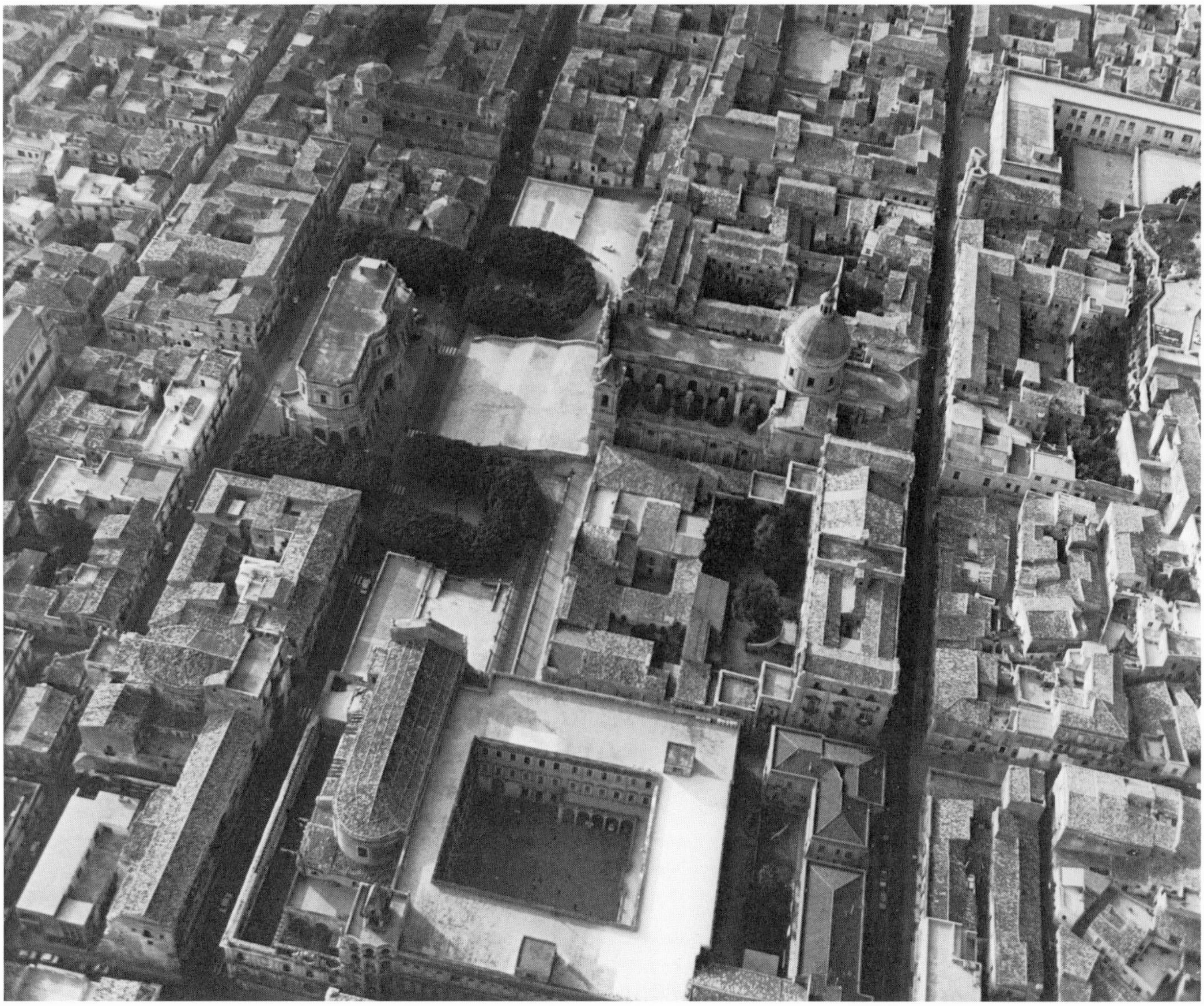

42 The main piazza seen from the east with the city hall on the left side of the photograph.

(Pl. 41). The stairs, although finished in 1818, were not strictly a product of the nineteenth century.[53] Funds for their erection were donated by the Marchese del Castelluccio as early as 1770, though work probably did not begin until much later. In November 1880, the two piazzas on either side of the stairs were lowered[54] (Pl. 44); these two horseshoe-shaped spaces were then planted with trees, which today further disrupt the expansive quality that the piazza once had. On the north-east side of the piazza, the new church of SS. Salvatore was built in the early nineteenth century, and required the porch in front of it. Stores were added to the south of this porch facing the Corso, and across the piazza on the western side a small block of stores also developed along Via Nicolaci. The dismembering of the piazza was complete. It no longer functioned as a unified space, but was totally fragmented as we see it today (Pls 42, 43).

But in the mid-eighteenth century the main piazza was unified by the positions of the buildings around it and the arrangement of the obelisk and fountains within it. The placement of the obelisk and fountains was influenced by High Baroque projects of seventeenth-century Rome. The fountains in Noto's piazza underscore the long narrow quality of the space while reinforcing its central axis.[55] This combination of an obelisk flanked by fountains recalls two Bernini projects.[56] The first is the Piazza of St. Peter's where the same elements are used to achieve a similar effect of centrality on the one hand and lateral tension on the other. The second is the Piazza Navona where Bernini mounted the central obelisk on the Fountain of the Four Rivers in the centre and flanked it with two lower lateral fountains: basically the same solution. The design of one of Noto's fountains itself was also copied from a Bernini work. The fountain of Hercules (Pl. 46), which now stands in Piazza S. Domenico, was originally intended to stand in the main piazza as a symbol of Noto.[57] Hercules, in an apish imitation of Bernini's Triton, blows a conch while holding a shield emblazoned with the arms of the city of Noto—an appropriate iconographical ornament for this piazza in which major civil and ecclesiastical buildings of the city stood.

The Roman Baroque employment of balancing symmetrically-placed church façades with one another also influenced the composition of Noto's main piazza. The south-eastern and south-western corners of the main piazza are defined by two churches: the church of the monastery of S. Chiara (Pl. 45, no. 4) and the church of S. Carlo

43 The main piazza seen from the east with the church of S. Nicolò and the staircase in front of it.

44 Main piazza with trees. Early twentieth century.

45 An aerial photograph of the main piazza from the north. Numbers correlate with Labisi veduta:

1 S. Nicolò
2 City Hall
3 SS. Salvatore
4 Monastery of S. Chiara
8 Monastery of S. Maria dell'Arco
17 Jesuit college
18 Abbey of SS. Trinità
41 Nicolaci palace (Villadorata)
42 Landolina palace (S. Alfano)
44 Present Bishop's palace
52 Landolina-Rau palace
53 Di Lorenzo palace
A Astuto palace
B Trigona-Frigentini palace (Cannicarao)
C Ferla palace

Borromeo (Jesuit College, no. 17). The two churches differ greatly in size, nonetheless the effect is that their façades and naves balance one another across the piazza (Pl. 45). Their façades, indeed, are almost the same height, which preserves the symmetrical relationship between them, and since they are not too close together, the difference in the sizes of their naves does not destroy the effect they produce. Their positions on the corners of the main piazza seem calculated to enhance the grandeur of the piazza by making it into a symmetrically-perfect Baroque statement. S. Nicolò and these two churches together form an isosceles triangle with its apex at S. Nicolò.

From the ground level the positioning of the two churches seems reminiscent of the placement of the two churches on Piazza del Popolo in Rome.[58] In the Netinese churches there is not the same illusionism at work to make them look more symmetrical than they actually are, as in Piazza del Popolo, nevertheless, the visual effect has the symmetry one feels in Piazza del Popolo. Very likely this was the model for the arrangement of the churches, as it was for so many other symmetrical combinations of façades in other cities.

46 Hercules Fountain seen from the south in its present position in Villetta Ercole on Piazza S. Domenico.

The Corso between the Main Piazza and Piazza S. Domenico

The stretch of street between the main piazza and Piazza S. Domenico is longer than that between the Piano of S. Francesco and the main piazza, but the effect is much the same. One feels the squeeze of the flanking buildings again as one proceeds west. The façade of S. Carlo Borromeo (Map 5, no. 17), probably the most exciting piece of architecture in the city, helps enhance this rest area between piazzas (Pl. 47).

47 The façade of S. Carlo and the Jesuit college on the Corso between the main piazza and Piazza S. Domenico.

Piazza S. Domenico

Passing the Jesuit College and the Seminary one arrives at Piazza S. Domenico, so named in the eighteenth century because of the Dominican church which faced it. After Unification it was dubbed Piazza XVI Maggio, but since its original name is still popularly used, I use it here. The addition of the nineteenth-century garden destroyed the total effect of unity created by the façade of the Dominican church which previously dominated the piazza (Pls 48–49). Called Villetta Ercole after the Hercules fountain which was moved here from the main piazza, this small garden with its palms and evergreens largely blocks the façade of the Dominican church which was strategically placed at the north-west in order to be seen from the eastern entrance to the piazza (cf. Pls 51 and 52), the same effect as is attained by the combination of the monasteries of SS. Salvatore and the church of S. Francesco in the Piano of S. Francesco. This position, if not blocked, would assure a view of the church on a diagonal, which means that not only its façade but its central cupola and tower would have been visible.

48 An early twentieth-century view of Piazza S. Domenico.

49 An early twentieth-century view of Piazza S. Domenico.

Other factors, like the nineteenth-century opera house in the south-western corner of the piazza,[59] make the piazza look quite different from Labisi's portrayal of it in his veduta (Pl. 50). But, in fact, the piazza probably never appeared as Labisi has portrayed it, at least on the north-eastern side. For here unmistakably we can see the completed dormitory block of the house of the Crociferi fathers which was only one storey high on the south side in 1787, years after the veduta had been drawn.[60] Labisi himself drew a map (Pl. 53a) in 1749 in which he shows that the property of the Crociferi was blocked from the piazza by the property of Giovanni Paredes. Although the church of the house was moved slightly to the south, it never occupied a site on the piazza. But by 1750 Labisi had completed his design for the house, and although it was not built, Labisi probably wanted to show how this important building would look in the context of the city. Therefore, to show it to advantage he subtracted the building to the south that would have obscured it on the veduta.

In spite of Labisi's deletion of the building, his depiction of the piazza gives us a

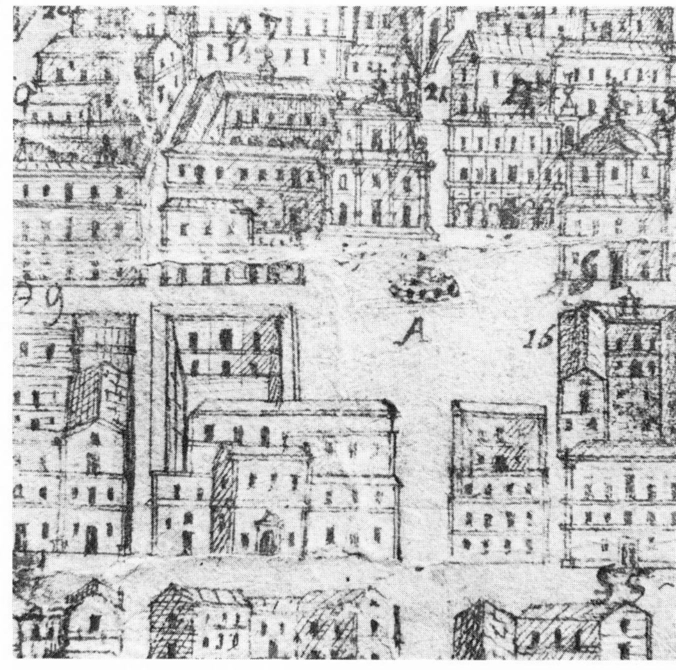

50 Veduta of P. Labisi, *ca.* 1750–60. Detail of Piazza S. Domenico.

51 The façade of S. Domenico seen from the west.

52 The façade of S. Domenico seen from the east.

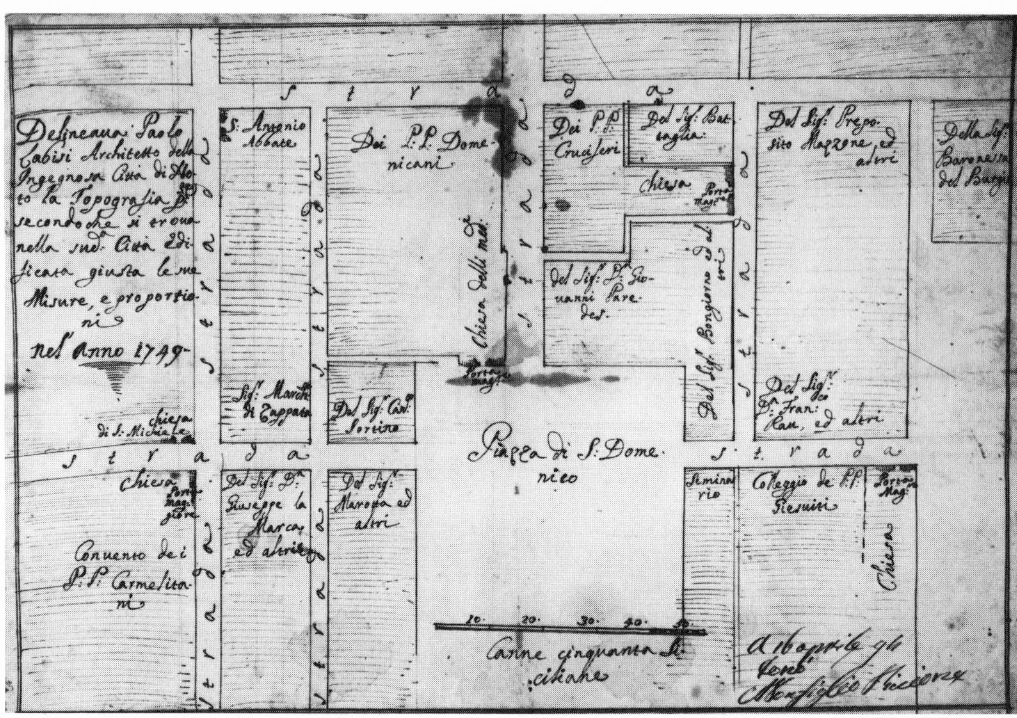

53a Map of Piazza S. Domenico drawn by P. Labisi, 1749.

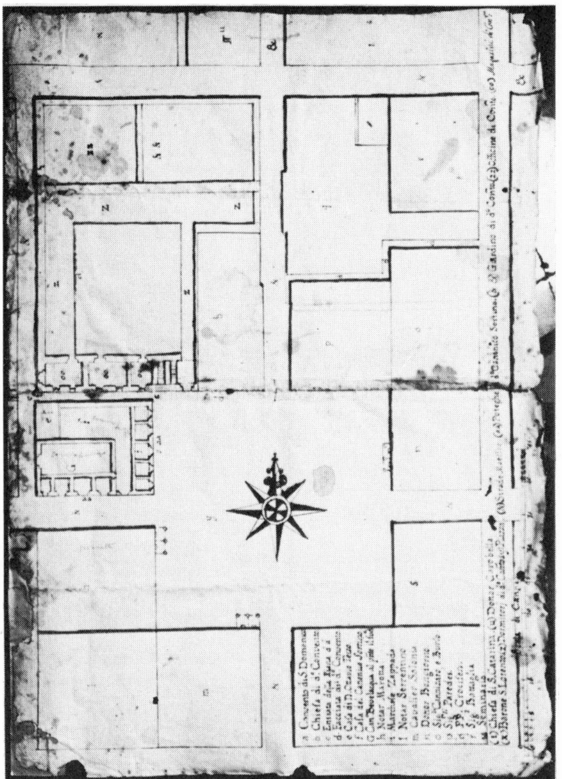

53b Anonymous map of Piazza S. Domenico, mid-eighteenth century.

good impression of how it must have looked as a relatively empty space. The gradient was slightly less than that of the main piazza but nevertheless considerable. This vast slanting piazza may have looked rather barren before the addition of the garden. In 1749, when Labisi drew his map of the area (Pl. 53a), he showed no fountain in the centre. In the veduta (Pl. 50) a fountain basin had appeared, and in the 1790s the Hercules fountain was set into this basin.[61] But up to that time this whole piazza was relatively unadorned, compared with the other two.

Tortora, in his description of Noto written in 1712, identifies Piazza S. Domenico as the city's market place.[62] On the veduta Piazza S. Domenico is called Area Principalis and that name denotes its significance as the most important non-ecclesiastical piazza in the city. Its large unadorned space may have been used by vendors to set up stalls when market day came, just as vendors regularly set up stalls on the southern part of the piazza today.[63] In the early nineteenth century the town market was still being held here, but for hygienic reasons it was later transferred to a site opposite the church of the Crociferi on Via Rocco Pirri.[64]

The Corso ends

Leaving the Piazza S. Domenico and proceeding west out of the city one has the definite feeling of leaving the heart of Noto behind. In 1749 the convent of the Carmelites stood on the south side of the Corso and the church of S. Michele on the north, but by the time the veduta was drawn, the Carmelite church had been demolished and rebuilt on Via Ruggero Settimo. The façade of the church of S. Michele, which looks essentially as it did in the eighteenth century, offers no real interest as a monument and does not in any way modulate the space around it. After passing these monuments the Corso unceremoniously descends to an ugly modern obelisk and stops. The exit from the town has little of the flair which characterizes its entrance.[65]

The Corso and the Open Spaces as Outdoor Rooms

The sequence of spaces down the Corso is so pleasing that it transforms the abstract geometrical grid plan on the slope into an experiential cityscape. The rhythm of street and open spaces combines with the site's gradient to give the city interest and diversity without destroying the feeling of control. The east-to-west statement of direction was clearly present in the eighteenth century, as the westerly positions of the church of S. Domenico and the SS. Salvatore—S.Francesco combinations on their open spaces prove. In the nineteenth century this emphasis was accentuated by the Arch of Ferdinand II, the Villa, and the lowering of the piano of S. Francesco. In this central core of Noto, the essence of Noto's special quality is distilled.

Paolo Labisi in an unpublished treatise that he wrote on civil architecture in 1773 extols the virtue of open spaces, like those along the Corso. Labisi states that open spaces provide ventilation and air, channel rainwater so that it will not endanger houses, and

> provide all of the inhabitants the ability to guard against earthshocks (from which God liberate us) by means of leaving their own houses and meeting in the open spaces to escape the perils of being hit by the ruins of buildings. And finally streets and open spaces are destined for everyone to enjoy the prospects of building, which rise around them for the ornament of the open spaces, and also for the inhabitants to lean out of their windows to enjoy public functions which are put on by the city. . . .[66]

Open spaces in eighteenth-century Noto were essentially like large outdoor salons in which the people could promenade and watch one another as they do today. Noto was a city of people watching other people, as it continues to be. The gaiety of the façades sealed out the problems which were apparent to any outsider: like other Sicilian towns, only a half of Noto's rich soil was under cultivation, largely due to the neglect of the landlords who owned it.[67] The landowners instead established an environment for themselves which revolved around outward show.[68] Open spaces and streets were essential for display and interactions. The sloping terrain of the city helped to make every open space very exciting when seen from windows or balconies. The sisters of the monastery of Montevergine wanted a tower from which to see processions, and most palaces have large balconies from which their owners and friends could survey the town and its vista of the sea.[69] Certainly, of all the views, those of the Corso and its open spaces were the most esteemed.

The Corso was also most likely the street on which the carriages of the aristocrats of Noto paraded. Throughout the eighteenth century in Sicily carriage rides, a

54a S. Girolamo, the church of the monastery of Montevergine. Exterior as seen from Via Nicolaci.

fashion established in Rome, were a popular aristocratic diversion; for aristocratic families the proper coaches and liveries were a social necessity, one's status being dependent upon them.[70] In eighteenth-century Palermo, the proliferation of carriages was so great that it posed a traffic problem: parking areas were assigned and traffic citations issued to ease the congestion. A tax proposed on carriages, intended to limit their use and acquisition, was suggested in 1740 but vigorously opposed. Among the important events that required a carriage (which was, if need be, hired out by the hour) was the evening ride to the seaside down the Cassaro, Palermo's main street. In a long line all the aristocrats of the city drove their carriages to the sea, exchanging gossip and visiting with one another.

In the provinces the aristocrats instituted similar customs where possible. The fashion was certainly present in Noto Antica, where there had been forty-three carriages.[71] The fact was that in the eighteenth century the roads throughout Sicily could not accommodate large carriages: many roads could not accept vehicular traffic at all.[72] So the carriages could only be used within the cities themselves, and had to be disassembled to be taken from one city to another. This led to some very

54b S. Maria del Carmine, church of the convent of the Carmelites as seen from Via Ducezio.

peculiar practices, in which carriages were used for in-town transportation, as the English traveller Algernon Swinburne describes in his visit to the hill town of Caltagirone, Sicily:

> After I had refreshed myself with a short but excellent meal, they took me to a very handsome coach. It was a singular circumstance to meet a string of carriages full of well-dressed ladies and gentlemen on the summit of a mountain, which no vehicle can ascend, unless it be previously taken to pieces and placed upon the backs of mules. . . . The hour of airing being expired, which consisted of six turns of about a half a mile each, a numerous assembly was formed at the Baron's house.[73]

The Noto Nuova aristocrats probably travelled back and forth, up and down the Corso, like the people of Caltagirone. But the road to the coast was level enough, and evidently well enough maintained to let them escape from their city environment for a while.[74]

In addition to the Corso, the east-west street above it – Via Cavour – took on social importance and visual appeal just after Labisi's veduta was finished.* For it was during the late eighteenth century that the Di Lorenzo family redecorated the exterior of their palace, that the Astuto family built their palace and that the Trigonas built theirs.[75] The street therefore became a kind of aristocratic thoroughfare with three religious houses, the monastery of Montevergine, the house of the Crociferi, and the oratory of S. Filippo Neri facing it. Neither the Astuto palace nor the Trigona palace can be seen on the veduta because of the late date of their construction.[76] Via Cavour can be seen as a new development, probably begun because space around the main squares and the Corso was no longer available.

*For Via Cavour see Pls. 76, 81, 85 and 154

A number of streets on the slope are enhanced by churches which stand at one end, defining a terminus and giving the whole street a scenographic effect. S. Girolamo, the church of the monastery of Montevergine (Pl. 54a), stands at the end of Via Nicolaci, the church of S. Maria del Carmine was moved to provide a visual terminus for Via Ducezio (Pl. 54b), and at one time (but no longer) the church of S. Pietro formed a fitting terminus to Via Roma.[77] The church and palace façades which line Noto's streets and on occasion dominate dead-end streets give the town the quality of a stage set, an orchestrated utopian experience which can be best appreciated riding or strolling down the Corso.

The Summit

From the slope below, the summit looks like a beautiful and interesting part of the city, a continuous silhouette of monumental buildings (skyline from no. 27 to 25, Pl. 21). In the eighteenth century the monastery of S. Agata, the Impellizzeri palace and the convent of S. Antonio di Padova were all standing on the southern edge of the summit, as Labisi portrays them.

The two eighteenth-century routes which led to the summit directly from the lower city were the present street of Via Galilei which led past the church of S. Antonio to Via Sofia, and Via Mauceri on the eastern side of town. Coaches

55 The northern façade of the Casa del Refugio with nineteenth-century basement.

proceeded up these streets until they reached the level ground of the summit.[78]

Like the streets of the lower city, the three main north-south streets of the summit—Via Umberto, Via Sallicano, and Via Garibaldi—have been lowered. The two or three metres of bedrock under the foundations of the former Casa del Refugio (Pls 19, no. 31, and 55; now the penitentiary) and the former convent of the P. P. Benefratelli (Pl. 19, no. 30) both illustrate the extent of this lowering. Behind the houses which face these streets the terrain rises sometimes as high as two metres. The bottom floors of many of the buildings on Via Sallicano were carved into bedrock, as recent demolitions show (Pl. 57).

In 1748 the population of the summit equalled less than half the population of the slope.[79] Still the population was 3,035, which would have caused it to be a good deal more built-up than Labisi's veduta indicates. Seven out of Noto's twenty religious

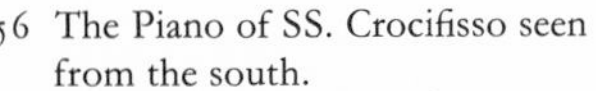

56 The Piano of SS. Crocifisso seen from the south.

57 Demolition on Via Sallicano showing the bedrock out of which the first storey of the demolished house in the centre was carved.

houses were located on the summit. But Noto's most powerful aristocrats shunned the upper city, probably because of its distance from the Corso; only the Impellizzeri family settled on the summit, and they chose a site which was at its extreme south-eastern edge.[80]

The Piano of SS. Crocifisso (present-day Piazza Mazzini) does not equal the visual excitement of any of the open spaces along the Corso (Pl. 56). On the veduta the piano looks rather amorphous, but its boundaries, according to Labisi, are a good deal larger than those of today. At the very least, the entire block in front of the church of SS. Crocifisso was open. It is also possible that the piano extended one or possibly two blocks further to the west, making it an east-west rectangle. In either case, however, the form of the piano is quite different from the one depicted by Formenti and illustrated in Map 5. The original plan was altered, probably because of the enlargement of the church of SS. Crocifisso. The crisp square of the turn of the eighteenth century seems to have lost its focus, perhaps because the Pianazzo itself was not a mecca for the powerful citizens of Noto. The piano today does not succeed visually because it lacks the rising elevations, the defined boundaries, and the expansive architecture of the open spaces of the slope. Even today few shops open on the piano and the everpresent guards of the penitentiary (on the right in Pl. 56) don't help to make it an appealing place to tarry.

Although there are numerous churches and religious houses on the summit, the architecture of these buildings is relatively undistinguished. The façades keep to themselves, rather than dominating streets or moulding space as façades do on the slope. Perhaps Gagliardi, Sinatra, Labisi, and the rest of Noto's architects interacted with the slope spatially whereas they could not invent with the same freedom on the flat summit. Also, in Gagliardi's case, the monastic houses on the summit came early in his building career at Noto so they are far less modulated than his later work on the slope.

All in all the actual buildings on the summit belie the impression one has of them from the slope below. The summit's more regular grid, its flatter topography, its lack of palaces, and its dull monumental architecture make it visually less successful than the slope. Although no documents record life in Noto in the eighteenth century, the summit seems the quieter of the two quarters of the city, having more the character of a village than a city. The summit represents what the rest of Noto might have been without its visually exciting site, its intriguing plan, and its fine architecture. It is the non-aristocratic part of the city, the embodiment of the relentless grid, relieved only by the organic qualities of the block interiors and by the edges of the grid which, spilling over the sides of the summit, disintegrates into alleys and wandering lanes (Pls 25, 26).

Influences on the Plan of Noto and its Position in European Urbanism

After examining Noto, the question which must be answered is, how does the city fit into the context of European urbanism? Sicily has always been a crossroad of cultures. What does the plan of Noto disclose about the tastes and society of the Sicilians who lived in the city? The question is not easy to answer because in the eighteenth century the Spanish Hapsburgs, the Spanish Bourbons, the House of Savoy, the Austrian Hapsburgs, and the Spanish Bourbons of Naples all ruled Sicily. Presumably each of these rulers left some imprint on the cities of Sicily. Given the heterogeneous nature of Sicily's rulers, how does Noto compare with other centres in Europe? What influences shaped its plan? And how up to date was Noto's plan in terms of other cities in Europe?

Since Sicily was a colony of Spain during the first twenty years of Noto's existence on the Meti, it might be argued that Noto was therefore a Spanish city. But as we saw in Chapter 4, Noto's plan derives from Italian treatise writers of the sixteenth century. Its four balancing piazzas relate it directly to Italian rather than to Spanish planning. Likewise, its scenographic streets terminating in church façades and its balanced central piazza all recall Italian precedents. To show how different Noto was

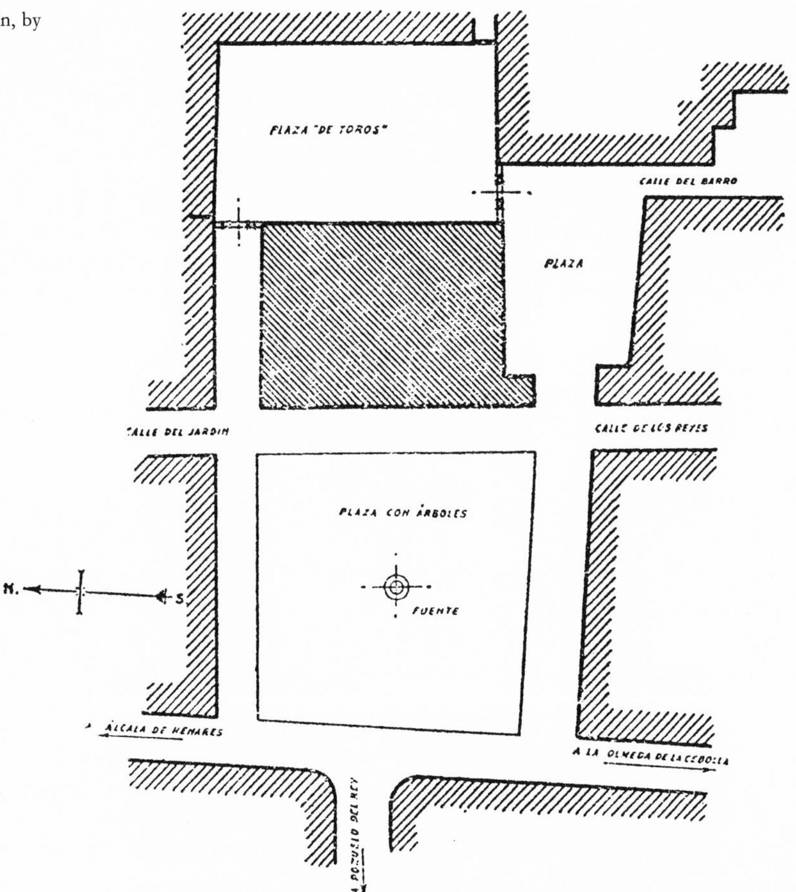

58 Plan of Nuevo Baztán, Spain, by J. B. de Churriguera.

in 1750 from contemporary Spanish towns we might consider several comparisons.

The Spanish town most comparable to Noto is a small plantation settlement in central Spain called Nuevo Baztán (Pl. 58) built between 1709 and 1713 by the noted Spanish architect José Benito de Churriguera (1665–1725).[81] Nuevo Baztán is unlike Noto because it lacks the kind of Renaissance Italian symmetry which can be found in Noto's plan. Churriguera very skillfully centred a constellation of three plazas asymmetrically around the town church and the plantation owner's palace. The two most interior of these plazas are arcaded. Arcades, a particularly Spanish characteristic, are rare in Sicily and not visible in Noto. The arcaded, closed character of the minor plazas behind the church and the palace at Nuevo Baztán is certainly not present in Noto's piazzas.

Churriguera's three-plaza combination is rather rare in Spanish cities, so a more typical *plaza mayor* arrangement might be considered in relation to Noto. The *plaza mayor*, a huge, arcaded plaza or open space, sometimes incorporating a church but more likely a city hall, was a Spanish institution.[82] The central activities of the community took place on this space with shops operating from under the porticos of the arcade. Typical *plazas mayores* can be found in Salamanca, Madrid, and Valladolid. But in Noto's veduta no such arcaded single huge plaza exists.[83]

Considering Noto's colonial status perhaps its plan should be compared with the edicts of the Spanish king Philip II, which established the criteria for designing towns in the New World from the sixteenth to the nineteenth centuries.[84] These edicts were not always followed, but the import of their general principles for Spanish colonial cities in the Americas cannot be denied.[85] Not surprisingly the ordinances prescribe a town which is governed by a simple grid plan, block modules of which are governed by the site of the oblong plaza in the centre of the town. This central plaza is the key to the entire settlement, for its size regulates the grid and indicates just how large its founders intend the town to become. No other space is either as large or as centrally located. Its predominance in the plan is guaranteed because the chief political and ecclesiastical institutions of the town will face it.

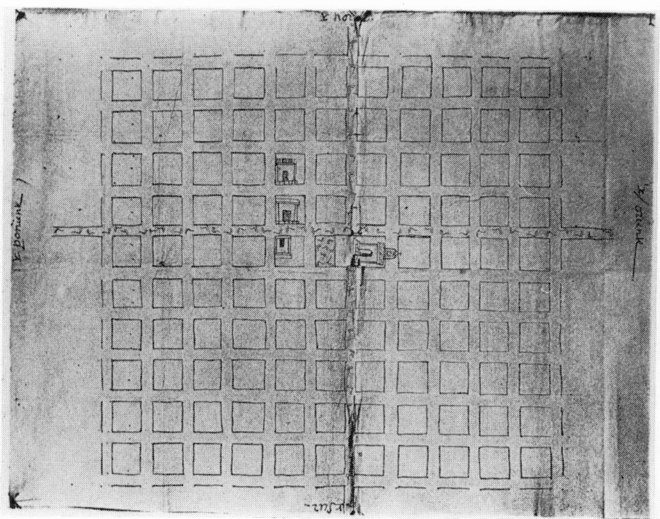

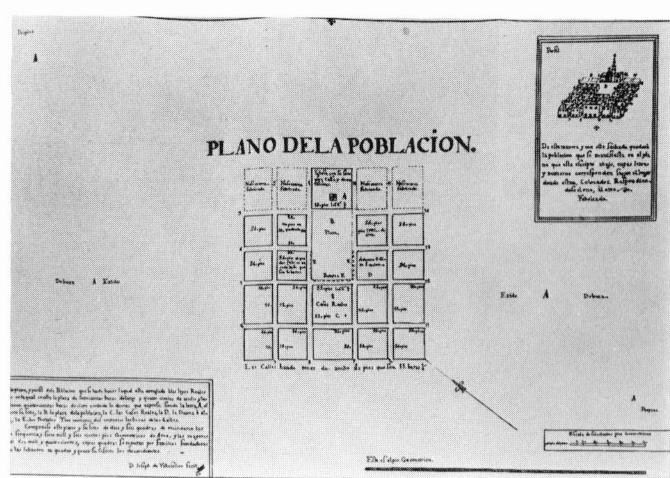

59a Plan of Nochistlan, Mexico.

59b Plan of S. Fernando de Béxar (S. Antonio), Texas.

Major streets run from the middle of each of its sides, and two streets from each corner. The plan of Nochistlan (State of Oaxaca), Mexico (Pl. 59a), drawn in 1581 gives an example of the kind of simple grid plan these ordinances could produce.[86] The plan of San Fernando de Béxar (San Antonio, Texas, *ca.* 1730; Pl. 59b) illustrates yet another example of the same kind of grid.[87]

Noto's plan in the 1750s certainly does not conform to several stipulations in Philip II's edict. First, the piazzas do not have two streets leaving from every corner and one from each side. Second, neither Piazza S. Domenico nor the main piazza establishes the exact dimensions of the surrounding blocks, which change considerably.

The simple grid plan used by Spain in the New World would have been repugnant to the Netinese nobility. For them it would have symbolized the kind of plantation towns that were established by Sicilian aristocrats in isolated areas to lure peasants to the countryside. These feudal towns abounded in sixteenth- and seventeenth-century Sicily. Between 1620 and 1650 alone twenty-five towns were founded (see Fig. 2).[88] Many of them have in common an occasional palace for the landowner and a principal church which usually faces the town's single large piazza. Their plans are usually based on unrelenting grids which produce a monotonous sameness relieved occasionally by a few major buildings or sloping terrain. But in most cases the unrelenting similarity of streets in towns like Vittoria (founded in 1607) is as depressing and confusing as some of the faceless blocks Lynch analyzed in Jersey City, New Jersey.[89]

Noto, while not resembling the grid-planned colonial towns of Sicily, likewise does not conform to the design of the polygonal towns of Avola (Pl. 12) and Grammichele rebuilt after the 1693 earthquake. These towns, while interesting from the air, appear to be rather vacuous intellectual exercises from the ground. Of course this is the kind of plan that the Netinese probably would have liked but the topography of the Meti and the confused genesis of the plan of Noto prevented it from taking the form of Avola or Grammichele.

Noto has about it the sense of symmetry and organization of plan which also distinguishes it from a centre rebuilt on the same site like Catania. Catania's aristocrats and clergy reconstructed their town in a more organized grid pattern with larger streets and piazzas than it had before the earthquake but the form of the plan was established by pre-existing monuments and fortifications. The main streets were imposed over the rubble of the medieval fabric but they had to lead from previous city gates to the marina, from the cathedral to the large Benedictine monastery in the northern part of the city. In a manner similar to Sixtus V's plan for Rome, Catania had straight streets leading from one monument or entrance to the next. Streets criss-crossed the city to provide better, safer communication in time of

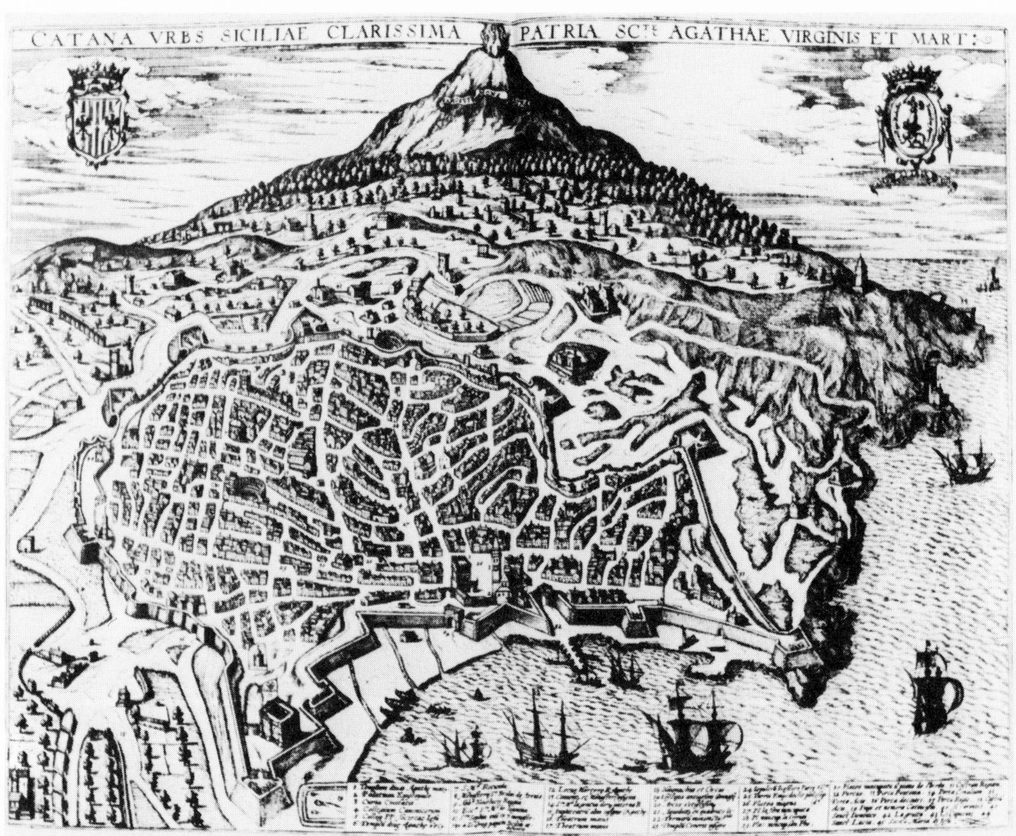

60a City of Catania prior to the 1693 earthquake.

60b City of Catania after the 1693 earthquake as it looked in the eighteenth century.

earthquake. Given the conditions of Catania's rebuilding, the control over the plan could not have been as absolute as in the case of Noto where nothing had previously stood. But even though main axes exist, linked piazzas are used, and Baroque scenographic effects are present, Catania does not have the composed quality of Noto's plan (Pls 60a and 60b). In Noto there is a distinct mental image of the city which orients one to his location within it whereas this is much less the case in the larger, less geometrically-composed Catania.

Noto's plan is also quite different from that of Ragusa Superiore (Fig. 1), the new town that rises on a slope above the medieval city of Ragusa Ibla. The new town planned after the 1693 earthquake is similar to Noto in that it is based on a grid applied to a sloping site which affords many views of the area around the city. The city is defined by two streets—Via Roma running north-south and Corso Italia running east-west. These two streets join at the central piazza where the major church is located and obviously follow the scheme of two major streets intersecting at right angles which had been used to modernize Palermo in the late sixteenth century. Ragusa's plan does not possess the same subtle equilibrium between central focus and satellite piazzas that Noto's has. And because most of the churches of Ragusa were reconstructed in the old medieval city, Ragusa Superiore has few of the monuments that Noto does to act as vertical embodiments of the foci of the plan in the city.

Only Ragusa's Piazza S. Giovanni, dominated by the cathedral, with the nineteenth-century façade of the Collegio di Maria Addolorata to the north, recalls Noto's main piazza in which much the same relationship between S. Nicolò and the church of SS. Salvatore is established. Likewise, the general longitudinal shape of Ragusa's Piazza S. Giovanni recalls that of Noto. But Ragusa's main piazza does not approach the complexity of Noto's either in the spaces it creates or the placement of important buildings around it.

In relation to main currents of French and German urbanism in the eighteenth century Noto's grid plan would have been old fashioned. Leblond's 1717 project for Peter the Great's capital of St Petersburg (Pl. 61) illustrates the newer trend in eighteenth-century urban planning which superseded Noto's rectilinear arrangement.[90] In Leblond's project streets run from significant monument to significant monument, often at 45° angles. Peter's palace, for example, forms the central focus of streets which approach it from principal churches. Each church is encircled by a rotary which is in turn surrounded by a square. The grid plan is thus overlaid by

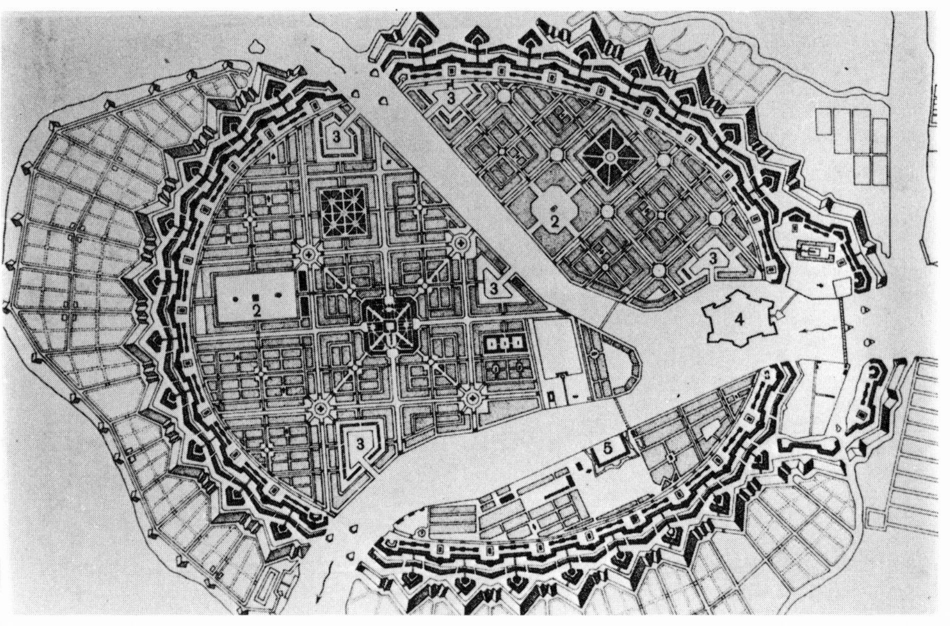

61 St. Petersburg Plan (unexecuted), J. B. A. Leblond, 1717. 1. Peter I's palace. Diagonal streets lead from the palace to four cathedrals (marked by crosses) each in the centre of its own square; 2. Market squares; 3. Harbours with storage buildings; 4. Peter and Paul Fortress; 5. The Admiralty.

circular open spaces and diagonal streets which reinforce its hierarchical organization.

The French architect Patte used a similar network of open spaces and angled streets in his renewal project for Paris of 1765.[91] Here the main open spaces in the city – *Places Royales* – were to surround principal Parisian monuments and be linked by a network of streets which sometimes ran right through the older urban fabric. At Karlsruhe (1727) in Germany the city plan was even more hierarchical: as planned, its centre was the governmental palace towards which evenly spaced streets ran in from a huge circle which incorporated both city and palace grounds.

Within the city of Noto curvilinear spaces which were popular in eighteenth-century Rome (the Spanish Steps, 1723–25; Piazza S. Ignazio, 1727–28) are absent. Nothing like John Wood's curving façades of Bath (The Circus, begun 1754) can be found in the city. Noto's plan, formalized in the first years of the eighteenth century pre-dates most of the curvilinear schemes. Of course rectilinear town plans were still the simplest means of organizing cities. They appear in schemes for two major European cities: Edinburgh and Lisbon.

Lisbon's Baixa district, rebuilt after the 1755 earthquake, is composed of a grid with a major street running between uniform façades to a plaza open to Lisbon's ceremonial quay.[92] Craig's plan for a new town in Edinburgh (1767) did not incorporate circular forms, nor did it acknowledge the beautiful view of old Edinburgh castle that the new town would have.[93] The concept was to tie together the new town by linking two squares together within a grid system by running a major street between them. On paper the end result lacks any dynamic relationship between view, buildings, and onlooker. However, by not building on the north side of Princes Street Craig at least left the view open to the south side of the street. The uniform buildings which were constructed along the streets succeed where the plan fails, in bringing a unified look to the new town.

Noto's plan has less in common with Lisbon or the new town of Edinburgh than it does with a family of eighteenth-century cities planned on the same basic sixteenth-century Scamozzian schema as it was.

More than a decade before the earthquake of 1693 Philadelphia had been planned similarly to Noto: a main open space is balanced within a grid at the confluence of two major streets with four satellite spaces (actually open commons) placed around it. Interestingly enough the Scamozzian schema of organizing cities was revived by planners trying to schematize two small late eighteenth-century European cities, Versoix and Carouge. In Versoix a central hexagonal open area defines the centre of the grid. Four open areas are placed symmetrically around it and linked to it by main streets. The plan for Carouge drawn in 1772 by Francesco Garella is similar to Philadelphia's plan in its positioning of open spaces but lacks main arteries leading from the principal square to the outskirts of town. Garella also had the problem of working with the pre-existing city which forced a diagonal street into his plan seriously compromising his design.[94]

In spite of Noto's dependence on a sixteenth-century plan, it manages, because of the sequential drama of the Corso and its open spaces, to be in style in terms of continental European design. When Noto was initially laid out in the late seventeenth century it is doubtful whether the dramatic potentialities of the Corso were considered. But dynamic building placement, the topography of the site and the architecture itself help to make the city a visual experience as much as an intellectual one. Ideas from seventeenth-century Rome, such as fountain placements, also helped to bring the staid plan to life.

The sequential spaces of the Corso unite Noto with the trend toward linked symbolic open spaces which lasted throughout the eighteenth century. The experience of going from place to place was as important as the arrival at one's destination, as projects like the Spanish Steps in Rome prove. Of the renewal projects which incorporated designed sequential spaces, perhaps the most famous is the centre of the small city of Nancy in Lorraine, designed in 1752 (Pl. 62). In Nancy, the joined spaces consist of a rectangular square (Place Stanislas) from which a triumphal arch leads to a long open space on axis (the Palais de la Carrière) which in turn proceeds to a rectangular open space with a semi-circular colonnade. The entire ensemble, with a unified architectural style, was planned as a unit. Its urbanistic function was to join the newer city of Nancy on the Place Stanislas side with the Palace of Government in the older medieval core of the city. But its social function was to make the centre of Nancy suitably grand for Stanislas Leczinski, the Duke of Lorraine, its ruler. The centre of Nancy is essentially a beautifully orchestrated promenade down diverse but not antagonistic spaces. In this respect as well as its carefully balanced character the centre of Nancy, while very different from Noto's, nevertheless illustrates a similarity in intent and organization.

Eighteenth-century Noto, like Nancy, was an isolated showpiece, a centre of taste and sophistication in the provinces. Noto's citizens wanted to have a city that rivalled the memory of Noto Antica, that surpassed such nearby centres as Avola, and challenged larger cities like Syracuse. The aristocrats donated money and land to erect Noto's churches and city hall. It was largely the aristocrats, not rich enough to go to Naples or Palermo, but solvent enough to be powerful in a small town like Noto, who must have wanted the image of Noto that we see in the veduta. Their investments in buildings probably did not occur without some indication of style preferences. They were far more aware than other citizens of what was going on in Europe, even if this awareness was dimmed by distance. It was probably their libraries, rich in imported books, from which came the ideas that shaped Noto's architecture. Noto as it appears in the veduta might be seen as a utopian vision of what a city in eighteenth-century Sicily could be. Netinese aristocrats and the architects they employed turned to Italy, not Spain, because Italian architecture and city planning were more stylish than Spanish. By that time all the documents within the city were written in Italian and on the basis of the plan and the architecture of Noto, one would have to conclude that the Netinese considered themselves Italians and not Spaniards. Thus Noto was an Italian city far removed from the rest of Europe and desperately trying to be in vogue. No longer a fortress, Noto's prestige was based on its buildings and open spaces designed for the most magnificent outward show.

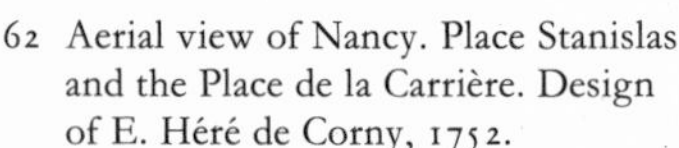
62 Aerial view of Nancy. Place Stanislas and the Place de la Carrière. Design of E. Héré de Corny, 1752.

Part III
Architecture and the Eighteenth-Century City

Chapter 6 Building Types and Life in Eighteenth-Century Noto

A city or territory is the principal edifice of the community, built and divided into many lesser structures which are commodious and useful to civil life, like convents, monasteries, colleges, palaces both grand and small, obelisks, pyramids, and fountains and other things for use of a communal society of many men and women who live there, subservient to a regent or to a particular prince.[1]
Paolo Labisi, Royal Engineer of Noto, in *Architettura Civile*, MS. *ca* 1773

Some urbanists might quarrel with Labisi's definition of a city because he sees it as a community of people served by the built environment rather than an economic entity. One contemporary historian, for example, defines a city as 'a tool for the production and exchange of goods and services'.[2] Such an economic definition would have been alien to Labisi who does not even include shops or markets among a city's attributes. For Labisi a city was composed of the building types which represented his society: convents, churches, colleges, and palaces. Sicilian cities, of course, do not often have obelisks or pyramids, but these antique monuments are nevertheless consonant with Labisi's definition which focuses on the notable and prestigious monuments of a city.

This chapter is devoted to the kinds of buildings which 'define' Noto as a city. Later, in Chapter 7, there will be a detailed stylistic analysis of façades. Here, the object is to examine the building types present in Noto, to compare and contrast their forms, and to hypothesize, using what little information there is available, how these buildings functioned in the 'communal society of men and women' who lived in Noto.

Religious Architecture and the City*

The most striking aspect of land use in Noto is the large percentage of property occupied by churches and religious houses. Monasteries, convents, and oratories often covered entire city blocks. Their churches, dormitories and cloisters formed the most distinctive part of Noto's urban character. As the French traveller Denon noted in the 1780s:

The city of Noto stands upon high ground and as if it were only meant to accommodate a people of mostly priests and nuns, their only object seems to have been to build churches and convents, which are so wide and numerous that there appears to be nothing else.[3]

The Frenchman Denon, who later joined Napoleon's government, had little patience with what he must have regarded as expressions of the power of the church in Noto.[4]

Like Denon, modern visitors are struck by the large number of churches and religious houses in Noto (see Map 7). In 1748 when Noto had a population of 10,083, it boasted 32 churches including 20 in religious houses.[5] If the religious houses in Noto seem more numerous than we might expect, it is instructive to bear in mind that Syracuse, with a population of 14,487, had 23 religious houses and Vizzini, in the interior of Sicily, with a population of 9,004, had 15 religious houses.[6] On the Italian mainland, particularly in the south, similar ratios can be found.

*In Noto Religious houses for women were called monasteries and those for men were called convents. In order to avoid confusion I have retained this designation in the case of individual buildings, but when discussing religious houses in general I use the English designation of convent for a religious house sheltering women, and monastery for a religious house sheltering men.

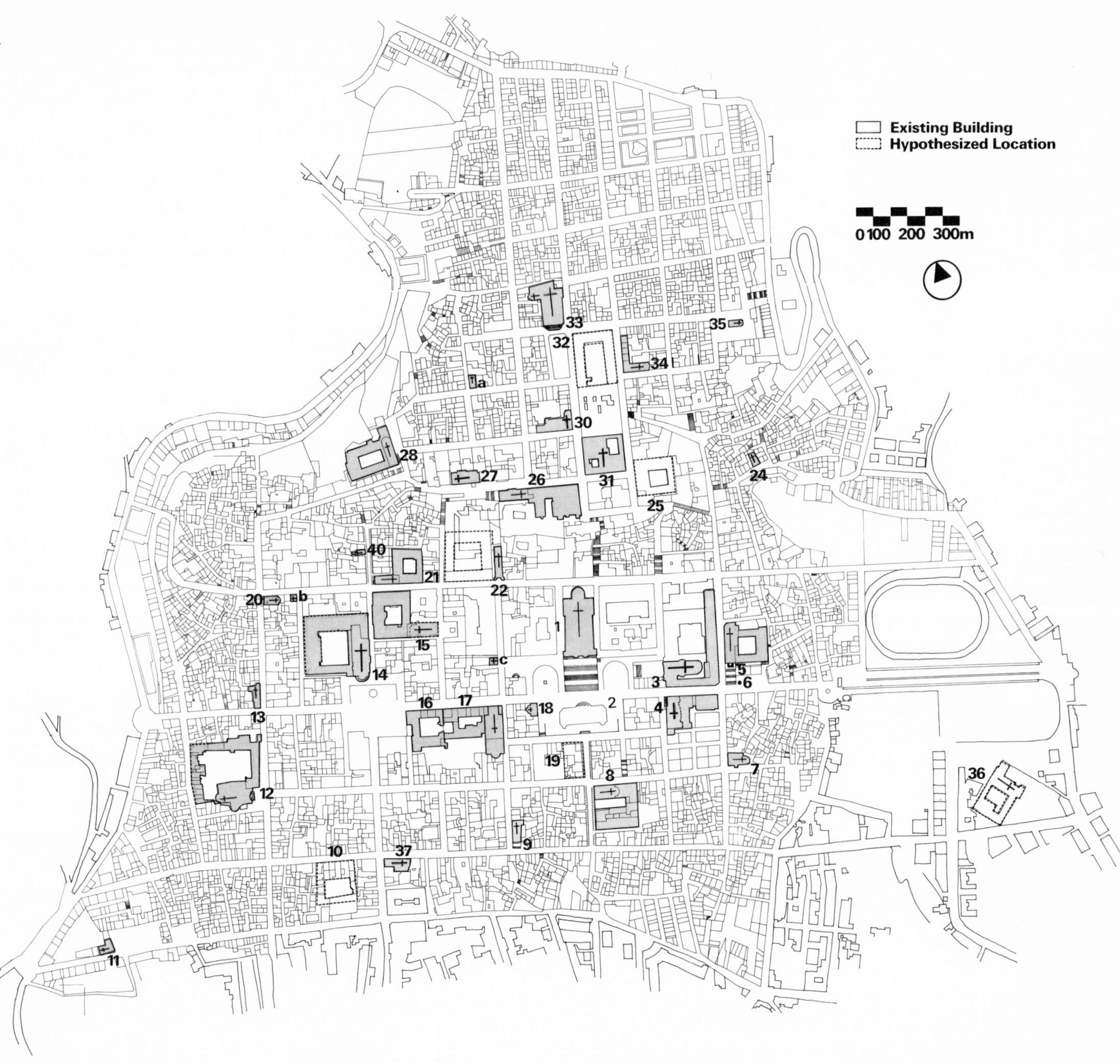

7 Noto's churches and religious houses.

1 S. Nicolò
2 City Hall
3 Monastery of SS. Salvatore
4 Monastery of S. Chiara
5 Convent of S. Francesco d'Assisi
6 Statue of Madonna Immacolata
7 Santo Spirito
8 Monastery of S. Maria dell'Arco
9 S. Maria del Purgatorio
10 Monastery of S. Giuseppe
11 S. Pietro Martire
12 Convent of S. Maria del Carmelo
13 S. Michele Archangelo
14 Convent of S. Domenico
15 House of the Crociferi
16 Seminary
17 Jesuit college
18 Church of SS. Trinità
19 S. Sebastiano
20 S. Antonio Abbate
21 Oratory of S. Filippo Neri
22 Monastery of Montevergine
24 S. Andrea Apostolo
25 Convent of S. Antonio di Padova
26 Monastery of S. Agata
27 Monastery of SS. Annunziata (Badia Nuova)
28 Convent of S. Maria di Gesù
30 Hospital of the Convent of PP. Benefratelli di Dio
31 Monte di Pietà, Casa del Refugio, called S. Teodoro
32 Monastery of S. Tommaso Apostolo
33 SS. Crocifisso
34 Convent of S. Francesco di Paola
35 SS. Pietro e Paolo
36 Convent of the Cappuccini
37 S. Maria la Rotonda
40 S. Isidoro
a Ruins of unidentified church
b Castelluccio family church S. Lucia
c Nicolaci family church S. Elia

Not shown are the convent of S. M. della Scala (Labisi's no. 29) and the church of the Trigona family on Via Gioberti which has been absorbed into the east wall of the Trigona palace.

We tend to think of size and number of religious institutions in proportional relationship to the population they serve.[7] But no direct relationship necessarily exists. The sanctity of a given area and the availability of patrons and donors were reasons enough to warrant the establishment of churches. Some monasteries and convents were so insulated from the communities around them that no interaction occurred. Yet even if the religious houses did not directly interact with the community at large they did carry its spiritual burden. They helped redeem the sinful cities of Sicily which citizens thought had been singled out for punishment by their wrathful God.[8] By giving to churches, monasteries and convents, citizens attained grace through their good works and helped forestall further catastrophes. In the logic of the time in Sicily the large number of ecclesiastical institutions must have made perfect sense: through prayer and perpetual privation the religious population helped to carry the spiritual burden of the rest of the citizenry.

In addition to securing the spiritual well-being of the community through prayer, the churches and some of the religious houses provided vital services without which the community could not function. Priests administered the seven sacraments and recorded deaths, births, and marriages.[9] Parishes established a kind of neighbourhood cohesion within the town.[10] Church confraternities or organizations provided a nucleus to which citizens could ally themselves.[11] Monastic orders ran hospitals, like S. Maria della Scala and S. Maria della Consolazione, while S. Teodoro was devoted to the care of orphaned girls.[12] The church also ran its own Monte di Pietà or pawn shop in S. Teodoro which lent money at a fixed rate in exchange for pawned articles. The Monte di Pietà was virtually the only place one could get credit in Noto. Some orders, like the Jesuits and Dominicans, also taught the children of Noto's upper classes.[13]

Aristocratic families used the religious houses to maintain their position in society. First, monasteries provided a means of limiting the dissolution of aristocratic fortunes.[14] Sicilian eighteenth-century inheritance practices favoured primogeniture. In order to keep the first son securely in possession of a family's property, the conventual or monastic life provided a way of disposing of an unwanted heir. Second, guarding young women's virginity was no less vital to society in the eighteenth century than it is in Sicily today. The cloister was an excellent way of insuring this virginity until the proper suitor came along, or sometimes for life. The life of seclusion was also an honourable way for widows, orphans, and women without sufficient dowries to exist in eighteenth-century Sicilian society.[15]

The religious houses seem to have been a distinct drain on the resources of the monied aristocracy. In Palermo the aristocracy lavished huge sums on fêtes celebrating the entrances of their daughters into convents.[16] The aristocratic competition for the most elaborate celebrations put them all heavily in debt. So bad did the situation become that the government tried to curb the number of ecclesiastics and limit the extent of celebrations.[17] The economic power and legal immunities of the religious orders became so extensive that the Bourbon king Charles III ruled in 1738, with the assent of the Sicilian Parliament, that no new houses could be founded and no old ones enlarged without his permission.[18]

Royal decrees limiting the establishment of religious institutions and the enlargement of established ones seem to have had little effect on Noto's built environment or society. By 1738 nineteen of Noto's religious houses had already been refounded in the new city. The house of the Crociferi fathers, founded in 1734, was probably delayed by the decrees, but finally foundations were laid in the 1750s.[19] The most energetic building campaigns of monasteries, churches and convents occurred between 1730 and 1760. Perhaps the ecclesiastical orders building in Noto began their projects before the ban was ordered and therefore were allowed to continue. But construction and revision of the monastery of S. Maria dell'Arco (Cistercian) and the monastery of S. Chiara (Benedictine) went on into the late eighteenth century.[20] It seems clear that King Charles III should not be seen as limiting the extent of monasteries and convents in Noto or discouraging the building boom.

It is not surprising to find that almost all the religious institutions built in Noto Nuova had their origins in Noto Antica.[21] Although the earthquake of 1693 destroyed Noto Antica's churches and religious houses, ecclesiastical property and revenues remained for the most part intact. Those churches and religious houses blessed with sufficient goods and property resurrected themselves after the earthquake; and, with the assistance of wealthy patrons and money from abroad, new churches and religious houses could rise on the virgin soil of Noto Nuova. Thus, by the mid-eighteen century, Noto Nuova, the city on the Meti, just exceeded its predecessor, Noto Antica, in its number of monasteries and convents.

Plans of Religious Houses and Churches

With only a few exceptions religious houses and churches in Noto share a single trait: both have very conventional plans. The most common church form in Noto is a simple rectangle, having altars placed against the side walls and a major apse separated from the nave by several steps.[22] Undoubtedly the rectangular church either vaulted or wooden roofed, perfectly adapted for preaching and relatively easy to construct, solved the problem adequately. But these staid plans are a far cry from the spatially adventuresome churches being built in Germany and northern Italy during the eighteenth century.[23] The type of church found in Noto is an end product of a development which began in sixteenth-century Rome, when vaulted rectangular churches became popular during the Counter-Reformation.[24] The major churches of Noto – S. Nicolò, SS. Crocifisso, and S. Carlo (the Jesuit church) – follow a different but equally traditional plan. They are arcaded Latin cross churches which in plan deviate little from sixteenth-century models.[25]

Only a very few churches in Noto are based on plans other than the rectangular: the church of S. Chiara is an oval, the church of S. Domenico is an elongated Greek cross, SS. Trinità an octagon, and S. Maria del Carmine a lobed rhomboid. These four plans were not in any sense new ideas; each has a long and very respectable lineage. The oval was first used in a plan by Giacomo Barozzi da Vignola for his Roman church of S. Anna dei Palafrenieri in the 1550s; the elongated Greek cross with a central dome and four subsidiary cupolas is found in Rosato Rosati's S. Carlo ai Catinari, a Roman church of 1612–20; the lobed rhomboid plan is a development of Borrominesque ideas of the seventeenth century.[26]

Like churches, monasteries and convents were planned with an eye to simplicity. The most important function of the religious houses was to provide privacy for the community which lived within them. Huge billowing iron gratings screen the windows, large gates close the portals, walls surround the cloisters. Typical religious houses in Noto flank one side of their order's church. While virtually all of Noto's convents and monasteries were intended to be built around a rectangular courtyard of cloisters, few complete cloisters still stand today. In some cases the cloister seems to have been left unfinished, in others it has been partially destroyed.

Although the layouts of many of Noto's monasteries and convents are now obscured by more recent buildings, the preserved plans for the monastery of S. Chiara illustrate what was probably the simplest typical arrangement (Pls 125, 126, Figs 5, 6). The rooms within the monastery were strung together in a row only one room in depth around four sides of an internal courtyard. No common halls provided for communication between the rooms in the original plans for the monastery. Rather one had to proceed from room to room until a final destination was reached or one walked from room to courtyard to room. This *enfilade* (hall-less) arrangement was rather primitive by eighteenth-century French standards, but common in Italy, even in palaces.[27]

The rooms themselves were shielded from the outside by high windows and massive grating. The law protected the light and view from windows in monasteries and convents from encroachments which might have compromised the religious community, and any buildings constructed too close to the windows were subject to being torn down.[28] Within the monastery itself monks and nuns could further be screened from the populace by special passages which allowed them to use the church without being seen by the public. A *parlatorio* (supervised meeting room) for the relatives of those in the cloister was also provided.

In the case of S. Chiara (page 161), spiritual functions (church, chapel, and 'chapter rooms', letters D, C, E) were housed in the west while daily necessities such as kitchen and storage areas were at the east. According to Paolo Labisi, the city architect, eastern or northern kitchens were most advisable because they were cool and had the most favourable ventilation. The best positioning of the monastery kitchens was crucial because chimneys were not common. The north-eastern magazine (K), or store-house, was huge, for it was needed not only to store foodstuffs for the monastery but to preserve saleable produce from monastery lands. The cistern in the middle of the central courtyard was indispensable to the monastery, for by catching and storing run-off rainwater, it served as an emergency water supply if the aqueducts to the city failed. Pit privies, the usual variety in eighteenth-century Noto, provided for waste disposal simply and efficiently. The 'black well' extended into the foundation of the building, where waste could interact with the lime in the soil, eventually disintegrating.

While the rather simple plan for the monastery of S. Chiara represents the basic monastic solution in Noto, the plan for the house of the Crociferi fathers, dating from 1750, represents the most elaborate solution (Pls 160–1). The complex building programme planned was never completed, but even the partially finished building can be described as vast and labyrinthine. As opposed to S. Chiara, the house of the Crociferi fathers incorporated shops on three sides, perhaps to increase revenue for the order by capitalizing on urban real estate. Parts of the plan, like the utilization of modular cells in varying combinations on either side of a central hallway, are ingenious. Strange contradictions nevertheless slip into the otherwise beautifully designed building: the kitchen faces south, in spite of the contrary advice of the architect who designed the building; and the privy shaft-seems unnecessarily close to the water storage system.

Upper- and Middle-Class Housing

The nobility of Noto, the patrons and donors who made possible the gigantic monasteries and convents of Noto, lived in dwellings that ranged from large, highly ornamented palaces to more modest apartments. In the census of 1748 no less than 194 aristocratic household heads appear, some with seven-member families.[29] Yet the Labisi veduta only identifies 14 houses of nobles, many of which can still be recognized today by their sumptuous façades which clearly differentiate them from other structures (Map 8). Where did the lesser nobles live? Many probably lived in more modest buildings which are difficult to identify today because they have few distinctive architectural features. Widespread renovation of these buildings—neither palaces nor lower-class dwellings—further complicates their identification.

The differentiation of the dwellings of the less solvent nobility from those of the rich commoners is difficult because sometimes the commoners' houses surpassed those of the aristocracy. For example, Brother Antonino Labisi was the head of a noble household including his two younger brothers, one of whom was a notary, his nephew, his mother, his youngest brother's wife, and three servants.[30] The six Labisis and their three servants lived in a five-room house (four rooms, one kitchen). On the other hand, the architect-commoner Vincenzo Sinatra with a wife, five children, and a servant occupied a two-storey eight-room house with a cistern.[31]. The two houses in question cannot be identified in present-day Noto, but it is clear that the Sinatras probably lived more comfortably than the Labisis and that the Sinatras' house was most likely more deserving of being called a palace than the Labisis'.

8 Noto's palaces. The numbers are those which appear on the Labisi veduta. Many of the numbers do not agree with where the important palaces of the town are today. See Appendix 2.

Differentiation is also difficult because the eighteenth-century architects left few clues for identifying the dwellings of the lesser aristocracy. Neither Paolo Labisi in his treatise on civil architecture nor Noto's tax assessors attempt to separate palaces from non-noble houses.[32] In the eyes of the assessors, buildings were valued by the cost of their materials, the number of their rooms, and their special features (stores in the basement, a well in the back yard). In these documents both palaces of the aristocracy and other dwellings were called 'tenements'. Undoubtedly the houses of the lower aristocracy and the well-off peasants would fall into the category that Valussi, in his book on rural buildings in Sicily, would call the 'casa del burgisi'.[33] The *burgisi* – well-off Sicilian peasants – lived in multi-roomed structures either one or two storeys, which were differentiated from the extremely modest one- or two-room houses of the lowest social class, the day labourers. Unfortunately the form of the houses of the pharmacists, notaries, and artisans of Noto—the homes of Noto's middle-class—are hard to identify. They were more elaborate than the houses of the day labourer (*uomo da compagna*) but basically not too different from them. Their façades can be seen throughout Noto (Pls 27, 51, 52, 56, 57, 65, 90) and although these houses have been altered over the years they still retain the general simple, two-storey elevations and interior room arrangements they had in the eighteenth century. Given the difficulty of differentiating between the houses of the 'middle class' and those of the lower classes I will make some very broad generalizations about structures which are neither peasant huts nor palaces.

The dwellings of the lower aristocracy and the more solvent commoners could be decorated, symmetrical and more than one storey, as can be seen in the Labisi veduta. Depending on the size of the tenement, each floor might be divided into several apartments or be left as one apartment. Upper floors usually have separate entrances from the ground floor. The entrance to the stairway which leads to the upper floors may appear in the centre of the façade, or to one side. The stairs themselves are usually dark narrow vaulted passageways which either rise to the upper floors in a single precipitous flight or 'dog-leg' their way up the building. Some stairways were open-welled, but on a very small scale, not at all grandiose or ceremonial. The exterior form of these buildings demonstrates scores of variants. Dwellings could be large, like Rosario Gagliardi's two-storey ten-room house (now destroyed) across the street from the monastery of S. Maria dell'Arco, or they could be quite small, like the two-storey building on Via Grimaldi on the summit (Pl. 64). They could be either symmetrical or unsymmetrical, with part of the structure being a single storey, another part two storeys. Like Netinese palaces, these dwellings are oftentimes the result of many alterations and additions, but unlike palaces they have the minimum of architectural pretension (as in Pl. 63).

63 Dwelling, Via Roma.
This building is representative of the ornamental treatment and façade composition of a middle-class dwelling in Noto, perhaps the house of a rich merchant or a craftsman. The door to the right leads up stairs to a series of small rooms arranged along a hall. The area behind the portal is comprised of a large room with the remains of a kitchen. This building has massive internal buttressing and arches. It is aligned with the Jesuit college which may indicate that it served the college at some time.

64 Dwelling, Via Grimaldi. These two small buildings are typical of hundreds of Netinese structures. An internal stairway links the ground floor with the first floor in the building on the left. On the right the owner has not yet rebuilt the first floor.

Netinese Palaces[34]

A Netinese palace differs from a lesser dwelling in its size and degree of ornamentation. The dwellings of the richer aristocrats could be very substantial. The largest and most ostentatious of these can still be identified in present-day Noto. Map 8 indicates the positions of the palaces identified on Labisi's veduta, and also identifies the structures which can be recognized as palaces today. Near the corner of the Corso and Via Rocco Pirri, the Sacristan Don Francesco Landolina e Rau owned a twenty-room house which was in part two storeys high. Farther down the Corso, between Via Galilei and Via Giordano Bruno, was Marchese Zappata's palace in a two-storey 17-room house in which only seven people lived.[35] North of Di Lorenzo's and Landolina e Rau's palaces stood Noto's largest noble residence, the palace of Baron Giacomo Nicolaci which can still be seen today (Pl. 70).[36] The Baron and three other people lived in a building which consisted of 48 rooms, three cisterns, and a number of outbuildings. When trying to compute the tax on the construction, Vincenzo Sinatra, the assessor, complained that the rooms were so numerous and lavishly decorated that they were practically useless.[37] He probably meant that the rooms were so arranged that they could not be rented out or adapted for purposes other than entertainment. He concludes that he cannot see the use of such a large palace in so small a city as Noto.

The interior arrangements of Noto's palaces are not as imposing or as integral as most of their façades might suggest. Many of Noto's most extensive palaces are amalgamations of humbler constructions or piecemeal products of many unco-ordinated building campaigns. For example, Francesco Landolina e Rau claims that part of his house, which later became a palace, was made of earth and built just after the earthquake of 1693.[38] Other palace plans are asymmetrical, complex and disjointed, which indicates that they too are cumulative constructions; an aerial view (Pl. 45) of the palace of the Landolina family, the S. Alfano palace, with its separate and random roofs and unfinished courtyard shows how an apparently 'designed' building can grow almost without premeditated plan in Noto. It is really not one but several buildings brought under a single façade.[39] The ground plan of the palace (Pl. 74), though generally symmetrical, has irregularly placed rooms, not only because of different building campaigns but because the terrain on which the palace is built was so uneven. The Bishop's palace on the eastern side of the main square (Pl. 84) has a Neo-classical façade which masks three earlier asymmetrical structures, whose thicker walls can be seen on a nineteenth-century plan (Pls 82–3).[40]

Evidence of the separate building campaigns can be seen on other palace façades as well. The ambitious Nicolaci palace is the product of at least three separate architects working at different times: the first architect is reponsible for the façade, the second for the interior courtyard on the south, and the third for the northern addition to the original building.[41] Although apparently built at almost the same time, the styles of the Trigona palace show that its façade and western wing were probably completed before its eastern façade.[42]

Noto's palaces almost invariably stand flush with the street with no setback. Behind these façades the palace's plan is usually U-shaped (see Pl. 45). The arms of the U, as in the Astuto palace, Landolina palace, Di Lorenzo palace, or the Battaglia palace lose definition as they move away from the façade, giving the buildings an air of incompleteness. The courtyards formed by these U-shaped buildings, with the exception of the one in the Trigona palace, are very bleak, and rarely have gardens to brighten them.

The rambling plans of Noto's palaces were suitable to the uses to which they were put by Noto's aristocracy. First, a landowner might use the basement of his palace as a secure storehouse for his agricultural goods. The large vaulted rooms in the basement of the Nicolaci palace may have been just so used. Second, a palace could provide revenue by providing areas for shops or rooms for rent (as was probably the case in the Astuto palace). Third, the palace was the family dwelling place and may therefore have contained numerous rooms for various family branches as in the Trigona palace, which functions today as two separate palaces divided by a central portal.

Important palaces incorporated a large ceremonial portal which could accommodate a carriage. Within this portal a side entrance led to stairs which in turn led to the *piano nobile* on which the owners of the palace received their guests and frequently lived. The stairs took one past the storage areas, the servants' quarters, and the other areas of the palace, to the ceremonial rooms. As a modern visitor to many of Noto's palaces, I was received and entertained in these formal rooms but usually not allowed to see the rest of the palace.[43]

Palace apartments are less sumptuous than one might expect from the exteriors of these buildings. The entrances and main stairways are far less elaborate or playful than those of the Baroque palaces of eighteenth-century Germany or mainland Italy and, in fact, appear poverty-stricken by comparison.

Likewise the decoration of the rooms is sometimes disappointing. Only in the Trigona palace are the private rooms of a quality which seems to match the promise of the exterior of the building. But even these rooms, decorated in the late 1770s, lack the grace of French eighteenth-century ensembles and seem more in harmony with the heavier, less imaginative Italian taste of provincial Italy.

Even if the palaces of Noto are not the most luxurious imaginable, they certainly provided an appropriate stage from which aristocrats could entertain, follow intellectual pursuits, and gaze over the expanse of Noto from their balconies. In the eighteenth century aristocrats stocked their palaces with antiques from the area, art works, and books. The aristocrats, from what we know about them, were anxious to keep abreast of the latest developments in Naples and on the continent, and so they imported foreign books which transmitted the latest styles to them. Don Giacomo Nicolaci, prince of Noto's aristocratic academy of dilettante scholars, amassed a huge library and a collection of optical equipment.[44] He was also a patron of the arts and may have lent books from his library to important architects of the city. The Astuto family displayed a sizeable numismatic collection and collected books, which were stored in their palace.[45] In short, Noto's palaces were repositories of culture and fashion. We can imagine Noto's aristocrats, like Lampedusa's Prince Fabrizio in *The Leopard*, engaged in intellectual pursuits and interested in current events as curiosities far removed from the placid urban scene they saw from their balconies.

Lower-Class Houses

If monasteries, convents and palaces are the most noticeable of Noto's buildings, certainly the small, whitewashed homes of Noto's less affluent citizens are the most invisible. Along the secondary streets of Noto and the winding alleys that lace through the grid, these lower-class dwellings—what we now call vernacular structures—line the streets (Pls 25–7). In general the types of lower-class dwellings which can be found in Noto differ little from those found elsewhere on the island. They are in fact closely related to the rural house-types of the day labourers which can be found in present-day Sicily. The Sicilian folklore expert Pitrè, writing at the turn of the century, wrote that there are three basic types of day labourers' dwellings: the simplest is a mean room with a narrow doorway, without pavement, which you might find to contain some chairs, two beds, an oven, a manger for a mule, some chickens, and a pile of manure in the corner. The second type is a structure which has a loft reached by a small wooden ladder. In the loft there is a single large straw mattress. The third type has a loft but is also divided down the middle by a partition which creates separate spaces within the ground floor of the structure.[46]

The identification of lower-class dwellings built in the eighteenth century is practically impossible since few bear dates and few have distinctive carving.[47] But the Labisi veduta illustrates many extremely modest houses which would have fitted into Pitrè's classification system.

In spite of the difficulty of identifying eighteenth-century lower-class buildings in present-day Noto, we know from the veduta that such structures existed. A typical example of a Netinese lower-class house (which would fall into Pitrè's second type) can be found in Vico Trigona, an alley running south from Via Ducezio just across the street from the Ferla palace (Fig. 3). It is the second house down the alley on the eastern side and has been declared a building of architectural importance by the Netinese authorities who believe it dates back to the eighteenth century (Pl. 65).[48] When I visited the house the people who had been living in it had died, and the new owner was preparing to make it as saleable as possible by restuccoing the walls and removing all of the former owners' ancient gear which still could be seen in the main room. The main unit of the house is an unpartitioned room measuring about 4.5 × 5 metres with its longest side facing the alley to the west. This western side bends slightly inward towards the south in order to accommodate a twist in the alley's path. On the south the main unit is joined to a second, trapezoidal room, which seems to have been added later. Many of the little houses of Noto are square or rectangular in plan, but many more, like this one, are fairly irregular due to the spaces available for building.

The walls of the building are probably constructed of rubble masonry with a coating of plaster.[49] The corners of the house, as well as all the apertures, are constructed of unornamented, harder dressed masonry (*pietra d'intaglio*) for greater strength and beauty. Dressed masonry corners and windows provide the only architectural accent on the otherwise undecorated façade. The first unit originally had a window facing south below the peak of the roof. But since this window is now being used as a passageway to the second unit, the only aperture in the first unit is the doorway which opens onto the alley; it is far more usual that such a room would have both a door and at least one window.

In this house, like most in Noto, the area around the doorway must have served as a porch. The women of contemporary Noto usually stay at home during the day and do their sewing on the threshold, with their backs to the alley so the light comes from behind them. Sometimes a straw mat is hung from the top of the architrave and pushed out into the alley with poles. This provides much more privacy for those

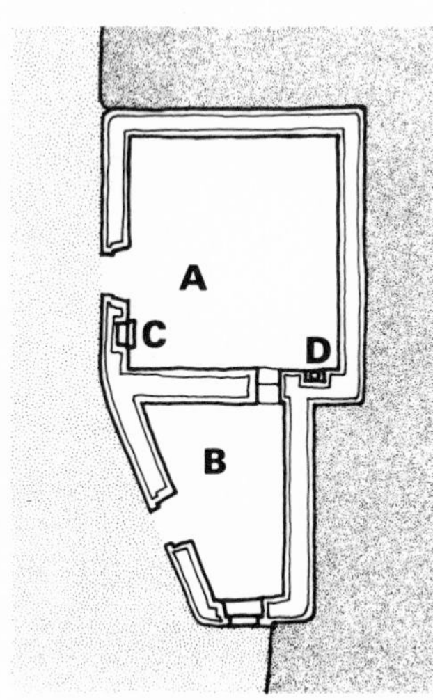

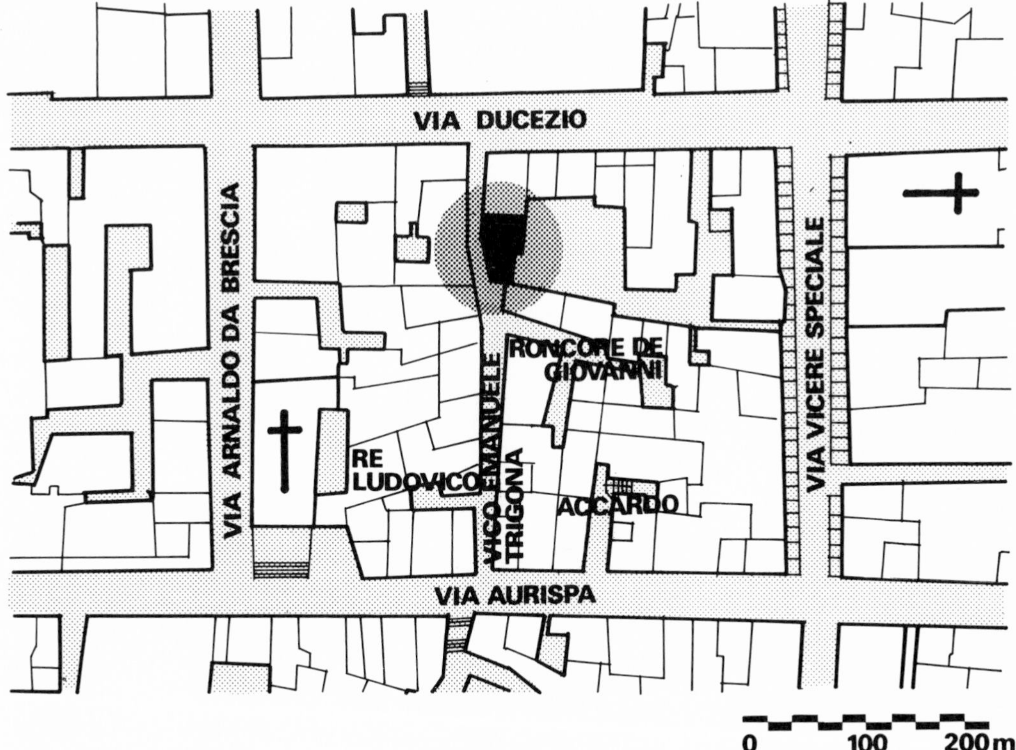

Fig. 3 Vico Trigona in the modern city of Noto. The block is honeycombed with alleys in which Noto's poorer citizens live. Above shows ground plan of a lower-class dwelling.
A main room
B addition
C former cistern
D former location of privy

sitting so close to the busy street or alley. In these houses there is less than a half-metre of semi-public space inside the threshold dividing the private world of the interior of the house from the public world outside.[50]

The first unit of the house has a hipped tile roof which for most of its length splashes water down on unwary pedestrians during rainstorms. However, to protect the threshold from inclement weather and thus assure its year-round use, a gutter is installed above it in almost every Netinese house of this type. In this house the gutter once had a secondary purpose; its outlet is positioned near a second gutter, built into the wall, which drains the depression between the roof and the first and second units; together these two outlets provide a source for fresh rainwater which was once tapped by putting a container under them.

In the interior of both units of the house a common Netinese device is used to increase the floor and storage space: the loft (*solaio*).[51] The people who lived in this house slept in a huge bed in one corner of the room of the first unit and used the loft for storage. Lofts in Noto today are still most commonly used for storage (never for sleeping).

The floor space of both units was undifferentiated allowing occupants to arrange the space as they wished. The washing area simply depended upon where the day's water supply was stored; sleeping depended on the location of the mattress; and cooking upon where a fire pit could be built or a brazier placed. Fire pits for the ovens were set into walls without chimneys, the smoke escaping through the door and windows. Noto's poorer population can still be seen using small braziers in lieu of an oven for heating and cooking.

In this house, as is generally the rule, the family toilet is inside, recessed into the wall in the south-eastern corner of the main room without any permanent division between it and the rest of the room. In most of the modernized Netinese houses of this vintage the privy is screened from view by a thin partition. But even in some modernized houses, in towns like Buscemi and Buccheri (in south-eastern Sicily), as well as in Noto itself, the privy may be in the kitchen separated from the stove by only a curtain. The privy in this house is now stuccoed over but other privies of this kind are still in use in Noto. Today their outlet pipes probably connect with the modern sewage system; formerly they ran through the wall into a cesspool at

65 Vico Trigona looking north with lower-class dwelling in the centre of the photograph.

the rear of the house or a 'black well' under the floor. Plumbing systems were essentially the same in small dwellings as in monasteries and palaces. Paolo Labisi, in his treatise on architecture, tells his readers that no one can stop them from sinking a cesspool because it is a necessary part of a dwelling. If they find their neighbour's cesspool is on their property, they can also use it without paying the neighbour who dug it.[52]

The Netinese, and in particular the poor who live in lower-class houses, do not keep their homes well lit, either at night or during the day. Since few people read much, electricity is used at night for television sets rather than for light. People talk in the dark or with only the flicker of the television at night, and they get up with the sun. In the day most activities are carried on in the doorway or outside the house.

Such is the Netinese lower-class house at its simplest. However, the house can grow with the needs and social position of the family, units being added as they are needed and as space is available. If money is available and space lacking, the first storey is topped by a second and the original house is reintegrated into a larger unit. In Noto the stairway connecting the second floor to the ground floor is on the interior. Sometimes a second doorway is opened on the façade from which a stairway ascends to the second floor. One can see how additions to the dwelling can easily upgrade the apparent social position of the owner.

One-storey lower-class dwellings appear throughout Labisi's veduta of Noto Nuova and in the panorama of Noto Antica. In the case of Noto Nuova, some that have been topped by a second storey also appear. These visual sources indicate that this house-type goes back at least to the seventeenth century. However, its origin, according to Axel Boëthius, may be far more ancient. Boëthius believes that this type of dwelling, common throughout south-eastern Sicily, is the descendant of Roman *tabernae*, used for trade and habitation by the lower classes of Rome.[53] Among the characteristics which distinguish tabernae from other Roman dwellings are their dependence on a single large aperture opening on the street, their row-like arrangement, and their interior organization which included a wooden garret or mezzanine above the first floor. The lower-class dwellings of Noto meet two of these criteria. In addition, they are in some locations arranged in rows of three or four with identical apertures. Thus it is possible that the dwellings are actually part of a very ancient tradition which was transferred to the new Noto from the old with no basic changes.

Social Status in Building: Differentiating Huts from Palaces

The use of costly *pietra d'intaglio* differentiates ecclesiastical and aristocratic constructions from lower-class dwellings. Whereas lower-class dwellings display little or no stone ornamentation, most palaces and churches have façades constructed of *pietra d'intaglio* (literally 'cut stone'), also called *pietra bianca* (or 'white stone').[54] *Pietra d'intaglio* is a medium-hard porous limestone which is indigenous to the Noto area. Because it is permeated with iron deposits, it takes on an orange colour with exposure to air and thus gives Noto its distinctive golden appearance. But when it is first quarried the stone is chalk white, only turning yellow after having been left to dry – hence, 'white' stone.[55]

Pietra d'intaglio is longlasting, strong in compression, and can, of course, be carved. Much of the *pietra d'intaglio* used in Noto Nuova probably was salvaged from ruined buildings in Noto Antica.[56] Testimony to the cost of having stones carved can be found on the exterior walls of churches and palaces: only the most important parts of the façade received this expensive treatment. The stylistically less important parts of both ecclesiastical and aristocratic buildings were constructed with cheaper materials. Walls could be constructed out of less durable stones – sandstone or even cheaper rubble—filled with mortar and protected from the elements by a thick-coat of plaster. Corners and decorative orders on the façade of S. Chiara were built of *pietra d'intaglio*, but the surface between the apertures and the corner pilasters of the façade is plastered over, indicating that rubble construction lies underneath.

The social status of an individual in Noto would be read from the façade of his dwelling. The more important the building and the greater the client's ability to pay, the more likely the building would be to have decorated door mouldings, window surrounds, or a façade proudly ornamented with the orders – all carved of *pietra d'intaglio*. For example, art historians discussing Noto always mention the unusually carved balconies on the façade of the palace of the Nicolaci family. What they fail to underscore is the prestige of possessing a structure which is composed of costly material expensively carved. The façades of the palaces of the Nicolacis, Impellizzeris, Astutos, and Landolinas were intended to be symbols of each family's wealth and power.

An Emphasis on Exteriors

Because life in Noto was oriented to the out-of-doors, all sectors of society seem to have been concerned with the best representation of what they possessed. Uniformly, the exteriors of buildings in Noto, whether churches, religious houses, palaces, or even lower-class houses, were more impressive than their interiors. Every building in the city presented its best image to the community.

As regards construction and materials, again Noto's buildings were very much alike. While façades of palaces and churches might be partly made of *pietra d'intaglio*, they also had areas covered by plaster as in the lower-class dwellings. A look behind the fancy upper-class façades shows us that they too had rubble walls and asymmetrical plans just as the lower-class dwellings did. In large expensive buildings and lower-class dwellings alike, walls rarely come together at 90° angles although they were intended to. Noto was a far less geometrically perfect city than its leading citizens probably desired. Its buildings were more organic in their growth than their façades indicate.

Chapter 7 A Netinese Style

> Most of these buildings and others of lesser importance seem to have been built at the same period, that is around 1702, after the 1693 earthquake, and by the same architect. I was told that he was from Catania (but I doubt it, not having seen anything in Catania in the style of the Noto buildings). In any case, they are all in the same style and built by someone who had studied Palladio, Inigo Jones, and especially Vignola; he therefore more or less copies their orders.
>
> Léon Dufourny, *Notes rapportées d'un voyage en Sicile fait par lui en 1789.*[1]

Dufourny saw a stylistic unity in the façades of Noto's palaces and churches which persists for the contemporary observer. All the major buildings of eighteenth-century Noto repeat similar themes, like furniture designed to decorate a sumptuous salon. The homogeneity in the treatment of the façades and interiors of Noto is even greater than that of other cities in Sicily reconstructed after the earthquake – but this homogeneity is *not* a consequence of the consistent effort of one architect as Dufourny concludes. Rather this stylistic unity he perceived has at least five sources. One, the architects of Noto shared a preference for traditional Renaissance usage of separate orders for each storey of a building. Two, their use of ornamental motifs in window surrounds and niches is similar. For example, although three different types of church façades can be discerned in Noto, they are united by the ornamental motifs they share. Three, the architects preferred spatially conservative façades and interiors. Four, they tended to fuse different styles and utilized decoration from varied and sometimes disparate sources. Five, the prolonged construction period for most Netinese buildings resulted in different architects with different styles contributing consecutively to the same buildings. And six, by a happy consequence of nature, Noto's buildings are unified by the golden colour of the stone native to the area, of which they are built. This chapter will examine these factors which contribute to Noto's homogeneity in more detail and will consider the Netinese style of European influence.

Orders on Palaces and Religious Houses

One feature of Noto's palaces and religious houses which makes them a cohesive group is the use of separate orders for each storey of a building. Noto's chaste façades offer the sense of continuity lost in many other townscapes where giant two-storey pilasters predominate. Although giant pilasters do appear in Noto's buildings, as on the corner of S. Chiara (Pl. 37) and the palace of the Nicolacis (Pl. 70), the one-storey orders make the greatest impression. Paired Doric and Tuscan pilasters articulate the lower façade of the monastery of SS. Salvatore (Pl. 36), paired Doric and Composite pilasters articulate the Landolina palace (Pl. 73), single Doric and Ionic pilasters can be seen in the courtyard of the Nicolaci palace, and paired Doric and Ionic pilasters appear on the façade of the oratory of S. Filippo Neri (Pl. 76). The Impellizzeris' palace is composed of three storeys of orders; the bottom order is banded Tuscan (Pl. 77). The façade of the Monte di Pietà (Casa del Refugio) is articulated by Tuscan pilasters (Pl. 55). The courtyards of the Jesuit college (Pl. 80) and the convent of S. Francesco are both surrounded by Doric arcades (Pl. 78).

The orders on these façades are taken for the most part from standard treatises of the period. The Netinese architects took some ideas from the Roman palaces illustrated in the engraved volumes by Falda and Ferrerio which were probably imported by Noto's aristocrats.[2] The architects sometimes painstakingly copied the orders from the printed treatises into their own manuscript copies. Paolo Labisi, for example, copied volume four of Christian Wolff's *Elementa Matheseos Universae* which applied Wolff's ideas to civil architecture. The book was a compendium of the thoughts and the orders of the most famous architects in Europe.[3] Labisi copied it with great fidelity, adding to his manuscript volume a series of designs he attributes to Albrecht Dürer. Gagliardi copied from Serlio and Vignola as well as Wolff.[4]

Motifs borrowed from these authors can be seen throughout Netinese architecture. The portal on the façade of the convent of S. Domenico (Pl. 48) is an adaptation of the portal from Vignola's Caprarola reproduced at the end of his book.[5] The portal of the convent of the Carmine (Pl. 79) comes from the same source. The Ionic order of the city hall is a copy of Michelangelo's capitals for the Capitoline palaces which the architects probably saw in Vignola's treatise.[6] Paolo Labisi specifically designated Wolff as the source for his Doric order on the sheets of his design for the house of the Crociferi (see p. 193 et seq).

Ornamental Motifs and Conservative Façades

Noto's architecture keeps ornament in check. The city has a hauntingly classical character which contradicts one's expectations of a provincial Sicilian city. For example, Noto's architecture is very different from the architecture of Lecce in the province of Apulia (Pl. 66). Both the southern Italian mainland and Sicily have an energetic and fanciful ornamental tradition. In Apulia, sculptors and architects loaded buildings with a myriad of imaginary creatures, religious figures and floral decorations.[7] A less energetic but equally busy variety of this decoration can be seen in Catanese architecture built just after the earthquake of 1693 (Pl. 67).[8] Common to both Lecce and Catania are caryatid figures and a profusion of putti heads and anthropomorphic architectural members. Although these elements of southern

66 S. Croce, Lecce. Upper part of the façade.

67 Façade of Palazzo del Barone Massa, Catania, begun 1694.

69 Nicolaci palace balconies.

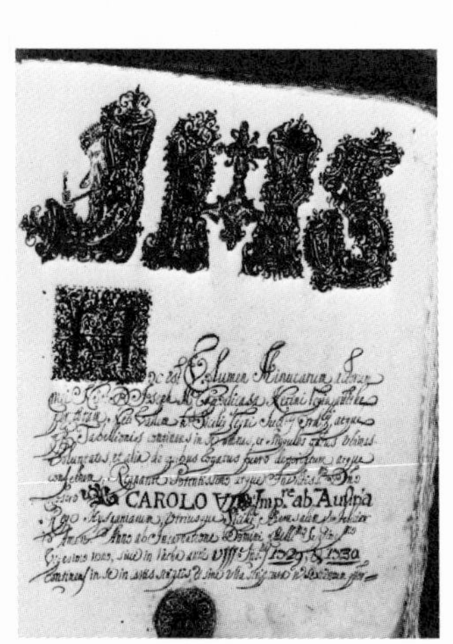

68 Minutes of Joseph Capodicasa, ASS, 1729–1730, R-1. First page illustrating Sicilian penchant for fanciful ornament which includes both abstract embellishments and realistic faces.

Italian ornament appear in Noto, they are always circumscribed and delimited; the overall effect remains one which has the quality of cool control.

The most boisterous decoration in Noto, the balconies of the Nicolaci palace, fit into a pristinely plain façade. Below the prancing horses, floating maidens and angry lions which support the balconies (Pl. 69), one finds a portal which is taken directly from Vignola's *Regola delli Cinque Ordini d' Architettura*.[9] This unlikely combination of provincial and classical ornaments explains some of the fresh quality of Noto's architecture: two very different styles appear to fit the same severe building.

When Noto was rebuilt after 1693, it retained the conservatism of Sicily. Washed by the currents of Renaissance and post-Renaissance styles, Sicilian architects concentrated on ornamental formulas which fit their tastes. They never seem to have accepted fully the more abstract geometrical ratios of the Renaissance but instead relied on applied articulation and ornament to carry their classical statement. In eighteenth-century Noto, ornamental motifs, even in their controlled formats, were preferred to spatially interesting façades and interiors which are the hallmarks of Baroque architecture in Rome. The Sicilians seem to have felt a reluctance to embark on experiments with the curved façades of Rome or the diaphanous domes of Guarini and Vittone in Piedmont. S. Anna, one of the first curved church façades of Sicily, was begun in Palermo in 1726, more than a half century after curved façades had become commonplace in Rome.[10] Even Gagliardi never developed the compound curved façades which Borromini had popularized. None of the spatial inventions of the Bavarian Baroque architects can be seen in Noto's eighteenth-century churches.

Netinese architecture, while definitely interesting and stately, is simpler and more direct than the architecture of Rome and northern Italy. While few of the buildings are outstanding, those that are often have interesting combinations of spatial experimentation and ornamental invention, each seemingly kept in check by the other.

70 Nicolaci palace. Façade.

71 Nicolaci palace. Portal. Compare with pl. 72.

72 Copy of Vignola's Ionic order with griffin frieze. Volume of drawings in the Mazza collection, Syracuse.

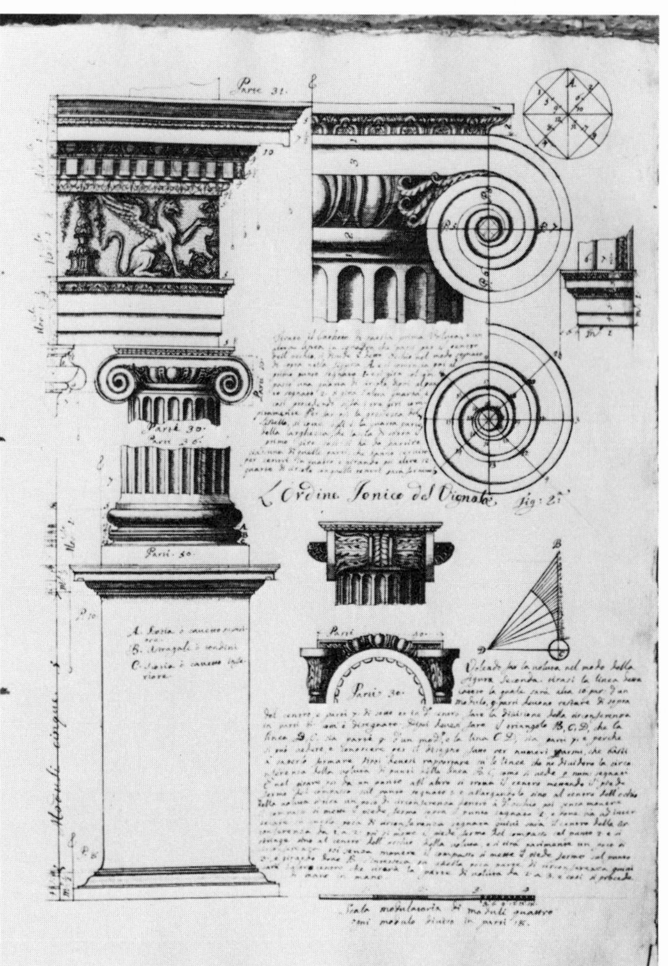

73 Landolina palace (S. Alfano). Façade.

76 Oratory of S. Filippo Neri. Façade.

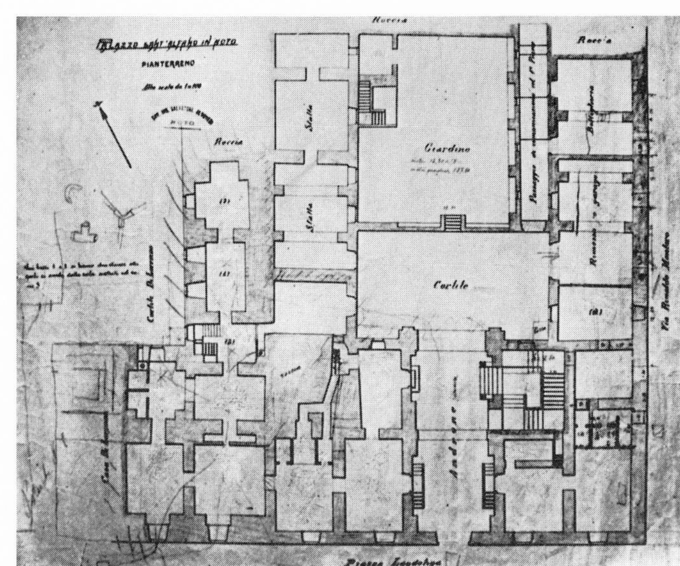

74 Landolina palace (S. Alfano). Ground plan. Nineteenth century. Collection of Francesco Genovesi.

75 Landolina palace (S. Alfano). First floor. Nineteenth century. Collection of Francesco Genovesi.

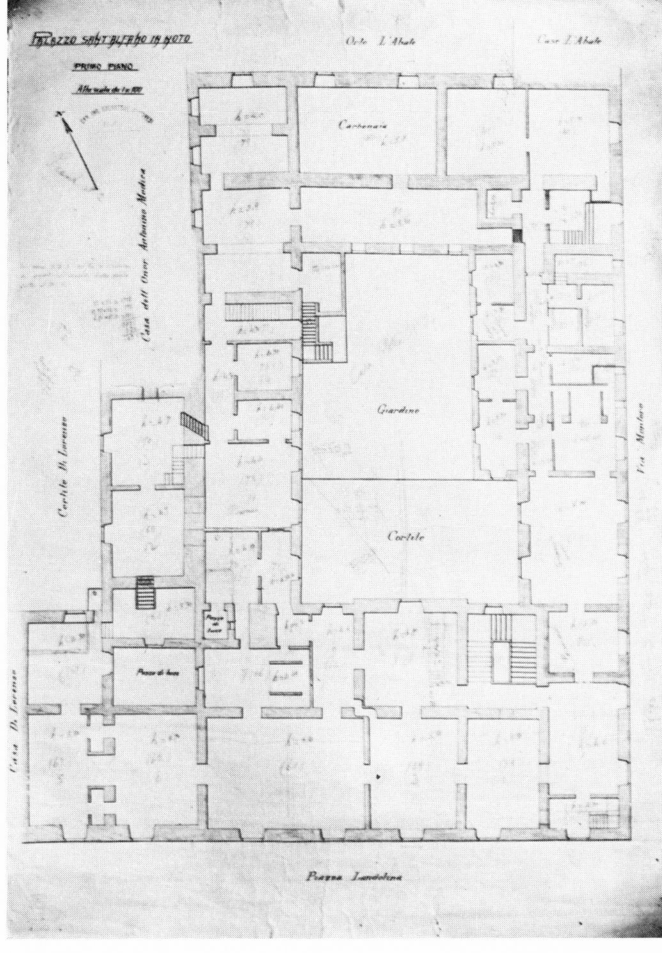

77 Impellizzeri palace (S. Giacomo). Façade.

78 Convent of S. Francesco. Courtyard.

79 Convent of S. Maria del Carmine. Dormitory portal.

Noto's Church Façades

Noto's church façades fall into three groups, which are related to one another through ornament and façade composition. The first group comprises buildings that remain faithful to flat two-storey façades articulated by pilasters in a sixteenth-century Late Renaissance manner. These façades, which include the convent of S. Francesco (Pl. 90) and the convent of S. Giovanni di Dio, are severe and very traditional, looking as if they were created by architects innocent of the seventeenth- and eighteenth-century advances made in church design. But because of the use of orders and the clarity and fluidity of their overall conception, Noto's church façades achieve a limpid quality typically Italian rather than the rigidity one finds in Spanish architecture. And while the framework may be conservative, often aperture mouldings show the influence of Borrominesque ornament. They are unusual façades because they do not rely on a volute to tie the upper and lower storeys together and they bring to mind some of the Roman church façades that G. B. Soria designed in the 1630s. This kind of two-storey façade remained popular throughout the eighteenth century as the late façade of S. Agata (Pl. 91) illustrates.

A sub-group relating to the first one are the single-storey façades articulated with great severity with Doric and Tuscan pilasters. These include the small church of S. Isidoro and an unidentified ruined church on the Pianazzo (Map 7, no. 40 and letter a respectively, page 111).

The second group of church façades looks much less classical and more eighteenth-century Sicilian. They commonly have block-like façades, visually defined by giant pilasters and often topped with belltowers. The church of the monastery of S. Chiara (Pl. 127), the church of the monastery of S. Maria dell'Arco (Pl. 119), and S. Maria la Rotonda are examples of this type of façade, and all seem to have a certain clumsiness, rigidity and flatness which is not a part of Italian

80 Jesuit College. Eastern courtyard looking north-west.

architectural tradition. Their primitive massiveness, superimpositions of windows over portals and concentrated ornament are reminiscent of Spanish architecture.

The third group of church façades incorporates seventeenth- and eighteenth-century Italian Baroque spatial concepts. Its examples are among Noto's most distinguished buildings. The churches of S. Carlo (Pl. 47) and S. Domenico (Pl. 52), with concave and convex façades respectively, break the flat plane while retaining a respect for the orders and a kind of Italian abstraction. Surface treatment never obscures massing and spatial plan. The tower of SS. Salvatore, cutting three concave twists skyward, has increased textural richness but is still firmly Italian. The concave façade of S. Maria del Carmine (Pl. 54b), with its Italian Rococo volutes and mouldings, is also a member of this group of façades. Another church in this group is S. Girolamo (Pl. 54a) with its concave façade and towers. In conception the church is Baroque, but it is articulated in an extremely restrained manner like the façades in the first group.

The decorative motifs found in each of the three church façade groups link together many of these buildings which might otherwise seem quite separate and distinct. The multi-lobed window surround, for example, is repeated in the Casa del Refugio (Pl. 55), S. Chiara (Pl. 127), S. Nicolò (Pl. 93), the convent of S. Domenico (Pl. 131), the Jesuit college (Pl. 47). The fleshy, broken, segmental arch appears on the façades of S. Domenico, SS. Salvatore, S. Chiara, and S. Maria dell'Arco. Low relief floral decorations sprout on many of the door surrounds throughout the town. The native Sicilian decorative tradition emerges in limited façade areas, like the capital of S. Chiara (Pl. 127) or the balconies of the Nicolaci palace (Pl. 69).

A Fusion of Styles

In Netinese architecture surprising combinations of disparate styles occur, belying any linear stylistic progression. What we see as several styles the Netinese may have seen as one. In the application of Rococo decoration, which appears at Noto in the 1750s, the Netinese proclivity for fusing styles is very apparent. Rococo ornament, light, lovely and asymmetrical, relied for its effect on sensual, delicate S-curved shapes suffused by gentle, even lighting. Rococo decoration used on interiors might be called anti-classical because it totally dissolved the orders in the organization of

81 Astuto palace. Façade from the west on Via Cavour.

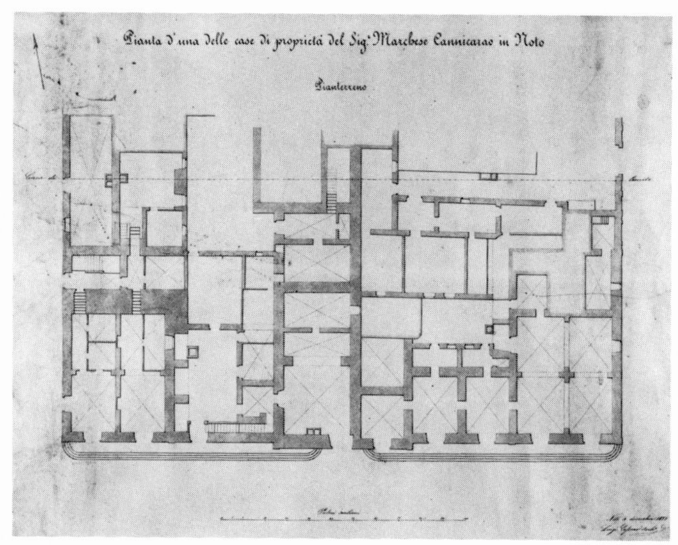

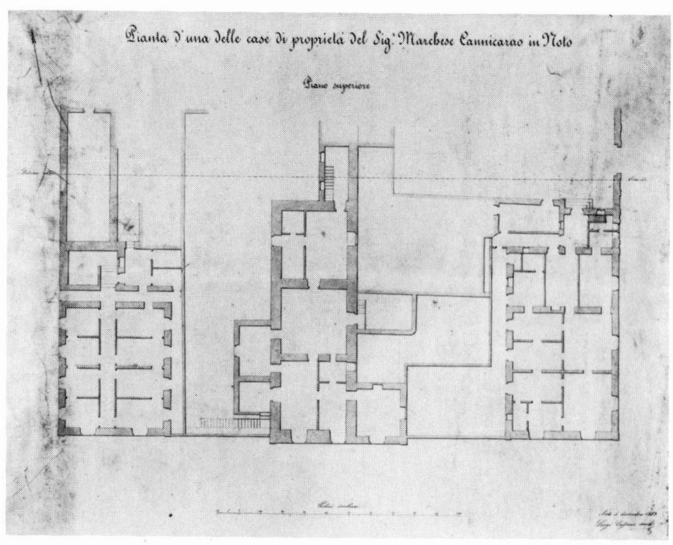

82 Bishop's palace. Luigi Cassone, 12 April 1853.

83 Bishop's palace. First floor. Luigi Cassone, 12 April 1853.

84 Bishop's palace in foreground, Trigona palace in the background. As seen from the upper terrace of the city hall.

wall space and had asymmetrical accents rather than remaining strictly symmetrical. The Netinese, perhaps influenced by French Rococo design, tried to use what they had learned, but either applied Rococo flourishes to otherwise staid façades, as in the exterior of the church of S. Agata (Pl. 91), or tamed the ornament as in the interior of S. Maria del Carmine. On the side of the nave of the Carmine (Pls 86–7) small putti frolic among Rococo ornaments in the form of S- and C-shaped wreaths. The Netinese took the idea of the Rococo but they classicized it by adding a more rotund balance to the forms. Along with Rococo, French and English Chinoiserie, a western version of Chinese design, appear in Noto. On the ecclesiastical furniture of SS. Crocifisso as well as along the aisles of the Jesuit church, Chinese figures with coolie hats mingle with Rococo arabesques. The stuccoing contract for the Jesuit

85 Trigona palace (Cannicarao). Main portal on northern side of building facing Via Cavour.

church of S. Carlo Borromeo states that this 'Bastard Chinese' ornament should be applied to the 'Vignolan' pilasters and arches of the nave.[11] Here the Netinese tried to reconcile the antithetical: the late sixteenth-century Renaissance classicism of Vignola is combined with non-classical, or even anti-classical Rococo and Chinoiserie ornament (Pls 88–9). Similarly the balconies of the Nicolaci palace with their fine provincial decoration have been combined with a copy of Vignola's Ionic order; sculptural decoration in the folk tradition, perhaps deriving from Noto Antica, appears next to ornament composed with the paradigm of classical correctness, almost as if the architect of the portal had chosen Vignola's Ionic with the griffin frieze as a means of uniting the classical motifs and the boisterous provincial ones.

86 S. Maria del Carmine. Nave.

87 S. Maria del Carmine. Detail of nave decorations.

88 S. Carlo Borromeo. Nave.

89 S. Carlo Borromeo. Detail of nave decoration.

Trying to establish a chronological progression of styles in Noto, based on the idea of a turn away from the Baroque to a kind of Renaissance-Revival cum Neo-classicism, is doomed to failure. While it might be said that the last third of the eighteenth century in Noto saw an increase in Neo-classical ornament in the Di Lorenzo palace, for example, construction of two of Noto's greatest Baroque palaces—the Astuto palace and Trigona palace—took place at the same time. Both discard single-storey orders in favour of gigantic pilaster strips. The Astuto palace (Pl. 81), ornamented with oversized *guttae* dripping from its balconies and pilasters, illustrates how uncanonical these late buildings could be. The Trigona palace, with a plan based on a prototypical Italian three-part division of central and flanking towers (Pl. 84), has wild ornamentation around its apertures (Pl. 85). But, while Baroque in its decoration, the palace is strangely self-conscious of order: the length of the façade and the rear of the palace are divided into modular sections by corbels which alternate with pilasters.

One Building—Several Architects

The slow construction rate of Noto's major buildings also played a distinct role in the homogeneity of its architecture. S. Nicolò is a case in point.[12] The first architect used five-lobed window surrounds and Baroque spatial sequences which can still be seen on the side of the church (Pl. 94). The style of decoration of the apertures is close to that of S. Domenico (Pl. 131). The original façade was probably to have been like S. Domenico, five-part/three-part, but without flanking towers. The first architect used a bolection frieze which can still be seen on supports for the dome. The entire side of S. Nicolò is treated with the care of a façade and articulated in evenly spaced Corinthian pilasters (Pl. 94). The pristine style of the façade (Pl. 96), continued by a second architect in the 1770s, is unlike any other in Noto both in its three-dimensionality, which separates it from the first group of church façades, and in its non-Baroque quality which separates it from the third group. But the pedimented niches are reminiscent of S. Domenico and S. Carlo (Pl. 47), while the pilaster repetitions on the bottom storey recall S. Maria del Carmine. A third architect

93 S. Nicoló. Western side. Five-lobed window surround.

94 S. Nicoló. Western side.

90 Convent of S. Francesco di Paola.
Façade from south.

92 S. Maria di Gesù. Façade.

91 S. Agata. Façade.

95 S. Nicoló. Cornice on western side.

96 S. Nicolò. Façade.

completed the towers of the façade in the eighteenth century. He did not even attempt to continue the pilaster arrangements, designed by the second architect, into the superstructure of the towers (Pls 95–6). Neo-classicism had displaced the Baroque as a popular style toward the end of the eighteenth century, so when the third architect designed the superstructure of the towers he deleted the repeated pilasters on the tower bases. The same kind of stripped style appears on the dome of the S. Nicolò, which was built in the nineteenth century to replace two others which collapsed because of earthquakes. The dome, which is stylistically identical to the dome of the church of SS. Crocifisso, is Neo-classical with touches of a nineteenth-century Neo-Baroque.

S. Nicolò is only one example but it is typical. Every major building in Noto was altered during the course of its construction in the eighteenth century or in later periods. Each revision added another dimension to a building's meaning and usually brought it closer to other evolving Netinese buildings. In the monastery of S. Chiara there were at least five building campaigns in the eighteenth century alone.

The Appearance of Stylistic Unity

If the pure statement of the principal architect of a building in Noto suffered over time, the complexity of the architectural relationships within Noto grew in a unique way. No structure in Noto is stylistically isolated from the rest. Parts of seemingly homogeneous buildings are actually creations of diverse eras and any number of aesthetic sensibilities. All of Noto's architects may have at one time or another worked on each of Noto's major buildings. Their use of ornaments and repeated motifs combine with an overall dependence on the same classical models to further strengthen the ties between buildings in Noto.

Noto has neither the appearance of a riotously ornamented provincial town nor of a completely up-to-date Baroque city. It hovers between the two extremes, creating a unique visual environment. In nearby Catania, Vaccarini and Ittar attempted to capture the Roman Baroque style in elephantine buildings of dark grey stone. Although Baroque influence appears in Noto's buildings it does not take Catania's sophisticated frigidity of form. The Baroque is integrated with freshness and grace in the golden stone buildings of Noto.

Part IV
The Eighteenth-Century Architects

Chapter 8 Rosario Gagliardi (1698?–1762?)

Who were the architects of eighteenth-century Noto? Since the study of architectural history in Sicily is in its infancy even the most famous eighteenth-century Sicilian architects practising in the island's capital, Palermo, lack adequate scholarly studies. All the standard resources for researching the biographies of architects are useless in the study of eighteenth-century Sicily. Therefore, the aim of this chapter is to supply crucial information which cannot be found elsewhere about three architects who worked in eighteenth-century Noto: Rosario Gagliardi, Vincenzo Sinatra, and Paolo Labisi. Because little has been written about the relationship of the architecture of Sicily as a whole to the rest of Europe this chapter also compares and contrasts the work of the architects practising in Noto with the work of their colleagues elsewhere.

Gagliardi, Sinatra, and Labisi were not the only architects working in eighteenth-century Noto, but their work comprises the most important fragment of Netinese architecture that we can now identify. Other than these three men, a number of less important architects and master-builders appear in eighteenth-century Netinese documents, among them Corrado Mazza, Bernardo Labisi, Joachim Gonzales and Antonio Mazza. Priests may have played a significant part in the designs of secular and religious institutions alike in the early decades of the eighteenth century but their role as architects remains undocumented.[1] However, it was undoubtedly Gagliardi, Sinatra, and Labisi who were the most important architects in Noto from 1715 to the 1780s when much of the city's architecture was built.

Although all three of these men may have been official architects of the city of Noto we know more about their individual buildings than their contributions to the city plan. Labisi and Gagliardi intermittently signed themselves 'Architect of the City of Noto' or 'Engineer of the City of Noto', particularly when engaged in civic projects like drawing a map of a piazza or building a city aqueduct, but whether they are perfunctorily stating their citizenship or signing their official titles is unclear. At least as early as 1757 Noto's Senators formed a special municipal committee called *i Deputati di acqua e strade* to administer the construction of streets and water courses in Noto's territory.[2] Whether such a committee existed previous to 1757 we cannot know, but after that time architects were employed by the Deputies to perform certain tasks.[3] According to Labisi, he occupied the position of City Architect from 1760 to 1784 although – so he complained – the Senators of Noto did not honour his appointment (see below). Labisi petitioned the central government to stop the Senators from employing someone else (probably Vincenzo Sinatra) either concurrently or in his stead. From Labisi's protestations we can deduce that the office of City Architect, which by his time bore the title of Royal Civil Engineer of the Senate and the City of Noto, was supposed to be filled by one person at a time. City Architects, according to Labisi, helped to determine who should build on vacant plots within the city.[4]

We know that City Architects also estimated buildings' values for tax purposes, as Sinatra did for the 1748 taxes.[5] Likewise, as a City Architect Gagliardi repaired an aqueduct, Labisi moved the Hercules fountain to Piazza S. Domenico and Labisi's son, Bernardo, studied the possibility of lowering the Corso.[6]

How these men, as City Architects, contributed to the city plan as a whole is unknown from the available documents.[7] The individual buildings they created or helped to create stand as the clearest record of who these men were. Each of their buildings is a microcosm of the uncertain process of evolution from artistic conception to built reality which repeats itself throughout the history of Noto. This chapter and the next address themselves to the task of studying the careers and buildings of Gagliardi, Sinatra, and Labisi and clarifying architectural expression and practice in eighteenth-century Noto.

Gagliardi Rediscovered

Since 1950, first one Netinese building then another has been attributed to a little-known architect: Rosario Gagliardi.[8] For years scholars have claimed that he was Noto's foremost architect yet only recently have documents come to light which prove this contention. Why the name of Rosario Gagliardi, Noto's most influential architect, vanished from every historical record is not hard to guess. First, Gagliardi was by birth a Syracusan, not a Netinese, which probably worked against his memory.[9] Second, being remembered was the exception, not the rule: of all the architects of eighteenth-century Noto, only Paolo Labisi – an aristocrat and a native – was remembered.[10] Third, personal animosity towards Gagliardi and jealousy of his prowess may have obliterated his memory. Paolo Labisi, for example, was a highly ambitious but deeply frustrated man who quarrelled violently with Gagliardi's chosen successor, Vincenzo Sinatra (see pp. 172–181). One can easily imagine Labisi destroying Gagliardi's designs or incorporating them into his own written and graphic works. Fourth, the Netinese seemed to respect ideas but not authorship. There is every evidence that Netinese architects borrowed from one another without noting the provenance of their ideas. Even within the last few years puzzling disregard for authorship still exists. The plans of a church by Antonio Mazza (1761–1826) were preserved by the Mazza family and donated to the city library. But for unknown motives, the signature of the architect was ripped off the edge of a sheet of the plans. Therefore, it is not surprising that the identities of Noto's architects are just emerging.

Recently discovered documents indicate that Rosario Gagliardi was a Syracusan. According to his tax statement he was born in 1698. If he listed his age correctly, he began to work as a carpenter in Noto at the early age of 10 which doesn't seem too likely. But he was probably in his 'teens when he first began to work in Noto.[11] Around the age of 15 Gagliardi may have emigrated to Noto where he worked from 1713 until he was incapacitated by illness in 1761.[12] During the four decades Gagliardi designed and built in Noto he influenced most major construction in the city. He first worked on the design for the monastery of S. Maria dell'Arco with Ignacio Puzzo, a Syracusan *capomaestro*, or foreman, in 1713.[13] By 1726 he is acknowledged as an architect, probably having worked himself up from carpenter.[14] In 1728 he designed portions of the church of SS. Crocifisso.[15] In 1730 he resumed work on the church and monastery of S. Maria dell'Arco.[16] While continuing to work on S. Maria dell'Arco Gagliardi designed the church of SS. Crocifisso. In the 1730s his commissions include the continuation of S. Chiara, work on the Casa del Refugio and S. Calogero, the design for S. Maria la Rotunda, and the design for the Battaglia palace. By the 1740s he had worked on the convent and church of S. Domenico and the dormitory of S. Maria del Carmine. In the 1750s he designed the dormitory and church for S. Agata, but it is unclear just how much of the latter survives.[17] Although undocumented his work in Noto probably includes the first campaign of S. Nicolò as well as the design for the Jesuit church of S. Carlo and the belvedere tower of SS. Salvatore.[18] While he was directing work on the buildings begun in the 1730s, he also designed buildings throughout southeastern Sicily in Comiso, Caltagirone, Ragusa, and Syracuse.[19]

In addition to actually designing buildings for Noto, Gagliardi's influence extended to the styles of the architects that followed him in Noto, as we shall see. The combination of his constructions and the influence he had on others makes Gagliardi Noto's most important architect.

97 Frontispiece, treatise by R. Gagliardi, Mazza Collection, Syracuse. From Albrecht Dürer's *Vier Bücher von Menschlicher Proportion*

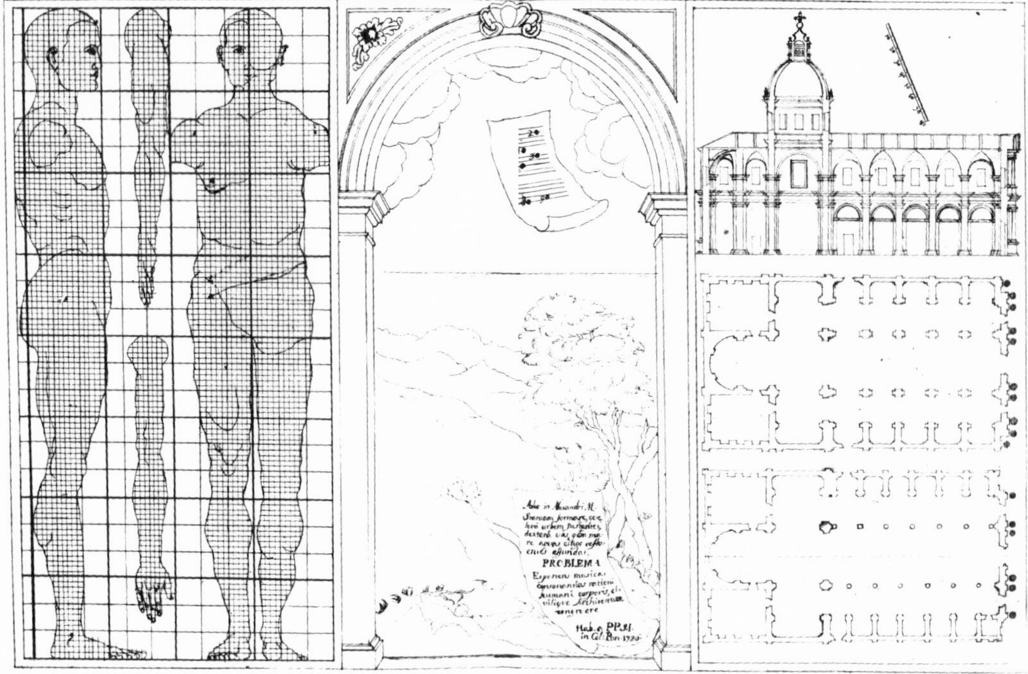

Gagliardi's Treatise

Although his name was forgotten, three volumes of Gagliardi's drawings miraculously survived.[20] These volumes, never finished, were probably intended to become a treatise on civil and ecclesiastical architecture. The first volume contains ground-plans, elevations, and sections of churches. The other two volumes bring together geometric exercises, column capital designs, military plans, and altars.[21] Some of the drawings in the last two volumes may in fact be by other architects consciously trying to complete Gagliardi's work in his style.[22] The volumes survived because they were handed down from city architect to city architect until the 1940s. They then fell into the hands of a descendant of Antonio Mazza, named Giuseppe Mazza, who in turn showed them to friends. The friends, Francesco. Genovesi and Luigi Di Blasi, privately published one volume in 1972. Although the authorship of the drawings in the second and third volumes can be debated, the first volume is wholly the work of Gagliardi, who even signed his name to two of the plans. Also, several drawings in the first volume (hereafter Gagliardi's treatise) are ground-plans, elevations and sections of buildings known to have been designed by Gagliardi, hence his authorship is fairly secure.[23] Since no documents have yet been found which tie Gagliardi's training to any particular region or master, the drawings in the treatise represent an invaluable source of information as to what he felt was important and where he drew his inspiration.

The treatise shows Gagliardi very much under the sway of Baroque ideas filtered through sixteenth-century Italian Renaissance concepts. Like Giovan Biagio Amico who wrote an architectural treatise in Sicily before him (*Architetto Practico*, Palermo, 1726 and 1750), Gagliardi did not venture far past re-examining worn Renaissance design problems. As the title page (Pl. 97) of his treatise demonstrates, he is at his weakest when he tries to restate these problems: the well-known theme of the title page is the relationship between the proportions of the human body, musical scales and proportions in architecture. Treatise writers since the early Renaissance were concerned with expressing the mathematical principles which account for perfection in proportions.[24] Gagliardi wanted to show this interrelationship so he complemented the division of the human body with two longitudinal ground-plans and the section of a church, presumably his most perfect designs. The representations of the churches seem in no way conceptually related to the geometricized man, which leads me to conclude that Gagliardi may not have understood either how to represent the relationships he sought or how to communicate them. His representations of proportions are wholly emblematic rather than explanatory. The aisled church-plan on the title page would have looked very old fashioned to an eighteenth-century Italian architect since it is typical of sixteenth-century churches.

Gagliardi designs his churches to answer archetypal Renaissance problems posed by Serlio and Palladio who were in turn inspired by Vitruvius. The questions which were repeated *ad nauseam* were how can one design a round church, a square church, an oval church, a pentagonal church, a hexagonal church, a longitudinal church? Gagliardi's plans answer these old questions with simple, direct, uninspired responses. He copied some of the questions and answers from his fellow Sicilian Giovan Biagio Amico.[25] Many plans seem close to Serlio too. But the plans are not pure copies; they are eclectic reviews.

Gagliardi, unlike his fellow countryman and contemporary Filippo Juvarra who worked in Turin, was not interested in spatial experimentations. Juvarra, born and raised in Messina, practised in Turin for the royal house of Savoy which briefly owned Sicily. He incorporated the soaring, seemingly weightless interiors of Guarino Guarini with his own interest in stage design to produce some of the most spatially innovative interiors of the eighteenth century. Gagliardi was simply not interested in complex spatial relationships or structural innovations, as his ground-plans and sections demonstrate. In most of his designs he confines his support systems to arcades of piers with pilasters. He uses pendentives only on small crossing domes. He refuses to clear the interior of his churches by transferring more thrust to exterior bearing walls. Whether longitudinal or polygonal, most of his buildings are aisled when aisles were not used in the most adventuresome architecture being built in the rest of Europe. In Piedmont, for example, architects were attempting to create more spatially unified and visually complex interiors while Gagliardi seems deeply entrenched in a more primitive system. Perhaps Gagliardi was designing with a conservative support system to eliminate earthquake hazards. But since he nowhere else in the treatise addresses earthquake-resistant construction, it is safe to surmise that his lack of interest in experimenting with daring vaulting techniques stemmed merely from innate conservatism.

While flirting with the problems of central-planned churches, Gagliardi is not much concerned with the abstract intellectualization of the fifteenth and sixteenth centuries either. In one of his most inventive plans he offers a solution to the problem of the pentagon by elaborating on a design published in Sebastiano Serlio's *Tutte l'opere d'architettura e prospetiva*, Venice, 1575. The beauty of the pentagon is that the altar, the entrance, and the side chapels are not exactly 90° apart and cannot all be on the major axes of the pentagon. In Serlio's temple (Pl. 99) the trilobed auxiliary spaces do not and cannot include both the entrance and the altar because of the nature of the pentagon; Serlio therefore includes four niches and the entrance as a minor theme to the major pentagon. But Gagliardi's solution (Pl. 98) to the pentagonal problem is simply to insert the similar lobed figure he used in his major theme in the doorway as well. He also adds two lateral doorways that play on the illusion that the viewer confronts a complete pentagon and symmetrical niches from any one of the three doors. By designing the lobed form into the main portal he breaks the strictures of the plan: either he does not understand the abstract problem or he chooses not to address it directly, instead diffusing it with visual trickery. If the latter is the case, Gagliardi was not alone, for many eighteenth-century architects seem to lose interest in the tensions that can be produced by the spatial ambivalence of the pentagons and hexagons. Even Bernardo Vittone, the adventuresome Piedmontese architect, lessened the impact of the hexagonal plan by differentiating his side chapels from the main chapel and entrance as in his chapel of S. Luigi at Corteranzo in Piedmont.[26]

Gagliardi's solution to the pentagonal problem illustrates that he sees scenically

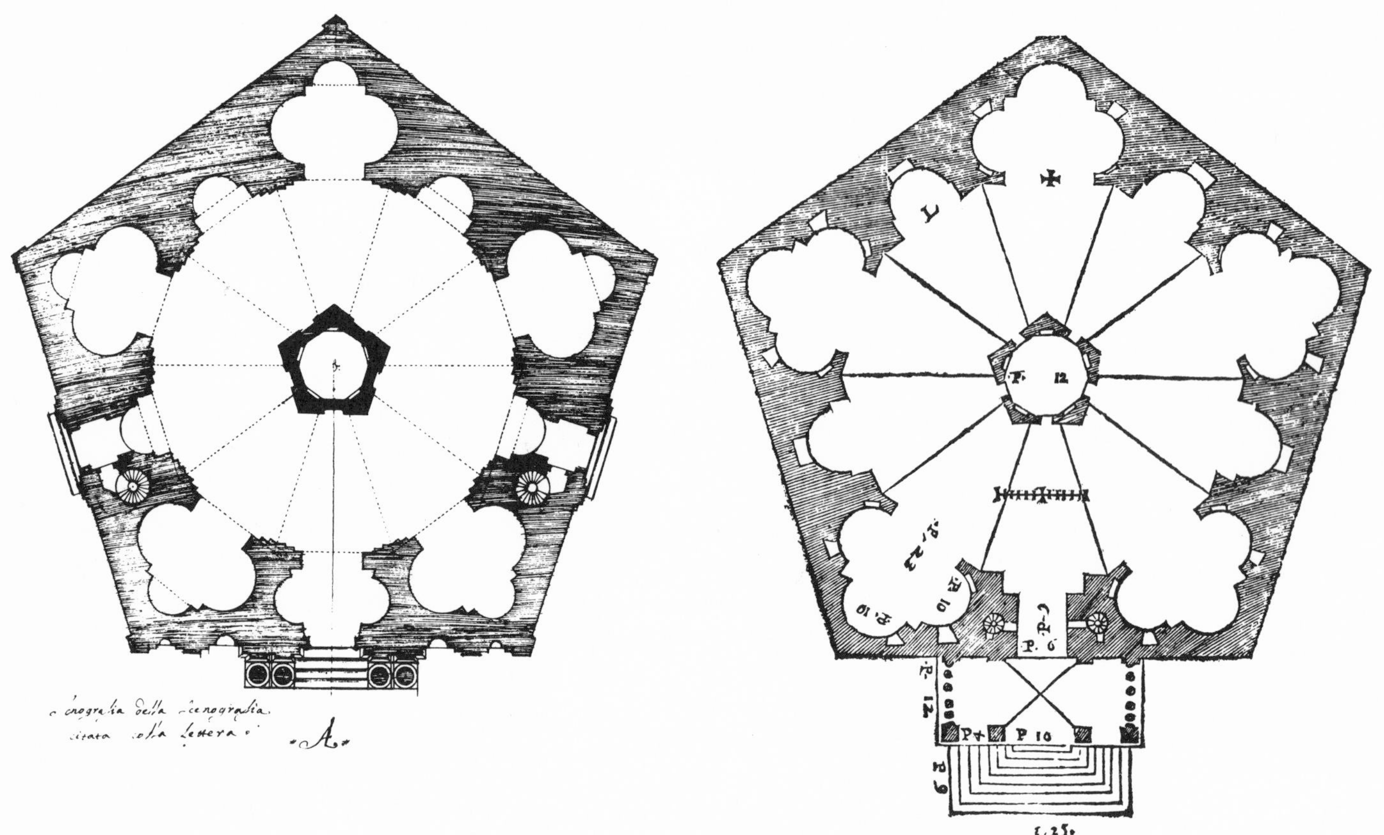

98 Ground plan for pentagonal church, Study A, treatise by R. Gagliardi, Mazza Collection, Syracuse.

99 Pentagonal temple. S. Serlio, *Tutte l'opere d'architettura et prospetiva*, Venice, 1619, p. 205 v.

rather than conceptually.[27] His solution is successful if considered not in relation to the plan but to sensual experience alone. Thus, from the main entrance of the pentagon church one gazes through the vast central area to the altar without realizing any discrepancy in plan. Churches like studies F (Pl. 100), E (Pl. 101), and H (Pl. 102) of the treatise are planned to let the visitor at the main entrance look successively through the column screen, a dark aisle, a highlighted arcade, a brightly-lit open space, another arcade, another dark aisle, another column screen, to the dim choir and main altar perhaps ablaze with candles. The important element is that Gagliardi's architecture is experienced as a series of two-dimensional stage sets rather than a cohesive spatial unit of plan and elevation. As with the churches of the seventeenth-century architects Carlo Rainaldi or Baldassare Longhena, it is the visual experience which seems paramount. That Gagliardi copies Michelangelo's plan for S. Giovanni dei Fiorentini (*ca.* 1559–60) for all of these churches is beside the point, since he destroys the built-in conceptual perfection of S. Giovanni by adding an extended choir (Pls 103–104).[28] Gagliardi shares this dilution through scenographic extension with other architects working in eighteenth-century Europe.[29]

Gagliardi's most inventive designs show him to be concerned with exterior massing and façade composition. His excellence is apparent in the façade elevation of Study F (Pl. 105), in which the powerful curve of the lobes on either side of the entrance portal expresses the massiveness of the turning wall. Gagliardi carefully limits decorative elements to corner pilasters and balustrades, to emphasize the contrast between the central portal and façade wings. The great restraint of the Ionic order of the pilasters and columns in the entrance portal, with its tightly closed architectural members, worked to contain the energy of the façade. Gagliardi's composition is more successful than Giovanni Battista Vaccarini's famous church of S. Agata in Catania (Pl. 106).[30] Like Gagliardi, Vaccarini, the most important architect working in eighteenth-century Catania, also used massive convex side walls to emphasize the monumentality of his shrine for S. Agata. But of the two,

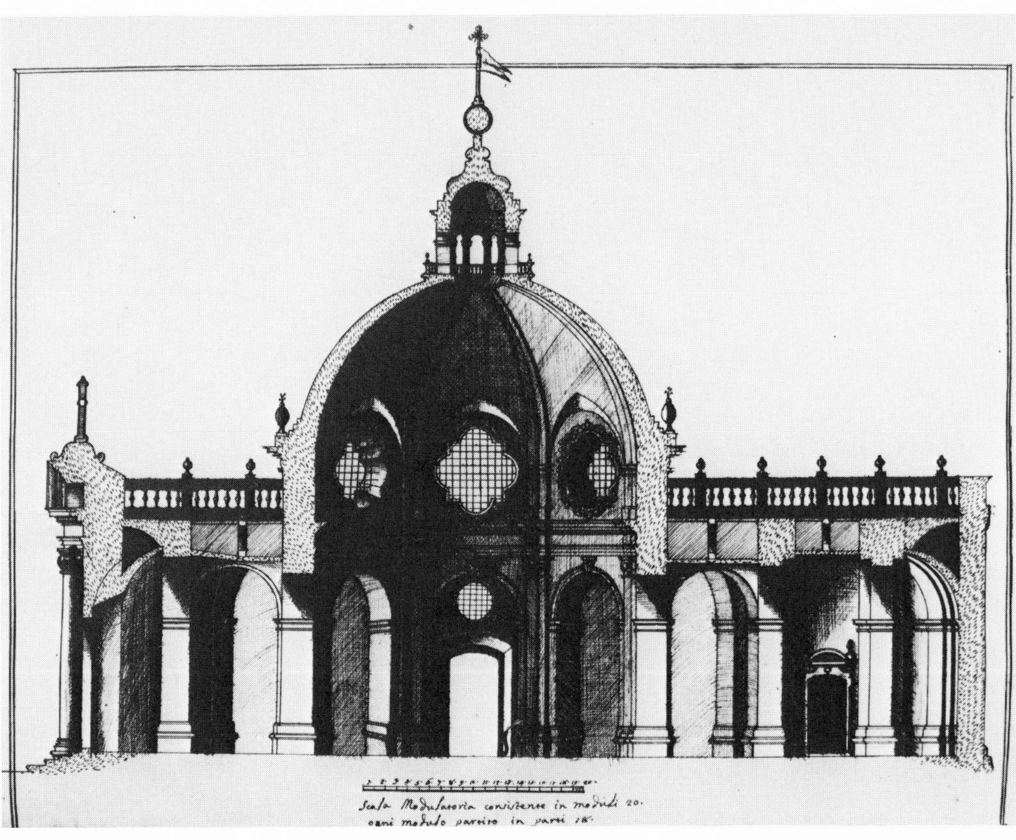

00 Section F, treatise by R. Gagliardi, Mazza Collection, Syracuse.

01 Section E, treatise by R. Gagliardi, Mazza Collection, Syracuse.

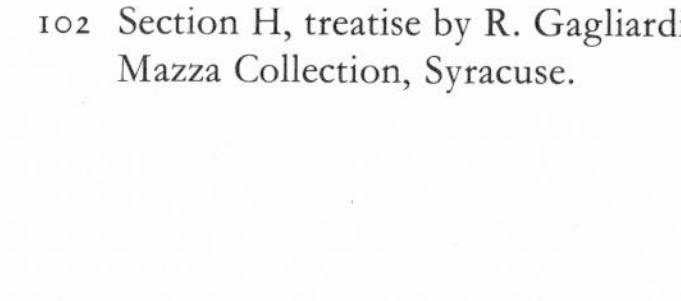

102 Section H, treatise by R. Gagliardi, Mazza Collection, Syracuse.

105 Elevation F, treatise by R. Gagliardi, Mazza Collection, Syracuse.

106 S. Agata, Catania, G. B. Vaccarini.

107 Elevation E, treatise by R. Gagliardi, Mazza Collection, Syracuse.

108 Façade study L, treatise by R. Gagliardi, Mazza Collection, Syracuse.

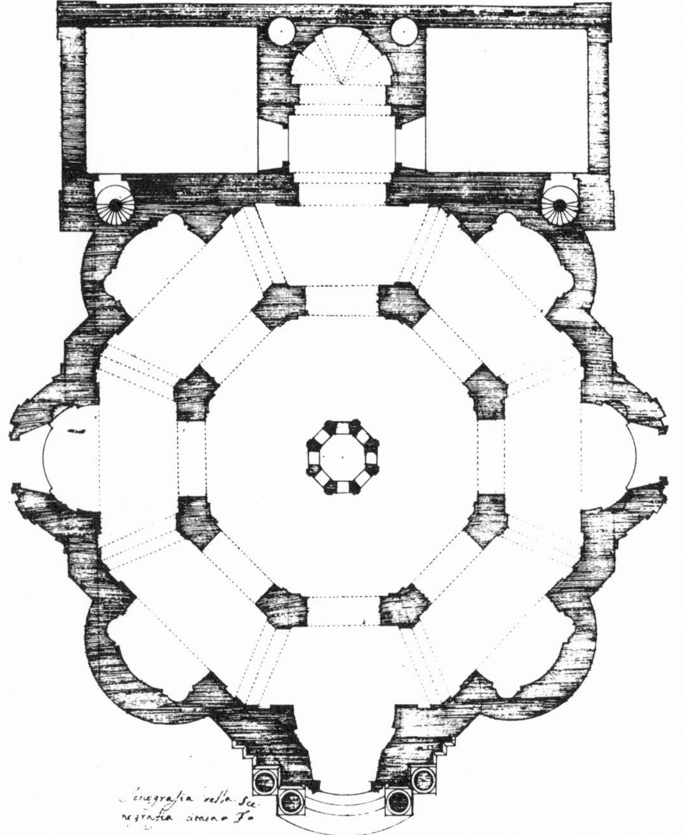

103 Ground plan F, treatise by R. Gagliardi, Mazza Collection, Syracuse.

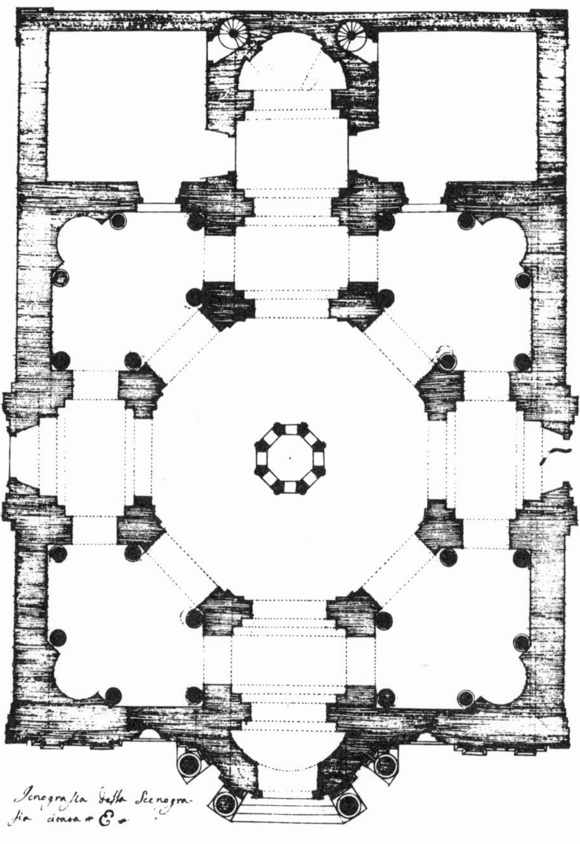

104 Ground plan E, treatise by R. Gagliardi, Mazza Collection, Syracuse.

Scala Modulatoria consistente in moduli 20.
ogni modulo partito in parti 18.
Scenografia della Senografia
citata ✠ F ✠

2. 4. 6. 8. 10. 12. 14. 16. 18. 20.
Scala Modulatoria consistente in moduli 20.
ogni Modulo partito in parti 18.
Scenografia della Senografia
citata ✠ C ✠

Scenografia della
Senografia citata ✠ L ✠
Scala Modulatoria consistente
in Moduli 20. Ogni Modulo partito
in parti 12.

109 Façade study K, treatise by R. Gagliardi, Mazza Collection, Syracuse.

110 Façade Study. R. Gagliardi, Di Blasi Collection, Noto.

Gagliardi's church more effectively plays off convex masses against the entrance portal. Vaccarini's gargantuan façade when compared with Gagliardi's loses its power through ornament, over-articulation, and the ungainly half-storey attic he adds to his façade.

Gagliardi's major success as a designer is in his handling of the façades based on the accepted superimposition of one unit over three (Study H (Pl. 108), K (Pl. 109)), with the transitions accomplished by means of volutes. Applying a formula widely in use in Sicily, Gagliardi often goes on to add an additional miniature storey, on which he places a single belltower.[31] Many times the façades curve forward as the lateral wings remain flat. To dramatize this convexity Gagliardi uses columns to concentrate the upward thrust of the façade, while they mark the outward movement of the façade through their placement.

Gagliardi was a master of the Sicilian belfry façade as his excitingly concentrated design for the façade of S. Giorgio in Ragusa illustrates (Pls 110–112). More than any other architect in southern Italy he realized the potential of a columnar façade which Martino Longhi the Younger's SS. Vincenzo and Anastasio (Rome, 1646–50) suggested.[32] He united columns with a repeated superimposition of ever smaller architectural members to bring façades ecstatically alive.

However, Gagliardi's façade designs are uneven. The squat awkward one-storey attic façades certainly do not seem to be his forte, although they were popular in Sicily, while the more Roman Baroque façade designs, or even the more classical façades like Study K are handled with consummate grace and skill (Pl. 109).[33]

While Gagliardi does understand how to design façades so that they can be viewed with greatest advantage from the street, he does not seem to understand that the domes he designs for his churches, because of their low drums, would not be visible from below (see Pl. 107). This is striking because in many of Gagliardi's studies, the dome is a critical part of the design, as in Study F (Pl. 105).

Two volumes of drawings which may not all be Gagliardi's accompany the treatise.[34] They show, through their borrowings from fortification treatises (Van Dogen) and Italian treatises (Serlio, Vignola), how indebted Gagliardi was to these sources. Direct copies are few but inspirations are many. He borrows from

111 S. Giorgio, Ragusa. Façade. Designed by R. Gagliardi.

Vignola's orders and then takes off, *à la Guarini*, inventing his own whimsical capitals as other eighteenth-century architects did. He takes his decoration from common Baroque sources. Although the decoration may be plentiful, he never breaks from the symmetry of Baroque ornament into the asymmetrical decoration of the Rococo. Although Gagliardi was open to influences from outside Italy as some of his designs show, he saw himself primarily as heir to the Italian Renaissance and Baroque tradition, and this is the stamp he put on the architecture of Noto.

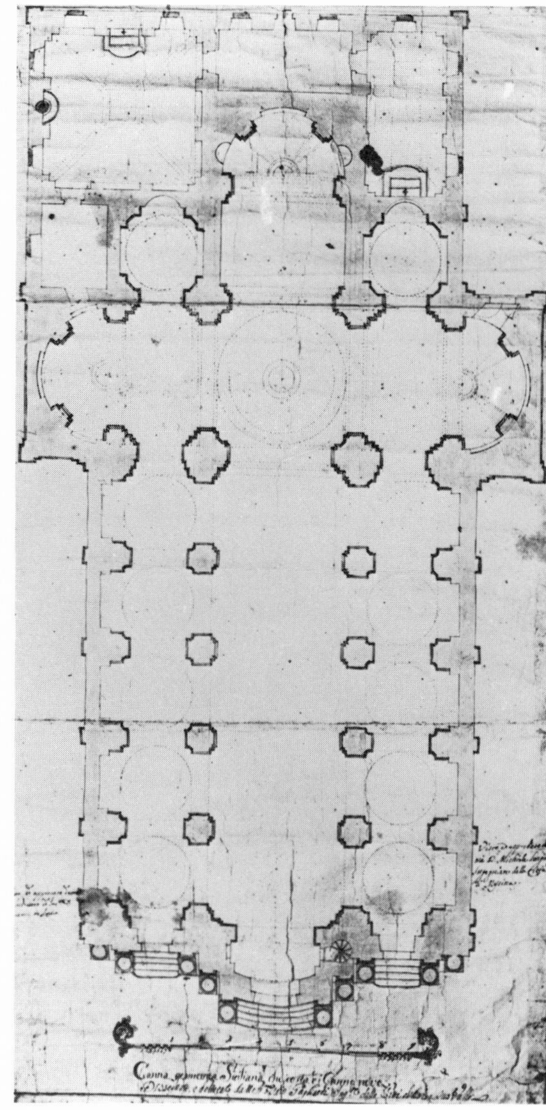

112 S. Giorgio, Ragusa. Façade elevation. R. Gagliardi.

113 S. Giorgio, Ragusa. Plan. R. Gagliardi.

Both drawings are in the sacristy, S. Giorgio.

Gagliardi in Noto

Gagliardi's work in Noto reflects in the same way as his treatise the uneven nature of his creative talent. Buildings with different styles and contrary approaches and concerns sometimes rose at the same time. He seems to have had no master plan for the architecture of Noto and makes only minimal attempts to produce continuities for the viewer. Nevertheless his personal style appears in whatever project he is attempting; and his design signatures, such as the segmental pediment with a bolection frieze or the multi-lobed aperture surround, invariably appear in his work.

The analysis of seven buildings designed by Gagliardi which follows illustrates the variation in his style. Four of the buildings (S. Maria dell'Arco, the church of S. Chiara, the church of S. Domenico, and SS. Crocifisso) are definitely Gagliardi's while three (S. Carlo, S. Nicolò and SS. Salvatore) are attributed to him on the basis of stylistic evidence. The buildings are arranged in a stylistic progression from the most primitive exteriors to the most sophisticated. Gagliardi's monastery of S. Maria dell'Arco is discussed first because it is his best documented, most conservative, and earliest monumental Netinese building. In examining both S. Maria dell'Arco and S. Chiara it should be borne in mind that Gagliardi may have been finishing structures begun by earlier architects. The conservatism of these buildings may be due to post-earthquake caution on the part of Gagliardi's patron, the church. But even taking conservative patrons and restricted original plans into account, Gagliardi still stamped the buildings with his own style. His other Netinese buildings, S. Domenico, S. Nicolò, SS. Crocifisso, S. Carlo, and SS. Salvatore, are all close to a High or Late Baroque style of the kind we found in his treatise.

114 S. Giorgio, Ragusa. Longitudinal section. R. Gagliardi.

115 S. Giorgio, Ragusa. Elevation of side. R. Gagliardi.

S. Maria dell'Arco

S. Maria dell'Arco, Gagliardi's first commission in Noto, presents typical problems in examining his Noto works: the structure has been added to for more than two hundred years, and at the same time it has been steadily decaying (Pls 117–118). During the first years S. Maria dell'Arco was a temporary structure.[35] Later, a permanent structure was built. Building was begun in 1713; sixty-six years later in 1779 construction was still continuing.[36] Much later, in the 1860s, the Cistercian order, which owned the building, was suppressed by the government, and the building was used as a bishop's administrative headquarters.[37] Later, the whole complex, falling into ruin, was subdivided into apartments (Pl. 118) and the church closed. Despite the deterioration and internal reconstruction of the complex, the building, with all its puzzling changes, today retains a simple forcefulness.

Gagliardi's part in the construction is defined by documents but his overall conception is hard to visualize and his rationale for various parts difficult to grasp. As the complex rose, his architectural and ornamental style matured, with all the changes registered on the building itself. Gagliardi began his participation in building the monastery and church in 1713, when it is recorded that he received a payment for having designed the monastery and assisted in measuring it. He is referred to as a carpenter, not an architect. By 1730 Gagliardi is an architect, assisted among others by Vincenzo Sinatra, a stone cutter who would later become another of Noto's foremost architects. In 1733 Gagliardi designed the plan of the church, in whose building he participated until it was vaulted in 1752 and 1754. He directed the stuccoing, wood carving, and metal ornamentation until his failing health put an end

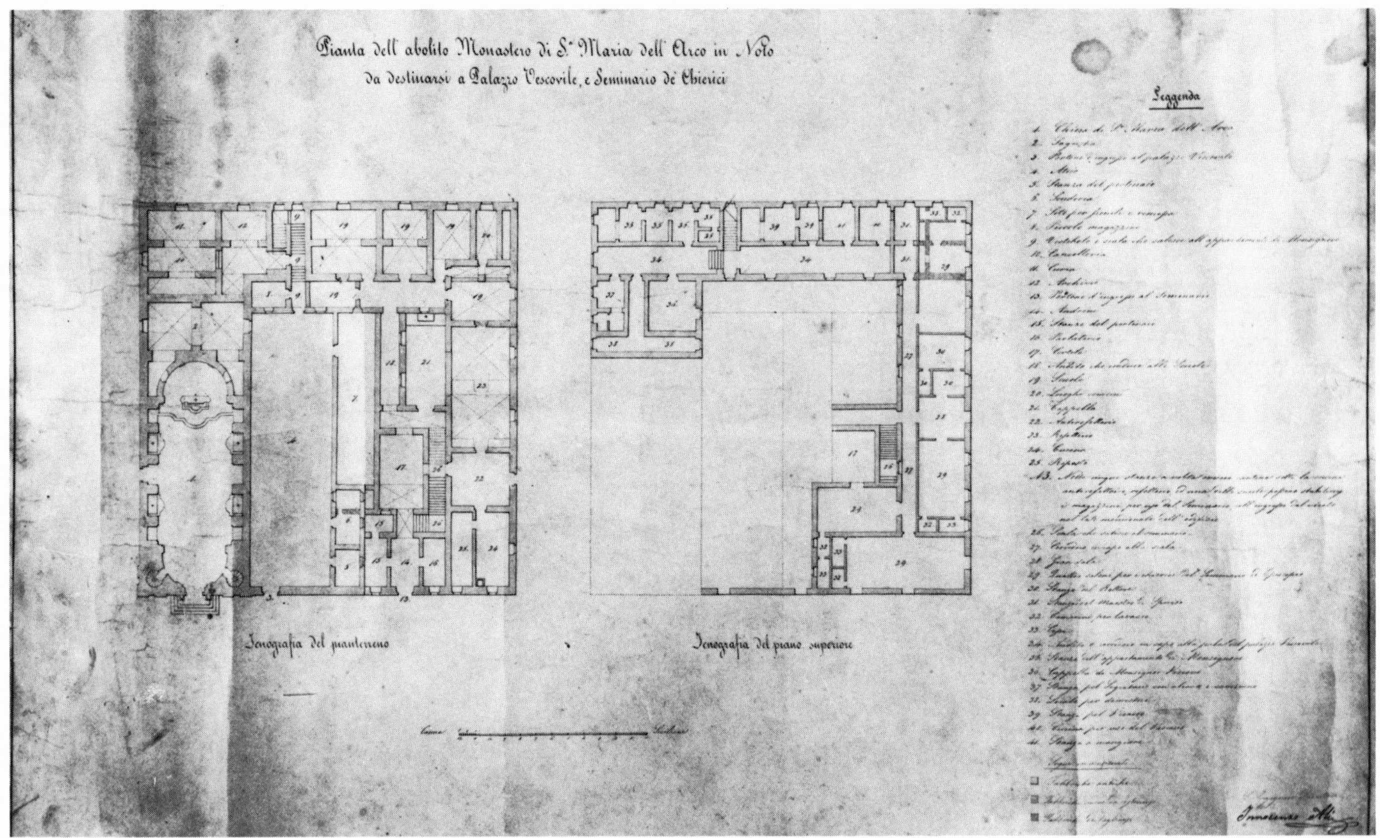

116 Plan of the abolished monastery of S. Maria dell'Arco with modifications.

to his work in the 1760s. Construction on the 'new monastery' and repairs on the church continued at least until the 1770s.

The church, while wholly inconsistent as a total architectural statement, is both easier to analyze and far more telling of Gagliardi's design interest than the monastery. While a few of the apertures of the picturesque ruined monastery dormitory seem to be Gagliardi's, the continued transformation of the monastery renders an analysis almost impossible. The focus here will be the church. The construction of the little church took twenty-five years, during which time the ornamental style seems to have changed so radically that the interior of the church has a completely different feeling from the exterior. Considering Gagliardi's disregard of interior and exterior continuities, this discrepancy is not surprising.

The exterior façade of the church is a single flat awkward block articulated by four low-relief Corinthian pilasters (Pls 119–120). Above the entablature two stubby ruined towers flank a lazy pair of naïvely-carved volutes. The very flat façade represents a fairly typical solution to church building in Sicily, appearing first in sixteenth-century Palermo churches such as S. M. dei Miracoli. Gagliardi drew a far more elaborate version of this kind of façade in his treatise which shows more sophistication. A case could be made that the façade style which appears here, as well as in S. Chiara and S. Maria la Rotunda, was Gagliardi's simple, most conservative solution which he later may have discarded. Patrons may likewise have requested this façade treatment because they were conservative in their tastes or they felt that such a simple construction would much more easily survive earthquakes. The diminution of proportions above the cornice, which seems to have been a standard practice in Sicily, makes it look as though the architect had a façade elevation in mind which was somehow never finished. Judging from other façades of the same type, this one would look incomplete even if the towers were repaired. The design represents Gagliardi at his most primitive.

Each of the three doors leading into the church is executed in a different style, all of which can be found in Gagliardi's work. The main portal in the east is carved very tightly in low relief with compact, slight, Solomonic columns (Pl. 119). Resting on

117 Façade of S. Maria dell'Arco. Looking north on Via Speciale.

the broken pediment of this portal is a window topped by a fleshy, high-relief Baroque pediment. The style of the upper window seems totally out of keeping with the style of the doorway. The northern door of the church (Pl. 122), in the Doric order decorated with bishops' mitres, seems most in keeping with the style of Gagliardi's treatise: but the iconography of the mitre suggests that the portal was probably altered by a later architect when the monastery became a bishop's palace in the nineteenth century. Most Sicilian of the doors is the southern one giving onto the monastery, decorated with beads and angels' heads with deeply undercut leaf-like ornament (Pl. 121). Gagliardi was at various times responsible for the designs of all these doors and they represent different components of his architectural style: the decorated late Renaissance, the High Baroque, and Sicilian-decorated Baroque.

Gagliardi minutely designed the interior of the church (Pl. 123) and it is here that his imaginative decorative skill can be seen. The church is a double-ended hall with four side chapels on either longitudinal wall. Side entrances equidistant from the altar and the entrance originally bisected the church. Gagliardi plays with the mirror image of the church by continuing the arcade into the altar apse and entrance apse, thus confusing the boundary between the nave and the altar and minimizing the difference between the altar and the entrance. In the elevation of the nave bays Gagliardi sets up a rhythm of decoration and void, a-b-c-b-a, which emphasizes the double-ended plan of the church.

Twenty-two years after he had planned the church, Gagliardi composed the design for the stuccoing which is so important to the interior. Onofrio Russo of Agrigento stuccoed the church according to the designs and models that Gagliardi gave him. His contract spelled out exactly what he was to do. The church:

> . . . must be stuccoed in the Ionic order of Michelangelo Buonarroti with capitals. In addition the architecture above the bases until the Bastard order

118 Exterior doorway and main courtyard, S. Maria dell'Arco. Looking through 3 to courtyard 4, to doorway in Plate 116.

119 S. Maria dell'Arco. Façade.

120 S. Maria dell'Arco. Façade.

121 S. Maria dell'Arco. South door of church.

122 S. Maria dell'Arco. North door of church.

123 S. Maria dell'Arco. Interior of church.

> must be done according to the design of aforementioned Gagliardi, architect, with the added stipulation of having to make four statues for the four niches as the reverend friar and fathers of the monastery request. . . . The architecture of the pilasters must be made following the designs with arabesques in the middle of the church and the models of the raised architecture by the architect. . . . The tablets above the six chapels are to be made in just form of the design. The sculptured bastard order must be made and striated as in the design. . . . The two middle arches must be left out, but so as not to leave the architecture without a finish two vases of flowers must be added to terminate the architecture with order.[38]

Because the ornament of the interior is so close to the detailed instructions of the document we can be assured that we are seeing Gagliardi's hand in the design and we can attribute to him the impressively conceived stucco decorations for this modest church. Festooned Ionic capitals patterned after Michelangelo are placed atop pilasters on either side of the nave. The pilasters themselves, decorated with panels of twisting ribbons of stucco, are boldly punctuated in the centre with heavily embossed eight-pointed stars like those used by Borromini in designs for the church of the Sapienza in Rome. Above the cornice of the nave, buckling acanthus leaves (like those which can be seen in many Roman Baroque churches, e.g. the Gesù) support a short fluted attic pilaster from which delicately carved garlands of flowers rise above the nave. In the centre of the nave, true to the contract, the garlands are replaced by beautiful three-dimensional flowers standing in decorated pots on top of the stunted attic pilasters. These are evidently the pilasters that the document calls Gagliardi's bastard order but as I mentioned earlier they are like others being used in attics throughout Baroque Rome. The flowing, low-relief stucco panels in the attic and the tight but intricately detailed garlands in the vault give the interior a richness which is delicate and interesting while not detracting from the main wall decorations, stuccoed low-relief cartouches. Instead of being three-dimensional, the cartouches are suggested by sinuous twisting stucco borders. These fanciful, flat cartouches call to mind the billowing stairway decorations Juvarra designed for the window decorations of his palazzo Madama in Turin. Above the windows of the nave are miniature broken segmental pediments bending into volutes with gill-like fluting which recall the work of Buontalenti in Florence. The accomplished interior, as a whole quite different from anything to be found on mainland Italy, is indicative of how Gagliardi could combine decoration associated with the Renaissance (Michelangelo), and Mannerism (Buontalenti), with Baroque (Borromini and Juvarra) and with the folk tradition in Sicily (the intricately carved floral decoration).[39]

The Monastery of S. Chiara and its Church

S. Chiara, like S. Maria dell'Arco, has had a long history of construction with accompanying important transformations in its design.[40] In May, 1693, the sisters of the strict Observant rule of the Benedictines requested funds for a temporary loggia which they occupied until a permanent building could be erected. The northern part of the permanent structure of the monastery dormitory probably went up first, as it bears the date of 1717 over its doorway. Either during the construction of the dormitory or in the 1730s, Gagliardi took control of the project, designed the church, directed the roofing of the monastery dormitory, and directed the stuccoing of the church which was carried out by Onofrio Russo before it was dedicated in 1758.

The history of the monastery involves even more transformations than S. Maria dell Arco. The first dormitory design was revised by Gagliardi himself and later probably by Bernardo Labisi (Pls 124–126, Figs 5–6).[41] Labisi is probably responsible for the bifurcated circular stairs (Figs 5–6, letter N) which now lead up to the upper floors of the monastery and are dated 1773 (over doorway, letter L).

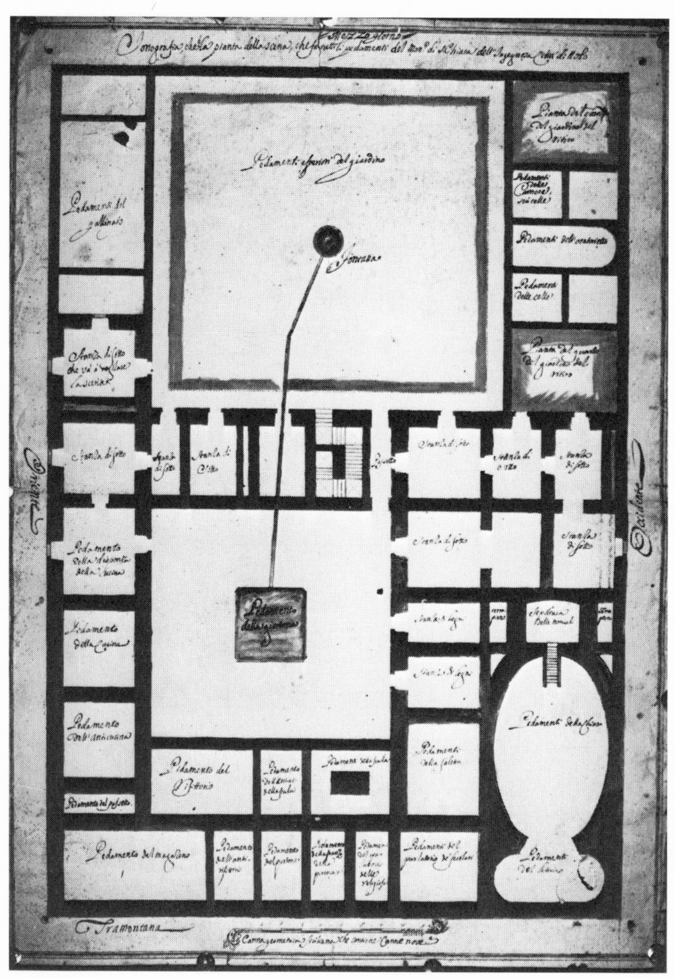

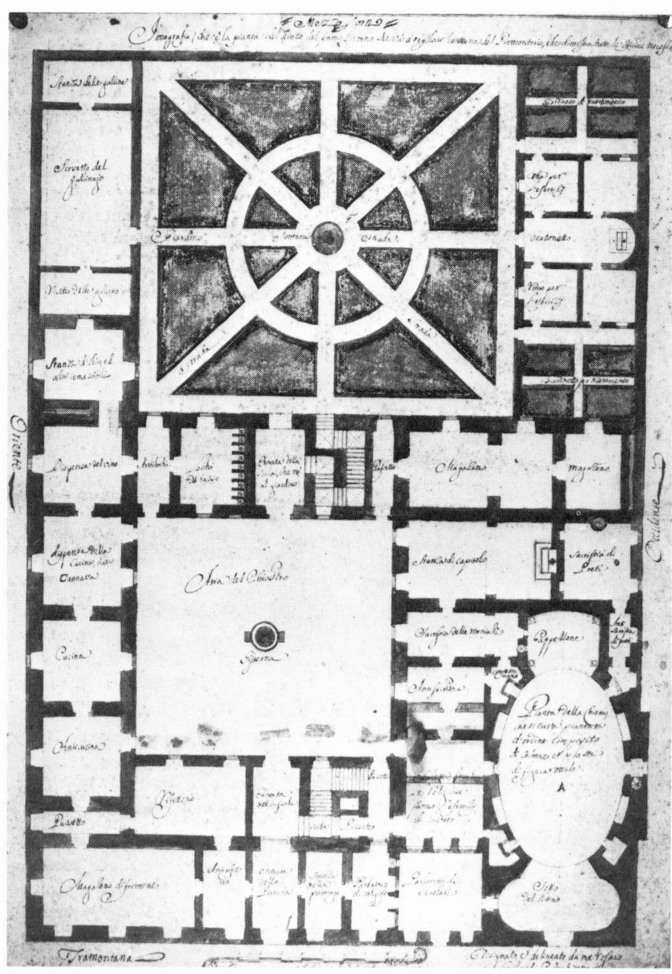

124 S. Chiara. Plan of foundations by R. Gagliardi. Collection of the Biblioteca Comunale di Noto.

125 S. Chiara. Plan of first floor by R. Gagliardi. Collection of the Biblioteca Comunale di Noto.

The project's southern extension remained incomplete and an eastern wing rose which was not in Gagliardi's plan (letter O).[42] Nuns inhabited the monastery until 1918, when, during World War I, it was converted into a barracks for soldiers. It then became a school, the function which it still serves today (letters A, P, B, I, K). During the 1930s, the upper room of the dormitory (letter P) became a dance hall in the summer and a cinema in the winter. In 1949 the city architect wanted to tear most of the structure down to construct a theatre, hotel, post- and telegraph office, but the scheme failed. A new cinema was, however, built on the first floor (letter K). The orchestra of the cinema now serves as a gymnasium for the school while the balcony seats are used by the town band (steps to balcony, letter I). In the 1950s the south-eastern wing of the dormitory (letter O) was demolished in order to construct a modern post office.

The church (officially called S. Maria Assunta, but referred to here as S. Chiara) has fared slightly better than the monastery attached to it. It has remained largely intact since 1758. A new western portal was added in the late eighteenth century for better access from the street west of the church as plans were afoot to lower the Corso on the north. When the street was lowered in the nineteenth century, the main portal of the church stood isolated from the roadway, which prompted a side door on the western side of the church to be converted into the only usable entrance to the church (letter H). The church, originally richly decorated in coloured tiles, has been redecorated with marble floor and its off-white walls whitewashed.

As in S. Maria dell'Arco, Gagliardi makes no attempt to express the interior of the church on the exterior of the monastic complex. His treatment of the whole exterior of the building shows an interest in massive forms with relatively unadorned, flat wall surfaces. However, in S. Chiara he added a tower to the solid mass which serves

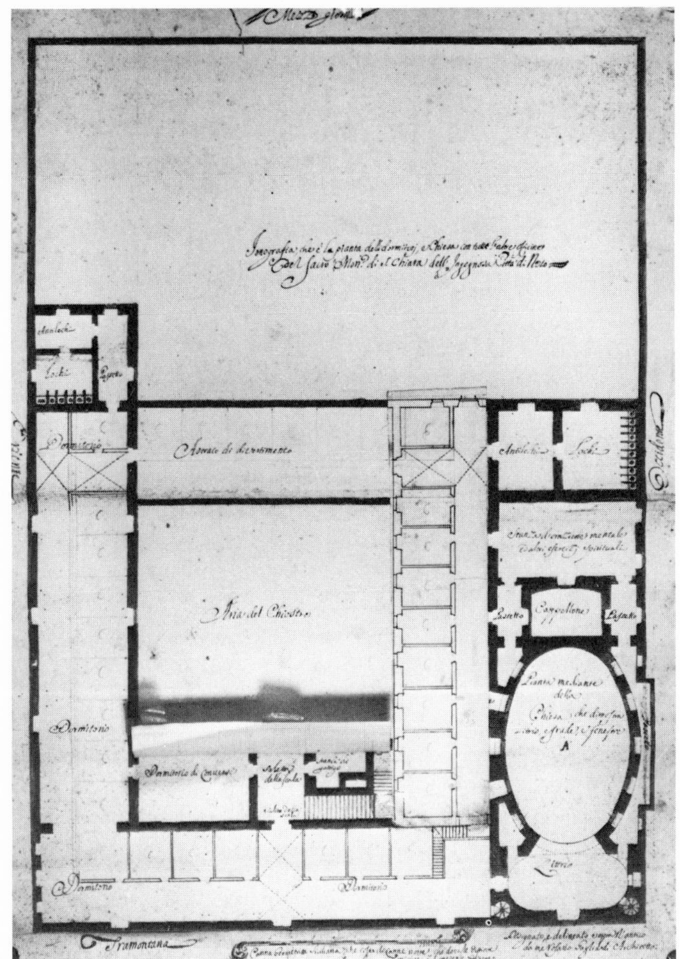

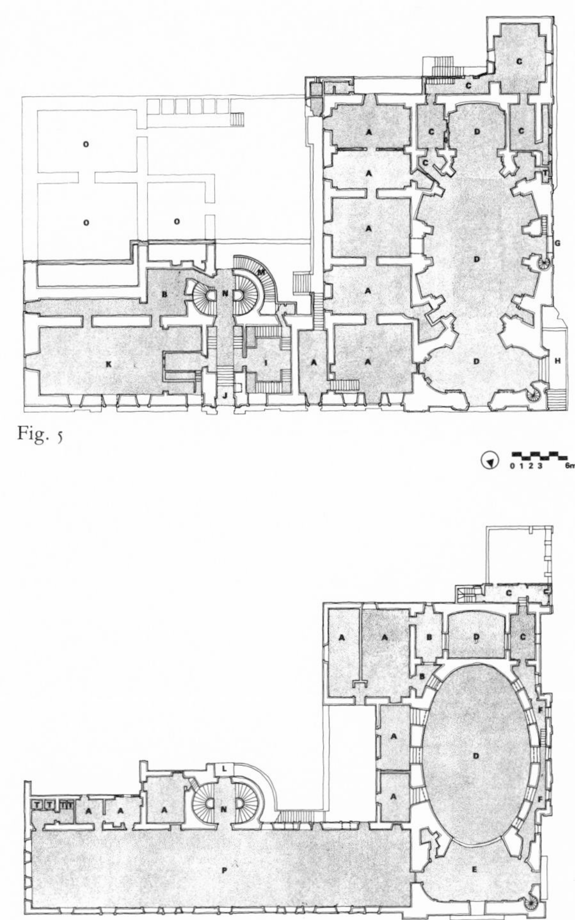

126 S. Chiara. Plan of second floor by R. Gagliardi. Collection of the Biblioteca Comunale di Noto.

Fig. 5 Former monastery of S. Chiara. First floor.

Fig. 6 Former monastery of S. Chiara. Second floor.

A school classrooms and offices
B school storage rooms
C nuns' quarters
D church
E choir loft
F nuns' passage
G blocked eighteenth-century portal
H added portal and porch
I modern stairs to theatre mezzanine
J entrance lowered to street level, nineteenth century
K old cinema, now school gymnasium
L inscription reading 1773
M twentieth-century stairs
N eighteenth-century stairs not in original plan
O demolished portion
P former cinema and theatre, now classrooms
T privy

as both bell-tower and belvedere (Pl. 127). The rigid western side of the monolithic church exterior unexpectedly juts out, side-stepping the protruding nave of the oval church. This side extension, with a single doorway (now sealed) flanked by two pilasters (letter G), was probably intended to present a façade of the church to the large main square of the town, much of which is now built over (Pl. 128).

Across the main square is the tower façade of S. Carlo (Pl. 47), the church of the Jesuit college. The great tower of S. Carlo is a more sophisticated version of the blocklike tower construction of S. Chiara. The third storey of the Jesuit tower in fact has a filled-in square arcade like that of S. Chiara which can be seen from the side of the building. The façade of S. Chiara might be seen as a step to Gagliardi's more sophisticated work on S. Carlo.

The handling of decorative details on the otherwise plain exterior of the building indicates a rejection of what we might call Baroque characteristics. The segmental arch over the doorway bears down like a lid over the façade, and is not broken in the Baroque style. There is a lack of flow between one part of the façade and another, and the decoration helps to reinforce this rigidity rather than lessen it. When separate decorative elements are superimposed upon one another, as in the doorway of the church and the window above it, they retain their individuality.

Many of the individual decorative elements of the façade have their own power and uniqueness in spite of the fact that they do not seem to work together. Though rejected overall, Baroque details creep in. For example, the window on the northern side of the church is very similar to that of S. Maria dell'Arco: its jubilant Baroque style seems particularly out of keeping with the rigid, almost brittle carving on the bell-tower. This same window also seems clearly out of phase with the Doric western portal. Likewise, the Doric portal and the articulation of the western side of

127 S. Chiara. Exterior from the north-west.

128 S. Chiara. Exterior from the south-west showing door originally opening onto the main piazza.

the building seem out of keeping with the rest of the aperture surrounds in the building; set in the Doric western side of the church is an exquisite, highly ornamented doorway, the final disjunctive Baroque element.

The most unusual features of S. Chiara's sombre façade are the decorative pilaster capitals laid over the Doric pilasters at the north-east and north-west corners (Pl. 129). They show the same acute attention to detail that was apparent in the stuccoing of S. Maria dell'Arco. But here the lightness of the stucco is replaced by a disturbing static quality. The pilasters are divorced from their role as supports: elements like volutes, which usually give capitals a sense of structure, here have been inverted in the style of Borromini and transformed into decorative strapwork. The little head in the centre, the decorative garlands, and the deeply incut, yet frozen forms have a vague similarity to Borrominesque experiments.

Either Gagliardi's stone carver did not interpret his drawing correctly or Gagliardi himself produced an unusually static capital design. In the carving of the capitals swiftness and delicacy are left behind for a slower rhythm in which distinct elements do not fuse together. Each equally weighted form contradicts the next: the heavy festoons break the upward movement of the acanthus leaves; whatever dynamism the volutes might have is contradicted by the compact and symmetrical cherub face which appears out of nowhere; the upper volutes cannot produce a directional energy because they are mimicked by lesser volutes which defuse them: they turn out and up while the ends of the shell between them turn down and out. On the bottom of the capital lesser volutes strapped together turn in and over while below tiny volutes turn in and up. It is no wonder the upper volutes seem static.

One wonders how much Gagliardi was influenced by the older seventeenth-century decoration he might have seen in the ruins of Noto Antica, and if fragments

129 S. Chiara. Pilaster capital.

130 S. Chiara. Interior.

131 S. Domenico. Façade.

of this decoration may have affected his conservative treatment of pilaster capitals. We know from documents that several capitals for S. Chiara were brought to the building in the first years after the quake.[43] These capital designs may be derived from those earlier capitals, or might even incorporate parts of them.

The only comparable invention in capital designs in eighteenth-century Sicily occurs in Vaccarini's capitals in Catania. Both Vaccarini and Gagliardi should be regarded less as provincial Sicilians than as participants in the wave of ornamental invention which had enveloped Europe from Sicily to southern Germany and France.[44] Vaccarini, perhaps directly inspired by Guarini, created thematic capitals to match the iconographic content of the churches they adorn. However, Gagliardi was not interested in any such statement in S. Chiara and opted instead for pure ornamental complexity.

Gagliardi's oval ground plan for the church is expectedly pedestrian, based on a model initiated by the church of S. Anna dei Palafrenieri (begun in 1572) and repeated in a host of oval churches built in the sixteenth and seventeenth centuries in Rome.[45] His plan for the church shows him once again using an essentially scenographic approach. One looks from the doorway through the atrium to columns which frame the sanctuary. The choir behind the sanctuary is set off by columns and an arch behind which the altar stands.

It is again through his ornament that Gagliardi captures the organic potentialities of the building. To the nave of the church he gives an a-B-c-B-a rhythm by modulating the distance between the twelve columns, the size of the bays, and the ornament (Pl. 130, Fig. 5). The carver, Onofrio Russo, was working on the church just before he began S. Maria dell'Arco in 1755. Gagliardi's decoration as interpreted by Russo is as free-flowing and bold as Juvarra's, particularly when Gagliardi emphasizes the roundness of the oval windows of the attic. The motif of figures standing upon pedestals above the entablature could probably be traced back to Palladio, whose treatise Gagliardi may have known.[46]

In order to provide the nuns of the monastery with private views of the service, Gagliardi raised a high attic above his cornice throwing the nine windows illuminating the sanctuary into the dome itself (Fig. 6) – as he did in Study E of his treatise (Pl. 107). Again he is drawing on another typical sixteenth-century solution, such as that of the interior of S. Giacomo degli Incurabili in Rome.[47] These windows are now blocked, but the iron or lattice grating which covered the oval windows of the sanctuary must have added considerably to the richness of the decoration of the church, and with the hidden nuns praying and singing, the church would have been alive with sounds and mystery which can still be heard and felt in parts of Sicily today.

In contrast to the exterior of the church where no attention is paid to its iconography, in the interior Gagliardi united the iconography with the plan and interior elevation. The church is dedicated to S. Maria Assunta – the Virgin who rises into heaven after her death. The Assumption of the Virgin takes place in a painting on the altar, but the twelve apostles stand on columns around the nave, so in effect the Assumption occurs not only in the apse but also in the centre of the church itself. Over the arch in front of the altar God the Father looks out into the nave; angels and clouds appear at the top of the vault. In the spirit of his church and in the motifs he uses, Gagliardi appears to have been aware of the High Roman Baroque concept which Bernini popularized of the church as religious theatre. The delicacy of this drama is protected from the outside world by the massive exterior of the church and the dormitory, which envelop it like a tight strongbox.

The Church of the Convent of S. Domenico

When Gagliardi began the façade of the convent church of S. Domenico (dedicated as SS. Annunziata) he inaugurated High Baroque architecture in Noto one hundred years after the heyday of the style in Rome.[48] What separates Gagliardi from his Roman contemporaries is the pure semi-circular curve of his façade which recalls the

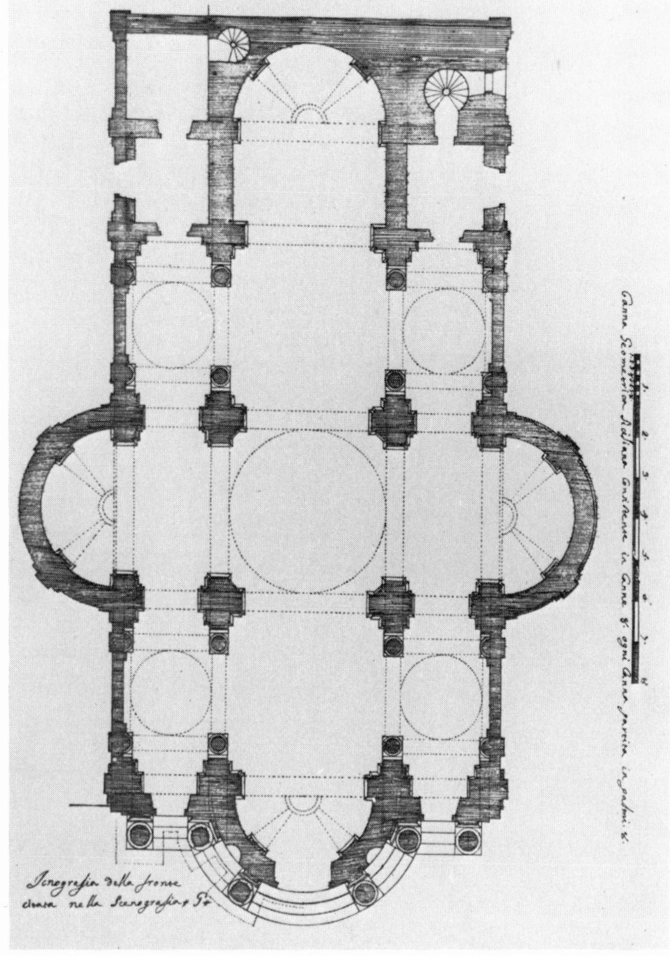

132 Façade study G. Treatise by R. Gagliardi, Di Blasi Collection, Noto.

133 Section study G. Treatise by R. Gagliardi, Di Blasi Collection, Noto.

134 Plan study G. Treatise by R. Gagliardi, Di Blasi Collection, Noto.

boldness of the rounded porticos used by Bernini (in S. Andrea al Quirinale) and Cortona (in S. Maria della Pace). Eighteenth-century Roman architects like Gregorini, Passalacqua and Raguzzini, although interested in curved façades, favoured compound, depressed curves. Gregorini's and Passalacqua's façade for S. Croce in Gerusalemme, for example, gains its interest through the subtle curving of the wall and the canting of pilasters, a solution quite different from Gagliardi's clear and emphatic curve which is underscored by freestanding columns placed on the orthogonal to it. Gagliardi's use of columns on his curved façade contrasts strikingly to the eighteenth-century Roman practice which favoured the use of pilasters on curved façades. The volutes have a robustness which is quite contrary to those used in Rome (e.g. the façade of the Hospital of S. Gallicano). The style of S. Domenico's façade therefore seems closer to that of seventeenth-century High Baroque buildings than to those of eighteenth-century Rome. However, Gagliardi's very energetic and assertive façade does not look like a nostalgic remembrance of what was, but a very persuasive assertion of what is. For him the components that he chose are relevant to his time and place and his aesthetic sensibilities.

S. Domenico (Pl. 131) differs from Gagliardi's earlier block-belfry façades such as S. Chiara because it is more articulated (organized in terms of Orders) and because it breaks the planar wall. Its façade follows a more common Italian division in which

135 S. Domenico. Interior of nave from altar.

136 S. Domenico. Arcade and clerestory window. The window decorations are not the same as those in Plate 134.

137 S. Domenico. Chancel. The gallery is not designed following the plans in the Gagliardi section: a window has been added (see Plate 133).

the second storey is not as wide as the lower one. It seems to be one of the earliest of Gagliardi's convex façades, though perhaps predated by the unfinished façade of SS. Crocifisso. As pointed out in the preceding chapter, Sicilian architects, Gagliardi included, were well behind Roman architects who used curved façades as early as the 1630s. Among the pioneers of curved façades in Sicily were Vaccarini, the Catanese architect, whose S. Giuliano was begun in 1739, and Amico, the Trapanese architect, whose S. Anna, Palermo, was begun in 1726.

Comparing his two-storey church façade with that of Amico's S. Anna in Palermo, we find Gagliardi's design seems to breathe with well-proportioned ease without tension. The transfer of momentum from side aisles to upper façade is accomplished through massive if lazy volutes, and the turning façade does not seem to be actively pushed and pulled. In the façade of S. Anna just the opposite is true: the outward twisting façade is unexpectedly pushed backward in the centre, seemingly capturing energy within it and thus creating tension. Gagliardi's curved façade of S. Domenico retains instead a kind of pure majesty and calm.

Unfortunately, Gagliardi left not a single sketch which discloses the thinking process he engaged in while considering the potentialities of the curved façade of S. Domenico. This façade is in contrast to the belfry-façade of his church of S. Giorgio at Ragusa designed in 1744.[49] In S. Giorgio, Gagliardi achieved the appearance of convexity by placing columns at the diagonal on either side of the central façade. Each pair of columns steps out a little farther than the one behind it, but the façade behind the columns does not turn. Unlike S. Giorgio, S. Domenico's façade is smoothed out into a pure semicircle with columns giving substantially less emphasis to its shape. Wall surface becomes more dominant than columns. The components of the S. Giorgio façade are present, but enter into an airy, convex composition in S. Domenico which is further accentuated by a curving stairway.

S. Domenico is the only completed project that Gagliardi designed which he included in his treatise (Pls 132–134); for him it must have represented an especially beautiful solution to a church plan and elevation. The plan has a respectable pedigree in the modified Greek cross quincunx (five-domed) plan used extensively in Italy during the sixteenth century and popularized again in the eighteenth century.[50] Gagliardi may have liked it because it provided a wide variety of scenographic possibilities. However, the plan, elevation, and façade of S. Domenico in Gagliardi's treatise do not correspond exactly to the church itself. Gagliardi would probably have preferred to have had apses at the ends of the transepts, as in the plan, but the street running north along the side of the church made them impossible. Ornamental surrounds within the church do not correspond to those on the section in the treatise (cf. Pls 133, 135–37) and the designs do not indicate the tower which was built on the eastern side of the church. But on the whole S. Domenico is a faithful actualization of the designs. Urbanistically, the church addressed the whole Piazza of S. Domenico from its commanding site and formed the perfect accent for the western part of Noto.

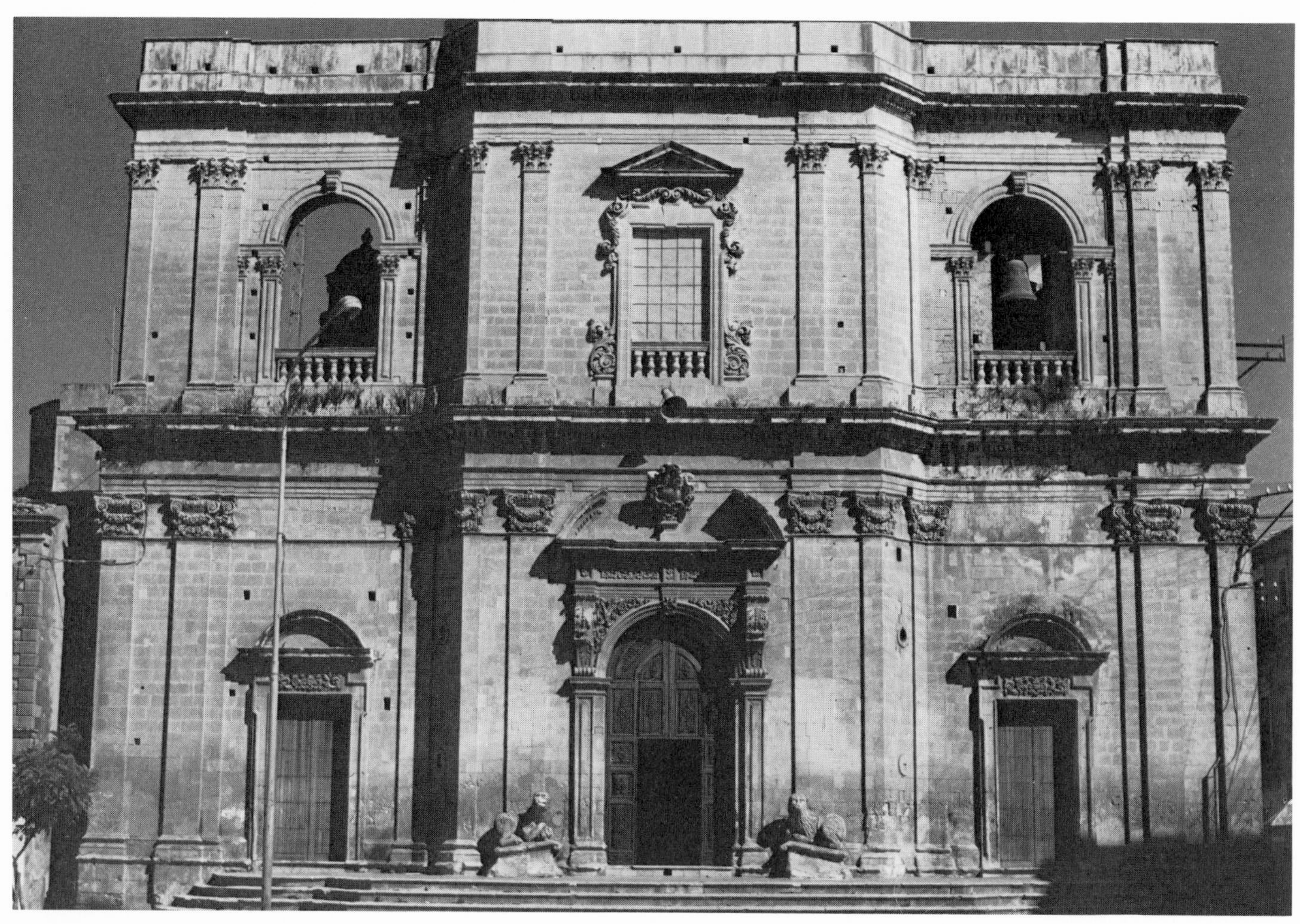

Gagliardi Fragments: SS. Crocifisso and S. Nicolò

Gagliardi appears to have participated in the design and construction of the two most important churches in Noto, S. Nicolò, the Chiesa Madre, on the main piazza, and SS. Crocifisso on the main square on the summit.[51] They are not only ecclesiastically the most important but also form the north-south axis of the city plan. Unfortunately neither is a particularly fine building architecturally. The plans for these churches were among the earliest in Noto Nuova, yet their construction continued into the last century. The façade of SS. Crocifisso was never finished.

As the most important church on the summit and the second most important in Noto, SS. Crocifisso had to be designed as one of the most imposing of Noto's churches. The first church on the site was probably temporary and must have been pulled down and rebuilt just as S. Nicolò was. The first church may have faced in an easterly direction, as I indicated earlier, and it may survive in part in the Landolina chapel in the western transept. The second church of SS. Crocifisso still remains incomplete (Pl. 138). Gagliardi is called the architect in several documents, so there is little doubt of his part in the planning and building of the church. A document of 1728 charges him with executing the designs for the capitals. These capitals can still be seen on the sides and façade of the building (Pl. 138). The pilasters with their elaborate scrollwork and garlands have the same stiff two-dimensional quality as the pilasters on the façade of S. Chiara by Gagliardi. The plan for the church, a three-aisled Latin cross very much like Gagliardi's plan for S. Giorgio in Ragusa, is an old formula which affords maximum internal space under the constraint of limited building technology. The façade with its stepped-out central portion is reminiscent of a plan accompanying Gagliardi's treatise. But the façade is less successful than many of Gagliardi's other buildings because of its lack of columnar emphasis. Exactly how it would have been completed is open to question but there is no doubt that this church was not one of Gagliardi's finest.

138 SS. Crocifisso. Façade.

139 Tower of old monastery of SS. Salvatore.

140 Tower of the church of S. Carlo Borromeo. Detail.

The ground plan of S. Nicolò, which is much like that of SS. Crocifisso, was probably designed by Gagliardi, as were the walls of the side of the nave. The distinctive towers of this church were added after the main façade was already constructed up to the upper cornice, as the change in cornice design on the substructure of the towers indicates. According to the date on the upper part of the façade immediately below the capital on the eastern tower, the façade (Pl. 96) was in construction in 1768 long after Gagliardi could have hoped to direct it.[52] The church was still under construction in the 1790s, perhaps because of eighteenth-century earthquake damage. Although the ornament on the façade and the stiff handling of the disposition of the columns does not seem Gagliardesque, the overall design of the façade was no doubt taken from a restrained two-tower façade design in Gagliardi's treatise (Pl. 109). If nothing else, the church façade illustrates the influence of Gagliardi's designs after his death.

Gagliardi and the Belfry Façades of SS. Salvatore and S. Carlo

Two of Noto's most interesting buildings, the monastery of SS. Salvatore and the Jesuit church of S. Carlo, are also the most difficult to date and attribute, but it is possible Gagliardi had a hand in both.

Part of the difficulty in discussing SS. Salvatore is the complexity of its construction history.[53] In addition to the problem of the discordance between the upper and lower portions of the monastery (discussed in Chapter 5), the building has been gutted. The most striking remnant of the older building is a tower which overlooks Piano S. Francesco. The tower (Pl. 139) looks as if it could have been Gagliardi's because of its bulging balustrades, and its dramatic though delicate ornament. In particular, the interlocking C-shaped volutes are unmistakably Gagliardesque. But unlike any other façades that are known to be designed by Gagliardi, this one has three cusps cutting out into space, as if in imitation of

Borromini's famous Baroque church of S. Carlo alle Quattro Fontane in Rome. Unlike Borromini's church, in which the central portion of the entablature recedes into a cusp on the top tier and billows out on the bottom tier, the SS. Salvatore tower repeats three cusps across its façade on each level, establishing a single repeated rhythm. But even with a single repeated cusp the undulating façade seems too Borrominesque for the more classically Baroque Gagliardi. Furthermore, the tower is stylistically united to the upper part of the monastery rather than to the lower part. Taken together the tower and upper part of the monastery appear to have been inspired by the hospital and church of S. Gallicano designed by Filippo Raguzzini, the master of Roman Rococo. The repeated quatrefoil and cusped façade of the tower are reminiscent of Raguzzini's work, and it is clear that whoever designed SS. Salvatore knew of it, possibly through engravings like those of Giuseppe Vasi's. But whether the unknown architect was Gagliardi or not remains a question.

The problem of the attribution of the belfry façade of the Jesuit church of S. Carlo is less difficult to solve than that of SS. Salvatore (Pls 47, 140).[54] The Jesuit college was built in several campaigns, but the church itself seems to have been the work of one man, probably Gagliardi. Gagliardi signed for materials used in the construction of the Jesuit college and he also worked on the Jesuit college in Syracuse. Likewise the aperture surrounds, the second-storey bolection frieze, the shape of the volutes, and the ornaments on the balustrade are Gagliardesque. The conservative three-aisled Latin cross of the church likewise seems in keeping with Gagliardi's style. The use of the quatrefoil void punched into the uppermost storey recalls Study G in Gagliardi's treatise. Even the superimposition of free-standing columns is a common Gagliardi motif in his façades. It is significant that Amico illustrates almost identical columnar proportions to those of S. Carlo in his treatise which Gagliardi seems to have known. What is distinctly non-Gagliardesque about the façade is the tension between the outer free-standing columns orthogonal to the street front and the interior pairs orthogonal to the curved portion of the façade. The central portion of each level bracketed by the interior pair of columns extends out from the convex façade, yet not as far out as the outermost columns. The relationship between the interior and exterior columns running up the length of the façade is therefore perplexing, and adds a discordant note in the composition which seems unlike Gagliardi. Nevertheless, the belfry façade of S. Carlo is probably the work of Gagliardi while attribution of SS. Salvatore is more questionable.

Rosario Gagliardi the Architect

Rosario Gagliardi was a provincial architect who never worked in important or prestigious Italian cities; he probably never went to Rome, never designed in Palermo, never even saw Naples. He worked in a seldom-visited obscure area, south-eastern Sicily. He seems to have had an innocence which many of his colleagues in Rome who were familiar with Baroque architecture of the seventeenth century lacked. It is likewise true that he had none of the spatial inventiveness of his contemporaries in Piedmont or Germany. But Gagliardi approaches architecture with a freshness that other architects in more central locations were often unable to give their buildings. For Gagliardi, Renaissance rules and High Baroque enthusiasm are real. Unlike some of his contemporaries, he is not a bored purveyor of worn ideas. He is struggling with his Sicilian identity, the freedom of the Italian Rococo, the rules of the Renaissance and the virtuosity of the Baroque all at the same time. Considering his distance from architecture centres, he absorbed new trends with sophistication. His medium for catching the current styles in decoration was the printed page. By means of books, engravings, and perhaps conversations with passing architects he tried to keep abreast of current developments. With his prodigious talent for lively façades, exquisite decoration, and constant decorum, he provided a hybrid Sicilian Baroque, an amalgam of Renaissance plans and order, Baroque massing, Sicilian decoration, and his own exquisite sensibility. It is Gagliardi's buildings which reproduce vertically and in three dimensions the plan of the city of Noto; his church of S. Domenico boldly steps forward with a convex façade to define the northern side of the Piazza of S. Domenico. The towers of both S. Carlo and S. Chiara are visual markers for the corners of the main piazza and make it understandable, just as the domes of SS. Crocifisso and S. Nicolò underscore the link between the upper and lower parts of Noto. Gagliardi, more than any other architect who worked in Noto, influenced our perception of the plan through his individual and diverse buildings. It is his vivid style and his sensitivity in responding to urban context which makes Noto so noteworthy as a visually successful environment.

Chapter 9 Sinatra and Labisi: Interpreters of an Idiom

During the late 1740s when Gagliardi was at the height of his career, two other architects began to practise in Noto. One was Gagliardi's assistant, Vincenzo Sinatra, and the other was Paolo Labisi, a Netinese aristocrat. From the buildings and drawings that can be attributed to them, it can be said that both men were profoundly influenced by their contact with Gagliardi. But while they borrowed liberally from his High Baroque Sicilian style, they sapped it of its vitality. They brought Netinese architecture into the European sphere of the Late Baroque and Rococo by lightening Gagliardi's style and infusing it with European grace. With their architecture contemporary European styles could be said to have reached Noto.

Political turmoil increased in Sicily during the eighteenth century. Over 430 years of Spanish rule ended for the perpetual colony in 1713 when Sicily was ceded to the House of Savoy. In 1720 it was ceded again, to Austria in exchange for Sardinia. The Spaniards received Sicily in 1735 but in 1759, Don Carlos, on inheriting the throne of Spain, gave that of the two Sicilies (Southern Italy and Sicily) to his third son who became Ferdinand III of Sicily. This remained Sicily's political status until 1860 when Garibaldi landed at Marsala.[1]

The change in architectural climate which affected Sinatra and Labisi may have been due to the influx of foreigners into Sicily in the mid-eighteenth century.[2] Foreign ideas would have a greater impact on them than on Gagliardi because they began practising almost thirty years after he began. The time lag usual in the dissemination of intellectual ideas in Sicily caused the major architectural developments of the early eighteenth century to emerge in Noto in the mid 1700s. In addition, Sinatra and Labisi were not as strongly traditional as Gagliardi and were, therefore, more susceptible to new sources. Renaissance treatises and Gagliardi's architecture still held sway, but Rococo and Neo-classical styles likewise began to appear.

Vincenzo Sinatra (active 1730–67)[3]

Sinatra's personality is not as well-defined as Labisi's, and not a single architectural drawing survives which might help to give an idea of his architectural style.[4] Yet his name appears on such quantities of documents that he is hard to ignore.

By the time Gagliardi was paralysed by a stroke in 1761, his nephew by marriage, Vincenzo Sinatra, was directing his affairs.[5] Sinatra worked alongside Gagliardi as his foreman or capomaestro for years and, like Gagliardi, was a commoner. Sinatra was born in 1707, presumably in Noto.[6] In 1726 he married Corrada Bianca and had four children by her.[7] Widowed, he married again in 1745 and in 1746 had a son, whom he christened Rosario, probably in honour of Gagliardi.[8] Sinatra's second wife was the daughter of Antonio Capodicasa and Agata Gagliardi, Rosario Gagliardi's older sister.[9] Sinatra's close family ties with Gagliardi most likely were important for launching him in his career.

Like Gagliardi, Sinatra started his career as a craftsman. He worked with Gagliardi as a stone-cutter in the 1730s on the monastery of S. Maria dell'Arco.[10] In 1742 he worked as the capomaestro for the new city hall being built in the main square of Noto.[11] During the extended building campaign of the city hall Sinatra is alternately referred to as capomaestro and architect. By 1747 when he adjusted property taxes throughout Noto, Sinatra is consistently called architect.[12] His

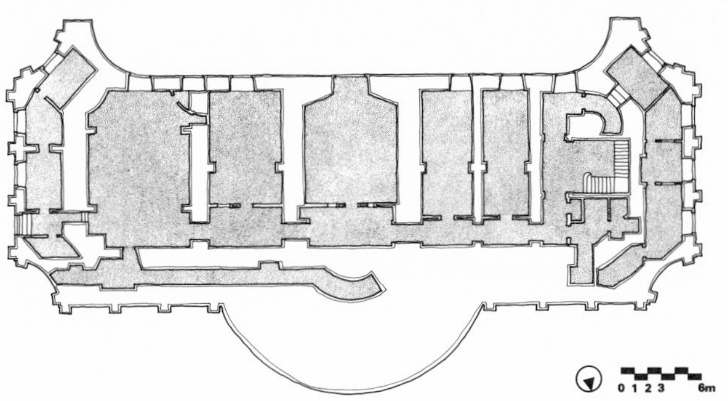

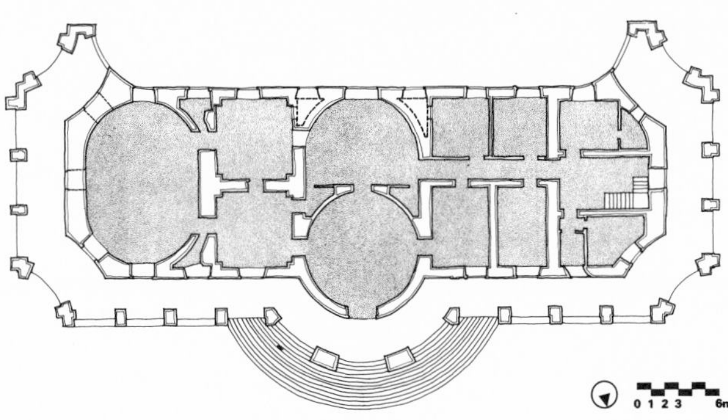

141 City hall from the steps of S. Nicolò.

ig. 7 City Hall. Basement.

ig. 8 City Hall. First Floor.

transition from capomaestro to architect took place as he was building the city hall and courting Gagliardi's niece. It would be improbable to presume that Sinatra did not seek some help from Gagliardi on his first important commission, the erection of Noto's city hall.

Noto's City Hall

For more than ten years Vincenzo Sinatra worked on Noto's city hall (Pl. 141, Figs 7–8). Sinatra is the only architect mentioned in the contracts with which Noto's leading aristocrats bound themselves to pay for the building in 1742, 1743, 1745, and 1746.[13] They probably chose Sinatra because of his reputation as a knowledgeable builder with fine technical skill. Year after year he alone directed the construction: he paid for the selection and transportation of the river stones for the foundations of the building, he supervised the stone-cutting and the laying of the walls, he made models for the capitals. But it is hard to think of the person who signed his name to a poorly drawn map in 1764 (Pl. 23) as the creator of the city hall, which is a truly exquisite and unusual building.

As originally conceived in the eighteenth century, the city hall was to be a single-storeyed, domed building. Nineteenth-century architects planned a second storey (Pl. 142) which was not called for in the original plans.[14] The earliest photographs of the city hall in the late nineteenth century show it in a state of construction with second-storey walls begun above the first storey (Pl. 143). To the detriment of the original conception, the second storey was completed in the 1950s.[15]

142 Nineteenth-century elevation for the city hall project. Francesco Cassone, 16 November 1880. Biblioteca Comunale di Noto.

The original building was drawn (Pl. 144) by the French architect Léon Dufourny in 1789.[16] He showed a single-storey building facing the north with a central dome. Because of the incline of the hill, the south side of the building would have had a single storey and a basement; this is exactly the arrangement that Labisi drew on his veduta of Noto. The veduta (Pl. 40) illustrates the building from the south, showing its rear elevation which would have appeared to be two storeys in height (i.e., basement and first storey).

The arches which adorn the north side of the city hall drawn by Dufourny recall the Italian loggia tradition which played a prominent part in public buildings. But here the similarity with Italian protoypes stops. The original one-storey elevation of the building, its semicircular entrance, its corners with their re-entrant angles, and its oval reception room and central dome are not Italian but French.

Arezzo Prado, a nineteenth-century Netinese historian, mentions in his history of Noto that Giacomo Nicolaci brought the design for the city hall, as well as the designs for the Nicolaci palace and his villa, from Montpellier, France. Giacomo Nicolaci, Baron of Bonfalà, was one of the group of leading aristocrats who founded and funded the city hall. All the aristocrats were somewhat style conscious, but Nicolaci was probably one of the most intellectually active of their number (see p. 118). He was prince of the Accademia degli Trasformati (an academy of noble dilettantes), a recognized astronomer, and something of a linguist who accumulated a rich library and corresponded with intellectuals and telescope makers throughout Europe. He is known to have travelled frequently to Montpellier. It is therefore possible, as Arezzo Prado reports, that Nicolaci brought a design for the city hall from France. Arezzo Prado explains that Nicolaci,

> returning from Montpellier, brought not only the design of his house, and of the Casino in the contrada Falconara, which through the merit of its architecture so decorates our marina of Calabernardo, but also that of the casa comunale,[16a] which was then executed by the celebrated architect Paolo Labisi.[17]

Arezzo Prado seems to be largely, if not completely, correct in his statement. Although the present Palace of Villadorata in Noto, with its wide Baroque balconies, does not fit too well into one's idea of a French palace, the casino that Arezzo Prado mentions does. The casino, called Villa Falconara, is a product of two campaigns. The façade which faces south-east dates from the early eighteenth

143 Late nineteenth-century photograph of the city hall. Mauceri Collection, Noto.

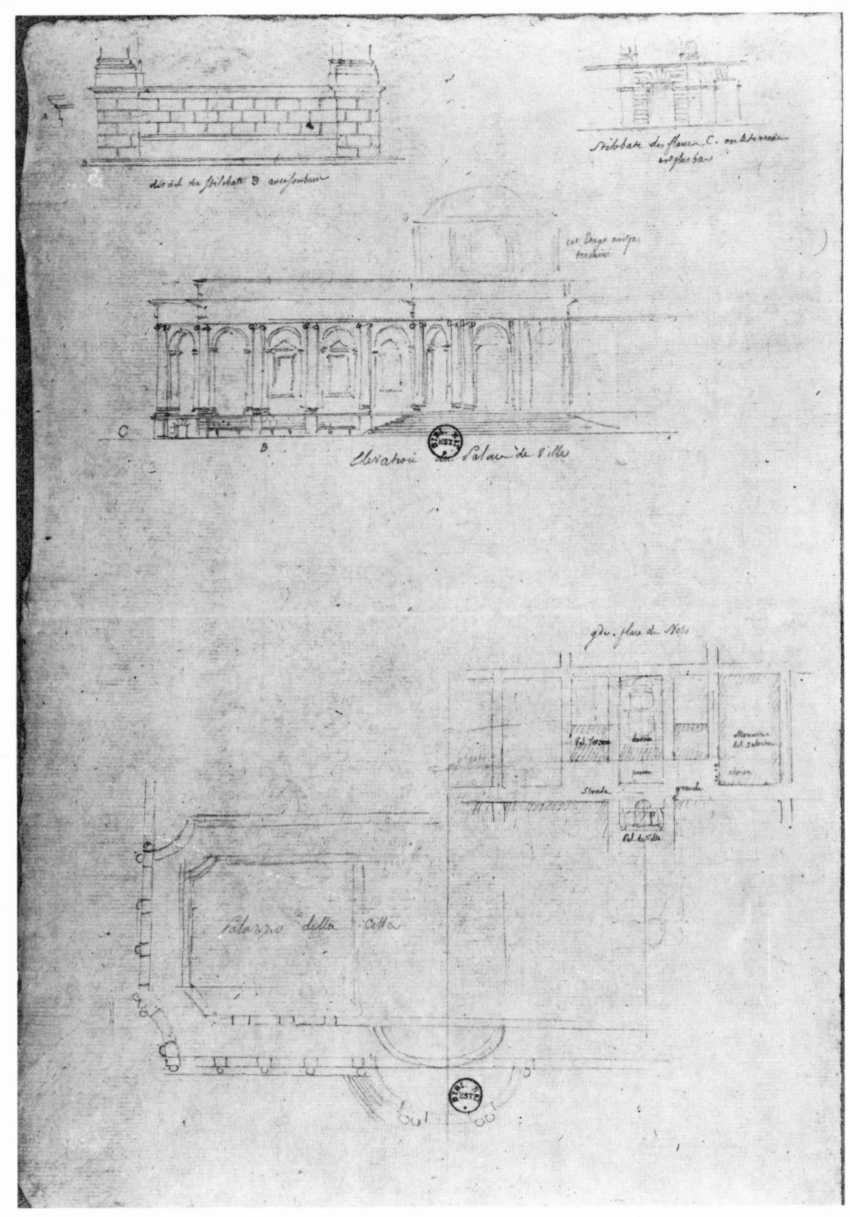

144 Léon Dufourny, *Notes rapportées d'un voyage en Sicile fait par lui en 1789*, MS Cabinet des Estampes, Bibliothèque Nationale, Paris.

century, when naïve Baroque forms were in style in Noto. But the north-west façade, rebuilt in the late eighteenth century, is definitely in a different genre (Pl. 149). The central portion of the façade, a high convex pedimented tower, contrasts with the low, one-storey screen along its base. The design of the gateways, which resemble jutting prows, might be completely original, but the rest of the building is not as unusual as it appears at first glance. The original sources for the conception of such a façade may have been Villa Aldobrandini in Frascati (Giacomo della Porta, 1598–1603). However, the French architect Jean Giral (1679–1753) seems to have picked up della Porta's original idea and classicized it, adding a convex façade in his Château de la Masson built outside Montpellier in 1723 (Pl. 150).[18] The close correspondence between this façade and the façade of Villa Falconara indicates that Arezzo Prado's statement might be in part correct. If, as he states, Labisi did have a part in the erection of the city hall, it was as interpreter of the designs which were sent from France.

The French origin of the design for the city hall is further confirmed by the comments of Dufourny, the Frenchman who drew the building and recognized its provenance.

> The town (city) hall or Palazzo di Città [*sic*] opposite the cathedral is nothing extraordinary, but has been built according to a very elegant design . . . the style has been taken much from our Decotte, Cartaud, and Blondel. . . .[19]

Strangely enough, the city hall of Noto is actually modelled on a French eighteenth-century concept of an Italian palace called *maison à l'italienne*. In reality what the French called Italian palaces had practically no resemblance to their supposed prototypes except in their low roofs and rangy plans. Some of the most famous eighteenth-century Parisian palaces (e.g. Palais Bourbon) were influenced by supposed Italian palace plans and elevations. The major feature of the elevations of these buildings was that they were lower, single-storey structures with unobtrusive roofs. Their plans were typically free-flowing with great attention paid to the arrangement of rooms for maximum utility (a singularly un-Italian trait).

Jacques François Blondel described just such an arrangement in his *De la distribution des maisons de plaisance*, published in 1737.[20] Blondel's treatise deals largely with garden palaces which he states should be one-storey buildings raised only a few steps above the ground. They are to have low roofs 'à l'italienne'. The advantage of the single-storey, low-roofed structures, according to Blondel, is that they eliminate overhead noises because there are no upper storeys, cut down on wasted space by eliminating large reception halls, and yield direct access to the garden.

Several buildings patterned on the *maison à l'italienne* look very much like the original eighteenth-century conception of Noto's city hall. None of the buildings discussed here is the prototype for the city hall. But these structures prove that Noto's city hall was one of a family of buildings whose plans and elevations were derived from a common French prototype. The most intimate structure which can be compared to the city hall is François de Cuvilliés' Amalienburg in the park of the Nymphenburg palace outside Munich, built between 1734 and 1739. The small hunting lodge, which was used as a resting place and dog kennel, has a low profile, re-entrant corner angles, a circular hall, a semicircular garden façade, and a recessed portion on its 'public' façade.

A building which seems even closer to the design of the city hall is Sanssouci (Pls 147, 148), the garden palace of King Frederick II of Prussia, begun in Potsdam in 1745. A comparison between its plan (drawn by Frederick II himself) and the plan of the city hall of Noto illustrates how closely they resemble one another in the outlines of their exterior walls. Both incorporate arcades in their elevation and have a central axis marked by a semicircular exterior. Both have central domes, both incorporate re-entrant angles.

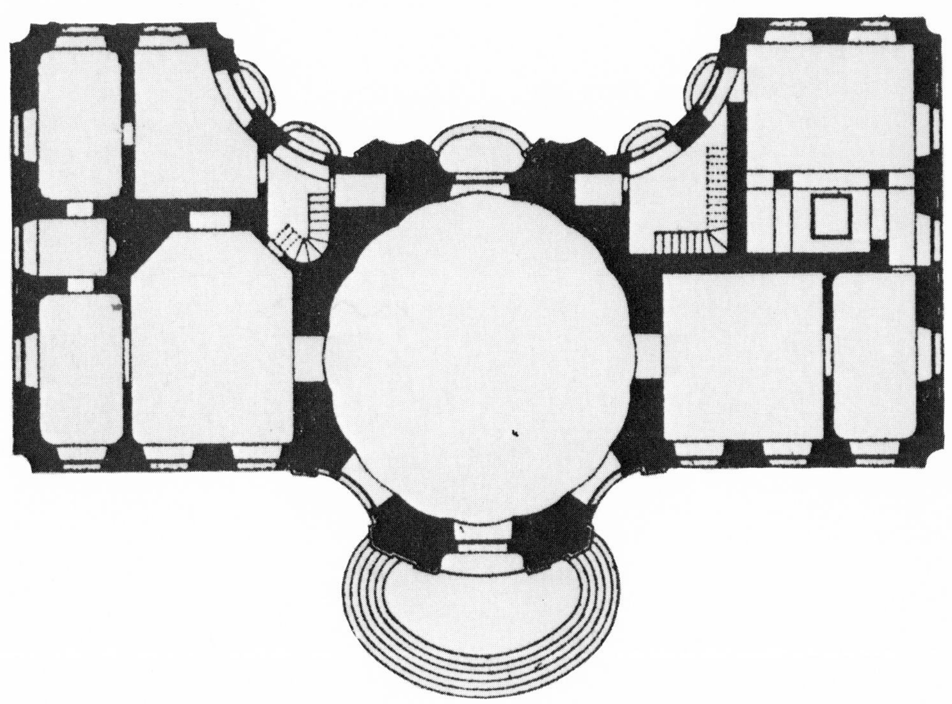

145 Amalienburg, Nymphenburg.

146 Mon Repos, Ludwigsburg Stuttgart, designed by La Guépière.

Pierre-Louis-Philippe de la Guépière's Château de Mon Repos (Pl. 146) near Stuttgart (1760–5) is also in the same tradition as Amalienburg and Sanssouci but composed on a larger scale.[21] The three-storey building hardly adheres to the advice given by Blondel, but it is one example of a large palace structure which has a semicircular arcade in the centre of its garden façade, re-entrant angles at the corner, and a concave 'public' façade. Above the semicircular projection is a dome, just as in Amalienburg and Sanssouci.[22]

While Sanssouci and Mon Repos were conceived and executed according to the spirit of the French conception of a garden palace, Noto's city hall was not a garden palace or an hôtel but a public administrative building. As such it falls outside the goals of French intentions. The Netinese took one building type to use as a model for another with different functional and ceremonial needs. In order to accommodate the foreign building to their city they had to invert it: the concave

147 Sanssouci, Potsdam. Garden façade.

148 Sanssouci, Potsdam. Sketch of proposed ground plan drawn by Frederick II, 1744.

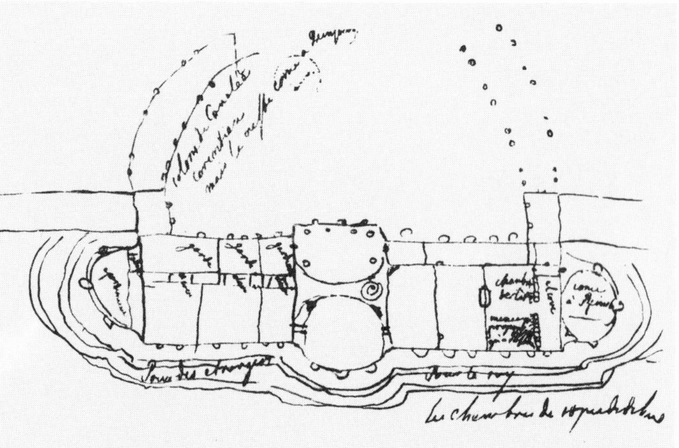

149 Villa Falconara. Northern façade.

150 Château de la Masson, Montpellier. J. Giral, 1723.

151a Garden of Landolina palace (S. Alfano). Pilaster.

façade which should be the public face of the building faces the wrong direction. In Noto the curved garden façade faces the street. The Netinese also created an arcade with Michelangelesque capitals which seems out of keeping with the model. Although the rhetoric of the curved central portion of the loggia was certainly acceptable (Bernini used it on his first Louvre project), the low height of the building makes it appear too small in scale for a city hall. S. Nicolò, the Chiesa Madre, fairly towers over the city hall, diminishing its ceremonial gravity and stature.

The aristocrats of Noto used a French building type which was not specifically adapted to their purpose because they did not understand the discrepancy. They wanted to be a part of the stylish, intellectual elite of Europe so they built the city hall to embody the most urbane ideas they could summon. It is doubtful that they were making an anti-clerical Enlightenment statement by using a French style. They were most likely interested in style only for the sake of style. Considering that the city hall was being built at almost the same time as Sanssouci and apparently came from the same source, they were successful in their attempt to be fashionable. The uniqueness of the city hall stems from the strange translation of a French garden palace into an Italian municipal building. The Netinese took the form, but inadvertently stripped it of its connotations. The result is a unique provincial version of a French idea as interpreted by an Italian, a fitting symbol for the aspirations of Noto's aristocracy, and a perplexing comment on Sinatra's architectural career.

An Elusive Personality

Sinatra's place in the history of Noto's architecture is difficult to discern. In 1750 he had a contract to design the window grating of the Corso façade of the monastery of SS. Salvatore.[23] In 1748, Sinatra was the city tax assessor.[24] He worked with Gagliardi on the monastery of Montevergine in 1747.[25] He worked with Paolo Labisi on the oratory of S. Filippo Neri (1753) (Pl. 76),[26] on a construction for the monastery of S. Agata (1751) (Pl. 91),[27] and on the house of the Crociferi (1770–87). Sinatra's main work seems to have been in conjunction with other architects; when his work appears alone in documents relating to the city hall, the monastery of SS. Salvatore, the dormitory of S. Maria di Gesù, the church of S. Francesco all'Immacolata, the church of S. Francesco di Paola, or the Chiesa Madre, it may not mean that he was the sole architect.[28]

No definitive stylistic traits emerge in the works which might be attributable to him on documentary grounds. The exteriors of S. Maria di Gesù (Pl. 92), S. Francesco all'Immacolata, and S. Francesco di Paola are among the most conservative façades in Noto yet they do not form a coherent group nor do they relate to the city hall. No architectural 'signatures' define Sinatra's artistic personality. In the case of the interior of S. Francesco all'Immacolata for which Sinatra designed two chapels, we find an overall dependence on the interior of S. Maria dell'Arco designed by Gagliardi. The design of S. Francesco is in fact attributable to Gagliardi on the basis of the positioning of the pilasters in the apse and the stucco designs. Likewise, the Chiesa Madre seems to have been liberally adapted from a Gagliardi design (see p. 219, note 18), and exactly how much Sinatra intervened in the design is unclear.

Further stylistic clues, which seem to contradict Sinatra's previously mentioned work, can be gleaned from his tragic association with Paolo Labisi, an architect much his junior. The two men appear to have at least been business partners until the 1770s when a building scandal separated them forever.[29] In 1750 Paolo Labisi drew plans (Pls 160–168) for the house of the Crociferi which was still under construction in the 1770s. Labisi intended the building to be his masterpiece. Sinatra was the 'second architect' of the building, probably supervising the construction. Unfortunately a scandal over building materials and construction costs forced Labisi off the job. Sinatra took over and completed the building in spite of Labisi's repeated protests. Everything in the final building which violates Labisi's plans is probably attributable to Sinatra.

Sinatra defined by the House of the Crociferi Fathers

In 1770, Paolo Labisi protested to the authorities about Sinatra's construction changes in the house of the Crociferi fathers. He specifically mentioned that Sinatra incorrectly designed the pilasters, the columns, and the ornament of the entrance and stairway of the building (Pls 156, 157), and he demanded that Sinatra remove them. When Labisi's designs (Pls 162, 165) are compared with the actual building (Pls 156, 157), the ornament of the present atrium and the main stairway differ only slightly from them. In the atrium, the niches on either side of the entrance are missing, and the extra columns and pilasters Labisi called for on the eastern side are not present. On the stairs the new elements are the pilasters which Labisi had not included. Sinatra treated these pilasters (Pl. 157) in an almost atectonic manner by literally dissolving their volutes to inverse lobes, their acanthus leaves to petals, and by enlarging their guttae in the manner of Michelangelo. The distortion of the capital to fit the slope is a device popularized by the Spanish treatise writer Caramuel, whose motifs appear in other areas of the building.[30] The smooth double arches of the refectory, which again follow Caramuelian distortions by being carved on angle (Pl. 159), are not in Labisi's plan (Pls 160, 166). On the landing of the stairway the ornament of the bearing columns, balustrade, and pedestal (Pl. 158) looks more Gagliardesque, as do the window and door surrounds.

In the house of the Crociferi, Sinatra seems to be quite at home in Gagliardesque and Rococo motifs, and seems to have had enough assurance to introduce a more varied plan for the refectory. His interest in Caramuelesque distortions and double pointed arches is amply apparent. He may also have been responsible for the stripped straight façade of the final church of the Crociferi (S. Camillo), which was directly contrary to Labisi's plan (Pl. 174).

151b S. Girolamo, the church of the monastery of Montevergine. Interior. Although this church is attributed to Sinatra on the basis of documentary evidence, the style of the capitals, the positioning of the columns around the apse, and the theatrical decorations link it to Gagliardi who was the architect of the monastery dormitory, and perhaps contributed to the church design.

152 House of the Crociferi. Western façade from north.

Sinatra's Style

Vincenzo Sinatra's contribution to Netinese architecture for the time being remains a question mark. Although he worked on many buildings in Noto, his artistic personality is still not clear. His work on the house of the Crociferi fathers shows that he could design ornament well and execute interesting spatial arrangements. His taste for the Rococo unites his work with Paolo Labisi's late work. Either one of these architects or both might be responsible for the Astuto or Trigona palaces, or the church of S. Maria del Carmine with its Rococo façade and interior.[31] The kind of Rococo capitals found in the house of the Crociferi fathers recur on several Netinese buildings, including the courtyard of the Landolina palace. But whether these capitals (Pl. 151) can be used to identify Sinatra's architecture in Noto, where even enemies traded ideas, is questionable. For the time being, the artistic personality of Vincenzo Sinatra is still largely a mystery.

Paolo Labisi (1720?–1798?)

Whereas Gagliardi was by birth a Syracusan and Sinatra a commoner, Paolo Labisi was both an aristocrat and a native Netinese. His aristocratic lineage and Netinese birth probably saved his name from the oblivion which enveloped both Gagliardi and Sinatra after their deaths. Arezzo Prado, Noto's nineteenth-century historian, left an account of his life;[32] his graphic work and theoretical writing is preserved in the city library; his frequent legal problems have left a paper trail of his personal and professional life. Because he is so thoroughly documented, Labisi offers the most complete picture of what an architect did in Noto and the problems of practising there.

Paolo Labisi was born *ca.* 1720 to Giuseppe Labisi and Bartoloma Labisi e Costanzo, wealthy members of Noto's lower aristocracy.[33] Of Paolo's several older brothers,

153 House of the Crociferi. Western façade from south.

154 House of the Crociferi. Northern façade.

155 House of the Crociferi. Southern façade.

156 House of the Crociferi. Atrium.

157 House of the Crociferi. Main stairway.

158 House of the Crociferi. Stairway landing.

159 House of the Crociferi. Refectory.

one became a town notary and the other a successful priest.[34] Paolo's parents knew Rosario Gagliardi and had asked him to be the godfather of one of their older sons.[35]

By 1748 when Labisi was about 28 years of age, documents refer to him as an architect. Although details of his education are unknown, it is safe to say he did not start out as a craftsman as Sinatra or Gagliardi did. In his later writings, Labisi heaps contempt on those people who assume the title of architect but are actually stonemasons and capomaestri.[36] In his eyes the architect had to be trained in the liberal arts, mathematics, and philosophy rather than the building trades. Presumably Labisi was educated in the way he prescribes for everyone else. Francesco Sortino, who signs himself Professor of Philosophy, Mathematics, and Fine Arts of the City of Noto, translated a mathematical treatise from Latin to Italian in 1746 for Labisi.[37] It is possible that Sortino was Labisi's teacher and that the book was a reward for his student's erudition. The fact that the book had to be translated for Labisi shows that his education probably did not include a reading knowledge of Latin. Given the presence of Gagliardi and the availability of books, Labisi need not have left Noto to produce the architecture he did.

Labisi's career in Noto opens with a flourish in the 1740s and 1750s. In 1748 he designed a roof for the apse of the new church of S. Caterina, in 1749 he drew a map of the existing Piazza S. Domenico, in 1751 he and Vincenzo Sinatra worked on a plan for minor construction for S. Agata.[38] In 1750 he designed the house of the Crociferi and worked on problems relating to its construction for the rest of his life. Outside of Noto he designed a villa for the famous Gargallo family of Syracuse and a church in the city of Ispica, both of which were only partially completed under his supervision.[39] Labisi was probably working for the city of Noto as its official architect as early as 1748.[40] From 1760 to 1787 he held the position of Royal Engineer of the city of Noto and City Architect.[41]

Labisi begins the House of the Crociferi Fathers

Attempts to establish a new religious house in Noto run by the Crociferi fathers began when Labisi was just 14 years old in 1734, but the church and central government delayed approval until 1749, when Labisi was 29.[42] The three religious administrators in charge of the project chose the young Labisi to be its architect. He drew up a plan of the plot in relation to the quarter of the city in which it was to be built in 1749. A year later he drew a set of seventeen plans for the church. These plans were at first unsatisfactory in some details and were redrawn, and were finally approved in 1753 (see Pl. 168).[43]

The plan of the building was unusual in that the church faced east while the main façade of the dormitory block faced west (Pl. 160). The most common arrangement in Noto was to position the church so that it flanked the cloister. In situations where such an arrangement was impossible the church was sometimes turned at a right angle to the dormitory block (as in the oratory of S. Filippo Neri and the monastery of S. Agata). But the house of the Crociferi is the only ecclesiastical building to have its church and dormitory facing opposite directions. This unusual plan was adopted because the space available for the new community was an irregular L-shape. The foot of the 'L' on Via Bovio accommodated the rectangular dormitory block but left little space for the church. The church had to be projected down Via Occhipinti to Via Pirri. This plan is represented by Labisi in his map of Piazza S. Domenico drawn in 1749 (Pl. 53a). This map may have been directly related to his project for the new church which was drawn the following year. The map illustrates the church farther up the hill than it appears in the 1750 designs because an important piece of property was not obtained until 1750. The addition of the new piece enabled the church and dormitory to be built on a continuous line on the south side. The obstacle on the north-east was the newly erected Battaglia palace, which cut into the rectangular shape of the city block. The palace forced Labisi to use an asymmetrical arrangement where he probably would have preferred a symmetrical one.

Labisi's plan of church and dormitory façades facing in opposite directions was

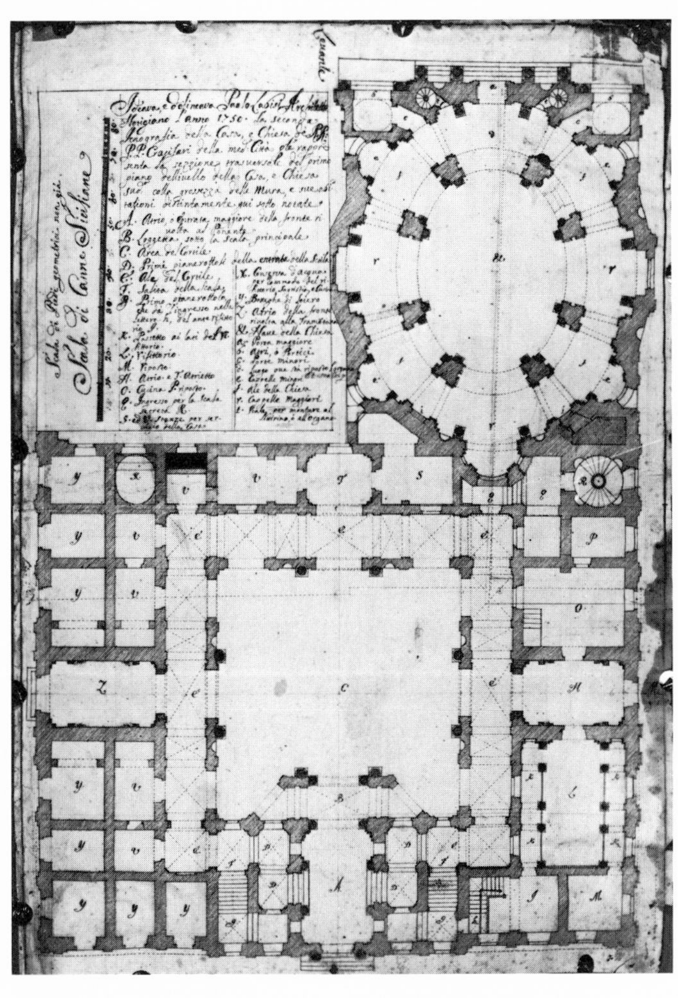

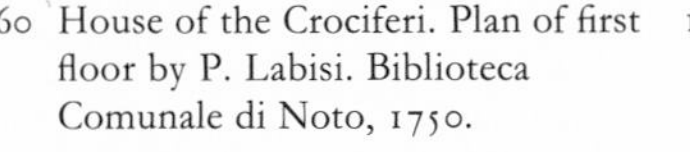
160 House of the Crociferi. Plan of first floor by P. Labisi. Biblioteca Comunale di Noto, 1750.

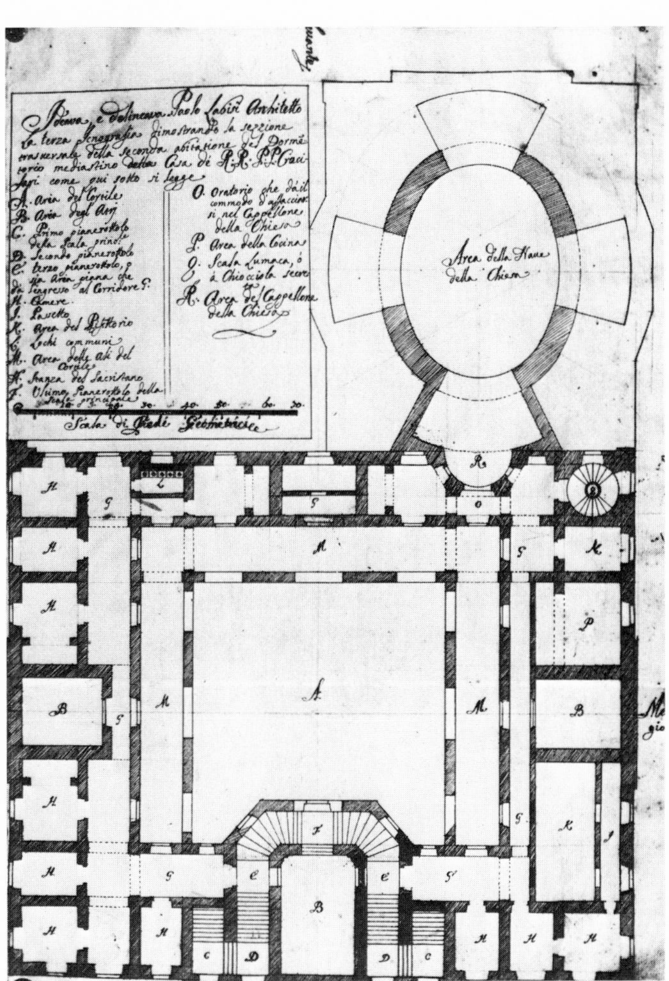

161 House of the Crociferi. Plan of second floor by P. Labisi. Biblioteca Comunale di Noto, 1750.

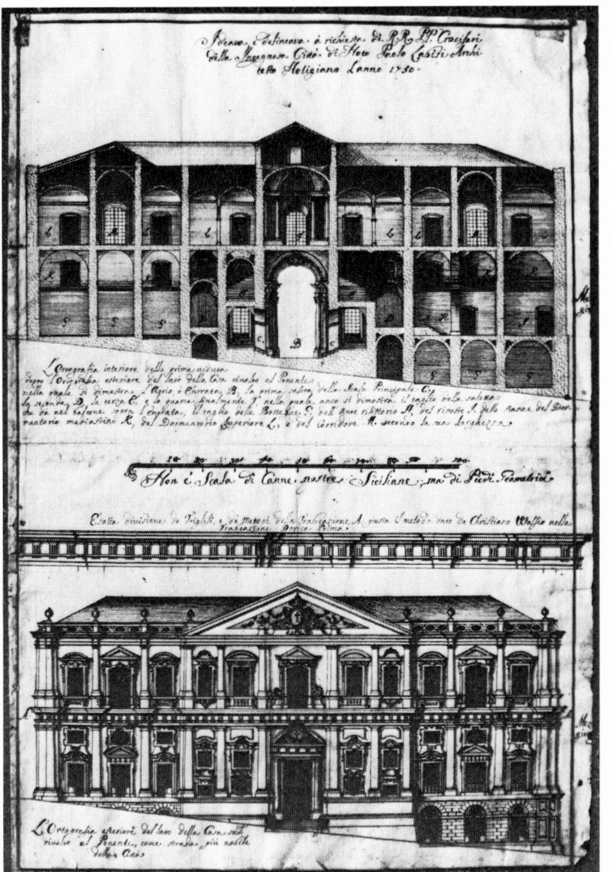

162 House of the Crociferi. Dormitory as seen from the west, by P. Labisi. Biblioteca Comunale di Noto, 1750.

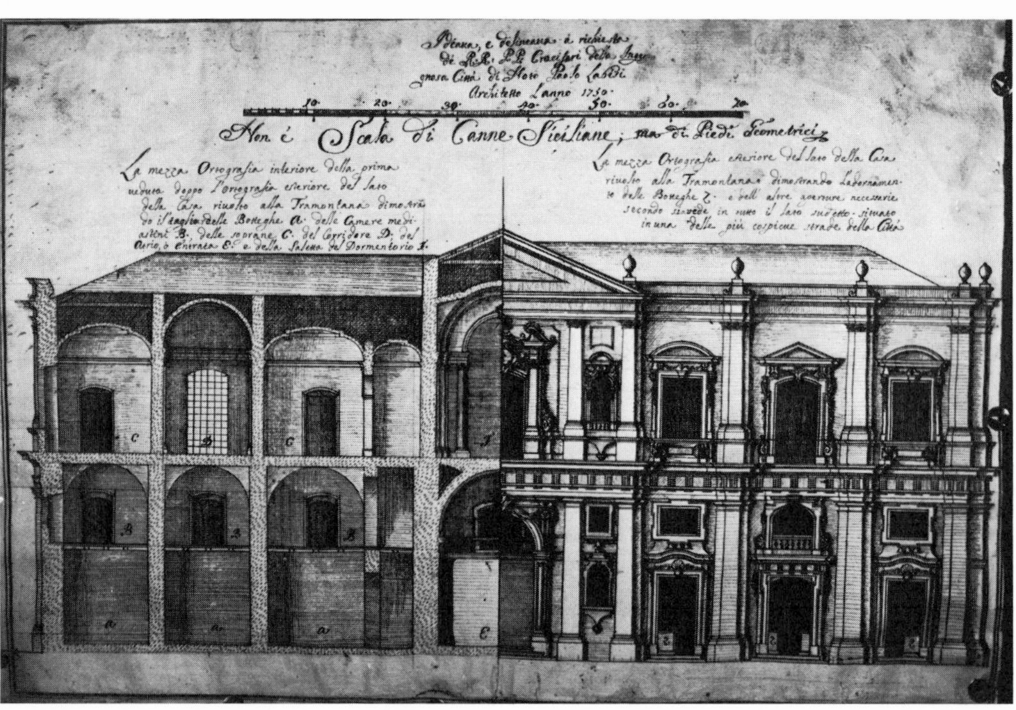

163 House of the Crociferi. Design of dormitory as seen from the north. P. Labisi, 1750.

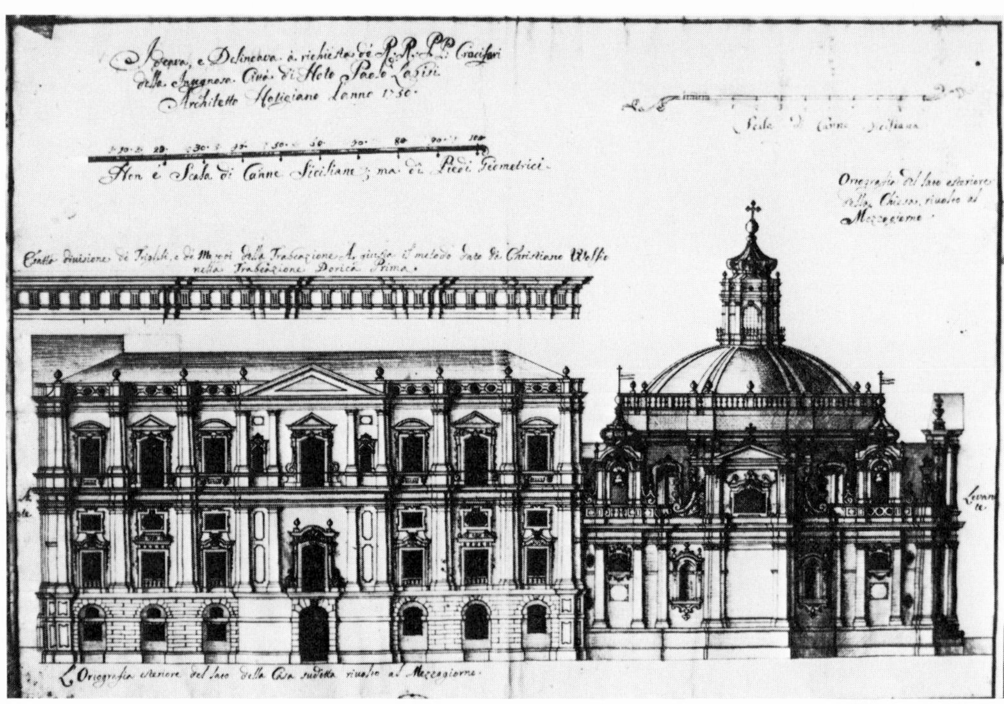

164 House of the Crociferi. Southern façade elevation. P. Labisi, 1750.

also occasioned by the positions of nearby churches. The Crociferi fathers were one of the last orders to establish themselves in Noto, and therefore may have been constrained by previous institutions which were not favourable to having a new church too close to theirs. With the exception of the churches of SS. Salvatore and S. Chiara, churches in lower Noto usually maintain about one city block or buffer zone between them (Map 7). Since the churches of the Oratorians and of the Dominicans were close to the plot of the Crociferi fathers, Labisi was probably compelled to build his church in the next street where it would not challenge the church of another institution.

Labisi's geometrically-balanced plan for the dormitory and church is extremely intricate and sophisticated. Throughout the design the symmetrical relationships between the centres of the three façades of the dormitory block (north, south, west) (Pls 162–165) are accentuated by entrance atriums and engaged columns on the

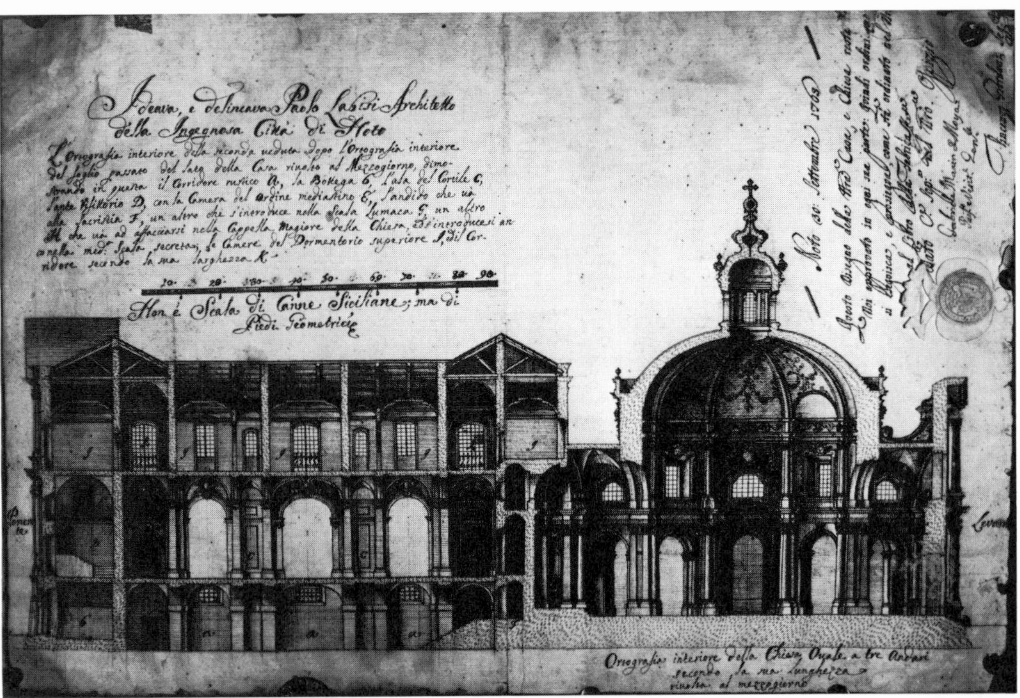

165 House of the Crociferi. Longitudinal section through southern portion of dormitory and church. P. Labisi, 1750.

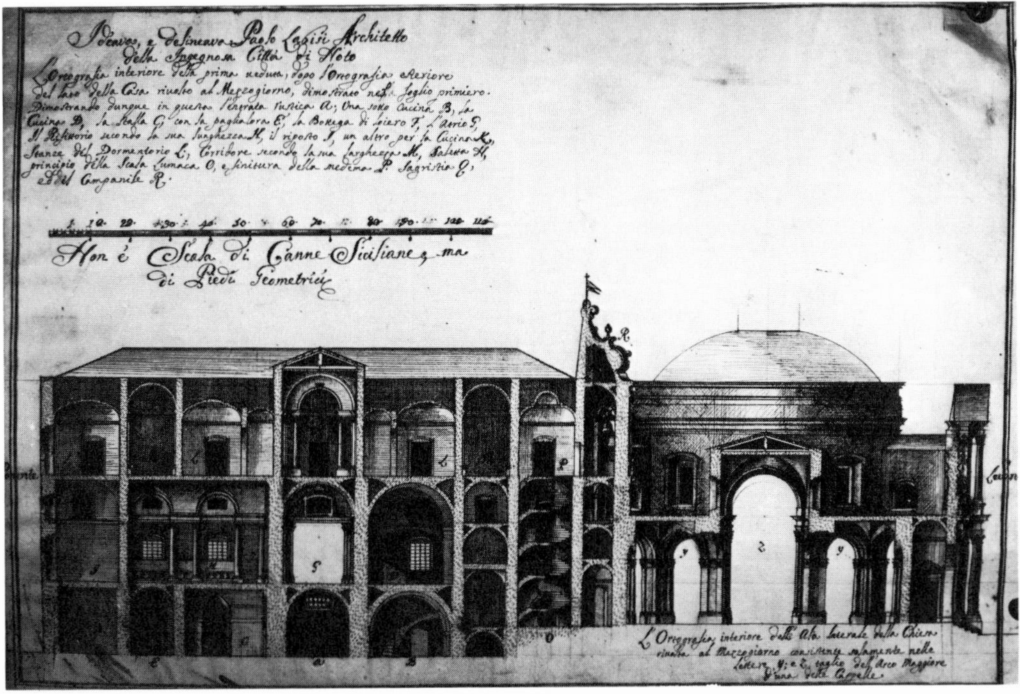

166 House of the Crociferi. Longitudinal sections through dormitory. P. Labisi, 1750.

interior courtyard (Pl. 160). The main entrance to the dormitory on the west is underscored by the trapezoidal projection for its upper staircases (Pl. 161) and its large entrance hall. It seems to call for an emphatic answer from the east side of the building. This would have been provided, of course, had the church been located in the centre of the eastern block. Then one would have looked from the entrance through a set of arches to the church. In overall conception such a design probably would have satisfied Labisi's aesthetic sense a little better than the present one does. It would have taken on the aspect of Juvarra's Superga with its church symmetrically centred at the head of the convent block.[44] Labisi, in fact, may have planned the structure around a much smaller centrally-located eastern church before the southern piece of land on Via Occhipinti was obtained. When this extra piece appeared he simply moved the church south.

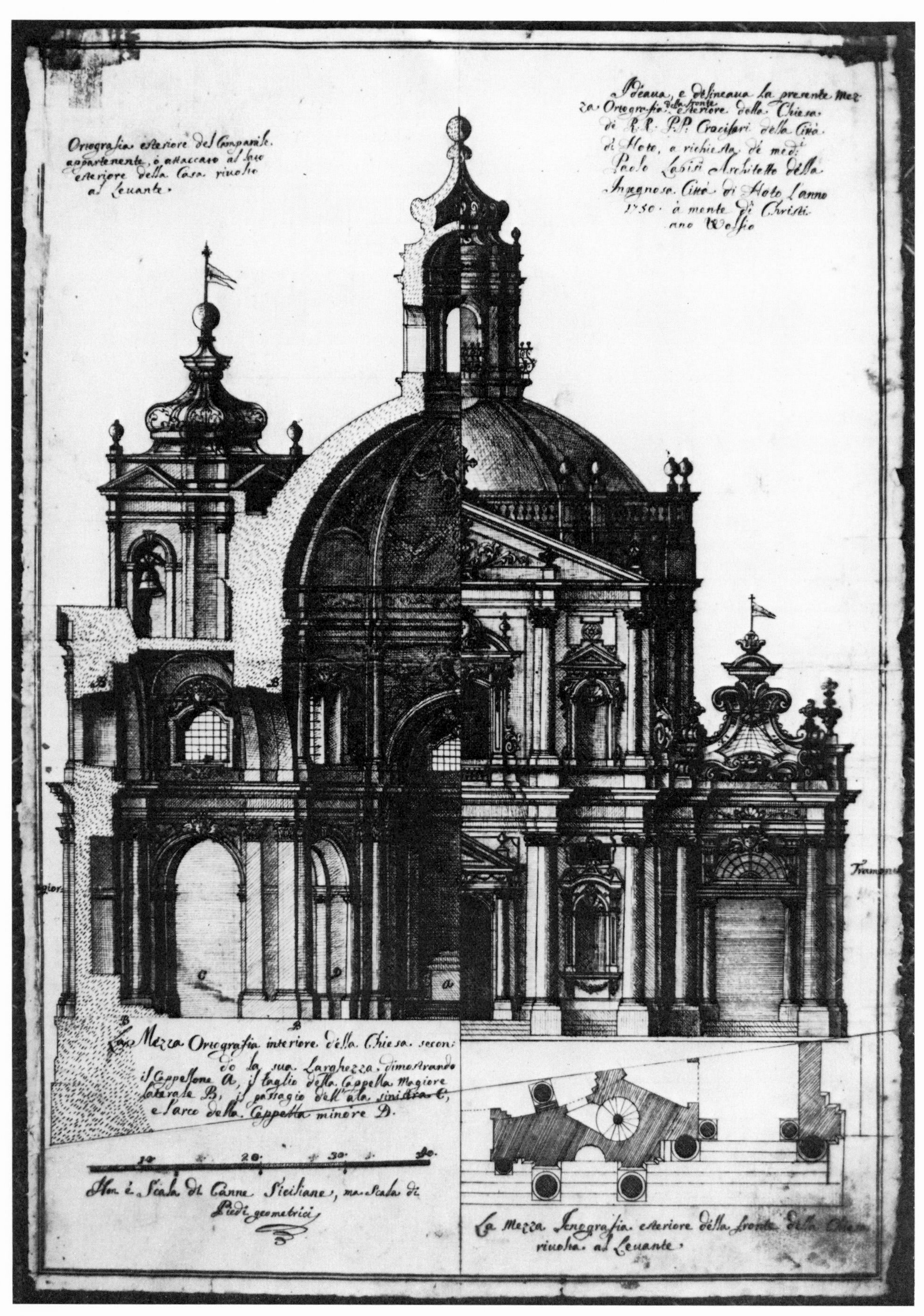

167 House of the Crociferi. Design of the church of S. Camillo. P. Labisi, 1750.

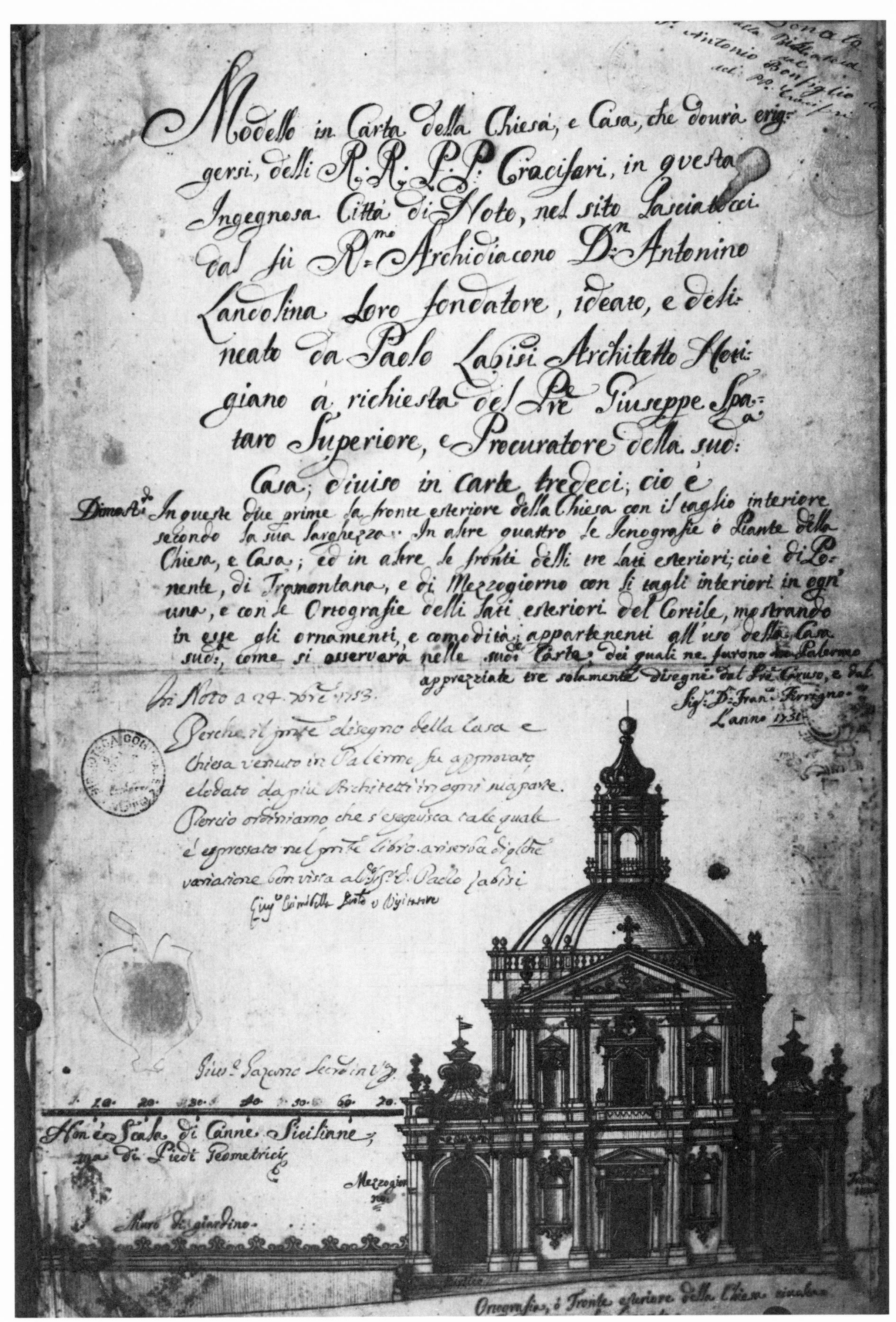

Modello in Carta della Chiesa, e Casa, che dourà erig=
gersi, delli R.R. P.P. Crociferi, in questa
Ingegnosa Città di Noto, nel sito Lasciatoci
dal fù R.mo Archidiacono D.n Antonino
Lancolina Loro fondatore, ideato, e deli=
neato da Paolo Labisi Architetto Neti=
giano à richiesta del P.re Giuseppe Spa=
taro Superiore, e Procuratore della sud:
Casa; diviso in Carte tredeci; cio è

Dimost.e In queste due prime la fronte esteriore della Chiesa con il taglio interiore secondo la sua larghezza. In altre quattro le Icnografie ò Piante della Chiesa, e Casa; ed in altre le fronti delli tre lati esteriori; cioè di Ponente, di Tramontana, e di Mezzogiorno con li tagli interiori in ogn'uno, e con le Ortografie delli lati esteriori del Cortile, mostrando in esse gli ornamenti, e comodità appartenenti all'uso della Casa sud:; come si osservarà nelle sud.e Carte, dei quali ne furono in Palermo apprezziate tre solamente disegni dal P.re Caruso, e dal Sig.r D. Fran.co Ferrigno. L'anno 1751.

In Noto a 24 ...bre 1753.

Perche il pnte disegno della Casa e Chiesa venuto in Palermo fu approvato e lodato da più Architetti in ogni sua parte. Perciò ordiniamo che s'eseguisca tale quale è espressato nel pnte libro a riserva di qualche variazione con vista al Sig. D. Paolo Labisi

168 House of the Crociferi. Design of the church of S. Camillo with description and approval of the project. P. Labisi, 1750.

S. Camillo, Church of the Crociferi Fathers, and the High Baroque

Labisi's church for the Crociferi fathers, called S. Camillo, shows him turning to Gagliardi for principal ideas in planning, elevation, and interior design. Labisi's church is based on Gagliardi's Study C. Study C (Pl. 169) in its turn is derived from a standard source, the sixteenth-century Italian treatise writer, Serlio. The plan of Study C might be called an oval version of Serlio's temple of Bacchus with the characteristic Gagliardi inner arcade added.[45] To be sure the rhythm of the repeating niches has been simplified, the circle is transformed into an oval, and the interior colonnade clumped into isolated piers, but the resemblance is still there: in both plans one sees a play between inner and outer niches (although Gagliardi is less consistent than Serlio), the insertion of niches between pairs of pilasters, and the same arrangement of chapels.

The resemblance between the plan of Gagliardi's Study C and Labisi's plan for S. Camillo (Pl. 160) leaves little doubt as to Labisi's debt to Gagliardi. Labisi changed the shape of the plan by basing it on a wider oval than Gagliardi's but otherwise the church plans look very much alike, with similar entrances, pier supports, niche design and spatial compositions. However, the foci of Gagliardi's Study C are the fragmentary spaces of the entrance, the altar, and the side chapels. The emphasis on side chapels is accomplished by means of strategically placed columns on the walls and the sides of the adjacent piers. Labisi, on the other hand, follows another study Gagliardi did for an oval church (Pl. 170) which clearly places the columns on the sides of the piers facing inward toward the central spaces of the building. Labisi was less interested in complex and puzzling effects than Gagliardi and wanted a clearer plan. But like Gagliardi, Labisi, in a strange perversion of architectural order, arranged the lateral entrances to his church so that they coincide with the positions of the piers. Thus entering the church one would be faced with a pier blocking the view of the nave. Both Labisi and Gagliardi may have taken this concept from the leading international architect of the day, Carlo Fontana, who used it in the design of his church of the Sanctuary for the Jesuits in Loyola, Spain.[46]

More than the plan, the façade of S. Camillo suggests that the relationship between the designs of Labisi and Gagliardi is similar to the relationship between Carlo Fontana and the High Baroque. Both Labisi and Fontana contained and

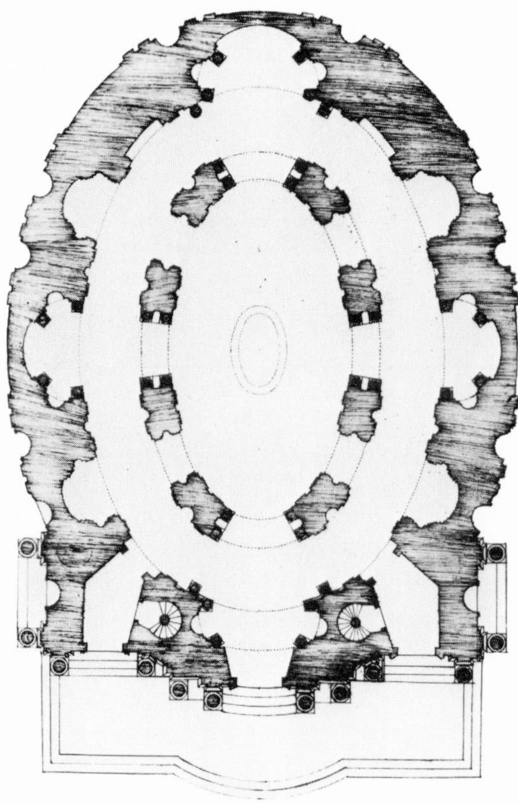

169 Plan for study C, treatise by R. Gagliardi, Mazza Collection, Syracuse.

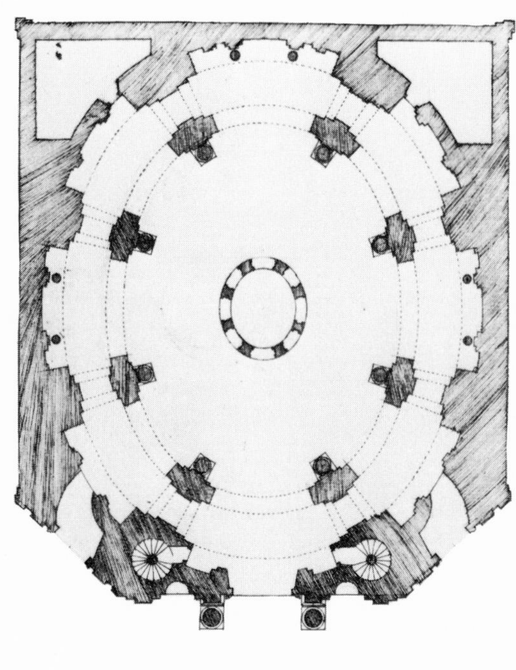

170 Plan for oval church, treatise by R. Gagliardi, Mazza Collection, Syracuse.

subdued the architecture of their predecessors. Carlo Fontana (1638–1714), repeated High Baroque themes but restrained their exuberance. Rudolf Wittkower eloquently christened Fontana's style 'Late Baroque Classicism'.[47] Labisi probably never went to Rome or studied under Fontana, but he was swayed by the classicizing of Baroque motifs which resulted as a consequence of Fontana's influence. Whereas some of the excitement of the High Baroque is still registered in Gagliardi's façade for Study C, Labisi's S. Camillo façade (Pls 167–168) has more of the characteristics of Late Baroque Classicism: elements that in the High Baroque would have been underscored by repetition remain single in Labisi's façade; towers that would have competed with their dome are low, feathery stumps; bold rolling volutes devolve to twisting vines; the assertive stepped advance of the aedicula façade degenerates into an ambiguous flat wall. These traits in particular emphasize the weakness of the façade of the church in relation to the High Baroque, exemplified by Gagliardi's façades. The weakness of S. Camillo is further accentuated by the side entrances of the church, which neither stand alone nor join the façade. In fact, the swing column, the column of the side entrances closest to the main aedicula, can be linked with either the main aedicula or the side entrances but positively joined with neither.[48]

Influence of Christian Wolff on the Design of S. Camillo and the House of the Crociferi Fathers

Considering the Italian origin of the components of Labisi's designs it is confusing to find him professing that he was following the method of the German philosopher Christian Wolff. In the dormitory façades as in the façade and plan of the church, there is a distinct dependence on Italian prototypes. On all three façades there is one decisive central accent on the main doorway framed by a pediment, and secondary accents on the second bays in from each side. Likewise, an even more subtle third rhythm is present in symmetrical repetitions on either side of the primary and secondary accents. This kind of rhythmic complexity in building façades was particularly popular in eighteenth-century Italy in the work of Fuga in Rome and Juvarra in Turin.[49] What differentiates the façade from practically every building being constructed in Italy during the mid-eighteenth century is its unrelenting dependence on a strict interpretation of the Doric and Ionic orders in its organization. However, above the designs for the Doric trabeations on both the south and west façades of the dormitory Labisi wrote that he was following the ideas of Christian Wolff (Pls 162, 164):

> Exact division of Triglyphs and of Metopes of trabeation A on the design according to the method given by Christian Wolff in the First Doric Trabeation.

On the design for the façade of the church (Pl. 167) he wrote:

> The present half elevation of the front exterior of the church of the R.R. P. P. Crociferi of the City of Noto, created and drawn by Paolo Labisi, Architect of the Ingegnosa City of Noto 1750. According to the thought of Christian Wolff [à mente di Christiano Wolfio].

It is extraordinary to find a Sicilian architect in a small town in Sicily referring to a contemporary German philosopher. Who was the philosopher whom Labisi sought to follow?

Christian Wolff was a German philosopher and mathematician who lived from 1679 to 1754.[50] Born in Breslau, he first studied mathematics and physics, and later philosophy. In 1703 he qualified as tutor at the University of Leipzig where he lectured until 1706, when he became Professor of Mathematics and Natural Philosophy at Halle, largely through the influence of Leibnitz, who had been his teacher. Wolff's ideal was to base theological truth on evidence of mathematical certitude. This aroused the Pietists who centred in Halle. In 1721, Wolff delivered his famous lecture 'on the Practical Philosophy of the Chinese' in which he used the moral precepts of Confucius as evidence of the power of human reason to attain moral truth. This succinct statement of the aim not only of Wolff's philosophy but of the Enlightenment in general led to a protracted fight between Wolff and his Pietist enemies which lasted ten years. Wolff asked Frederick William I for protection but the latter, afraid that Wolff's deterministic view might sanction mutiny in the army, expelled him. Wolff then went to Saxony, but on the accession of Frederick the Great, was welcomed back to Halle.

One of Wolff's most important books was his *Anfangsgründe aller mathematischen Wissenschaften* (1710) which was translated into *Elementa Matheseos Universae* (1713–1715). This mathematical treatise was one of the most popular in eighteenth-century Europe. Not only was its quality extraordinarily high, but its popularity was no doubt stimulated by Wolff's mathematical view of the universe which was hotly debated during the first three decades of the century. Over 200 books were written either attacking or defending his position. But by the 1740s, however, his philosophy had lost its glamour in continental Europe. Nevertheless, his book on mathematics retained its renown.

As Wolff's philosophy became less popular in continental Europe, it began to reach Sicily.[51] Descartes had slowly become popular in Sicily in the 1730s, but his philosophy was gradually supplanted by Leibnitz and his follower, Wolff. In 1750 the Benedictine monks of S. Martino della Scala near Palermo publicly professed Leibnitz's doctrines. These same doctrines became popular in Messina and Catania. Wolff's popularity in Noto and Syracuse can be judged by the large number of editions in Latin that one finds of his work in both public and private libraries. Labisi had his own copy of *Elementa Matheseos Universae* translated from Latin into

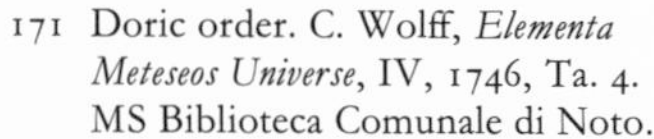

171 Doric order. C. Wolff, *Elementa Meteseos Universe*, IV, 1746, Ta. 4. MS Biblioteca Comunale di Noto.

Italian by Francesco Sortino.[52] Sortino translated the book in 1746. The handwritten Italian copy is inscribed: 'For the personal use of the Royal Architect of the City of Noto: Don Paolo Labisi.' All the illustrations in the text, which were copied by hand from a Latin edition of the *Elementa* in tiny scale, are testimony to Labisi's expertise as a draftsman. His copy of Wolff's work includes only a selection (but a lengthy one) from the fourth volume in which Wolff considers the subject of civil architecture.

Labisi probably saw the original edition of the book in the library of Giacomo Nicolaci who is known to have owned one. He may also have been introduced to Wolff's work by Sortino, who apparently thought he should have the book. In either case, the philosophical fashions of the rest of Europe reached Sicily through books purchased by aristocrats and scholars who had learned by word of mouth, or by letter, what was being discussed in the French and German salons. Labisi understood the significance of the book as a useful and authoritative compendium and thus wanted it translated for his own use. Perhaps his knowledge of Wolff helped him obtain the commission for the designing of the house of the Crociferi in the first place.

It is significant that Labisi does not seem to have included Wolff's name or his trabeations on the designs when they were first drawn. The 'according to the thought of Christian Wolff' ('a mente di Christiano Wolfio') is tacked on to the inscription at the end, perhaps because there was nowhere else to insert it. Likewise the trabeations are placed above the already drawn façades in an awkward fashion which suggests that they were not originally intended to be there. Other changes in the designs, like the conversion of Sicilian *canne* (a Sicilian measurement, approximately two metres) to feet, also indicate that Labisi may have made some last-minute changes, ostensibly to please his clients who did not find the drawings completely to their liking. In fact a document of 1754 which records a misunderstanding over the price of the drawings hints that one of Labisi's clients was not satisfied with them.[53] What then would the addition of Wolff's name remedy, and was the insertion an idea of Labisi himself or a requirement of a client? These questions must for the time being remain undecided, but it is probable that Labisi was trying to show that his designs had a desirable and reliable source. That the gist of Labisi's church design came from Gagliardi and the Italian tradition didn't seem contradictory to his claim that his building was designed 'after the thought of Christian Wolff'.

Wolff's illustrations, which were copied by Labisi, are for the most part conservative representations of the orders and offer little insight into the process of Labisi's design and its relation to the German philosopher. There are exceptions: Labisi took the Doric order he uses from Wolff (cf. Pl. 171 and 164) and there are other instances in which Labisi seems to have taken some inspiration from Wolff. In the arrangement of the stairs on the interior of the eastern side of the dormitory and in the composition of all three façades, Labisi seems to have followed Wolff's instructions for constructing a building (Pl. 172). Wolff flanks the central entrance to the façade of the two-storey building he illustrates with windows and crowns it with a pediment. On either side of this central pediment he places three rows of windows. The second row in from each side is slightly more accentuated by its frame than the other two, setting up the same rhythm which occurs in Labisi's façades. Aside from the trabeations which Labisi draws on his design these are the only direct ways in which his conception appears to be influenced by Wolff.

At the back of Wolff's treatise, after Wolff's plates, Labisi includes what appear to be his own inventions which he used to embellish the apertures of his design for the house of the Crociferi. The fifteen pages of drawings depict doorways and windows in Late Baroque or even Rococo designs (Pl. 173). Though they recall the designs of Andrea Pozzo and the Italian Rococo group working in Rome in the eighteenth century, they do not seem to have been copied directly from any Roman sources.[54] They incorporate some of the broken-, split-, and splayed-pediment motifs so popular in Rome and even a touch of Borrominesque revival, but there is also the

172 Elevation of building. C. Wolff, *Elementa Meteseos Universe*, IV, 1746, Ta. 17. MS Biblioteca Comunale di Noto.

173 Aperture designs. Drawn by P. Labisi in C. Wolff, *Elementa Meteseos Universe*, IV, 1746, unnumbered plate. MS Biblioteca Comunale di Noto.

intricacy and fussiness that is reminiscent of Gagliardi. Even if Labisi did not copy Gagliardi directly, his style was greatly influenced through close contact with the older architect. The legacy of Gagliardi is definitely part of Labisi's drawings in some of the more energetic passages in the window surrounds, in the strapwork, the leaf designs, the festoons, the bowing friezes, the repeated use of putti heads, the finical use of details and the momentary emergence of a rather clumsy motif (the shell atop the window entablature). Many of these original aperture surrounds were used by Labisi in the design of the elevations of the church and dormitory of the Crociferi fathers.

Problems with the House of the Crociferi Fathers

The extravagant and fanciful ornament that Labisi had incorporated into the plan for the house of the Crociferi fathers unfortunately was eliminated because of high cost and a construction scandal involving Labisi himself (cf. Pls 152–5 with Pls 162–4). In 1753 the designs were approved and building commenced. Shortly thereafter, as mentioned earlier (p. 180), a bitter controversy erupted over the work in progress. Documents dated 1770 outline a scandal involving the costs of construction, the stability of the work, and control of the entire project.[55] Clearly the dispute must have been going on for some years by that time.

Although Labisi was still formally the architect of the building in 1770, he does not seem to have been in direct control of the building operations. If he had been, none of the alleged violations of the original design would have taken place. There is a twist in the story that is not clear from Labisi's complaint. In a document of the same year Corrado Pizzi stated that the construction built during Labisi's 'time' was threatening to collapse. Likewise, he said, the design was extraordinarily expensive to build. What seems to have happened is that the incomplete building fared very poorly during an earthquake which struck Noto in 1766. Because of the damage, particularly to the southern side of the building, Labisi's patrons lost faith in his expertise, hiring Vincenzo Sinatra to assist him. It was this unasked-for assistance which probably fostered Labisi's resentment and his claim that Sinatra was making errors, such as ordering the wrong kind of stone for a wall. It is hard to believe that the veteran Sinatra would miscalculate the kind of stones and their cost as Labisi alleges.

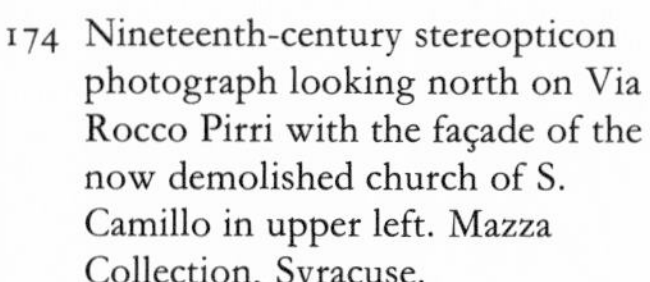

174 Nineteenth-century stereopticon photograph looking north on Via Rocco Pirri with the façade of the now demolished church of S. Camillo in upper left. Mazza Collection, Syracuse.

Perhaps he was trying to avoid the collapse which threatened under Labisi's supervision. From the limited facts available it seems that Labisi was at fault, if anyone. The subsequent history of the building is not in his favour. Perhaps Labisi's use of huge arcades in the courtyard of the convent did not give it the stability to endure in Noto where minor earthquakes are frequent. The use of huge open arcades to support upper stories was not a common building practice in Noto.

By 1770, the time of the above controversy, the first of the three planned floors had been finished up to the gateway of the convent on the west side. By 1787, the entire first floor on the south side was also completed. After that time no dates record the progress of the construction. Perhaps the south side of the building was never completed. Whether it was or not, in the nineteenth century the north side of the building collapsed. In the twentieth century a quarter of the façade of the south side of the building either collapsed or was demolished.[56]

Despite Labisi's protests to the contrary, the dormitory building in general does follow his design, but all the details (such as the apertures) have been changed. While Labisi's rhythms have been preserved, his ornament has been drastically simplified, so that his façades lose much of the novel effects they display on paper. On the interior neither the entrance hall nor the stairways are decorated as Labisi indicated they should have been. In a final ironic note, the refectory which was planned by Labisi as a simple rectangle was transformed by Sinatra, who usually moved in the direction of greater austerity, into a more complicated design with different column intervals and decorative touches.

S. Camillo, the Crociferi church designed by Labisi, was never built, probably because of financial problems. A nineteenth-century stereopticon photograph of the street on the eastern side of the Crociferi building shows that a church was indeed constructed, but this church was not Labisi's: it had a plain longitudinal hall with the most minimal façade decorations (Pl. 174). These decorations included an oval medallion of S. Camillo, which can be seen in the photograph and which is now in the foyer of the Communal Library of Noto. The church, which may have been the work of Sinatra, eventually developed construction flaws in the late nineteenth century and was demolished to make way for the town market on Via Pirri in 1925.[57]

Labisi's Treatise

After the Crociferi débâcle Labisi sought to re-establish himself as an authority by writing a book on civil architecture for the rest of the architects of Noto. The date of the manuscript he wrote reads 1773, but it is unclear whether he began or concluded on this date. He entitled his signed treatise 'Volume IV' although it was an introduction to architecture.[58] One wonders if he intended to incorporate into his own work the three volumes of designs which include Gagliard's treatise.

Labisi's volume deals almost exclusively with architecture and the law, an apt subject for a person like Labisi forever afflicted with legal difficulties. Labisi thought that *servitù* was a major problem to be considered in the construction of buildings and discussed it at length. *Servitù*, roughly defined, is how the building will relate to the rights and duties of the neighbouring property owners around it. Labisi's interest in *servitù* led him to write a treatise on city planning in the same volume. Unfortunately he wrote only furtively of his own experiences as royal architect and engineer of Noto.[59] Instead, a large part of his treatise is devoted to condemning those who are appointed as architects though they are not trained in the liberal arts. It seems clear that Labisi is attacking Sinatra, the capomaestro who rose through the ranks.[60]

More than two thirds of the Labisi volume is windowdressing, copied out of books that have nothing whatever to do with the conditions in Noto. He copied from a bewildering variety of architectural treatises and lawbooks. But by far the most frequently used sources are Wolff's *Elementa Matheseos Universae* (to which no credit is given by Labisi), Giovanni Battista De Luca's *Il dottor volgare* (Rome, 1673; a law book), and Giuseppe Secondo's *Ciclopedia ovvero dizionario universale delle arti, e delle scienze* (Naples, 1754). Among the other works Labisi used are various editions of Vitruvius, including Perrault's, the works of Plato, the hermetical treatise on Ezekiel's Vision of Solomon's temple by Villalpando, and the architectural treatise of the Sicilian Amico. Many of the books Labisi used were in the library of the Nicolaci family; he probably had access to them because Giacomo Nicolaci was his patron.[61] Labisi's volume proves, more than anything else, that he had humanistic aspirations. From the books he read he could grasp what was occurring in the rest of Europe and adjust his view of himself to what he perceived was happening. Interestingly enough, he was not alone in his use of Wolff as a dependable authority of his concern with the education of architects in relation to the laws under which they worked. Several treatises citing Wolff and also explaining *servitù* were written in Rome and Naples within ten years of Labisi's book.[62]

S. Agata: More Frustration for Labisi

Gagliardi may have been the first architect to actually design and supervise the construction of S. Agata. From 1760 to 1761 he is documented to have contracted stones for the monastery and during the same period to have supervised the construction of a model of the building.[63] But in 1770 the dormitory was still incomplete, and the church, because of earthquake or poor maintenance, was in need of remodelling. Labisi was contracted by the Marchese of Cannicarao, the Procurator and Commissioner General of the monastery, to design the offices and dormitories as well as other portions of the building.[64] But the Marchese went on a trip to Palermo taking the designs with him. For four years, from 1770 to 1774, the Marchese kept the project in limbo. Since the total design seemed stalled, the abbess asked Labisi at least to draw a design for the remodelling of the church, which he did. For six months stonemasons worked under Labisi's supervision, redecorating most of the interior and some of the exterior of the church (Pl. 175). The ornament on the exterior

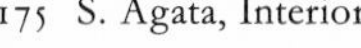

175 S. Agata, Interior.

doors of the church, the façade, and the interior can all clearly be attributed to him (Pl. 91).

On the interior of S. Agata Labisi uses brittle garlands of feathered ornament to break up the spaces of the vault. Usually in the Rococo style the orders are neglected in favour of a planar, non-articulated wall. However, in S. Agata the order is preserved, following Gagliardi's practice, in spite of the Rococo decoration of the vault. On the exterior of the church Labisi dresses up the older façade, placing Rococo flourishes over the more restrained Baroque apertures of the façade. S. Agata was the last building that Labisi is known to have worked on in Noto.

Labisi and Noto's Architecture

Labisi was not a great architect, but he was a good designer and an excellent draughtsman. His work demonstrates what a provincial eighteenth-century architect could do in a town the size of Noto. A self-taught virtuoso at designing churches and composing decoration, he never went further than Ispica, fifty-five kilometres from Noto, to seek commissions. He seems to have run into a spate of bad luck, perhaps brought on by his own inexperience and pomposity. This bad luck is manifest in the hulk of his Crociferi project on which his hopes for recognition in the community must have hung. Begun in a lavishly financed and beautifully planned campaign, the building soon became a ruin in its own time. Its disintegration, accelerated by neglect and wilful disregard, is sad to watch. The badly planned walls are buckling in the courtyard, the beautiful Wolffian cornice is ripped apart by an intervening modern drain. The collapse of Labisi's dream, like the forgotten pages of his unpublished volume, might be seen as signs of the futility of practising architecture in Noto. But Labisi did in fact leave his stamp on the city, even though over the years it has grown less and less visible. He should be included as one of the men, like Gagliardi and Sinatra, who created a very unique and visually successful city.

Part V
The Eighteenth-Century City Endures

Chapter 10 Noto frozen in Time

In spite of the passage of more than two hundred years since Labisi drew his veduta in the 1750s, Noto looks remarkably the same. Isolated from the modern world with its inevitable and devastating progress, Noto remains preserved as an island of eighteenth-century urban culture. After decades of headstrong urban redevelopment in the United States, architects and planners are only belatedly turning to the possibilities that rehabilitation of older buildings offers; older neighbourhoods are now sought by those who want to return to the humanity and charm of past ages. But in Noto the evolving city never suffered the kind of destruction that has befallen other urban centres. The city remains rooted to its initial conception.

One reason for the exquisite preservation of Noto is the stagnation of its agriculturally-based economy.[1] Noto's air is clean and devoid of industrial smoke because there are no factories; Noto's core is free from large Italian department stores because there is no market; Noto's streets are empty of foreigners because there is no tourism. Apartment buildings have been kept at bay on the edge of town. Rusting hulks of doomed constructions, presumably stopped by economic uncertainty, stand in the lower section of the city. Poverty has forced old buildings to be reused, rather than being torn down.

176 The main piazza of Noto. Late nineteenth-century photograph taken before alterations completed. Collection of Mauceri, Noto.

Another reason for the preservation of the eighteenth-century city is that the Renaissance-Baroque-Rococo continuum established in Noto's early architecture could incorporate a wide range of divergent styles from Neo-classicism to Art Nouveau. Even with the retirement of Sinatra and Labisi in the 1780s, the Baroque tradition in Noto was far from dead, for while in other areas of Italy Baroque architecture had gone out of style decades earlier, it still had adherents in Noto. Bernardo Labisi, son of Paolo Labisi, probably designed the renovation for the parlatorio of S. Chiara in the 1780s: his window surrounds are stiff and ungiving but they are most definitely Baroque.[2] He also worked on the Trigona palace which carries on the style of his father and Gagliardi. It is hard to decide whether Corrado Mazza, who worked in Noto in the 1780s and 1790s, was returning to a simpler Baroque tradition or embracing Neo-classicism; his design for the church of S. Michele in Palazzolo shows him using great restraint but essentially the same kind of solution that Gagliardi might have chosen almost seventy years earlier.[3] Cantor Antonio Mazza, who also worked in Noto in the late eighteenth and nineteenth centuries, carefully collected the designs of the city's architects before him. His designs for the oratory of S. Filippo Neri (1795) and the church of SS. Salvatore (1791), conserved in the Biblioteca Comunale, show him assimilating a chaste and frigid version of the Late Baroque. The church of SS. Salvatore, which he may have helped design, is in a Neo-classical style similar to the deadly academic Baroque-Neo-classicism which surfaced all over Italy after the mid-eighteenth century (Pl. 176).[4] Nevertheless, SS. Salvatore does not disturb the homogeneity of the main piazza which it faces because its decoration and proportions are not dissimilar from other buildings around it and the entire church is submerged into the older fabric of the monastery. Similarly the arch dedicated to King Ferdinand of Naples in 1838 (Pl. 30), does not add a new note, but repeats the tonality of the eighteenth-century city.

177 The main piazza from the top of the city hall looking north-east. The rebuilt section of the monastery of SS. Salvatore (on the right of the church) illustrates how the Netinese 'restored' the building to a Baroque appearance it never had (compare with Plate 176).

Like the monumental architecture, the smaller private buildings of Noto present a continuity, less because of style consciousness than because of traditional building practices and dwelling types. Since stuccoed stonework is still competitive with concrete, the traditional materials are used even today in Noto. Many of the buildings are constructed with *pietra d'intaglio* from quarries near Noto Antica. The rock is shipped down in blocks of proportions similar to those that Labisi lists in his treatise of architecture. Sometimes huge blocks of stone arrive at a site to be cut to size by two men working a handsaw, a method which goes back to the Middle Ages. When poured concrete is the material, often the overall shape of the building, the simple arrangement of its apertures, helps it to blend with previous buildings. In Noto's domestic architecture one can fine a plethora of styles and approaches and even a range of materials, but the buildings seem to recede from view, becoming foils for the more monumental churches, monasteries and palaces.

Noto's monumental buildings have been preserved because they were too expensive to be replaced and because they were considered a valuable part of Netinese heritage. In 1837 the provincial capital of the area which encompassed both Syracuse and Noto was transferred to Noto by the Bourbon government of Naples. Briefly, from 1837 to 1865, Noto's political importance matched its magnificent image. It was more than just a rich town with vast communal territories, it was a governmental centre. Thus the monasteries and convents which were no longer needed for their original purposes were converted to other uses. The monastery of S. Antonio di Padova became a barracks remodelled to look like a medieval fortress complete with crenellations. At last the Netinese had the fortress for which they had lobbied throughout the eighteenth century. The monastery of S. Maria dell'Arco became the seat of the Bishopric. To enhance its Baroque character the town added new embellishments which could have been equated with Neo-Baroque École des Beaux-Arts styles popular in France.

Even when Noto was demoted from provincial capital and divested of its Bishopric in favour of Syracuse its populace held fast to the image of a centre of culture and politics. In fact Noto's convents and monasteries, being dissolved by the unified government of Italy, were transformed into schools for the children within the city's territory. As schools they were both used and preserved to the present day.

Over the years, while interiors were gutted and altered exteriors remained intact. The Netinese consciously tried to preserve their cityscape. In the late nineteenth century when the façade of S. Michele, a well-known landmark, collapsed, it was reconstructed following the same design.[5] After a wall of the house of the Crociferi fathers collapsed, a concerned citizens' group formed in 1915 and attempted unsuccessfully to raise funds for its reconstruction.[6]

An even more interesting example of restoration occurred in the 1940s after a fire destroyed part of the façade of the church of SS. Salvatore and a portion of undecorated wall south of the church adjoining the monastery (Pl. 176). Instead of rebuilding the undecorated wall, the Netinese extended the monastery façade to cover the destroyed portion (Pl. 177). So accurate is the extension of the monastery façade it cannot be differentiated from the original building.

Equally important to the preservation of eighteenth-century Noto is the relative continuity in the appearance of the streets and squares. The levelling and straightening of the streets in the nineteenth century strengthened Noto's Late Baroque character. Long vistas were part of Late Baroque fashion in eighteenth-century Rome. When the Corso was levelled the original effect of surprise was lost and replaced with a panorama of open spaces through the central core. Although the levelling altered the proportions of Noto's eighteenth-century buildings, their dramatic scenographic qualities were accentuated by being raised above the street.

Conclusion

Noto's history is that of a beautiful city emerging from horrible catastrophe, terrible loss of life, chaos, indecision, social repression and poor planning. A review of Noto's early history produces a certain awe that any city stands at all, much less what one admirer called 'the perfect Baroque city'. Though far removed from the course a Utopian planner might envisage, the events in Noto's complex history are not unusual in the making of eighteenth-century cities. The first plan of St Petersburg in Russia was aesthetically undistinguished and its site on a swampy and malaria-ridden river delta was certainly as unfortunate as Noto's. Heavy losses occurred because of the inhospitable site, and the plan was altered several times to make it more successful. In Sicily itself other towns such as Lentini and Ragusa were plagued by the same chaos and indecision about a post-earthquake site as characterized Noto. The Spanish government evacuated Antigua Guatemala in 1773 in spite of the opposition of its inhabitants. The government of Portugal under Pombal unilaterally decided upon the form of the new city of Lisbon to be rebuilt after the 1755 earthquake.

What is uncommon about Noto's genesis is the newness of its plan and architecture in relation to the form of the old abandoned city. The council held after the 1666 fire in London did not adopt Sir Christopher Wren's visionary plan for the city, probably because of the chaos it would have caused among property owners. Pombal's plan for Lisbon only reorganized a central portion of the city, leaving much of the rest to be built on the pre-earthquake pattern. But Noto, like Ragusa Superiore, Catania, Avola and Grammichele, was built on a totally new plan. These new plans were attempts to remedy previous planning blunders exposed by earthquakes; they represent some of the first documented efforts of people to design specifically in response to seismic disaster.

Like the eighteenth-century town of Carouge, south of Geneva, Noto's plan was neither conceived nor implemented in one stroke. The first grid plan for the city proved too small, poorly positioned, and undistinguished. It was similar to the undifferentiated grids that had been used in the establishment of feudal colonial towns in seventeenth-century Sicily and may not have been acceptable to the Netinese aristocracy. This first undifferentiated grid was succeeded by an Italian plan, conceived as an intellectual framework for uniting the upper and lower cities. The Italian plan was more acceptable to the aristocracy, who settled along its main coordinates, than the earlier grid had been. However, the Italian plan did not cure the problems posed by the topography of the city's site. It was not an ideal solution for a sloping city. Nevertheless, this plan almost by accident provided the views, vistas, and dynamic terrain which produced Noto's unintended scenographic qualities. The intellectualized Italian plan was the perfect foil for the experiential and sensual treatment that the city received at the hands of eighteenth-century architects. The balanced piazzas and symmetrical positioning of churches created the order into which the excitement of Baroque scenographic effects could be injected.

No plan existed for imposing a stylistic homogeneity on the major buildings of Noto. But, through a process of borrowing motifs and sharing sources, structures in Noto were designed with much consistency and decorated similarly. The fine buildings of Rosario Gagliardi set the style for many of the important structures which were built during and after his career in Noto. Because the buildings share forms and are constructed of the same kind of golden stone they give the city a planned appearance not unlike eighteenth-century Nancy – a city which was built by a single architect.

The aristocrats of Noto probably knew too much to settle for the strange, anthropomorphized architecture current in pre-earthquake Catania and Lecce, Apulia. Instead they gave commissions to architects like Gagliardi, cognizant of the styles of the day in Rome. Gagliardi reproduced the grandeur of eighteenth-century Roman Baroque for the aristocracy of Noto, giving the city an oddly cosmopolitan air that seems to belie its position so far from the mainland. In addition Gagliardi brought to the city architectural maturity and sophistication which set the tone for the work which was to follow him. In Sinatra's and Labisi's work the same Italian stylistic persuasion is present, at times combined with features borrowed from French architecture.

Preoccupation with fashion on the part of patrons and architects alike explains many of the peculiarities in the architecture of the city. The French design for the city hall, the obvious knowledge of stylistic developments in Rome, the awareness of contemporary philosophical treatises shown in Labisi's designs for the house of the Crociferi fathers, the use of Chinoiserie in S. Carlo, all indicate that the architects and designers were conscious of the developments outside of Noto and were anxious to incorporate them into the city.

The traditions of eighteenth-century Noto were carried on in the nineteenth century when the city briefly assumed the role of provincial capital and became a Bishopric. Urbanistically and architecturally the eighteenth-century buildings were on the whole improved by the embellishments added by the city, anxious that its political potential should finally match its image.

With the transfer of the provincial capital and Bishopric back to Syracuse, Noto lost its power and its economic base. Its largely agricultural economy sank to its present depressed state. The lack of a strong merchant class has only accentuated the situation. The tiny town of Avola, a few kilometres from Noto, has been energized by the workers who live there. Syracuse itself is becoming a modern metropolis. But Noto remains, with the exception of a few high-rise apartments for the well-to-do, much as the Sitwells saw it.

But if present day Noto is a backwater in a depressed area of Italy it is also a three-dimensional document of the culture of eighteenth-century Sicily. The symbolic image it tried to achieve unites it with the greatest Baroque city of the eighteenth century, Rome itself. We as onlookers may disagree with the values of those who built Noto, but it would be hard to ignore the visual success of their effort. Noto was one of the most beautiful cities of eighteenth-century Sicily, and it remains as an exquisite tombstone for eighteenth-century urban culture.

Notes

Introduction

1 The population figure was valid for 1970. For the altitude see *Sicilia, Guida d'Italia del Touring Club Italiano*, Milan, 1968, p. 668. The distance measurements given here and those quoted throughout the book are measured from point to point on topographical maps and are not – unless otherwise stated – computed on the basis of the length of roads between one point and another. Hence *Sicilia, Guida d'Italia* . . . (p. 674) quotes Noto's distance from the sea as 7.7 kilometres derived from the length of the road from Noto to the sea, whereas the actual distance as the crow flies is 5.5 kilometres.

2 S. Sitwell, *Southern Baroque Revisited*, London, 1967, pp. 29–31.
Sitwell (ibid., p. 29) states:

> It must have been in the winter of 1922–23 that I went to Noto, drawn there by the statement I had read somewhere that it had been rebuilt after the earthquake of 1693. . . . I really believe that my brothers and myself were the first persons of any nationality to take note of them since they [the buildings] were built.

Several foreigners visiting Sicily in the eighteenth century saw and described Noto before the Sitwells: J. Houel, *Voyage pittoresque des isles de Sicile, de Malta et de Lipari*, Paris, 1735, Vol III, p. 119, and R. de Saint-Non, *Voyage pittoresque ou description des Royaumes de Naples et de Sicile*, Paris 1829, Vol 4, p. 429, both wrote briefly about Noto. D. V. Denon, *Voyage en Sicile*, Paris, 1788, translated into *Travels through Sicily and Malta*, Perth, 1790, gives the most complete printed eighteenth-century description, which repeats the judgement of Saint-Non concerning the vast number of religious houses in the city (see Chapter 6). The most useful description is the manuscript of L. Dufourny, *Notes rapportées d'un voyage en Sicile fait par lui en 1789*, MS Cabinet des estampes, Bibliothèque Nationale, Paris, which is used throughout the latter half of this book.

Noto was also fully and appreciatively described in an English guidebook: *A Handbook for Travellers in Sicily* . . ., John Murray Handbook, London, 1864.

For the Sitwells' impressions also see O. Sitwell, *Discursions*, London, 1931, pp. 200–214.

3 The script of the scene from *L'Avventura* can be found in *Screenplays of Michelangelo Antonioni*, New York, 1963, p. 186. For Antonioni's symbolic use of Noto's buildings, ibid., p. 192–3.

4 Douglas Sladen quoted by J. J. Ide, 'Noto – the Perfect Baroque City', *Journal of the Royal Institute of British Architects*, No. 66, 1958, p. 15.

5 J. Vance Jr., *This Scene of Man*, New York, 1977, p. 4.

Chapter 1

1 The Noto-based Istituto per lo Studio e la Valorizzazione di Noto Antica (I.S.V.N.A.) publishes an annual called *Atti e Memorie* which includes a review of yearly events concerning the preservation of the site as well as articles on Noto Antica by local scholars.

2 Noto is rarely mentioned as other than a fatality in the earthquake of 1693 in J. de Burgigny's *Histoire générale de Sicile*, The Hague, 1745 (later published as *Storia generale de Sicilia*, Palermo, 1792) or in G. B. Caruso's *Memorie istoriche di quanto è accaduto in Sicilia*, Palermo, 1744. Similarly neither G. E. Di Blasi e Gambacorta's *Storia civile de regno di Sicilia*, Palermo, 1811–21 nor D. Mack Smith's *History of Sicily*, New York, 1968 devotes more than a sentence to Noto.

3 Noto probably reached the height of its administrative importance under Moslem rule in the tenth century and thereafter only wielded similar administrative powers during a brief period in the nineteenth century when it wrested control of the vast province (which encompassed all the territory between Biscari, Lentini, and Pachino) from Syracuse (G. Passarello, *Guida della città di Noto*, Noto, 1962, p. 8, and C. Gallo, 'Il trasferimento del capoluogo di provincia da Noto a Siracusa nel 1848', *Archivio Storico Siciliano*, VIII, 1956, pp. 197–259). Since the cities of Sicily are nowhere ranked in importance I am deducing Noto's position from statements in the earthquake reports (Document Section I) as well as the claim, on the part of those who wanted the city rebuilt on the same location after the earthquake, that Noto's fortress was useful, not in and of itself, but for securing Syracuse's flank (see Chap. 3, note 29). After the earthquake many of the decisions about Noto's location emanate from the Bishop in Syracuse, and the whole ecclesiastical population of Noto is of course under his direction (Chap. 3, pp. 49, 50).

4 The political history of Noto Antica is beyond the scope of this chapter. The most important sources for the history of the city are Tortora, 1891 and 1972, Littara, 1593 and 1970. V. Amico, II, p. 213 includes an interesting physical description of the city from the introduction of Littara's book which does not appear in the 1970 translation. C. Gallo's two major articles on Noto Antica, 'Arte e monumenti dell'Antica Noto', *Archivio Storico Siciliano*, V, 1952–53, pp. 18–19, and 'Opere di pubblica utilità e abbellimento in Noto Antica . . .' *Archivio Storico Siracusano*, XV, 1969, pp. 30–44, are helpful in reconstructing the city. For the ecclesiastical history of Noto Antica see R. Pirri, *Sicilia Sacra Disquistionibus et Nobiliis Illustrata*, Palermo, 1733, pp. 660–669. A short description of the city can also be found in T. Fazello, *De Rebus Siculis*, Palermo, 1749, I, pp. 293–296. An extensive compilation of earlier local histories can also be found in a manuscript written by Antonino Tedeschi (1745–1823): *Comentari sacro-politici dell'antica ingegnosa città di Noto*, MS, Biblioteca Comunale, Noto, 1780. Modern commentaries on the history of Noto are published yearly in *Atti e Memorie*, the organ of I.S.V.N.A. (see note 1 above).

5 For the history of the Sikels in Noto Antica see A. Freeman, *History of Sicily*, Oxford, 1891, II, pp. 17–18. For the story of king Ducetius, see ibid., pp. 369–387, 563–568. Ducetius is known only through the work of Diodoros and may be a wholly fictional character. He is said to have led the Sikels in rebellion against the Greeks from about 459–440 B.C. Freeman (p. 563) identifies Ducetius' birthplace as Mineo. But he is puzzled by a second reference to a town which Ducetius established on a hill called Neas. Neither Freeman nor M. I. Finley (*Ancient Sicily*, New York, 1968, pp. 63–64) seem to be aware that the Netinese have associated themselves with Neas and the king Ducetius legend. The Netinese humanist Vincenzo Littara (1550–1602) (Littara, 1970, pp. 1–13) claims that king Ducetius was born in Neas on the coast and founded the inland city which we know as Noto Antica. In the eighteenth century Filippo Tortora (Tortora 1891, p. 5) repeated the same legend. It is still held to be true by the Netinese (Gaetano Passarello, *Guida della città di Noto*, Noto, 1962, p. 4). For a discussion of the problem see Vito Amico (Amico, II, p. 213).

6 Amico (ibid. p. 215) recounts the following legend about the city's name:

> Occupando i saraceni la Sicilia dopo alcuni secoli . . . essersi Noto loro resa, poichè non mai per la fortezza del sito cadde per violenza, perciò detta 'Noto' dai barbari, cioè 'eminente', e per la sua celebrità si ebbe nome da Noto una della tre regioni dell'isola.

At first appraisal it would seem more probable that 'Noto' is a simple Italianization of the Latin 'Netum'; however, several words in modern Arabic come close to the name of the city and mean high hill or prominent hill (see Hans Wehr, *Dictionary of Modern Arabic*, New York, 1966, p. 941); among them are the following which derive from the 'NT' root in Arabic: 'Nutu' ' and 'Nat'a', which both mean high, eminent hill.

7 For a discussion of the Moslem and post-Moslem divisions of Sicily and the importance of the Val di Noto see Michele Amari, *Storia dei Musulmani in Sicilia*, Catania, 1937, III, pp. 608–609.

8 See E. Bresc, 'Il casale suburbano e la sua eredità: l'esempio di Noto' in *Il problema Siciliano dei villaggi abbandonati nel Medioevo*, proceedings of Gruppo Ricerche Archeologia Medievale, Palermo, 1972, pp. 7–9, for the extent of Noto's territory and the parcels its nobility controlled. For a list of the *feudi* and conjectures about how many there were see Tortora, 1972, p. 20, Tortora, 1891, p. 7, and A. Tedeschi, *Comentari sacro-politici* . . ., f. 18v. Tedeschi also lists the foodstuffs produced within the territory of Noto (ibid., ff. 17–21).

Within its territory Noto enjoyed a number of privileges. It could call itself by the complimentary title 'Ingegnosa' granted by the Spanish government (Tortora, 1891, p. 27) and enjoy a number of rights which helped to preserve some of its local autonomy (Littara, 1970, pp. 55–56, 67–68). For a complete list see V. LaMantia, *Antiche consuetudini delle città di Sicilia*, Palermo, 1900, pp. cxlviii–cliii.

The exact number of nobles living in Noto is in doubt because of conflicting data: Antonino Tedeschi (*Comentari* . . . ff. 27–29) lists 120 families. Tortora (1891, p. 26) states that there were only 87 aristocrats in Noto Antica in 1693 (presumably before the earthquake). See note 13.

9 For contributions to ecclesiastical institutions see L. Boglino, *La Sicilia Sacra*, Palermo, 1900, II, p. 252–259. For the prestige of having many churches in town see W. Braunfels, *Mittelalterliche Stadtbaukunst in der Toskana*, Berlin, 1953, pp. 131–173.

10 For descriptions of Noto's fortifications see Littara, 1970, pp. 69, 92; Amico, II, p. 213; and Tortora, 1891, p. 27. A good analysis of the ruins of the fortress above Porta della Montagna can be found in B. Ragonese, 'Ricognizione preliminare per lo studio ed il restauro del Castello Reale,' *Atti e Memorie*, Anno 1, 1970, pp. 83–96.

11 Tortora (1891, p. 27) lists all of Noto's products and mentions the variety of the city's stores. For Noto's wool trade and its commerce in general see C. Gallo, 1964, pp.

46–47. A more specific discussion of the wool trade can be found in C. Gallo, 'Industria e mercanti di albascio nel Cinquecento netino,' *Atti e Memorie*, Anno 2, 1971, pp. 103–112.

12 For the general economic condition of Sicily with comments on trade at this time see D. Mack Smith, *Medieval Sicily, A History of Sicily*, II, N.Y. pp. 177–208.

13 For Noto's population see Tortora, 1891 p. 27. Figures at this time are often untrustworthy so it is no surprise to find Rocco Pirri giving a conflicting population figure. According to Pirri the city had 3,046 hearth fires and a population of 14,416 persons. (See Amico, II, p. 220 for Pirri's population figures.) The official government population figure is 12,043 (see Chap. 2, note 8). A useful study of the population problem in general can be found in E. Pontieri, 'Sulla distribuzione della popolazione in Sicilia nel secolo XVIII,' in *Atti* of the XI Congresso Geografico Italiano, Naples, 1930, II, pp. 299–308.

14 Roger Mols, *Introduction à la démographie historique des villes d'Europe du XIVᵉ au XVIIIᵉ siècle*, Louvain, 1955, II, pp. 441–452; for populations of Lisbon and Florence ibid., II, pp. 518–519, 508 respectively.

15 See Amico, II, p. 513 for the population of eighteenth-century Syracuse; ibid., I, p. 288 for the population of Catania. For current population figures see *Sicilia, Guida* . . ., pp. 520, 598, 668.

16 The engraved view I have chosen to illustrate is one of three I analyzed extensively in my doctoral dissertation *The Architecture and Urbanism of Noto, an 18th-Century Sicilian City*, Harvard University, 1971, pp. 11–21. Concurrently Lucia Cugno published her article 'Per una valutazione della pianta del padre Antonino Maria Tedeschi', *Atti e Memorie*, Anno I, 1970, pp. 99–112, which also treats some of the questions that the views raise.

17 Tortora (1891, p. 7) calls this street Via Piana; Littara is probably referring to the same street in his discussion of the growth of the city (Amico, II, p. 213). The ancient name for the church of SS. Crocifisso was S. M. del Castello. For descriptions of the piano see Littara, 1970, pp. 107–9.

For the name Via Piana see Tortora, 1891, p. 7. Littara (in Amico, II, p. 213) is probably referring to the same street in his discussion of the growth of the city.

18 (Gallo, 'Arte e monumenti . . .', pp. 14–16).

This building (no. 14) was more of a place for the king and his ministers to reside while visiting the town than a city hall. It was a symbol of Noto's status as a privileged town ruled by the central government of Spain rather than a free commune. The siting of such an administrative building in the centre of the city agrees both with current Italian practice at the time and the advice of Alberti (1404–72) (Leone Battista Alberti, *Ten Books of Architecture*, trans. James Leoni, 1955, Book V, ix, pp. 92–93). Perugia, San Gimignano, and Piacenza, just to mention a few, are among the large group of Italian cities in which the Casa della Città or Casa di Magistrato is in a central location.

A variety of local conditions played an important part in the siting of civic buildings; for some examples see W. Braunfels, *Mittelalterliche* . . ., pp. 198–208; J. Paul, *Der Palazzo Vecchio in Florenz, Ursprung und Bedeutung seiner Form*, Pocket Library Studies in Art, XXI, Florence, 1969.

19 S. Nicolò, Noto Antica's Chiesa Madre, was the spiritual hub of Noto – the most important church in the city. Around it stood the five parish churches which took care of the daily spiritual needs of their parishioners. The parish churches depicted on the views and the panoramas are:

Identifying numbers*

	Views	Panoramas
S. Spirito	11	24
S. Andrea		52
S. Teodoro		115
S. Maria della Rotonda	40	133
S. Michele	23	167

The churches in the view seem to be widely separated; those pictured in the panoramas (S. Andrea and S. Teodoro) likewise appear to be well spaced so that their areas would not overlap. Each was neither too close to the surrounding walls nor to the centre of the city, but in a convenient middle ground from which it could have directed community affairs.

Neither the convents nor the monasteries seem to be confined to any particular part of town. Monasteries in which strictly cloistered Benedictine nuns were enclosed (e.g. S. Chiara, no. 37) could be in the centre of town while mendicant friars like the Padri Conventuali (no. 27) who observed a more relaxed rule might be on the periphery. Probably the availability of land played the major part in deciding where a religious house should be rather than ecclesiastical requirements.

The seminary was, as we might expect, near the Chiesa Madre (no. 39) while the city hospital, run by the Padri Benefratelli di San Giovanni di Dio, was in the northernmost part of the city (no. 7), perhaps to help travellers and natives coming into Porta della Montagna.

For identification of the ruins of S. Nicolò in the city today see F. Balsamo, 'Proposta di identificazione dei ruderi detti di S. Nicolò', *Atti e Memorie*, Anno III, 1972, pp. 115–132. I heartily concur with Balsamo's argument that the ruins indentified as those of S. Nicolò by G. Santocono Russo are actually the church and façade of the Jesuit college.

20 Littara, 1970, p. 109; C. Gallo, 'Arte e Monumenti . . .'

21 Noto's organic plan, with streets radiating out from its central piazza, also superficially resembles that of Toledo, which is generally considered Moslem. However, it does not have what Torres Balbas would call Toledo's Moslem characteristics (L. Torres Balbas, *et al., Resumen historico del urbanismo en España*, Madrid, 1954, pp. 9–33). Also see Ira M. Lapidus, *Muslim Cities in the Later Middle Ages*, Cambridge, 1967, for concepts of the 'ideal' Muslim city.

For example, one of the characteristics of Moslem towns is that they have maze-like streets which often end in the centre of a cluster of homes. Certainly there are some alleys in Noto which are not portrayed in the views. But of the streets that are depicted there are hardly any that terminate in dead ends; instead Noto's streets are wide and easy to read, at least on the views. In addition, unlike Moslem cities, Noto had not only two central piazzas but many smaller open spaces called *piani*. Most Moslem cities, on the contrary, were composed around one major open space in the medina on which the main mosque (la mezquita mayor) and the bazaar (the Kaisariya) were located. Finally, Moslem cities are known for their labyrinthian streets in which invaders or those unfamiliar with the city might lose their way. The simplicity of Noto Antica's plan and the connective nature of its streets, which all lead to the centre, again suggest that it does not fit into the definition of a Moslem city.

Spain was under Moslem domination for centuries and was well colonized, as numerous monuments still surviving in southern and central Spain demonstrate. Sicily, on the contrary, retains only a few tangible traces of Moslem occupation, mainly in Palermo. When Noto was captured by the Moslems it was already a fully developed medieval city and aside from the erection of a few administrative buildings the effect of the Moslems on it would have been minimal. It therefore seems logical to deduce from the evidence at hand that Noto's plan was not a Sicilian hybrid but one of the family of organic city plans which were common in Europe.

22 See E. Detti, *et al., Città murate e sviluppo contemporaneo*, Milan, 1968, pp. 120–140, 154–161.

23 There are three views and two panoramas depicting Noto Antica, all of which were copied from a set of lost originals drawn before the earthquake. Antonino Tedeschi drew a view and panorama in 1780, an anonymous artist engraved a view in the eighteenth century (Pl. 2), and another anonymous artist painted a view and panorama in 1887. See note 16.

In their general depiction of Noto Antica the views and panoramas agree, but in representations of particular buildings they often disagree. For example the engraved view (Pl. 2) illustrates buildings which crowd together seemingly fighting for whatever space is available while the 1887 view illustrates a much less crowded condition. The panoramas depict an even higher urban concentration than the views do.

The credibility of the panoramas is at least in question: some of the buildings illustrated seem to be fantastic embellishments which are present only to add interest to the skyline. For instance, a number of very improbable three- and four-storey domical towers with windows and doorways appear just below the skyline (below nos 17, 43, 98, 28, 63, etc.*), as if placed there to show the richness of the city's architecture. Furthermore, building-types seem to be repeated at will: in the panorama of 1887, Tedeschi palace (no. 34), high, block-like, with two registers of rectangular windows and a domed gazebo, looks surprisingly similar to the Cistercian monastery (no. 42) just to the south of it. The strange bowed tower which is the Rizza palace (no. 44) closely resembles the tower of SS. Trinità (no. 47) next door. The steepled gazebo on the palace of the Daniele family (no. 150) reappears over the monastery next door (no. 153).

Any attempt to analyse the architecture of the city by correlating all the views and all the panoramas is doomed to failure because in most cases they disagree with one another. For example, the convent of the Carmelitani (no. 41), and the monastery of Montevergine (no. 20) have definitely Moslem domes if we consult the view of 1887. But these domes are not present on the same two buildings in Tedeschi's view and the engraving. Nor are the domes present on the same two buildings in the panoramas (nos. 123 and 183); in addition, the positions of the buildings in the panoramas are completely different from those shown in the views. Many other buildings, while retaining their positions, are depicted entirely differently in the views than they are in the panoramas. Some of these are the following:

*Numbers are for comparison with originals and do not appear in plates.

Identifying numbers

	Views	Panoramas
SS. Salvatore	22	163
Monastery of the Repentite	9	29
S. Tommaso Apostolo	35	53
Monte di Pietà	17	69
Monastery of S. Agata	21	125
Cavalry quarters	24	180

24 For Moslem domes in Sicily see S. M. Zbiss, 'Documents d'architecture Fatimite d'Occident', *Ars Orientalis*, 1959, III, pp. 27–31.

25 The arcades which appear on the view and panorama are probably 'Spanish'. In Spain in the sixteenth century, loggias were transformed into a decorative device which differed from the Roman belvedere, for example. The Spanish emphasized the upper-storey arcade and de-emphasized the rest of the building, creating an essentially atectonic effect. Façades often take on the character of decorated hanging carpets with the upper stories seeming more substantial than the lower (for examples, see F. Chueca Goitia, *Arquitectura del Siglo XVI, Ars Hispaniae*, Madrid, 1953, II, figs 232, 270, 273, 244; and G. Kubler and M. Soria, *Art and Architecture in Spain and Portugal and their American Dominions, 1500–1800*, New York, 1959, plate 4b).

26 J. Vallery-Radot, *Le recueil de plans d'édifices de la Compagnie de Jésus conservé à la Bibliothèque Nationale de Paris*, Rome, 1960, pp. 56–61.

Chapter 2

1 For the use of the term 'new town' see E. Y. Galantay, *New Towns: Antiquity to the Present*, New York, 1975.

2 For the reaction of the people of San Francisco (who refused to emigrate to Oakland across the Bay after the 1906 earthquake) see W. Bronson, *The Earth Shook, the Sky Burned*, New York, 1958. After the recent earthquake in Managua, Nicaragua it was decided to remain on the site and to rebuild the city as safely as possible (*The New York Times*, 4 September 1973, p. 3). A discussion of a city which was moved – Guatemala City – can be found in Chapter 3, p. 43.

3 *Sicilia, Guida d'Italia*. pp. 424–425.

4 Catania was half destroyed in an eruption in 121 B.C.; an earthquake in 1169 killed 15,000 people; it was inundated by lava in 1669, wiped out in 1693. Ibid., pp. 521–22.

5 For the history of the reconstruction of Lisbon and the political problems the earthquake created see J.-A. Franca, *Lisboa pombalina*, Lisbon, 1965. For psychological effects of the earthquake on the rest of Europe see T. D. Kendrick, *The Lisbon Earthquake*, Philadelphia, 1957.

6 For an analysis of the psychological effects of the physical rebirth of Hiroshima see R. Lifton, *Death in Life, Survivors of Hiroshima*, New York, 1959, pp. 92–93, and pp. 270–75. For an analysis of collective stress situations see A. Barton, *Communities in Disaster*, New York, 1969; G. W. Baker and D. W. Chapman (*eds.*), *Man and Society in Disaster*, New York, 1962, and R. R. Dynes, *Organized Behaviour in Disaster*, Lexington, Mass., 1970.

7 Tortora (1891, p. 29) was the witness.

Observation of natural disasters stimulated a catastrophe literature in Sicily which dwelt upon the details of seismic destruction. Earlier in the seventeenth century foreigners had been morbidly fascinated by the lava which flowed down the flank of Etna around the walls of Catania and into the harbour (see G. F. Ridwell, *Etna, a History of the Mountain and its Eruptions*, London, 1878, pp. 90–6). In 1693 patriotic Sicilians described in great sorrow how their home towns were destroyed. Among the most notable in addition to Tortora are P. Francesco Privitera, *Dolorosa Tragedia*, Catania, 1695, quoted by F. Fichera in *G. B. Vaccarini e l'architettura del Settecento in Sicilia*, Rome, 1934, I, pp. 36–7; D. Pietro Mataplana, *Vita e miracoli di Santa Rosalia*, Palermo, 1693; A. Burgos, *Lettera per le notizie dei danni cagionati in Sicilia da' tremuoti a 9 e 11 gennaio 1693 con una Elegia in fine*, Palermo-Naples, 1693; P. Domenico Guglielmini, *Catania distrutta*, Palermo, 1695.

8 A. Mongitore (*Biblioteca storica e Letteraria di Sicilia*, ed. G. di Marzo, Palermo, 1871, VII, pp. 103ff.) reproduces a list of damaged towns from a report of the Viceroy to the office of the Reale Patrimonio. The locations of these towns can be found on Map 1. (p. 26).

See table

9 D.S. I, 1.

10 J. Vicens Vives, *Manual de Historia Economica de España*, Barcelona, 1959, pp. 375 ff. and J. DeVries, *The Economy of Europe in an Age of Crisis, 1600–1750*, Cambridge, 1976, pp. 51–5; D. Mack Smith, *Medieval Sicily*, pp. 199–208, 231–40.

11 D. Mack Smith, pp. 211–19.

12 Ibid., pp. 220–30.

13 For anarchy, confusion and looting see Gallo, 1964 pp. 27–31. Never once do the documents record efforts of citizens from one city coming to the aid of another, more stricken, community.

Town	*Pop. before*	*Fatalities*	*Destruction*	*No.*
Aci Aquilia (Acireale)	12,895	839	almost all	
Aci S. Antonio				3
Aci S. Filippo	6,363	1,335	almost all	4
S. Agata	1,402	20	half	a
Agosta (Augusta)	6,173	2,300	almost all	5
Aidone	6,000	50	in part	b
Avola	6,225	300	all	2
Biscari	983	200	all	6
Bonacorsi	844	94	almost all	7
Borello o Stella Aragona	172	2	all	8
Buccheri	3,295	452	all	9
Buscemi	2,192	900	all	10
Caltagirone	12,339	800	in part	c
Carlentini	2,751	100	all	11
Castel d'Aci	331	32	half	d
Cassaro	1,458	15	all	12
Catania	18,914	16,000	all	13
Chiaramonte	4,830	303	almost all	14
Comiso	5,305	90	some buildings	e
Fenicia Moncada	1,651	104	almost all	15
Ferla	3,610	800	all	16
Floridia	1,037	20	all	17
Francofonte	2,039	345	all	18
S. Giovanni la Punta	1,082	15	almost all	
Lentini	10,063	3,000	all	19
Licodia	4,898	753	almost all	20
Mascali	1,300	15	2/3 damaged	21
Massa Nunziata	394	55	all	27
Melilli	5,480	900	all	22
S. Michele	1,838	1	in some parts	g
Militello	6,438	1,276	half	h
Mineo	5,740	1,355	almost all	23
Modica	18,203	3,400	half	i
Monterosso	2,340	200	all	24
Naso	4,000	1	1/8 damaged	j
Nicolasi	844	4	all	25
Niscemi	1,483	–	in great part	26
Noto	12,043	3,000	all	1
Occhiolà (Grammichele)	2,910	1,407	all	28
Palazzolo	5,571	700	all	29
Palagonia	1,862	40	half	k
Patti	4,237	–	little	l
Pedara	1,562	475	all	30
Ragusa	9,946	5,000	almost all	31
Scordia	907	30	major part	32
Siragusa (Syracuse)	15,399	4,000	major part	33
Scichili (Scicle)	9,382	2,000	all	34
Sortino	6,316	2,500	all	35
Spaccafurno (Ispica)	5,982	400	1/3 damaged	o
Tre Castagne	3,264	1,000	all	36
Tremestieri	992	90	almost all	37
Troina	5,954	1	little	m
Trizza (Aci Trezza)	–	200	almost all	38
Via Grande	–	200	all	39
Vittoria	3,950	200	half	
Vizzini	10,678	2,000	major part	40
Total Fatalities		59,700		

14 D.S. I, 2.

15 Ibid.

16 For an excellent outline of Sicily's government and the utility of the Vicar General appointment, see H. G. Koenigsberger, *The Practice of Empire*, Ithaca, New York, pp. 9–35.

17 Gallo, 1964, p. 117 and Tortora 1891, p. 35 for Camastra's appointment. For Aragona's gout, D.S. I, 2.

18 D.S. I, 10 and F. M. Emanuele e Gaetani, *Della Sicilia Nobile*, Palermo, 1754–57, parte seconda, libro II, pp. 42–3.

19 Asmundo had been appointed to the court in 1692. F. M. Emanuele e Gaetani, *Della Sicilia Nobile*, parte prima, libro IV, p. 243.

20 Carlos von Grunemburg's career has never been studied. He is referred to in Maria Accascina's *Profilo dell'Architettura a Messina dal 1600 al 1800*, Rome, n.d., p. 67 as Carlo Norimbergh. A guidebook of 1864 (*A Handbook for Travellers in Sicily . . . John Murray Handbook*, London, 1864, p. 474) gives his name as Carl Nurimburg.

A short bibliographical sketch of his life and works appears in Q. Hughes, *The Buildings of Malta*, London, 1956, p. 215. But Grunemburg's importance in the rebuilding of Sicily is mentioned nowhere. As the documents in D.S. I prove, he was instrumental in the relocation and reconstruction of towns and fortresses in Sicily. His fortress plans for Messina and for the modernization of Syracuse and Augusta can be found in the Archivo General de Simancas, Mapas y Planos Section XIX–113, X–5, IX–17, V–103.

21 D.S. I, 3, Gallo, 1975.

22 Gallo, 1970, pp. 77–8.

23 Ibid., pp. 78–9.

24 Ibid., pp. 12–13.

25 For Camastra's role in Noto and the history of the reconstruction of the city three documents are indispensable: Filippo Tortora's *Breve notizia*, an anonymous chronicler's account, and a history of Noto in a manuscript version of the life of S. Corrado.

The original manuscript of Padre Filippo Tortora's *Breve notizia della città di Noto prima e dopo il tremuoto del 1693* was written in 1712 and placed inside the silver arc of S. Corrado, the patron saint of the city; according to some people it still remains there. The Biblioteca Comunale of Noto owns what appears to be a half-finished eighteenth-century copy of the original (the MS is undated and uncatalogued, and preserved in the Library safe with another copy transcribed in a volume known as the *Libro Rosso*). The Messina family (Via Ducezio, Noto) owns a nineteenth-century copy of the original. Another nineteenth-century copy can be found in Corrado Puglisi's *MS Donato alla Biblioteca di Noto*, MS Biblioteca di Noto, 1–35. Bonfiglio Piccione published a good translation in 1891 and Balsamo corrected minor textual errors in his 1972 edition of the work.

The name of the author who wrote the second most important history of Noto during and after the earthquake is lost, and he is here referred to as the 'anonymous chronicler'. The anonymous chronicler's history of Noto can be found in Corrado Puglisi, *MS Donato*, pp. 3–14. Part of the MS was first published as a 'mystery document' without citations by Lucia Cugno ('Episodi storici e cronologici sulla ricostruzione della nuova Noto', *Città di Noto, Bollettino del Comune*, 5, 1955, pp. 5–7). The MS was again published without reference to its location by Gallo, 1964, 107–25.

A third version of the history of the city is contained in *S. Corrado*, an anonymous MS of the eighteenth century, owned by Francesco Genovesi, a Netinese. This version largely agrees with that of the anonymous chronicler.

L. Dufour, B. Huet, and H. Raymond (*Urbanistique et société baroques*, Institut d'études et de recherches en architecture et urbanisme, Paris, 1977, pp. 113–16) published a fourth source for the history of Noto: an account written by Giuseppe Asmundo in the 1690s, addressed to the Viceroy in justification of his rôle in the foundation of the city. Asmundo's version of the events in Noto on the whole follows Tortora's account. Significant new information Asmundo gives can be found in the notes which follow.

26 Gallo, 1964, p. 117.

27 Gallo, 1966, pp. 4–6.

28 Asmundo, like Tortora, states that Camastra first wanted the people to rebuild on the old site but that they refused, because they thought the hill of Monte Alveria might collapse. L. Dufour *et al., Urbanistique . . .*, pp. 113–16; Tortora, 1891, p. 35.

29 Gallo, 1970, p. 79.

30 Tortora, 1891, p. 35; Gallo, 1964, pp. 117–18.

31 Tortora, ibid.

32 For Noto and Avola see below. Ragusa's problems are discussed on p. 26. Grammichele's history is recounted in Giuffrè, 1966, pp. 49–63; for Sortino see Amico, p. 532; Ispica, in G. Bellafiore, *La civiltà artistica della Sicilia*, Florence, 1963, p. 231; Buscemi ibid., p. 218. Ferla may have been moved as well (Amico, p. 443). For attempts to move the city of Lentini see D.S. I, 3, 6.

One Sicilian city was moved three times: Belpasso was first called Malpasso and was destroyed by lava in 1669. Reconstructed at a lower site the town was rechristened Fenicia Moncada. But the lower site, prone to malaria, was badly damaged during the 1693 earthquake, and the city was moved again in 1695 to its present location. See *Sicilia, Guida d'Italia . . .*, p. 563.

33 D.S. II, 2.

34 Ibid.

35 F. Fichera, *G. B. Vaccarini*, Rome, 1934, pp. 217–25.

36 The causal analysis of earthquakes and possible warning conditions appears in D.S. I, 9.

37 Gallo, 1970, p. 13.

38 For communiqués, see D.S. II.

39 D.S. II, 1.

40 D.S. II, 2.

41 Vitruvius, *De Architectura*, trans, F. Granger, Cambridge, Mass. 1952, Book I, iv, pp. 35–7.

42 See note 55.

43 The Asinaro River must have had far more water in it during the seventeenth and eighteenth centuries which would have created even better conditions for breeding mosquitos. The principal source of the river, the Cava del Carosello, has been tapped for an aqueduct serving the city of Pachino. See B. Ragonese, 'Le porte di ponente e gli impianti artigianali nella valle del carosello', *Atti e Memorie*, Anno III, 1972, pp. 97–114.

44 For a contemporary description of the tower see Pierre del Callejo y Angulo, *Description de l'isle de Sicile et de ses côtes maritimes . . .*, Amsterdam, 1734, p. 31.

45 Gallo, 1964, p. 118.

46 Ibid.

47 Passarello, *Guida*, p. 182.

48 Tedeschi, *Comentari . . .*, seems particularly taken with Noto's antiquity. A modern description of the ruins can be found in M. Guido, *Sicily: An Archaeological Guide*, London, 1967, pp. 158–59.

49 The map of the Feudo of the Falconara (AdSN, Archivio Pignatelli-Avola, Scaffo IV, no. 3944, 1369–1695((see my Pl. 5) schematically depicts the coastal strip between the Cassibile river (no. 2 upper border of map marked 'Fiume di Cassibile che sfoggia a mare') on the north to an area well past the Asinaro River (marked 'Il detto fiume di Noto sfoggia a mare fra fegho della Falconara e di Cardello', letters C, H, G) on the south. The Feudo was half owned by Noto and half owned by Avola. Presumably the Netinese wanted to settle on their own side but, if the choice of the Meti as a site is any indication, they also may have wanted to settle across the river (where number 7 can be seen on my Map 2).

50 For more information about the choice of Madonna della Marina see Tortora, 1891, p. 23, and Gallo 1964, p. 118.

51 For a commentary on the choice of the site see Gallo 1970, pp. 13–14. Although Romanello is easy to find because a grammar school is now located there, I cannot locate the Carubba dell'Avvento. (For Romanello see *Indagine demografica, scolastica e socio-economica svolta nel Comune di Noto*. Progetto C/4, Ufficio studi e programmazione, Provveditorato agli Studi di Siracusa, 1963, p. 44.)

52 Gallo, 1970, p. 18.

53 Tortora, 1891, pp. 29–31.

54 The figures given here are only approximate. The cliff between the Pianazzo and the slope may have been accentuated by quarrying in the area of Montevergine and street levelling along the slope.

55 The very poorly drawn and painted map (AdSN, Archivio Pignatelli-Avola, Scaffo IV, no. 3944, 1369–1695, Pianta on last page) is one of two such maps. The second is apparently a copy of this one. Neither bears a date nor an indication of authorship.

Written on the Noto side of the Asinaro River which snakes its way past the new city of Noto are several cursive 'Falconara' notations. Near one of these notations a smaller script note reads 'dove anche si prendono l'acqua li notiggiani secondo dispose[?] il J. D. Giu. Asmondo' which may mean that Asmundo acquired the water rights along the Asinaro for the Netinese.

56 The legend around the map reads: La nuova città di Noto situata nel fego delli Meti il que e de i SS.ri.[?] dello stato d'Avola e da loro concesso che la Secretria [sic?] in percepisce il censo annuale.
I interpret 'SS.ri.' to mean the Seigneurs, probably derived from the Italian Signori. The secretria might be a part of the local government, or, less likely, a branch of the Spanish government, as in Secretarias Provinciales.

57 For the Duke of Terranova owning Avola, see D.S. I, 2. According to F. San Martino de Spucches (*La storia dei feudi e dei titoli nobiliari di Sicilia*, Palermo, 1927, VIII, p. 27), Giovanna Tagliavia Aragona was named the Duchess of Terranova in 1654. She married Ettore Pignatelli, the fourth Prince of Noja, and died in 1692. Their son from this marriage was Andrea Fabrizio Pignatelli Tagliavia Aragona who married Teresa Pimentel Mendoza. Giovanna Pignatelli Pimentel was the daughter of the union and it was

she who received the title after a battle of succession with the rest of the relatives (ibid., p. 179) in 1695. In 1694 Nicolò Pignatelli helped to manage Avola (see G. Gubernale, *Brevi cenni sulla città di Avola*, 1910).

58 Paolo Labisi, *La scienza dell'architettura civile*, MS Biblioteca Comunale di Noto, 1773, IV, 38–40, explains that the Senate rents Noto's land from Baron Sirugo:

> Il sito Vacuo è Libero è q.to, che non è occupato da nessuna fabrica, e che non appartiene a nessuna persona particolare, ma al solo Magistrato o Senato della Città, il quale ha la facoltà di concederlo e distribuirlo ad ogn'uno dei singoli di essa Città che ne averà il bisogno, e quantunque una tal giurisdizion non sia in tutte le Città e Terre del Regno di Sicilia, in quanto i Singoli ne sono i proprietarii per averlo ogn' uno comprato; ciò non di meno però nella Città di Noto perche il sito della Città med.a è proprio Uni.ta in quanto nè paga l'annuale censo il Senato al B.ne Sirugo d'Avola, nè ha la facoltà di concederlo e distribuirlo ad ogn'uno dei singoli iscritti per q.ta quantità, che gli bisogna colla consulta ed approvazione dell'Architetto o sia Ingegn.re Civile colla privativa della med.a Città, affine di comodamente fabricargli la sua casa, e che quando mai non gliel'aveva fabricata o che dopo d'essere stata fabricata no si rovinerà e dopo non sarà riedificata; in q.to caso il sud.o Senato la riconcederà ad altra Persona che ne averà di bisogno, com'è stata l'osservanza dell'anno 1693 sin oggi . . .

The surname Sirugo appears throughout *Volume per la causa coi Signori Barone Sirugo e Verona Marchesi di S. Floro e consorti per l'uso dell'acqua del fiume Asinaro in Noto* (AdSN, Archivio Pignatelli, Scaffo IV part 2, LVIII 4051) which is the record of a long dispute over the water and mills on the Asinaro River in the feudo of the Falconara. Documents contained in the volume date from 1695 to 1814. Asmundo may have begun the dispute by dividing the water in the Asinaro River on 8 January 1695 (ibid. ff. 86–8). In a review of the dispute dated 10 February 1801 the following is disclosed (ibid., f. 247v.):

> Le concessioni della Falconara per le più furono fatte alli naturali di Noto, Città vicina, e costadamente se era da essere stata riedificata nel fondo di essa falconara dietro che l'antica fu rovinata del terremoto del 1693.

An earlier concession is explained:

> Fra le altre delle do. concessione nel 1606 fu a Nicolo e Sebastiano Astuto fatta della tenuta chiamata la stagliata di Meti e Coffittelli vicino il luogo del monastero del Salvatore, vicino altro luogo dello Ereso [?] Astuto a tanti altri confini nel contratto individualizzati per l'anno censo di 4: 4 di frumenti e 1.6 di onze . . .

From the above documents it seems that Sirugo himself rented the land to Noto for an annual sum. But on the same page we read that the Sirugos involved in this document are Baron Corrado Sirugo and Don Antonio Sirugo, who were both inheritors of Giuseppe Sirugo's estate. Giuseppe Sirugo was the person whose claims are covered in the volume and he is only known to have been in possession of the land from 1736–37. However, these documents corroborate Labisi's statement that someone outside the city owned its site. It is likely that the rest of the comments that Labisi makes in this section are likewise trustworthy.

59 San Martino de Spucches, *La storia dei feudi* . . . V, p. 9. explains the history of title:

> È un titolo di B.ne concesso sopra fondo allodiale a Melchiore Sirugo per sé e i suoi discendenti, con diploma del 15 dicembre 1790 . . . Il nuovo posessore non aveva obbligo di investirsi. Era di Avola e figlio di Dorotea Astuto . . .

60 AdSP, Riveli di Noto, 3744, f. 19v. Payments:

> 'Al Padrone del Sito Nuovo della Città, ed altri onze venti sei, tarì ventisei e grani diciotto . . .'

Under the heading, 'Gravezza Esito dell'università di Noto secondi la plana del Tribunale del Real Patrimonio stabilita in [illegible] d'ordine in data de venti febraro 1744 . . .' the following appears: AdSP, Riveli di Noto, 3744, f. 28v.

> 'Al Padrone del sito nuovo della città ed altri onze ventisei tarì ventisei, e grani diciotto . . .'

61 By being situated on a foreign noble's territory Noto therefore would not have given up its sovereignty, and from all that can be found in the documents Noto's 'padrone' had nothing to do with Noto other than receiving an annual rent payment from it.

62 For an early case of feuding see C. Gallo, 'Episodi di anarchia nella Noto del Cinquecento', *Archivio Storico Siciliano*, XXI, XXII, pp. 195–232.

63 Document stating Don Giovanni Battista Landolina's intention to settle in Avola is AdSN, Archivio Pignatelli-Avola, Scaffo IV, Part 2, LVI, 4050, f. 205.

64 For a penetrating commentary on the situation see Gallo, 1966, p. 57. Accounts describing the rebuilding of coastal fortifications can be found in D.S. I, 3, 8, and 9. For Noto's inability to pay taxes see Gallo, 1966, pp. 9–12. On suspension of taxes in Noto: ibid., pp. 19–27. For the inability of other communities to pay taxes: ibid., pp. 51–71.

65 For Avola's relationship to the designs of Scamozzi and Cataneo as well as others see M. Giuffrè, 1966, pp. 41–73. For Scamozzi and Cataneo's part in the development of the radial city see Horst de la Croix, 'Military Architecture and the Radial City Plan in Sixteenth Century Italy', *Art Bulletin, XLII*, 4, 1960, pp. 263–72.

66 A discussion of the cities designed by Vauban (1633–1707) and the urbanistic view they reflected can be found in P. Lavedan, *Histoire de l'Urbanisme*, Paris, 1959, II, pp. 222–26. Also see P. Lazard, *Vauban*, Paris, 1934, and R. Blomfield, *Vauban*, London, 1938.

67 The painted plan from which the engraving in Amico's book was probably made can be found in the Archivio di Stato, Naples, in the storage room of Archivio Pignatelli.

68 Amico, I, p. 115:

> 'Agli angoli ed ai lati dell'esagono sono dei forti, ma ancora imperfetti, ai quali sono appoggiate quattro porte primarie, che corrispondono ai quattro punti cardinali.'

69 For the fortification situation in early Noto and later see Gallo, 1970, pp. 18–19.

70 For Sicily's poor road system see Chapter 5, note 72. Asmundo mentions that the position of the city of Noto would benefit the crown if it were on the coastal road by increasing commerce and therefore tax revenue. L. Dufour *et al.*, *Urbanistique* . . .' p. 114.

71 For the colonization of Sicily by Sicilian and Spanish nobility see A. Mori, 'Sulla formazione di nuovi centri abitati in Sicilia negli ultimi quattro secoli', *Rivista Geografica Italiana*, Anno XXVII, Fasc. IX–XII, Sept–Dec., 1920, pp. 149–183, and G. Savioli, 'Le colonizzazioni in Sicilia nei secoli XVI e XVII', *Vierteljahrschrift für Social und Wirtschaftgeschichte* (Leipzig), Band I, 1903, pp. 71–9.

72 See L. Torres Balbas, et al., *Resumen historico*.

Chapter 3

1 Tortora, 1891, p. 36, C. Gallo, 1964, p. 118, and Gallo, 1970, p. 79.

2 On 10 May 1693 Asmundo wrote that he transferred the city to the feudo of the Meti 'con animo di non tornare più sopra le rovine di Noto' (Gallo, 1964, pp. 2 and 107).

3 On 30 June 1963 according to the anonymous chronicler (ibid., p. 118) the arc of S. Corrado, patron saint of the city, was transferred to the new site:

> per maggiormente stabilirli e fissarli fe' trasportare il 30 giugno 1693 l'arca dove sta riposto il glorioso protettore S. Corrado, la quale egli in unione del Senato in toga andò a ricevere fuori il nuovo recinto e fe' collocare in una capanna che si formò dove oggi è il cortile di S. Domenico presso al pozzo.

The Di Blasi-Genovesi MS. also records:

> . . . e più obligarono fece trasportare la Sacra Cassa di San Corrado sotto li trenta Giugno dell'anno medesimo 1693, che il medesimo in toga col Senato, Magistratura, Clero, secolare e regolare andò ad incontrarla nella ripa del fiume di Noto e nel passo denominato di Commaldo, e transportata processionalmente fu conservata in una capanna a tale effetto eretta nella piazza di S. Domenico.

According to Tortora (ibid.) this procession may have ended in the Chiesa Madre of S. Nicolò; only later was the arc moved temporarily to the location mentioned by the Di Blasi-Genovesi document.

4 Impellizzeri states the following (Gallo, 1970, p. 79):

> S'incominiciò a mettersi in effetto il detto trasporto e si principiò a conoscere la difficoltà che nè popolo è tutti uniformi non volevano lasciare la loro patria, . . .

5 Impellizzeri recounts (ibid.):

> . . . Signor D. Giuseppe Asmundo il detto trasportò il quale con rigore forzò tutti li cittadini a calare.

The anonymous chronicler writes (Gallo, 1964, p. 118):

> Il Vicerè per dar principio alla nuova fabbrica inviò col titolo di Vicario Generale D. Giuseppe Asmundo, Giudice della Gran Corte Civile, il quale capitato nella distrutta città obligò i nobili e la miglior parte del popolo che ivi sopravanzata era ad abbassare nel luogo dove al dì d'oggi costrutta si vede.

6 V. Annis, *The Architecture of Antigua Guatemala, 1543–1773*, Visalia, Ca., 1968, pp. 11–14.

7 Gallo, 1964, pp. 68–9.

8 Ibid., pp. 69–70. In a dispatch the Royal Secretary advises Asmundo to clear up the disorders caused by the nobles and others. The secretary solemnly advises (p. 69) that the huts of the nobles should be completed first. There is no doubt that the nobles were not all pleased at being forced to leave the site of Noto Antica and some, like Antonino Impellizzeri, were causing disturbances. In a later dispatch (ibid., pp. 70–1) Asmundo reports that the nobles, who were presumably recalcitrant, were finally persuaded to settle in the new city and thereby were an excellent example for the rest of the populace.

9 For the orders of the Bishop of Syracuse see note 22.

10 On the jail, ibid., pp. 81, 82, 85; on mills, ibid., pp. 85, 87; on water, ibid., pp. 88–9.

11 Ibid., pp. 71–2.

12 For the account of the anonymous chronicler see ibid., p. 118.

13 Text of the report, Gallo, 1968, p. 41. Asmundo himself states in retrospect that he had doubts about whether the site was healthy. In an effort to suppress what he understood was bad air he closed and drained several rice paddies near the site. Although he did not know it, he was effectively combating malaria. But it remains to be seen how effective his programme was in controlling malaria breeding grounds around the site. L. Dufour *et al., Urbanistique* . . ., p. 115.

14 The gravity of the mosquito problem is underscored by Sinatra's map completed in 1764 which shows the area within Noto's territory where the air is good (see Chapter 5, note 12).

15 For documents relating the early outbreaks, see D.S. I, 2. The theory that a water-born disease may have been the cause of the epidemic is supported by a letter to the Bishop of Syracuse, dated 7 November, 1693 (Gallo, 1964, pp. 87–8).

16 Gallo, 1967, p. 33.

17 For victims of the plague see Gallo, 1964, p. 119 and Tortora, 1891, pp. 37–8.

18 Tortora (1891, p. 36) mentions Camastra's command to transfer the churches and religious houses to the summit. Giuseppe Asmundo, in a letter to the Royal Secretary dated 14 October 1694, wrote the following description of the incident (Gallo, 1964, pp. 97–8):

> . . . ha stimato detto Ill.te Duca condescendere alle suppliche universali di questo pubblico in lasciar la Collegiata Matrice di S.to Nicolò nello stesso sito, e trasferir nel Pianazzo la Collegiata Parrochiale del SS.mo Crocifisso, con tutte le persone che si tovano le lor capanne di tavole, e turgurij fuori le Mete . . .

The anonymous chronicler wrote the following about the move (ibid., p. 120):

> vedendo che l'aria grossa e insalubre per la vicinanza del fiume Asinaro . . . abbandonarono quel luogo, tra quali la Chiesa del . . . Crocifisso, i Padri Paulini e . . . altri . . . e sceltosi un sito più eminente, nel luogo che oggi Pianazzo si addimanda . . . ma . . . il sito del Pianazzo sembrò troppo angusto a ricevere interamente una città, che di giorno in giorno dovea aumentarsi, come pure scoraggiati per la mancanza dell'acqua che non potea in alcun conto ivi salire, ma soltanto giungere al pendio dov'è al presente, perciò contentaronsi di restare nella declività del colle Meti, dove al presente si vede.

The anonymous chronicler's statement about the difficulties of erecting a city on the Pianazzo is corroborated by a document asking for a road to be built to it in 1701: D.S. VII, 1.

19 Gallo, 1964, pp. 101–102.

20 See Chapter 2, note 58 for Labisi's version of the ordinance enforced from 1693 until his time.

21 See M. Beresford *New Towns of the Middle Ages*, London, 1967; for Sicilian new towns see Chapter 4, note 8.

22 For church scandals see Gallo, 1966, pp. 31–4. The Royal Secretary wrote to Asmundo on 18 August 1693 (Gallo, 1964, pp. 74–5) saying:

> . . . me manda encargar a VS. que se aplique con el mismo cuidado con la conclusion de las varracas de la ciudad nueva, y particularmente las de las religiosas por lo mucho que importa se reduzcan en su clausura, para evitar los escandalos . . .

The office of the Bishop of Syracuse sent a directive to the clergy of Noto on 27 July 1693 (ibid., pp. 110–11) giving precise instructions about the form of the temporary cloisters.

> . . . dette baracche con spazio conveniente fra mezzo si faccia clausura di fabrica all'altezza di due canne, o di tavole alla medesima altezza, chiesa per potervisi celebrare la S. Messa con la porta di fuori, medesimamente locutorio con doppie grate e spazio intermedio di due palmi, dove possa l'Abbadessa trattare li negotij occorenti ed altre religiose con li suoi parenti nel tempo e conforme le constituzioni sindolai di questa Diocesi, ed anco porta regolare per l'entrata di detti Monasteri capace di passare una cavalcatura . . .

23 In order to continue to serve the needs of the people and rebuild its churches at the same time the church asked for a special tax which would require the government to pay an annual sum for the sacraments performed by the clergy (ibid., pp. 15–17, 75–6). The civil administrators denounced the church's request as 'shameful', but it was granted nonetheless. According to G. Gangi (*Il barocco nella Sicilia orientale*, Rome, 1964, p. 17) the Bishops of Catania and Syracuse asked Innocent XIII for permission to rebuild their churches, convents, monasteries, and cathedrals with the money provided from bequests and donations made to ecclesiastical bodies for masses to be said after stability was restored. The bequests and donations flowing into the church coffers must have been prodigious. For evidence of the church's wealth and disputes among the juntas concerning tax credits that the church enjoyed see D.S. I, 4, 8. For a discussion of rents and gabellas and their place in post-earthquake reconstruction also see L. Dufour, *et al., Urbanistique*, pp. 51–7.

24 A full account of this vote is given in Gallo, 1970. His conclusions about the vote agree with those already stated in my doctoral dissertation and restated here. The documents supporting the discussion of the 1698 referendum can be most conveniently found in Gallo, pp. 69–90. On the discovery of these documents see Canale, p. 221, note 40.

25 For the tally of the vote see Gallo, 1970, p. 76.

26 Ibid., p. 6.

27 Gallo (ibid., pp. 6–8) divides the vote taken among the lower classes into small landowners and day labourers, artisans (artigiani), workers (operai), small industrialists (piccoli industriali) such as makers of tiles, bells, curers of wool, etc., small merchants (piccoli commercianti) such as small shopkeepers, and staff (semi-impiegati) such as servants.

	In favour of old site	*In favour of new site*
artisans	14	31
workers	89	24
small industrialists	25	6
small merchants	5	8
staff	12	21
total:	145	90

28 Ninety-eight members of the aristocracy and the clergy (ibid., pp. 71–6) voted to remain on the site of Noto Nuova. The only strong dissent was raised by Antonino Impellizzeri in an allegation appended to his vote.

29 Ibid., pp. 77–83.

30 For the investigation of Impellizzeri see Gallo, 1966, pp. 4–6.

31 For the relationship between the two families see Gallo, 1970, p. 11.

32 Chapter 4, p. 60.

33 I am thankful to Prof. Maurice Aymard for his views on the reasons for the class division in voting. Since very little economic data is available, my statements about the economic advantages and disadvantages of the move are conjectural.

34 C. M. Cipolla, 'The Decline of Italy, the Case of a Fully Matured Economy,' *The Economic Decline of Empires*, London, 1970, pp. 196–214.

35 Chapter 2, note 58 for Labisi's explanation of land distribution.

36 For the text of the entire document see Gallo, 1968, pp. 40–3.

37 Ibid.

38 For the anonymous chronicler's sentiment see Gallo, 1969, p. 119.

39 For Bellofiore's letter, ibid., pp. 43–4.

40 For Ruling of the Royal Patrimony, ibid., pp. 46–7.

41 Gallo, 1966, pp. 55–6. Also see Bruno Mare, 'Il Barone Don Mario Leggio Schinina . . .', *Colli delle 2 Raguse*, Rome, 1961, pp. 55–7.

42 D.S. VII, 2.

43 D.S. VII, 1.

44 D.S. VII, 4.

45 Gallo, 1964, p. 119.

46 This quotation and the information and quotations which follow derive from a copy of Giudice's report in Spanish and Italian in *Libro Giallo del Comune di Noto*, MS Biblioteca Comunale di Noto, ff. 568–70.

47 The anonymous chronicler's statement was 'las fabricas han deciso la lite', Gallo, 1964, p. 119.

48 *Libro Giallo del Comune* . . ., f. 570.

Chapter 4

1 The anonymous chronicler states (Gallo, 1964, p. 120) that a major part of the inhabitants had set up their huts on Cozzo della Fiera, and 'anche più abasso nel vicino lavinaro [sic] che al dì d'oggi si noma piazza lorda, vedendo che l'aria grossa ed insalubre per la vicinanza del fiume Asinaro, che alle falde del Colle scorre . . .' The Cozzo della Fiera, or area of the fair, is still remembered by locals as being on the site of the present housing development which was built on Piazza del Risorgimento on the northern side of the Pianazzo, but no one could remember ever having heard of a Piazza Lorda. In both Italian (Garzanti, *Comprehensive Italian-English Dictionary*, New York, 1961, p. 477) and in Sicilian (G. Cavallaro, *Dizionario Siciliano-Italiano*, Acireale, 1964, p. 112) *lordo*, or *lordu*, means dirty or filthy. In the context of the anonymous chronicler's statement the dirtiness is associated with the river itself which was so close to the piazza.

It is possible that this piazza was abandoned. It could also be that the unnamed piazza Formenti drew in his map of 1699 here illustrated in Map 5 (letter h and h'), was in fact the anonymous chronicler's Piazza Lorda. The piazza Formenti drew was closed during the first half of the eighteenth century. It is also possible Piazza Lorda survives as Piazza Calatafimi, the southernmost piazza of present-day Noto and one of the closest to the river.

2 For epidemic see Chapter 3, note 15; for the fire see Gallo, 1964, p. 121, and Tortora, 1891, p. 39.

3 Chapter 3, note 18.

4 See Labisi's statement Chapter 2, note 58.

5 AdSS, Registered Acts of the Senate, Noto, 636(34), 1705–6, ff. 81–2. The ecclesiastics of the convent of San Domenico address the King with a plea to stop the erection of a building near their institution. In the course of their argument they mention that the site they occupy was given to them by Camastra and Asmundo.

6 AdSS, Registered Acts of the Senate, Noto, 634(32), 1700–1, f. 30. See D.S. VII.

7 Chapter 3, note 19.

8 Menfi, Ramacca, Comitini, Floridia, Scordia, Trabia, S. Flavia, Canicattini Bagni, and Alimena are just a few of the grid-planned seventeenth-century cities that were founded in Sicily. S. Stefano is a strange exception to the rule, being planned as a series of 'X'-like streets repeated one after another. See Giuffrè, 1966 and 1969 and G. Bellafiore, *La Maniera italiana in Sicilia*, Palermo, 1963, p. 141 ff.

9 The royal jail, indicated on the Labisi veduta (Pl. 19, no. 23) was probably in place on the edge of the Pianazzo by December, 1693 (Gallo, 1964, p. 85 for document relating its completion). The portion of the city on the edge of the Pianazzo was called the area of the castello because the jail was also called 'el castillo'. That the jail was not part of a larger defensive network is proven by the repeated requests for a fortification and walls put forth by the population of Noto (Gallo, 1970, note 21, pp. 18–19). The request for a fortress and walls was never granted by the central government.

10 The legend on the Labisi veduta (Pl. 19) identifies the Monte di Pietà as being in the same building as the Casa del Refugio, no. 31. The façade of this building on Via Trigona is now part of the state penitentiary. An inscription over the easternmost doorway on Via Trigona proves that the building was dedicated to being a refuge for orphans by proclaiming just that in Latin and including the name of the founder, 'Carlos Javantus', and the date of foundation, 1606. According to R. Pirri, the Refugio di S. Teodoro was founded in Noto Antica in 1610 with funds provided through the will of Carlo Giavanti, written in 1606 (see Balsamo's note in Tortora, 1972, p. 34). Hence the identification of the building as the Casa del Refugio. Local guidebooks mistakenly refer to the building as the old monastery of S. Tommaso Apostolo, which is in fact behind the Casa del Refugio in the centre of the penitentiary complex (see Labisi veduta, no. 32, directly behind no. 31 in the veduta).

I believe that there is no reason to doubt that the Labisi veduta legend is correct in ascribing to one building the function of being both a Monte di Pietà and a Casa del Refugio. That the two were linked in Noto Nuova seems consistent with Tortora's comment (1891, p. 34) that the seventh monastery in Noto Antica was 'il Monte di Pietà, o vero Casa del Refugio'.

11 For the establishment of the city clock see D.S. VIII, 1879. The City Hospital, called Ospedale Trigona, was established in the dormitory quarters of the old monastery of S. Agata. A modern hospital on the road north of the Pianazzo is still incomplete. On the eastern side of the church of S. Nicolò are the present administrative offices of the bishop, transferred here from S. Maria dell'Arco.

12 The orientation in degrees given here is only approximate, not exact.

13 Guarino Guarini *Architettura Civile*, Turin, 1737, I, trat. II, Cap. III, pp. 48–52; A. W. Richeson, *English Land Measuring to 1800: Instruments and Practices*, Cambridge, Mass., 1966.

14 Vitruvius (*De Architectura . . .*, Book I, VI, pp. 53–67) sets out the theory of the eight winds which was followed by treatise writers up to and throughout the eighteenth century. Scamozzi, for example, uses it (Dell'*Idea . . .*, Parte Primo, Libro II, Cap. XX, pp. 52–3). Guarini, however, substitutes a compass reading for Vitruvius's elaborate solar computations, to establish wind directions. According to Vitruvius one must avoid the quarters of the eight winds by setting out streets and buildings so that they face the winds on angle. This means one has to work with fairly small angles of about 20° but nothing as small as 4°. At any rate, I am not convinced that the Netinese were all that particular about the position of their city in relation to the points of the compass or the direction of the winds. Even making allowances for the changes in declination which have occurred in Noto (declination is the amount of degrees magnetic north wanders both from location to location and from year to year in a given location as opposed to true north) Labisi, in his veduta (Pl. 17), and Sinatra, in his map (Pl. 23), make contrary judgements as to the orientation of the city. Labisi shows the city facing south-east, while Sinatra shows it facing south-west, This indicates that precise directions were not accurately or consistently noted in the eighteenth century and probably were not in the seventeenth century either.

15 Scamozzi in his ideal city (Pl. 16), for example, systematizes an obstacle, like the bed of a river, into his overall design. The idea was to keep the city's blocks and axes as regular as possible. However, Jean Baptiste Alexander Leblond in his 1717 design for St Petersburg (Pl. 61) shifts the axes of his plan much in the manner of the shift grid between the Pianazzo and the slope of the Meti. Between the Market of St Petersburg on one side of the river and the Storehouses on the other side of the river, the whole city moves to the east and the grids of the two sections diverge about 7° – a small but significant shift. About this shift, the most puzzling aspect of the plan, I. A. Egorov (*The Architectural Planning of St Petersburg*, trans. E. Dluhosch, Ohio, 1969, p. 15) has this to say:

> It is questionable that Leblond would have permitted such a shift of axes without some important reason. It may be that he did so because he incorporated parts of the existing fortifications into the geometry of his fortification system.

16 Asmundo wrote the following dispatch in 1694:

> ed è di mestiere star tutto il giorno misurando terreno, e designando strade, per falta di Capo Maestro; e mi ha giovata assai l'assistenza del capitan d'armi Don Nicolò Garces, il quale con lasciar complire colle sue obligazioni animando a tutti a transportarsi, in questo pianazzo . . .'

Gallo, 1964, pp. 100–102.

17 The Formenti map, preserved in the Archivio di Stato, Palermo, was published for the first time by L. Dufour *et al., Urbanistique*, p. 88. Although I have only examined a photograph of the map I have no doubts about its authenticity. Formenti illustrates the city as if seen from directly overhead. Using hatching he indicates the contours of the edge of the Pianazzo and the slope of the Meti. Existing buildings are indicated by solid shapes of varying intensity. To illustrate how these buildings fit into the grid plan, Formenti drew lines around the perimeter of each block. Whether Formenti was totally accurate in his depiction of the city is hard to ascertain. He sees the Pianazzo as being far longer in a north-south direction than it is. Likewise his estimation of distance between the present Via Cavour and the southern edge of the Pianazzo seems to be too generous. The map has many puzzling aspects in relation to the individual buildings portrayed. Map 5 is a conservative treatment of the information the map will yield, simply presenting the open spaces and grid of the city, both of which are updated to 1712.

18 Gallo, 1964, p. 101. The intake for the Coffitella aqueduct, on the western slope beneath the hermitage of S. Giovanni detto la Lardia, does not appear to have either the force of flow nor the elevation to send water to the Pianazzo (examined source, Summer 1972). Unfortunately, I was unable to trace the path of the aqueduct (which still supplies the city with water) to its junction with the underground intake pipes. But it would seem logical if the aqueduct were planned in 1693 that it could supply the Pianazzo, since the Pianazzo was the area first selected as the site of the city. I cannot at present satisfactorily answer this question. I am assuming that it would have been difficult to get water to the Pianazzo.

19 Dufour *et al., Urbanistique* . . . p. 114.

20 The ecclesiastical buildings either temporarily or permanently established by 1702 (see Map 5 and Map 7) included S. Nicolò (no. 1), SS. Crocifisso (no. 33), S. Antonio (no. 25); the convents of S. Francesco di Paola (no. 34), and S. Maria di Gesù (no. 28); S. Francesco (5), S. Domenico (14), and the Jesuit College (17); the monasteries of S. Maria dell'Arco (no. 8), SS. Salvatore (no. 3), S. Chiara (no. 4) Montevergine (no. 22), and S. Tommaso (no. 32), and SS. Annunziata (27), S. Agata (26) and S. Giuseppe (10). See Gallo, 1964, pp. 108–109. For S. Maria dell'Arco see ibid., p. 93. For Piano of San Francesco d'Assisi in 1704 and evidence that church and religious house had been erected, see Tortora, 1891, p. 42. For S. Antonio, see Gallo, 1964, p. 88. For the existence of the church of S. Domenico before 1704, see Tortora, 1891, p. 39.

21 On the state of the piazzas: Tortora, 1891, pp. 49. For the existence of Piazza S. Domenico, ibid, p. 42.

22 Of all the open spaces in Noto depicted by Formenti, only Piazza S. Domenico has remained totally intact. In addition to the Formenti map two others drawn in the eighteenth century (see Pls 53a and b) document its appearance. Written documents include the following: Tortora refers to the piazza as a market place in 1712 (see note 21 above). The ecclesiastics of the convent of S. Domenico mention that their building was to face the piazza pubblica, presumably the present piazza, in 1705 (see note 5 above). They also seem to indicate that the site, given to them by Camastra and Asmundo, was to be on the piazza, which would suggest that the piazza was planned from the very beginning of the occupation of the slope. The piazza itself was important in the history of the city because it was the place that the fateful vote on the future of the city was held in 1698.

23 The question of how to interpret Formenti's illustration of the piano is extremely difficult. He shades the area from Via Cavour to the letter e and all the way around the perimeter of the convent to letter d. (See Maps 4 and 5.) No building of this shape

ever occupied the area that Formenti indicates. Just what he had in mind when he drew this particular area is a mystery. The convent itself is represented by a thin solid area well behind but parallel to its present southern façade. No church is indicated. Below the convent are two very small solid squares – too small to be houses. The area of the piano itself, while open, is circumscribed by a thin line along the Corso, turning 90° north along the border of the present steps, on Via Dogali.

24 The information as to the location of the Landolina and Rau palace comes from the Noto census documents of 1748 (AdSP, Riveli di Noto, 1748). My initial idea was to reconstruct the city from the notices in the archives referring to the location of taxable property. But documents list only the names of the property owners on each side of the building described and rarely mention landmarks or street names. In order to pin down one piece of property one had to have at least three property owners identified. Placing each building in the context of the plan roughly approximated the children's game of 'pen the pig'. Because of the difficulty of getting information on at least three sides of each property from more than 20,000 pages of tax accounts, my method was difficult to use. But one of its successes was to locate the Di Lorenzo and Landolina and Rau palaces. The entire north-eastern portion of the block between the Corso on the south, Via Cavour on the north, Via Pirri on the west, and Via Nicolaci on the east (see Map 4) was occupied by the Nicolaci palace. According to the tax document (AdSP, Rivelo 3755, 1748, p. 459) Baron Giacomo Nicolaci owned a house 'confinante colle case dell' Eredi del fu Sr. Dn. Lorenzo di Lorenzo, case del Rever. Sac'te Dn. Francesco Landolina e Rau colle case del Rever. Preposito Dn. Mariano Mazzone strade publiche . . .' Mazzone's house, indicated on the anonymous plan of Piazza S. Domenico (Pl. 53b), is in the north-western corner of the block. The southern part of the block along the Corso was occupied by two property holders, Francesco Landolina e Rau and the di Lorenzo family. Rev. Sacto. Dn. Francesco Landolina e Rau (AdSP, Rivelo 3756, 1748, p. 55) lists as his property: 'una casa terrana dove abita di corpi no. 20: in parte loggia solarata in parte fabrica di terra fatta nel tremuoto del 1693: in q.a città di Noto quartiere del Collegio, conf: colla casa del B.ne di S. Giacomo Nicolaci colla casa del fu d. Lorenzo di Lorenzo e strada publica.' The report continues stating that Landolina and Rau owned 'Più sette Botteghe nell'istesso compreso fabrica di terra fatta nel tremuoto dell' anno 1693 . . .' The south-eastern corner of the block on the Corso next to the Landolina-Raus was the property of the Lorenzo family (AdSP, Rivelo 3744, 1748, p. 415). 'Rivelo che fa D. Vincenzo di Lorenzo come contutrice di D. Mariano, D. Simone, D. Corrado Tratelli minori di Lorenzo ed assenzo Figli legit'. (Lorenzo himself is evidently deceased as the Landolina e Rau document above indicates by the statement 'casa del *fu* d. Lorenzo di Lorenzo . . .'). The property is described as 'un tenimento di case palazzato consistente in otto corpi, cioè 4 di sopra e 4 di sotto (ed uno Mag. non con cisterna) es.nte in questa sud. città ed in Frontispizio del Ven. Colleg: della Compagnia di Gesù, con confinante di una parte colle case del Rev.do Sace. Dn Francesco Landolina Rau, dall' altra parte colle case di D: Giacomo Nicolaci, e Bellia B.ne di Bonfala, strade publiche da due lati, . . .' If the Lorenzo's property were opposite the frontispiece of the Jesuit college church then it would have occupied the south-eastern corner: if it were opposite the college building doorway, then it would have occupied the south-west corner. So even with bountiful information available uncertainties are still present. But from the documents we can certainly say that the southern part of the block was definitely occupied since 1693 which means that Piazza S. Domenico and the main piazza were never joined together as a single open space.

25 See Chapter 8, notes 40 and 53.

26 Some years ago when I was in Noto I was sure that the small blocks between S. Chiara and the Jesuit church of S. Carlo were laid out after the churches had been designed. The elaborate west door of S. Chiara, and a corresponding east door on S. Carlo seemed to be designed to façade a piazza. The two towers and façades would have been far more powerful than they are today if the small blocks didn't exist. I still believe that my idea of the main square has some merit, but the Formenti map and the existence of the religious complex of SS. Trinità (Map 7, no. 18) both mitigate against my hypothesis.

27 The date 1715 is inscribed over the main portal of the church of SS. Crocifisso.

28 The extension of Via Rocco Pirri between the seminary and the college of the Jesuits is clearly indicated on the anonymous map of Piazza S. Domenico (Pl. 53b). Part of the legend of the map (t, and x) is actually in the street. The street is much smaller on Labisi's 1749 map of the piazza (Pl. 53a). Although present property lines on Noto's catasto mark the division between the seminary and the college on the location of the street, the street itself no longer exists. S. Maria del Carmine was originally located on the Corso according to Labisi's map of 1749. The change in location might be explained by hypothesizing the ruin of the original church. The new church was built in its present location blocking what used to be the westward extension of Via Ducezio.

29 S. Elia, which was built just south of the Nicolaci palace on via Nicolaci, functioned as the Landolina family chapel. Another example of the same phenomenon is the Castelluccio chapel across Via Cavour from the family palace called S. Lucia. From the style of the façade of S. Elia it appears to have been built in the nineteenth century.

30 Tortora (1972, p. 52) writes the obituary of Giambattista Landolina e Salonia:

> . . . Nell'istesso anno 1693 dal mese di luglio principiò un'epidemia di pestifera febbre, colla morte circa di tre mila persone tra quali in brevi giorni si morì il nobile e virtuoso giovane D. Giambattista Landolina e Salonia, figlio di D. Francesco. Egli fu il principale disignatore di questa citta ed a morire in essa de' nobili il primo.

As Professor Corrado Gallo of the University of Palermo pointed out to me (conversation, 1970) the word 'disignatore' is ambiguous: it could mean designator of the site or designer of the city plan. In the earlier 1891 publication of Tortora's MS the word was mistakenly transcribed as 'disegnatore' according to Gallo. I have not had the opportunity to examine the Tortora document in question, but I trust Gallo's and Balsamo's interpretation of the word.

31 The anonymous chronicler's account can be found in Gallo, 1964, p. 120:

> Quietandosi alla fine i nobili e plebei, e si diedero a maggiormente insistere alla nuova costruzione, avendo fatto disegnare le strade con più ordine e proprietà da un fratello Gesuita nominato Fra [blank space in MS] Italia, che ne cavò il disegno da un libro di piante di città.

32 L. Dufour *et al., Urbanistique* . . ., pp. 113–14.

33 The most authoritative research on Italia's life can be found in M. Stella, 'L'architetto Angelo Italia', *Palladio*, XVIII, 1968, p. 172ff. and in A. Toscano Deodati, 'La Riedificazione della Chiesa di S. Maria dell'Elemosina (Collegiata) in Catania dopo il Terremoto del 1693', *Archivio Storico per la Sicilia Orientale*, LIII, 1957, pp. 109–41, in particular pp. 119–20.

Italia may have been more of a consultant than a supervisor. That and his death in 1700 would explain why his plan for the town was never completed.

34 Pietro Cataneo, *I quattro primi libri di architettura di Pietro Cataneo Senese*, Venice, 1554, Libro Primo, pp. 11 verso, 12 verso, 13 verso, 14 verso, 17, 20, 22, 24 are all illustrations of Cataneo's arrangement of piazzas within polygons. Illustrated here are Cataneo's fort on land, Pl. 14, and his city on the sea, Pl. 15.

35 For Scamozzi's discussion of his own plan see V. Scamozzi, *Dell'Idea della architettura universale*, Venice, 1615, Parte Prima, Libro Secondo, Cap. XX, pp. 164–72. The illustration and its legend (Pl. 16) can be found in ibid., p. 164.

Chapter 5

1 The population figures are from Tortora, 1891, pp. 26 and 56.

2 The population of Noto in 1748 is recorded in census documents AdSP Rivelo 3758, p. 248. Aristocrats are identifiable by the titles (such as Don) in front of their names but non-noble members of the population, for example Masters, are not differentiated by the census takers.

3 The Senate of Noto could dispense vacant land to whomever would build on it. See Ch. 2, n. 58.

4 The anonymous chronicler mentions that in 1693 wood for huts was imported from Calabria (Gallo, 1964, p. 16), but reports that the dwellings constructed from this wood were far from satisfactory:

> Riuscendo perciò i medesimi troppo incommodi e perigliosi per il continuo incendio, essendo dalla Calabria arrivata gran quantità di legname, formaronsi le abitazioni un poco più rade sode commode a via di travi e tavole, con sopraporvi le tegole. Ma queste, e per il sole e per l'acqua, formando delle varie fissure, intonacarono le medesime con pietre e fango, ed in tal guisa restò la città per lungo tempo con tetti simili edificata.

By 1702 at least the religious institutions must have been under construction in stone judging from Cardinal Giudice's report (Gallo, 1964, p. 122 and my p. 52).

5 Evidence that stone from Noto Antica was used in Noto Nuova can be seen in Noto itself, as in the lions in front of SS. Crocifisso (Pl. 138). Documents describe the positioning of fountains from Noto Antica in the new city, yet another example of sculpture being moved in the new Noto (Gallo, 1964, p. 100). Great quantities of stone and architectural sculptures were probably transported to the new city but these are difficult to document and identify. For stones used in the construction of Noto's buildings see D.S. VII, 3.

6 See p. 164.

7 The anonymous chronicler recounts that for a long time after the earthquake people were afraid to build higher than one storey (Gallo, 1964, p. 121). Given the aftershocks which the area felt (see p. 227) the Netinese were prudent to keep their buildings low. It would have been wise for the Netinese to adhere to lower building heights even today since unreinforced rubble and stone buildings react poorly to seismic shocks.

8 The anonymous chronicler wrote an account of the earthquake of 1727. It was this earthquake which evidently spurred him to write his history of Noto. See Gallo, 1964, pp. 116–25. For corroborating evidence that an earthquake did occur in 1727 see Canale, p. 265, no. 58.

9 Ibid., p. 24ff.

10 The veduta ((Pls 17–19) pen and ink, green and brown water colour, width approximately 14 × 20 cm., watermark impossible to examine) is in the collection of the Biblioteca Comunale of Noto. It was donated to the library by the Messina family of Noto. The legend on top of the veduta, many of the identifying numbers within it, and its inscription all appear to be later additions, confusing the dating of the document. The legend on top is not in the same steady hand as the legend on the bottom and its placement is so informal as to seem to be an afterthought. The first set of numbers on the veduta is confused by a second set which is penned in the same style as the upper legend; while the original numbers are formal and rectilinear the second set is scrawled in cursive style. The inscription in the cartouche on the upper right (Pl. 18) is written over an earlier inscription. The most recent inscription reads:

Excell.mo Dno
Francsó de Nicolaiis ex
Dynastibus Bonfalá Padro
Guisire: paganovum Al:
baccarie et Gisirotte: Spi:
nagalli Ricalcaccie
Oleastri et Gisire Bis
colensi Et Prici
Villeaurcati
Anno Domini
1783

Upon close examination it can be seen that the patron's name, the last two lines, and the date have been altered. It originally read:

Excell. mo Dno
Jacobo de Nicolaiis ex
Dynastibus Bonafalá Prado
Guisire: paganovum Al
baccarie et Gisirotte: Spi:
nagalli Ricalcaccie
oleastri et Gisire Bre
colensi Ec. D.D.D.
D. Paolus Labisi
Architectus
17—?

The original patron, Jacobo or Giacomo Nicolaci, lived from 1711 to 1760, during which time he played an extremely important role in the political and cultural life of Noto, and was the patron of Paolo Labisi (I. Murè Ruiz and G. Leante, *In memoria di Corrado Nicolaci Principe di Villadorata*, Noto, 1902, p. 180). Giacomo was eulogized at his funeral with his official title which appears in doggerel Latin on the veduta; in Italian he is called:

D. Iacobo Maria Nicolaci e Bellia . . . Barone di Bonfala, Prato, Gesira e Gisirotta di Pagno Calaccia, Ricalcaccia, Spinagallo, Agliastro, Gisira d'Agosta (ibid., pp. 196, 199).

The inscription was changed when the veduta was inherited by Franzo Nicolaci (1744–1807) after the family had acquired the title of Principe di Villadorata some years before on 24 August 1764 (ibid., pp. 195, 199). When Franzo substituted his name for that of his deceased relative he also had to insert the Latinized epitaph 'Principibus Villaeauratae' which meant that Paolo Labisi's name had to be obliterated to make room for it. The date of the inscription coincides with both a strong Calabrian earthquake and the reopening of the arc of S. Corrado (ibid., p. 199). Either one of these events could have caused Franzo to update the veduta. In the first instance, because he wanted to show that Noto, which had suffered through an earthquake just as disastrous as the one which had occurred in Calabria, had recovered and still existed; in the second, perhaps the commemoration of S. Corrado and the repair of his arc suggested to Franzo that the veduta should be 'repaired' too. Unfortunately the digits of '1783' completely obliterate the original date of the veduta, but we can assume that the year Giacomo died, 1760, is a stable *terminus post quem*. Since Labisi drew the designs for the house of the Crociferi Fathers in 1750, we can assume the veduta dates from between 1750 and 1760. In the text I consistently refer to the 1750s as a date for it.

11 I base my idea that Labisi climbed the hill to the south-west of the city to draw his veduta on the close correspondence between the view he drew (see Pl. 19) and the view from the hill (see Pl. 22).

12 The map can be found in the Biblioteca Comunale of Noto. It measures approximately 29 × 25 cm. and is glued to a cardboard backing (watermark impossible to examine). It is drawn in ink and painted in watercolour. The legend reads as follows:

I. BBBBB Linea equidistante dal perimetro della Città di Noto pel tratto di miglia due, la quale determina i confini per dove postanno li Canapi, e far bonache [?] acciochè l'aria che viene ammorbata dalla di loro mala qualità restasse sana. Essendo tutto ciò stato ordinato da questo Illustrissimo Senato nell'anno 1764 al ben publico di questa città esatta geometricamente da me Vincenzo Sinatra Architetto della sudetta Città di Noto.

Thus the map was intended to indicate the regions around the city where malaria (during the period described as bad air) was not present.

13 Labisi's map measures 28 × 22 cm. and is in the collection of the Biblioteca Comunale of Noto. An inscription on the lower part of the map reads: 'a 16 Aprile, 94, Dono Bonfiglio Piccione' which most likely refers to the donation of the map in 1894 (since Piccione was active in Noto around that time). The legend of the map reads:

Delineava da Paolo Labisi Architetto della Ingegnosa Città di Noto La Topografia P.z. secondo che si trova nella sud.a Città edificata giusta le Sue Misure, e proporzioni nell'anno 1749.

The anonymous map is in the collection of Francesco Genovesi of Noto. From the style of the drafting and the people mentioned in the legend (such as 'Notar Marotta' who can be identified as Natale Marotta, Netinese notary from *ca.* 1716–61) the map can be said to date from the mid-eighteeenth century.

14 For eighteenth-century reference to Piano di Chiesa Madre e Casa Senatoria see D.S. VI. The names for the parts of the main piazza are the following: Piazza Municipio, loosely applied to area in front of the city hall; Piazzetta Landolina, space above stores on north-west; Piazza Landolina, horseshoe piazza on west; Piazza Trigona, horseshoe piazza on east.

15 The building was approved for construction in 1753, and therefore was not as complete as Labisi illustrates it.

16 For the history of the church see p. 184.

17 See p. 139.

18 Evidently the church of the Carmelites was moved from a position on the Corso (see Labisi map Pl. 53a) to its present location. That the church was in fact newly erected is recorded in a contract of 1770, Vincenzo Labisi (AdSS 007239, 1769–70, 10 July 1770, f. 585) which refers to the 'nova Ecclia' or new church. But in 1776–78 the church is going to ruin (Vincenzo Labisi, AdSS 007246, 1777–78, ff. 147). It is therefore possible that the present church has a different vault than the one Labisi drew, and that the previous vault and dome fell in.

19 The present oval dome of the church of S. Chiara is probably original; Labisi is in error. A plan for the construction of the dome survives: the longitudinal section and plan of the dome (pen and ink, with yellow watercolour; 45 × 30 cm.; watermark of three crescent moons; collection of the Biblioteca Comunale di Noto) is interesting in light of the unusual construction of the roof. It illustrates the curved wooden beams which serve as a framework for the plaster ceiling. The beams are hidden in the plaster today, however. For after the coating of plaster became thick enough the contoured, crescent-shaped beams were laid across the vault of the church, lathed and then plastered. When the church had to be restored recently Msgr. Tranchina directed the workers to use this original technique to reinforce the stability of the vault.

20 See Chapter 8, p. 160

21 There is no evidence that the southern extension of the Jesuit college that Labisi illustrates was ever constructed; no wall can be found, no remains that would indicate the uniform walls he shows. The only support for his depiction is that a large portal of a building on Via Roma (Pl. 64) is vaguely in the same position as the main entrance to the college on the block above. Perhaps the two were correlated.

22 The property in front of the monastery was probably sought after because of its location on the piazza. It is doubtful that the property was ever vacant as Labisi depicts it. On both maps of the area (Pls 53a, 53b) the property is occupied.

23 For Noto's lack of defensive walls see Gallo, 1970, pp. 18–20. Early in Noto's history, during the reassessment of the site by Cardinal Giudice, his report (*Libro Giallo* MS . . ., f. 569) recommends:

y pa. defenderlos . . . de enemigos se podra disponer un castillo . . . en la situacion mas eminente dicha del planazo que ora domina toda la ciudad . . .

But the proposed castle for the Pianazzo was never erected, and the small jail on the Pianazzo was evidently of no use in protecting the city. Hence the request for a fort and walls that Gallo (ibid.) quotes. The walls illustrated by G. Gangi in his article on Noto ('Forma e avventura della città di Noto'. *Palladio*, XVIII, 1968, pp. 133–44) have no basis in fact.

24 On the establishment of the jail see Gallo, 1966, p. 8.

25 The discussion of Noto's roads which follows should be considered only an introduction to the problem since a survey of the old roads in the Noto area would be essential to isolate exactly where the eighteenth-century roads were. Contemporary

maps of Sicily are of little help because they are inaccurate. Both Noto Nuova and Noto Antica are depicted by Guillaume Del'Isle in his somewhat inaccurate map bearing the title *Insulae et regni Siciliae novissima tabula*, published by Joachim Ottens in Amsterdam and dated 1717. Although Del'Isle's map distorts the outline of Sicily it does have the virtue of depicting the roads which existed around the two Notos. He illustrates a single road leading from a too-far-inland Noto Nuova to Noto Antica and then to Palazzolo Acreide. A coastal road bypasses Noto. Agatino Diadone's slightly more accurate map of 1720 (legend: Opera di Agatino Daidone della Città di Calascibetta, Architetto nella Città di Palermo, e ristampata pel Sollievo che spera godere questo fidelissimo Regno sotto il potente ed augusto dominio della Cesarea e Cattolica Maestà di Carlo VI Imperatore e Il Re delle Spagne) illustrates Noto closer to the Asinaro river but unfortunately confuses Noto Nuova with Noto Antica. He places the 1720 city of Noto on the pre-earthquake location. But the roads he depicts are the same as those of the Del'Isle map. Both the Del'Isle and Diadone maps are contradicted by Samuel Schmettau's map of 1719 which records a road leading from Noto Nuova to Modica and deletes the one leading from Noto Nuova to Palazzolo. It is possible that Schmettau does not illustrate the road to Palazzolo because it was blocked by the earthquake and had become unusable; while the other two maps might be combining pre- and post-earthquake details Schmettau may be illustrating only what remained, or had been built, after the earthquake of 1693. For these maps and others see Giuffrè, 1969, p. 67ff.

26 See note 72.

27 Gallo, 1964, pp. 121–2

28 These roads are clearly seen on the aerial photograph of Noto (Pl. 9). The two southeastern roads which branch in a 'y' from the lower part of the city toward the Asinaro River can still be seen from the air, though they are so rough in places that they are not fit for a cart or a jeep. One road appears to end in the loop of a railway right-of-way while the other leads down on a diagonal to the Asinaro and crosses, where the Commaldo joins the Asinaro River, and reappears on the hills across the bank as a deep gully. The westernmost road crosses a small hill (from which I think Labisi drew his veduta), and then continues south. The configuration of these roads looks very much like that which can be seen in the Labisi veduta and the Sinatra map.

29 See pp. 179ff.

30 I experienced how the interior blocks of the city could grow during the Winter of 1969 when I lived on Via Aurispa in the lower part of the city. One of my neighbours wanted to build over a small gap which ran between his house and the back wall of the house I was renting. The space was about 3 metres wide and 4 metres deep. He chiselled a notch in the wall of the house I was renting and put a beam in it. Using other notches he beamed the space and closed it off.

Sometimes an obviously new addition to a building cut an open space in two. When I asked whether the builders who had erected the new additions – like the one next to the house I rented – had permission from the city, most answered they did not. This encroachment on space and non-regulated building activity is for me the model of uncontrolled organic city planning which can produce some very interesting street patterns. In my discussion of Noto Antica (Chapter 1, note 21), I explained that the plan was not Islamic, but more like other medieval towns throughout Europe.

31 The argument might be made that the maze-like alleys of Noto Nuova are Islamic. Although these alleys may be maze-like, I do not believe their appearance throughout south-eastern Sicily is due to Islamic influence. Rather they are the results of the situation in which the lower class agricultural workers found themselves. Because only so many dwellings could be built along the perimeter of a block they arranged their houses (one after another) along alleys which ran through the block. A medieval 'organic' pattern of streets thus developed. Furthermore, if the small alleys and dead-end streets reflect Islamic influence then why are the structures which line them so unIslamic, lacking the central atrium and gardens so much a part of Islamic culture? Formalistically these maze-like streets may look Islamic on a map but they do not have the same character. I think of them as part of the Mediterranean building tradition rather than as strictly 'Islamic'. Aldo Pecora ('Insediamento e dimora rurale nella regione degli Iblei,' *Quaderni di Geografia umana per la Sicilia e la Calabria*, IV, 1959, p. 28) gives another reason for the alleys and small open spaces within Noto's grid system. He explains that a common courtyard in the centre of a block is the result of the storage needs of the agricultural community, and gives as an example of such an arrangement, the eighteenth-century town of Pachino near Noto. In fact common courtyards where equipment can be stored are present in Noto; often such areas have a common gate.

32 Today, these inner-core houses are in a much better state of preservation than those on the straight streets of Noto. The exterior houses, the first to be built, were also the first to be torn down or improved, and they have often been remodelled so completely that their original date of erection is hard to guess.

33 Corrado Tafaro (*Notizie storico-religiose e civili dell'antica e moderna città di Noto*, MS Biblioteca Comunale di Noto, II, March 1928, p. 285) writes:

> Le nuove intitolazioni alle strade di Noto, che portarono ancora quelle tradizionali delle vecchie contrade furono eseguite nel 1873. Riportato dal giornale locale 'La Gazzetta Netina', 14 Aprile anno 1873 . . . La proposta per le dette intitolazioni era stata fatta dal Consiglio Comunale nel 1861. La commissione per le dette intit. era composta da Ascenso Mauceri, Francesco Connello, Giuseppe Labisi, e scelsero tanti nomi: Vittorio Em, Garibaldi, Cavour.

34 V. Arezzo Prado, *Cenni sugli avventimenti netini, Noto*, 1862, cites the old names of Noto's main streets.

35 See D.S. VI, f. 61 for Bernardo Labisi's use of the name Cassaro.

36 Noto's main street looks nothing like Palermo's. In Palermo the Cassaro crosses another main street (Via Marqueda) and at this crossroads the famous 'quattro cantoni' were erected in the seventeenth century; on each corner a concave façade was raised. However, in a ceiling painting which adorns the salon in Noto's city hall a map of the new city is shown in the hands of a founder; the painting, surely dating from the nineteenth century, shows Palermo's quattro cantoni in the centre of Noto, and very clearly shows an identification on the part of the Netinese with the cosmopolitan city of Palermo. (Passarello, *Personalità netine di tutti i tempi*, Catania, 1969, p. 131, credits Antonio Mazza with the painting.)

37 For a popular but reliable account of streets in Rome see M. Andrieux, *Daily Life in Papal Rome*, London 1968, p. 15ff.

38 See Chapter 4, note 24.

39 C. Lévi-Strauss, *Tristes Tropiques*, New York, 1970, pp. 125–27.

40 For the late nineteenth-century planting of the Villa see D.S. VIII, 1873. The plans for the planting of flowers and trees still survive uncatalogued in the collection of the Biblioteca Comunale of Noto.

Exactly where the fill came from is difficult to say. Most probably it is all the topsoil from the city and particularly the piazzas, which was carted away when the streets were lowered.

41 F. Boyer, 'Les promenades publiques en Italie du centre et du sud au XVIIIe siècle', *La Vie Urbaine*, IV, 1960, p. 241.

42 Ibid., p. 266.

43 I am indebted to Prof. Paul Hofer for pointing out the importance of Piazza Taranto to me.

44 G. Passarello, *Guida della città* . . ., p. 16.

45 For Bernardo Maria Labisi's proposal see D.S. VI, ff. 61–6.

46 See D.S. VIII for accounts of lowering the streets. F. Cassone (*Osservazione intorno al basolamento del Corso Vittorio Emanuele in Noto*, Noto, 1875, p. 4) in his diagnosis of the ills of the Corso says the following:

> Gli inconvenienti continui che vogliano evitarsi, e pei quali si vuole il basolamento sono il fango nello inverno, la polvere nella stagione estiva.

47 The previous level of the street can only be ascertained from the height of the false basement façades added to cover their original foundations. For the undermining of foundations that the excavation of the roads caused see D.S. VIII, 1873.

48 The width of the Corso was measured from the wall of S. Chiara to the fountain across the street on the wall of SS. Salvatore. The exact width is 9.4 m. The following widths of streets in Noto were also taken from the wall of one eighteenth-century building to the wall of another: Via Dogali (measured from SS. Salvatore to S. Francesco d'Assisi): 7.8 m; Via Rinaldo Montuaro (measured from the first pilaster of the Landolina palace to the tower of S. Nicolò): 4.7 m; the same street measured from the side of the palace to the nave of S. Nicolò: 7.9 m; Via Cavour (measured from the old oratory of S. Filippo Neri to the house of the Crociferi): 7.8 m; Via Rocco Pirri (measured from the Buongiorno palace to the eighteenth-century gate opposite): 7.8 m; Via Sovio (measured from the old wall of S. Domenico to the corner of the house of the Crociferi): 5.6 m; Via Trigona (measured from the north side of S. Giacomo palace to the south side of the former Casa del Refugio): 8.8 m; Via Sallicano (measured from the old hospital of the Benefratelli to the side of S. Tommaso): 9.7 m.

It should be noted that Via Dogali, Via Rinaldo Montuaro (before the erection of the side towers of the S. Nicolò, (see Chapter 7, p. 139)), and Via Rocco Pirri all approximate to 7.8 or 7.9 metres, a little more than three *canne*. They are all north-south streets and this measurement may have been prescribed for such streets. However, Via Cavour is also close to this measurement. I think it is safe to assume that we are hitting on a standard street measurement of the city.

Another interesting point about

the widths of the streets is that Via Sallicano on the Pianazzo is a little wider than the Corso itself. Via Sallicano is the street which runs past the church of SS. Crocifisso on the Pianazzo and continues south in the direction of S. Nicolò. It establishes the axis between the two churches. Thus the width of the street may be indicative of its importance in the minds of the planners of the city. Perhaps one might say that the Corso and Via Sallicano were the most important streets in the city while the others were secondary arteries.

However, there is no distinction made in the documents between these streets. They are all called *strada maestra*, or just *strada*. It is therefore difficult to judge how much the Netinese themselves distinguished between them according to their widths and importance.

In his treatise (*La scienza* . . ., p. 42) Paolo Labisi states that the Strada Maestra del Re should be at least 38 Sicilian *palmi* (there are eight *palmi* to the *canna*) wide, which makes the street 4.6 *canne* or 8.7 metres in width.

According to Labisi, who takes his standards from a European treatise writer, Christian Wolff (*Elementa Meteseos Universe*. MS Biblioteca Comunale di Noto, IV, copied 1746; see Chapter 9, p. 225, and Chapter 9, note 37), only Via Trigona and Via Sallicano would qualify as *strade maestre*.

49 See Fichera, *G. B. Vaccarini* . . . p. 221.

50 These statements about the eighteenth-century piano are based on visual observation corroborated by the Labisi veduta. The wall behind (north of) the shops is divided from them by a small narrow space. The wall, which appears to be the one illustrated in the veduta, is shown in my Figure 4.

51 The edges of the treads on the uppermost flight of steps are rounder than those of the lowermost flights.

52 Tortora, 1972, editor's footnote, p. 57, Passarello, *Guida della città* . . ., p. 22.

53 Passarello, *Guida della città* . . ., p. 24; N. Pisani, *Barocco in Sicilia*, Syracuse, 1958, p. 57.

54 See D.S. VIII, Nov. 1880.

55 See D.S. VI, f. 3 for description of the fountain.

56 For an explanation of Bernini's aesthetics see Timothy Kitao, *Circle and Oval in the Square of St. Peters, Bernini's Art of Planning*, N.Y. 1974.

57 See D.S. VI, ff. 44–44v.

58 For arrangement of the churches on Piazza del Popolo, see R. Wittkower, 'Carlo Rainaldi and the Architecture of the Full Baroque', *Art Bulletin* XIX, 1937, pp. 242–313.

59 For notes on the nineteenth-century theatre, the present teatro comunale, see Gaetano Passarello, *Noto, guida della città* (2nd ed.), Catania, 1970, p. 39. Also see Francesco Balsamo, *Una visita a Noto la 'città d'oro'*, Noto, 1973, p. 30.

60 The date of 1787 is inscribed over the first storey of the southern façade of the convent.

61 See D.S. VI, f. 44v on the transfer of the fountain. Also see Balsamo, *Una visita a Noto* . . ., p. 29 for the nineteenth-century history of the fountain. It was in the hands of this statue on 16 May 1860 that a group of local patriots placed the tricolor. Hence the present official name of Piazza XVI Maggio.

62 See chapter 4, note 22.

63 Such stalls can be seen on a map of the Piazza in the possession of Francesco Genovesi of Noto.

64 See D.S. VIII, April, 1880.

65 The western exit from Noto I refer to here is Piazza Nino Bixio. The ugly obelisk was erected in 1958 (Passarello, *Guida della città* . . ., p. 97). According to Passarello the statue that adorns the top of the obelisk was taken from an exterior niche in the façade of the oratory of S. Filippo Neri.

66 Labisi, *La scienza dell'architettura* . . . ff. 9 verso, 10.

67 Paolo Balsamo, in his *Giornale del viaggio fatto in Sicilia e particolarmente nella Contea di Modica*, Palermo, 1809, pp. 199–200, is astonished by the size of the uncultivated land within the city's rich territory:

> Fa maraviglia, come in 38000 salme di terre ve ne siano 19000 incolte, e come in tutte non vi siano più di 12000 abitanti: e si può domandare, se mai vi è poca coltura perchè vi è poca gente? Diversi su di ciò diversamente opinano; e dovendo anch'io sullo stesso argomento il mio guidizio proferire direi, che in un paese nuovo, e disabitato, quale fu un tempo, ed è ora in molti distretti l'America, può esservi molto di terreno greggio, ed infruttifero perchè vi sono pochi uomini; ma in un paese antico, e da remotissimi tempi popolato, qual'è la Sicilia, ciò non si può verificare: cosicchè il mancamento in questa di uomini indica sicuramente difetto di coltura, ossia di richezza, di capitali, d'industria, e di tutte le cose, che la stessa promovono, e principalmente di pronta, ed utile consumazione . . .

68 For a similar conclusion about the landowners of Sicily see D. Mack Smith, *Modern Sicily*, pp. 288–9.

69 See D.S. VII, 4.

70 D. Mack Smith, *Modern Sicily*, pp. 290–91.

71 Tortora, 1891, p. 26.

72 For travellers' laments about the deplorable road system and poor inns see H. Tuzet, *La Sicile au XVIIIe siècle vue par les voyageurs étrangers*, Strasbourg, 1955.

73 A. Swinburne, *Travels in the Two Sicilies*, London, 1790, III, pp. 53–4.

74 The anonymous chronicler claims the road to the coast was quite good, Gallo, 1964, p. 121.

75 The Di Lorenzo family referred to here has the inherited title of Marchese di Castelluccio. Although a palace existed on the Via Cavour site when the veduta was drawn, its façade is the product of a later campaign. Neither the palace of the Astutos nor that of the Trigonas appears on the veduta. For their positions see Map 8, 45 and 44b respectively. See also Appendix 2.

76 See Appendix 2.

77 For the way S. Pietro Martire used to look at the end of Via Roma, with the street skirting around it, see the Labisi veduta (Pl. 19). For the building of the church of the Carmine at the end of Via Ducezio see Chapter 4, note 28. For the church of S. Girolamo, see Chapter 9 note 25.

78 The procession of carriages to the upper part of the city along the present street of G. Galilei is recorded in a description of the feast of S. Corrado in *Libro Giallo* . . .

79 AdSP, Rivelo 3758, 1748, f. 248 gives the population of the city by parishes as follows:

Quarter of the Chiesa Madre (S. Nicolò)	3,200
Quarter of SS. Crocifisso (the Pianazzo)	3,035
Quarter of S. Spirito	485
Quarter of S. Michele	2,229
Quarter of S. Maria della Rotonda	789
Total	9,738
Total of monks and nuns	345

80 There is a legend that the Impellizzeris would not settle on the slope because of a fight with the Marchese of Castelluccio who owned the slope, so they settled on the edge of the Pianazzo. Certainly Antonino Impellizzeri who fought so vigorously against the new site, might have wanted to settle his family away from the rest of the aristocracy on the slope. For details about the palace see Appendix 2.

81 G. Kubler, and M. Soria, *Art and Architecture in Spain and Portugal, and their American Dominions*, Harmondsworth, 1959, p. 33. For illustrations and a discussion of Nuevo Baztán see E. A. Gutkind, *Urban Development in Southern Europe: Spain and Portugal, International History of City Development*, New York, 1967, p. 273; and Torres Balbas *et al.*,*Resumen Historico del urbanismo en España* . . . p. 125.

82 Torres Balbas, Ibid., pp. 93–7.

83 A print from the nineteenth century in the Biblioteca Comunale di Noto illustrates the church of S. Nicolò during a festival of S. Corrado. The building to the east of the church on the main piazza has an arcade in front of it. The artist who drew the portrayal of the festival shows the building (now the Bishop's palace) divided in three separate blocks. The walls of these three separate blocks can still be seen behind the unified nineteenth-century façade of the present building. So the print may be trustworthy. If so Noto did have at least a partial arcade.

84 For the Spanish ordinances in their original form and in translation see Z. Nutall, 'Royal Ordinances Concerning the Laying Out of New Towns,' *The Hispanic American Historical Review*, IV, 1922, pp. 249–54.

85 For examples of how new towns deviated from the ordinances see D. Stanislawski, 'Early Spanish Town Planning in the New World', *Geographical Review*, XXXVII, Jan., 1947, pp. 94–105.

86 For a discussion of Spanish colonial urbanism see G. Kubler, *Mexican Architecture of the Sixteenth Century*, New Haven, 1948, pp. 68–102, in particular p. 102. For a good bibliography of sources on Spanish, French, and English colonial practices in the United States, see J. W. Reps, *The Making of Urban America*, Princeton, 1965, pp. 554–62.

87 For a discussion of the plan of San Fernando de Béxar, see Reps, ibid., p. 37.

88 G. Bellafiore, *La Maniera italiana* . . . p. 141.

89 K. Lynch, *The Image of the City*, Cambridge, Mass., 1960, p. 31.

90 I. A. Egorov, *The Architectural Planning of St Petersburg*, Ohio, 1969.

91 C. Norberg-Schulz, *Late Baroque and Rococo Architecture*, New York, 1974, pp. 15–60 and P. Lavedan, *Histoire de l'Urbanisme*, Paris, 1959, I, pp. 358–64.

92 J.-A. França, *Lisboa pombalina* . . ., pp. 71ff.

93 A. J. Youngson, *The Making of Classical Edinburgh, 1750–1840*, Edinburgh, 1966, pp. 70–110.

94 André Corboz, *Invention de Carouge, 1772–1792*, Lausanne, 1968, p. 120ff.

Chapter 6

1 Paolo Labisi, *La scienza* . . ., f. 7. Labisi's complete definition of a city or village follows (ibid., 8–10ff.).

> Della Città e Villaggio
> La Citta o Terra è un Edificio principale, fabricato, e diviso in molti altri Edifici minori ben commodi ed utili alla Vita Civile,

come a dire Chiese, Conventi, Monasteri, Colleggi, Palazzi, cose grandi e mezzane, obelischi, Piramidi, Fontane, ed altro per uso della commune società di moltissimi Uomini e Donne, che ivi abitano, sottoposti ad un Regnante o ad un Principe particolare.

8.

E perchè lo scopo principale degl'abbitanti quello di voler principalmente godere una perfetta sanità e la diversa condizione delle persone esige un' abitazione diversa dall' altra; l'Architetto ha l'obbligo di dover eriggere un tal Edificio o Città o Terra in un sito commodo, e d'un' aria perfetta, con la divisione delle strade, e Piazze, non solo commode, ma anche situate in maniera, che gl'abbitanti medi non vengono ad esser soggetti alla mala qualità dei Venti nocivi, ma che le case o abbitazioni loro possono essere commodamente situate, senza che ogn'una di loro avesse dependenza dall'altra, con essere libere, sciolte d'ogni servitù di Porte, Fenestre, di entrate, di cadim. ti delle acque piovane, imperochè la legge generale delli Padroni di esse Città o Terre e q.ta di doversi distribuire con ordine e proporzione tutto il sito di essa.

9.

Città ad ogn'uno degl'abbitanti per commodo della loro abitazione particolare affine di essere difesi dalle ingiurie dei Tempi, e restar sani e comodi nelle proprie lor case, colla facoltà di poter ogn'uno di essi alzarle in un'altezza proporzionata e commoda, rispetto al proprio stato e condizione; distribuite con quell'ordine, che si ricerca nell' Architettura, non solo per la stabilità delle fabriche, ma pur anche per la commodità loro, e del Publico tutto, portando quell'avvenenza che si richiede in una Città, per delizia, e decoro tutto il complesso del Popolo, che si abbita con allegria, devozione, e sincero trattamento, giusta la norma che si richiede in una assemblea di Cristiani seguaci della Legge di Gesù Cristo. Le Città, per legge d'Architettura sogliono essere formate, e divise

[no number].

dagl'architetti con ottima simmetria, per mezzo della distribuzione delle Strade, dei Piani, e dei quartieri ch'eglino fanno dappertutto, per norma e regolamento, degl'abitanti, e per poter ogn'uno di loro fabricare commodamente all'intorno di esse strade, Piani, e vicoli, le rispettive case, con dover situare le lor Porte e fenestre nel prospetto delle m.e. Strade e Piani, per così ogn'uno poter avere in esse l'uscita libera, il lume chiaro, e l'Aria salutare; e perchè le Strade ed i Piani oltre d'essere d'ornamento e decoro della Città sono anche destinate non solo per l'esercizio del Publico commercio con dar il commando ad ogn'uno degl'abbitanti per poter passeggiare a piedi ed in Carrozza per tutta la Città e specialmente nelle Piazze per godere in essi Piani medi ed in.

10.

ogni quartiere il necessario esate [?] e ventilazione dell' aria salutare; ma pur anche son destinati per escludere dagli Edificij il molesto corso delle acque piovane, e le alluvioni, che potrebbero dannegiarli, com'anche, per avere ogn'uno degl'abbitanti il commodo di poter guardarsi dalle scosse della Terra (che Dio ci liberi) col mezzo di poter uscire dalle proprie case e ricoverarsi nei Piani med.i per così sfuggire dai pericoli di poter essere colpiti anche dalle rovine delle lor case; e finalmente son destinati le strade ed i Piani per ogn'uno godere i prospetti degli edificij, che si fanno all'intorno, per ornamento delli medi piani, e per aver anche gli abbitanti il piacere nell' affacciarsi dalle lor fenestre, godere le funzioni publiche, che si fanno in esse Città dal Popolo stesso;

[new page, unnumbered]

Ragione vuole che le strade ed i piani si lasciasseno nella sua primiera situazione, senza che da nessuno ufficiale locale, subalterno di S.R. potesse alterarli, in pregiudizio del Publico commodo, ed uso dei singoli ancora, che il fine per cui essi portano il nome di piani e strade reggie.

2 H. Saalman, *Medieval Cities*, New York, 1968, p. 11.

3 V. Denon, *Travels Through Sicily and Malta*, Perth, 1790, p. 191.

4 Larousse, *Dictionnaire du XIXe siècle*, 1870, VI, p. 443 for Denon's life.

5 For Noto's population in 1748, see Chapter 5, note 79. The number of churches operating in eighteenth-century Noto fluctuated so the numbers given here are only valid for 1748, when the churches and monastic institutions were listed in the census documents.

6 A. Leanti, *Lo stato presente della Sicilia*, Palermo, 1761, pp. 139ff. and 125ff.

7 The paragraphs which follow touch upon only a few of the major points concerning the size and functioning of religious houses. For a more complete discussion of the built forms of religious houses see W. Braunfels, *Monasteries of Western Europe*, Princeton, N.J., 1972.

8 The people of Noto believed that the earthquake was God's punishment for their wrongdoing. After the earthquake there were penitential processions which eye witnesses describe (see D.S. I, 1). A similar phenomenon occurred after the Lisbon earthquake. See T. D. Kendrick, *The Lisbon Earthquake* ....

9 The only documents recording the births and marriages of the architects discussed in this book were compiled by priests. D.S. III, IV, and V.

10 The dispersal of Noto's parish churches throughout the city was consciously planned. The parish churches of eighteenth-century Noto occupied the most peripheral straight streets on the north, east, south and west sides of Noto. Thus the church of SS. Crocifisso (Map 7, no. 33), which was both a college and a parish church, defines the northernmost part of the grid; S. Maria la Rotonda (no. 37) the southernmost part; S. Michele (no. 13) the westernmost part; and S. Maria del Purgatorio (no. 9) the easternmost part. The positions of these parish churches indicate that the planners expected the city to grow enough around the periphery of the grid to supply parishoners from future outlying neighbourhoods. Today, for example, these four parish churches are in perfect positions to be the foci of four areas of the city. (For the present parish churches, which number ten within Noto itself, and sixteen including those in the territory around it, see Passarello, *Guida della città* ..., p. 42.)

11 Confraternities still exist in Noto. During the festival of S. Corrado these lay confraternities, which have special costumes and banners, parade with the arc of S. Corrado. One of the most active currently is the confraternity of S. Domenico. On confraternities see C. Policastro, *Catania nel Settecento*, Catania, 1950, pp. 67–88.

12 Very little documentary evidence exists about the functioning of these institutions in Noto Nuova. See Appendix 1 for their inhabitants in 1748. For the identification of the Casa del Refugio see Chapter 4, note 10.

13 The Benedictine monastery of S. Chiara certainly had a significant share of the children of Noto's richest families. See Appendix 1.

14 D. Mack Smith, *Modern Sicily* ..., pp. 288–89.

15 G. Pitrè. *Palermo nel Settecento*, Palermo, n.d., pp. 389–463.

16 Ibid.

17 D. Mack Smith, *Modern Sicily* ..., p. 288.

18 L. Bianchini, *Storia economica e civile di Sicilia*, Palermo, 1841, II, p. 101.

19 See pp. 184ff.

20 See Chapter 8, notes 37, 40 and 41.

21 See Appendix 1 for the affiliations of the religious houses; with the exception of the house of the Crociferi fathers and the problematic abbey of SS. Trinità, all the other religious houses in eighteenth-century Noto originated in Noto Antica.

22 The churches (identified by Order if in religious houses) which have or had rectangular naves and side altars and a main apse are: the church of S. Maria dell'Arco, the church of S. Francesco d'Assisi, the church of the PP. Crociferi (demolished), the church of the oratory of S. Filippo Neri, the church of Montevergine, the church of S. Agata, the church of SS. Annunziata, the church of S. Francesco di Paola, the church of the Casa del Refugio, the church of the Benefratelli (gutted), the new church of SS. Salvatore, the church of S. Maria di Gesù, the churches of S. Michele, S. Maria la Rotonda, S. Pietro Martire, SS. Pietro e Paolo, S. Antonio, S. Maria del Purgatorio, and Spirito Santo.

23 See C. Norberg-Schulz, *Late Baroque and Rococo Architecture*, New York, 1971.

24 M. Lewine, 'Roman Architectural Practice during Michelangelo's Maturity', *Acts of the 21st International Congress of the History of Art*, Bonn, 1964, Berlin 1967.

25 The plans of these churches are based on the same schema that Gagliardi used in S. Giorgio, Ragusa (see Pl. 113). The very simple repetitions in the nave of the church are reminiscent of Early Renaissance church plans. The churches are equally conservative in their interior elevations which are closely related in the placement of apertures and the breaking of the entablature to Maderno's and Della Porta's S. Andrea della Valle in Rome.

26 For a discussion of S. Anna dei Palafrenieri and other oval churches in Rome, see W. Lotz, 'Die ovalen Kirchenräume des Cinquecento,' *Römisches Jahrbuch* ..., VII, 1955, p. 5ff. For S. Carlo ai Catinari see C. Norberg-Schulz, *Baroque Architecture*, New York, 1971, p. 142.

27 See C. Norberg-Schulz, ibid., pp. 199–298.

28 See D.S. VII, 5.

29 This figure was derived from the Riveli di Noto, 1748, Archivio di Stato, Palermo; it is only an approximate figure because it is based on counting the tax statements of people whose names were preceded by a title, as in Don, or Baron. Eighty-seven non-religious people had titles, and virtually all the 107 religious leaders of the community had titles. It is possible that the religious personages were called 'don' out of respect rather than on account of noble birth. If that is the case, Noto would still

have a disparate proportion of noble family heads to large palaces.

30 See D.S. V, 3.

31 See D.S. IV, 1.

32 Labisi never differentiates between a house and a palace in his *La scienza dell'architettura civile*, p. 21ff. He divides the house into components such as walls, windows, and kitchens but never gives a composite picture of what a house looks like. The tax assessments are likewise useful only in a general sense, giving us little information about how a building elevation looked, i.e. there is no description of ornament or façade style.

33 Giorgio Valussi, *La casa rurale nella Sicilia occidentale, Ricerche sulle dimore rurali in Italia*, vol. 24, Florence, 1968, p. 38.

34 For a list of the palaces in Noto and a discussion of their identification, see Appendix 2.

35 For Sac. Don Francesco Rau e Landolina's house, AdSP, Rivelo 3756, 1748, f. 55. For discussion of how buildings are located using tax records see Chapter 4, note 24. Marchese Zappata's palace: AdSP, Rivelo 3745, 1748, f. 338.

36 Source for Nicolaci house: AdSP, Rivelo 3755, ff. 451–55.

37 AdSP, Rivelo 3755, 1748, f. 459. In an unusually expressive assessment, Vincenzo Sinatra comments on the style and utility of the Nicolaci palace:

> il revelante ha fermamente procurato di fabricare sul moderno e nella struttura, e nella commodità delle stanze, . . . delle quali sono o pompa, o p. puro divertimento, sul che la suddetta casa quantunque sia di qualche prezzo ciò non ostante atteso la picciolezza della città in cui è fabricata riesco la Revelante di nessun utile e però uniformandosi a gl'ordini di S.E. alla Deputazione locale communicati nell'istruzione, . . . Fede di M.ro Vincenzo Sinatra Architetto, e Capo M.ro.

38 See Chapter 4, note 24.

39 See description of the palace in Appendix 2.

40 This building was owned by the Trigona family whose present palace lies just to the north. The building was donated to the church in the nineteenth century and adapted to its present use by Monsignor La Vecchia (1871–75) (F. Balsamo, *Una visita a Noto 'la città d'oro'*, Noto, 1973, p. 20). Consulting the plans for the building drawn by Cassone in 1853 (Pls 82, 83) we can see that it once had a single ground floor above which there were three separate second-floor sections; a central core and one at either end of the building. These three sections were joined by a low wall on the second-storey level. So the building looked like three separate buildings joined together. (See Chapter 5, note 83.) This very strange three-part façade does not appear on the Labisi veduta. On the veduta (Pl. 19, no. 44) this building is illustrated with a façade that does not match the present one either, but is certainly similar to it. Labisi shows the palace with pilasters that do not appear on the present building. But the form of the building, with a central pediment over a two-storeyed façade, is similar. The metamorphosis of the building is yet another example of the complex building campaigns which characterize Netinese palaces and ecclesiastical construction.

41 See Appendix 2.

42 See Appendix 2.

43 I tried to visit all of Noto's palaces but was unable to do so. Many of Noto's remaining aristocrats were very kind in letting me into their homes. Understandably they were reluctant to let me see their more private living areas, so I did not insist. In a few cases aristocrats refused to let me into their palaces. One palace I was unable to visit was that of the Nicolaci family.

44 For Nicolaci's accomplishments see I. Murè Ruiz and G. Leante, *In memoria di Corrado Nicolaci*, pp. 179–203. Giacomo Nicolaci, according to Leante, could speak six languages and was extremely interested in geometry. He also studied philosophy, geography, astronomy, and was interested in archaeology. He carried on a correspondence with a French astronomer, Abbate Caille, who was interested in Nicolaci's optical experiments. The Nicolaci collection of books must have been quite large judging from the number of books donated to the Biblioteca Comunale di Noto. See *Catalogo Alfabetico della Biblioteca Comunale*, Noto, 1889.

45 Among the visitors who commented on the Astuto collection was Leon Dufourny (*Notes rapportées . . .*):

> This palace is worth visiting, not so much for its architecture which is in very bad taste, but for the various curiosities that its owner, Baron Astuto di Fargione has collected there and still is collecting day by day. These consist mainly of a very fine sequence of consular and imperial medallions in gold and silver and above all a great number of very well preserved Sicilian ones. Amongst the latter those from Syracuse and Selinunte are some of the most perfect. There are altogether five or six thousand . . . There is a very fine library, where some very old volumes . . . can be found and also some fine original manuscripts . . . Finally a museum of ancient artifacts where there are several pieces of terra-cotta, funeral urns, inscriptions many of which are of interest . . . A number of busts, bas-reliefs and statues, amongst the latter many have been restored . . . There is also one of those candelabras made by Piranesi which are in no way antiques . . . .

46 G. Valussi (*La casa rurale* . . ., pp. 24–47) discusses the house of the *viddanù*. In his review of the nineteenth-century literature on the subject, he includes an extensive description quoted from M. Salvatore-Salomone, *Costumi ed usanze dei contadini di Sicilia*, Palermo, 1896, as well as the one G. Pitrè wrote in his *La familia, la casa, la vita del popolo siciliano*, Palermo, 1913, which is given here.

47 A few non-monumental buildings in Noto bear dates over their portals. No. 117 Via Umberto (Pianazzo) bears the date 1738, but the gate on which the year is inscribed doesn't seem to relate directly to any of the buildings around it. The same situation occurs in Vico Caramanna (near Vico Nizza); the gate with 1776 inscribed on its arch does not seem to relate directly to the buildings around it. The same pattern occurs in Via Cairoli at no. 25, dated 1808, and no. 3, dated 1810. These gates which stand alone probably indicate that some Netinese houses had their own private courtyards, or perhaps that gates to communal courtyards were dated.

48 An official map drawn from the Comune of Noto in 1970 indicated that this building was to be preserved because of its historical merit.

49 Short of destroying a wall it is difficult to tell whether it is constructed of rubble or roughly cut stones. It is probably that this wall is constructed of rubble. A magnificent example of such construction can be seen in a stone office and oven for the gypsum quarries called 'Cava di Gesso' on Capo Passero.

50 A. Rapoport, *House Form and Culture*, Englewood Cliffs, New Jersey, 1969.

51 G. Valussi, *La casa rurale* . . ., p. 30, defines a solaio:

> Il solaio (sularu o paglialoa) è sostenuto da travi sporgenti e da canne saldate assieme da legacci di agave (cannizzata). Talvolta occupa solo il settore dell'alcova o della stalla, altre volte sovrasta gran parte della stanza. Serve per il deposito della paglia, della legna e come ripostiglio. In case di famiglie numerose, vi può anche dormire qualche figlio.

52 Paolo Labisi, *La scienza* . . . ff. 76–77:

> La Cloaca o Lochi comuni è quella parte cavata sotto terra per introdurvi gli escrimenti del corpo, ed è una parte di Edificio molto necessaria agli abitanti di quella casa; e questo non può impedirsi da nessuno. Se caso mai una tal cloaca sarà stata cavata nel fondo anche del vicino; questo potrà farne l'apertura nel suo sito, e servirsene, per la ragione detta nella Cisterna.

Under Cisterna (f. 75):

> La cisterna o pozzo esistente in un Cortile comune deve servirsene communemente tutti quei vicini che ivi abitano. Se una tal cisterna o pozzo si trovasse cavati o in tutto o in parte nel fondo della casa vicina o laterale, il Padrone di questa casa può liberamente servisi dell'acqua con far un'apertura nel suo sito, senza che venisse obligato a pagare . . .

53 A. Boëthius, *The Golden House of Nero*, Michigan, 1960, pp. 145–65.

54 F. Rodolico, *Le pietre delle città d'Italia*, Florence, 1953, pp. 445–51. Labisi discusses estimating the price of buildings constructed of *pietra d'intaglio* (*La scienza* . . ., pp. 167–68):

> L'intaglio sia la pietra bianca, come che serve per formare gli adornamenti di architettura ed il di lui lavoro si applica alla diversa disposizione dell'architetto, per si rimette la stima al prud.te stimatore, che sarà per osservarlo, dovendo sempre considerare, prima il prezzo della pietra a tenore della sua grandezza, e poi la qualità del lavoro considerandone il tempo, che vi sia stato impiegato per poi determinare il prezzo . . .

55 *Pietra d'intaglio* is still actively quarried near Noto at S. Corrado di Fuori, at Villa Vella, and in parts of the feudo of Testa dell'Acqua and the feudo of Porcari. Deserted quarries of the softer *pietra arena* or sandstone can be seen near the Lido di Noto. See F. Rodolico, ibid.

56 See D.S. VII, 3.

Chapter 7

1 Dufourny repeats several times that the architecture of the city is distinctive because of the repetitions of the orders:

> The new city which was almost entirely built at the same time as we have already stated, around 1703, is surrounded with palaces, churches and other constructions. The architecture is not always in the best of taste, but at least the orders of architecture, which are magnificent especially the Doric, excel there on all sides and some aspects of them remind one of Vienna.

Again:

> Besides in Noto (just as in Vienna, the style of Palladio is still used) they are still building in the same style.

An individual building:

> The Palace of S. Giacomo . . .

Amongst the palaces, that of San Giacomo deserves first place, for its size and the rich quality of its decorations. It is close by the Convent of Observants where I was staying. The façade is decorated with two architectural orders. That of the ground floor is Tuscan with pilasters and casement windows with backing according to the manner of Inigo Jones; the second is Doric with roses and other motifs in the metopes and above it there is an attic with a roof more or less in the style of Mansart, the whole thing is very well done and creates a pleasant effect.

2 P. Ferrerio, *Palazzi di Roma de' più celebri architetti . . .*, Libro primo. G. B. Falda, *Nuovi disegni dell'architettura, e piante de' palazzi di Roma, de' più celebri architetti . . .*, Libro secondo, Rome, 1680.

3 For Labisi's copying of the plates to Wolff's work see p. 219.

4 For Gagliardi's copies of Vignola see notes 5, 6, and 9 below. Copies of Serlio appear in Gagliardi's Treatise, vol. II.

5 Gagliardi may have seen either an early edition of Vignola (*Regola delli cinque ordini d'architettura*), or A. C. d'Aviler's *Cours d'architecture qui comprend les Ordres de Vignole*, Paris, 1728. For the Caprarola portal, see Aviler Pl. 43.

6 Aviler, ibid., Pl. 80.

7 For examples see M. Calvesi and Manieri-Elia, *Architettura barocca a Lecce e terra di Puglia*, Milano-Roma, n.d.

8 Just after the earthquake and before the arrival of Vaccarini this decorative style flourished in Catania. See A. Blunt, *Sicilian Baroque*, pp. 18–19.

9 Aviler, *Cours . . .*, Pl. 18.

10 The upper storey of this façade was ruined by an earthquake in 1823 and replaced, changing the tone of the façade. But it still lays claim to being one of the first, if not the first, façades to break away from the simple planar solutions into a concavity.

11 For S. Carlo's Bastard Chinese decoration see AdSS, Notary Vincenzo Labisi, 007226, 1756–57, f. 489, Obligation Pro Contu S.ta Maria Jesus Syr.a Cum Francesco Sajola. Sajola is to do the stuccoing for the church in the same manner as he did the stuccoing in the new church of the Collegio with 'Bastard Chinese' decorations. For the original contract for the Jesuit college stucco work see Di Blasi, p. 63.

12 S. Nicolò is one of the least interesting and most discussed buildings in Noto. No one has pointed out in print that the building's façade does not relate at all to the design of its sides (see A. Blunt, *Sicilian Baroque*, p. 149; G. Passarello, *Guida della città . . .*, pp. 38–41; N. Pisani, *Noto la città d'oro*, Syracuse, 1953, pp. 19–24; N. Zappulla, *La cattedrale di Noto*, Noto, 1963). It has been established, however, that the present façade was not completed until late in the eighteenth century (Blunt, ibid.). This evidence is verified by the inscribed date of 1768 on the second storey of the eastern tower of the church. Likewise documents in the *Libro Giallo*, ff. 291, 239, 240 indicate that from 1767 to 1771 functions of the Chiesa Madre were performed in the church of San Carlo (Jesuit College) because S. Nicolò was still under construction (see Canale, p. 291, note 184, p. 292, note 189, p. 295, note 198).

Léon Dufourny, who visited the city in 1789, mentions (*Notes rapportées . . .*) that Stefano Ittar of Catania was erecting what was the second dome of the church. He attempted to solve the problem by reinforcing the crossing.

Dufourny explains the dome which had already been erected, fell a short while ago, because it had insufficient support . . . in order to make amends for this the architect Stefano Ittar, a Roman married to a woman from Catania, merely changed the shape of the casement windows nearest to the archstones on which the new dome is to be erected, from square or Romanesque as they were to oval: time will tell whether this slight change will suffice.

The ovals that Ittar built and Dufourny illustrates in a small sketch can still be seen on the exterior side of the building.

C. Tafaro (*Notizie . . .*, pp. 36–40; 47–8) in a lengthy inquiry into the history of the church, states that the second dome fell on 11 January 1848 in an earthquake. He believes the first dome fell in 1760. I would say it fell later based on the date 1768 on the right side of the façade. But by 1769 the festival of S. Corrado had to be held elsewhere because the church was ruined; therefore the first dome collapsed in the 1760s.

Chapter 8

1 The most important buildings that are known to have been constructed during the early years of the eighteenth century on the Meti were churches and religious houses. The architects of these buildings may have been priests. Tortora, 1891, (p. 48) mentions that Padre Baccelliere Giovanni 'built' the dormitory of S. Domenico, facing Piazza S. Domenico, before his death in 1710. Padre Luigi Frasca, who died in 1708, is also described as having 'built' the church and part of the convent of S. Antonio di Padova (ibid.). Whether the ecclesiastics were chief fund-raisers for their enterprises or actually the architects is unclear. But it is certainly possible that they planned and executed the buildings themselves since architect-priests are not unknown in Sicily (Fra Angelo Italia is an excellent example). Paul Hofer (in conversation, 1969) even believes that Tortora himself was an architect: his name is inscribed on the tower of his convent of S. Francesco: 'R. P. Phus Tortora GNV'.

2 Paolo Labisi (D.S. V, 10) was evidently fired as architect of Noto by the city's Senators who elected someone else instead. It is almost certain that the Senators and Mayor of Noto were also the Deputati of the Committee on Streets and Water.

3 See D.S. V.

4 For the duties of the *architetto della città*, see Labisi's discussion of a vacant plot, Chapter 2, note 58. Labisi (*La scienza . . .*, pp. 14–16) also describes the job of the *architetto della città* when a wall threatens to fall:

> . . . in tal caso può e deve essere obligato il Padrone dell'Edificio o fabrica, dal Vicino, med.º dal Magistrato ò Senato della Città, a dover dar riparo, con far, che non rovinasse, e portasse danno alle case vicine, o al Publico, che suole passare per quella strada; ma quando mai non sarà il caso di potersi riparare, si ordinasse, che si buttasse a terra, per così togliersi l'imminente pericolo, che potrebbe accadere ad un Publico; e tutto ciò deve procedersi con l'esame di un visoloco dell'architetto della Città, e se ve ne fossero più d'uno, coll'intervento di tutti quanti, per fare un esatto esame di quello che si dubbita, talmente che non trovandosi tale quale abbiamo descritto . . .

The description of the duties of the architect of the city sound almost identical to those of the *maestro di strada* in Rome (see T. Magnuson, *Studies in Roman Quattrocento Architecture*, Stockholm, 1958).

5 Labisi's treatise (*La scienza . . .*) dwells extensively upon how to assess the value of a property for tax purposes. Many documents in the volume of the Committee on Streets and Water contain estimates for future work. In private practice too, estimating costs was important (see D.S. V). Vincenzo Sinatra, who was called an architect, was important as a tax estimator in the census of 1748. He estimated the worth of the buildings people in Noto owned. Sinatra signs himself 'Vincenzo Sinatra come Esperto eletto d'ordine dell'Ill.mi Deputati delli Riveli . . .' (AdSP, Rivelo 3745, 1748, f. 135).

6 D.S. VI, ff. 5, 3, 62.

7 Other than Bernardo Labisi's plan for the lowering of the Corso we have not a single proposal for urban change written or drawn by one of Noto's architects.

8 Rosario Gagliardi's activity in Noto was rediscovered in the twentieth century after his name had literally been forgotten in the city. The first notice of Gagliardi appears in Corrado Tafaro's *Notizie storico-religiose . . .*, p. 74. In a letter to Prof. M. Riefstahl of New York University in 1935, Tafaro mentions that he has seen plans for the church of S. Chiara signed by Rosario Gagliardi. Nicolò Pisani (*Noto barocco . . .*, pp. 28, 33, 35) first started attributing buildings to Gagliardi, but without much evidence. No progress in the study of Gagliardi was made until Stefano Bottari began to have his students study the architecture of south-eastern Sicily. Lucia Cugno, now a school teacher in Noto, went through all the volumes of Notaries in the Archivio di Stato of Syracuse over a period of several years. Based on her evidence Bottari published the best article on Gagliardi to appear thus far: S. Bottari, 'Contributi all' architettura del'700 in Sicilia, nota sull'architetto siracusano Rosario Gagliardi,' *La Giara*, IV, 1955, pp. 14–27. In the article Bottari attributes S. Maria dell' Arco, S. Domenico, the Jesuit College, SS. Crocifisso, S. Chiara, the Carmine, and S. Agata, to Gagliardi based on Cugno's documents. Some of Cugno's documents were published in Canale, 1976, pp. 253–300.

Two other Netinese, Luigi Di Blasi and Francesco Genovesi, became interested in Gagliardi after they discovered architectural documents in the Genovesi family collection. Likewise, Genovesi's friend, Giuseppe Mazza, intensified their interest by showing them drawings which they rightly attributed to Gagliardi. From 1969 to 1972 they worked in the Archivio di Stato in Syracuse looking for Gagliardi documents. The outcome of this work is a highly reliable book which they published privately (*Rosario Gagliardi, Architetto dell'ingegnosa Città di Noto*, Catania, 1972; abbreviated as Di Blasi). Much of the archival information published here would not have been available without their pioneering effort. Although the documents that Di Blasi and Genovesi published are for the most part accurate, they do not cite the exact page or volume from which the information was extracted, nor do they differentiate between actual contracts in the books of the town notaries, and notes of the contracts which can be found in special indices called the 'bastardelli'. For some of the documents relating to Gagliardi's life see D.S. III.

9 See D.S. III, 1, 3.

10 See p. 218.

11 Di Blasi, p. 33.

12 In 1713 he is referred to as 'Rosarius Gagliardo Fabri Lignariis Netini' (Di Blasi, p. 34).

13 See D.S. III, 4.

14 Di Blasi, p. 38.

15 See D.S. III, 7.

16 See below pp. 182–88.

17 S. Chiara, see notes 40–42; Casa del Refugio, see D.S. III, no. 11; S. Calogero, see Di Blasi, p. 50; Carmine see Di Blasi, p. 46; S. Maria la Rotunda, see Di Blasi, p. 44; S. Agata see Canale, 1976, p. 295; Battaglia palace see Canale 1976, p. 264.

18 I attribute the original design of S. Nicolò to Gagliardi on the basis of the following: 1) the present plan of the church closely follows the longitudinal aisle churches Gagliardi illustrates in his treatise (Di Blasi, ta. XVII); 2) the exterior sides of the church present the kind of rhythmic play of apertures that Gagliardi used and the decoration details are identical to those used on the works firmly attributed to him; 3) the upper portion of the buttressing of the first dome which is still in place (although the dome itself collapsed) carries a bolection frieze, Gagliardi's hallmark; 4) according to Labisi's veduta the original façade of the church was to be more Baroque than the present one and the more Baroque design may indicate Gagliardi's authorship.

19 Gagliardi's work throughout south-eastern Sicily needs to be uncovered. There is a danger in attribution without firm archival documentation, so I only list fairly obvious Gagliardi buildings, some corroborated by documents. S. Giorgio, Ragusa was built after a signed design of Gagliardi (see note 49). The Chiesa Madre in Comiso, towerlike with repeated volutes, belongs to the same family of façades as S. Giorgio. The oval plan, capitals, and aperture surrounds of the church of S. Agata in Caltagirone are certainly Gagliardi's. Both the exterior and interesting pentagonal plan of S. Giuseppe in Caltagirone also link it directly to Gagliardi (for illustrations of the interior of S. Giuseppe see F. Minissi, *Aspetti dell'architettura religiosa del Settecento in Sicilia*, Rome, 1958, pp. 28–30). Di Blasi and Genovesi publish a plan signed by Gagliardi for work he was to do on the Jesuit College in Syracuse.

I do not believe that Gagliardi designed the beautiful tower façade of the church of S. Giorgio in Modica (A. Blunt, *Sicilian Baroque*, pp. 27–28) because the ornamentation of the façade is too florid for his style.

Considering Gagliardi was a Syracusan it is peculiar that the only evidence of his Syracusan work that we have are the plans for the renovation of the Jesuit college. Several other buildings, while undocumented, seem close to his style. One of the most prominent is S. Lucia del Sepolcro, which has Gagliardesque window surrounds and capitals. The church was begun in 1629 on the plans of Giovanni Vermexio. G. Agnello (*I Vermexio*, Florence, 1959, pp. 47ff., 168ff.) attributes the whole building to Vermexio. But as Sir Anthony Blunt points out (*Sicilian Baroque*, p. 148, and review *Burlington Magazine*, CII, 1960, p. 124), work was stopped in 1631, and a new foundation stone was laid in 1665. Although the foundation dates from the first phase, the capitals, and the door and window surrounds, all date from the first half of the eighteenth century and suggest the hand of Gagliardi.

20 The volumes belong to Giuseppe Mazza, who now lives in Syracuse, Sicily. The volumes, which are of different sizes, are bound in unmarked vellum. From the arrangement of the pages which in some cases are out of sequence, it seems probable that Gagliardi would have arranged the drawings in a different sequence. Likewise, many sheets are loose, so whatever the original order of the drawings was is difficult to perceive. Sig. Mazza generously gave Di Blasi and Genovesi the drawings directly related to Noto studies, thus dismembering the volumes further. Evidence that all the drawings may not be Gagliardi's can be found in the first volume; here a drawing is included which is labelled 'piccola della Ven.le Chiesa di S. Michele di Palazzolo ideata, e pensata da me Corrado Mazza della città di Noto . . . 18 Feb. 1788 . . .' Perhaps other unsigned drawings are by later architects; certainly at least two hands can be discerned in the writing on the drawings themselves. But the writing on the drawings may have been added after they were already drawn, so handwriting analysis is not conclusive.

21 Volumes II and III of Giuseppe Mazza's collection have never been published. Volume II is composed of column capital studies on the recto and verso of each sheet. Usually two capitals share a page. There are in all 27 pages of capitals. These are followed by pages of church altars, which are in turn followed by twelve pages of fortification drawings, bearing random figure numbers. Some are inscribed with the name of the French fortification engineer Vauban. Eight drawings copied from Vignola follow the fortifications. The volume ends with an altar plan and four church plans which appear to be connected with the church of S. Giorgio in Ragusa.

Volume III seems to be the best preserved of all the volumes, having 48 foliated pages bearing sequential numbers. The entire volume comprises copies of Flemish forcication treatises with no explanatory text.

22 The drawing styles of Labisi and Gagliardi are so similar that sorting out different hands in the Mazza volumes is extremely difficult. Nevertheless, the drawing labelled 'Cornice del Vignola' in Vol. II bears Labisi's handwriting, and could possible be his work. Labisi copied the plates in Wolff's book with such proficiency that there is little doubt that he was a first-rate draughtsman who could copy as well as Gagliardi could.

23 Di Blasi and Genovesi (*Di Blasi*) do not directly address the problem of attribution. They present no direct argument that the Mazza drawings must be Gagliardi's instead of Labisi's, for example. However, two of the drawings are signed by Gagliardi. One (the design for S. Chiara now in Di Blasi's possession) is close in style to a Gagliardi drawing for the same building. Four (the elevation of S. Giorgio and the set of drawings for the church of the convent of S. Domenico) are nearly identical to finished buildings that we know Gagliardi designed. All the drawings in this volume seem to be by the same hand and seem to have a definite unity of architectural thought. The style of the buildings depicted comes closest to Gagliardi's.

24 Just one of the many treatises that inspired Gagliardi's title page is Albrecht Dürer's *Vier Bücher von Menschlicher Proportion*, Nuremburg, 1528. The central portion of the title-page concerns a statue of Alexander the Great to have been carved on Mount Athos which is described by Vitruvius (*De Architectura* . . ., Book I, Preface, p. 73). The problem was to adapt musical harmonies to the law which governed the human body and civil architecture. The end of the legend indicates that this question was debated by the Jesuit order in their college in Palermo in 1726.

25 Gagliardi's oval and square churches (Di Blasi, tav. 43, 44, 41, 42 respectively) closely follow Amico's designs (*L'architetto practico*, Palermo, 1726, vol. I, figs 9, 10, 15, 16).

26 See C. Norberg-Schulz, *Late Baroque* . . ., pls 241, 242, 243.

27 The differentiation between scenic and conceptual compositions is taken from R. Wittkower, *Art and Architecture in Italy*, 1973, p. 194.

28 For an illustration of Michelangelo's centralized plan for S. Giovanni dei Fiorentini, see J. Ackerman, *The Architecture of Michelangelo*, London, 1961, pl. 68.

29 For Fontana's influence, see R. Wittkower, *Art and Architecture*, pp. 244–46.

30 Good plans and fair analysis of G. B. Vaccarini's S. Agata can be found in S. Boscarino's *Studi e rilievi di architettura siciliana*, Messina, 1961, pp. 143–48. The only major book on Vaccarini is still the unsatisfactory work of F. Fichera, *G. B. Vaccarini e l'architettura del Settecento in Sicilia*, Rome, 1931.

31 The miniature belfries appear in the churches of S. Sebastiano in Acireale, Spirito Santo in Syracuse, and S. Placido in Catania. It is possible that Guarino Guarini may have added to the popularity of these miniature belfries which surmounted façades when he included a small niche on the top of his Theatine church of SS. Annunziata in Messina. For an illustration of Guarini's church see M. Accascina, *Profilo dell'architettura a Messina dal 1600 al 1800*, Rome, 1904, pp. 54–5. Also see G. Guarini, *Architettura Civile* . . ., II, no plate number. Note that Guarini designed his façade to take a niche where a bell would naturally have been placed in other Sicilian churches. The actual bell for the church was housed in a tower directly behind the façade.

32 R. Wittkower, *Art and Architecture*, p. 187.

33 One of the many façades with the same squat proportions as Gagliardi's can be seen on the church at the Four Fountains in Messina (destroyed). See M. Accascina, *Profilo* . . ., p. 61.

34 See notes 20 and 21.

35 S. Maria dell'Arco was probably a temporary structure just like S. Chiara. See Chapter 4, note 20.

36 See note 37 below.

37 G. Passarello, *Noto, guida della città* (2nd ed.), p. 44. The history of the construction of S. Maria dell'Arco is the following:

- 1713: Gagliardi makes design for the monastery and assists Ignatio Puzzo of Syracuse in measuring it (perhaps in measuring the terrain?) (see D.S. III, 4).
- 1730: Sinatra and Gagliardi work on the church (Di Blasi, p. 44).
- 1733: Foundations of river stone laid for the church, the dormitory roof erected, and Gagliardi measures the plan for part of the church (Di Blasi, pp. 46–7).
- 1752: The roof of the church is to be constructed according to Gagliardi's designs (Di Blasi, p. 59).
- 1754: The forms necessary for the vaulting of the church in stone are ordered, the gessoing of the vault is

arranged. (Evidently the walls and wooden-trussed roof were built first, then the forms erected for the stone vault constructed and set in place below the finished roof, as was the practice in the Renaissance.) (D.S. III, 20.)

1755: Onofrio Russo, a stuccoist from Agrigento, stuccos the church according to Gagliardi's instructions (D.S. III, 21a).

1756: Francesco Guadegna, stuccoist from Piazza, is to finish stuccos left incomplete at Russo's death (D.S. III, 21b).

1757: Wooden doors are to be made like those of the convent of S. Francesco (D.S. III, 22).

1758: Iron for doors which is to be like that of the Collegio church is ordered (Di Blasi, p. 66).

1758: Gagliardi is paid in wheat for his part in designing and supervising the stuccoing (D.S. III, 24).

1760: Gagliardi is paid for having designed and installed the wooden 'coretti' or choir lofts on either side of the chancel (Di Blasi, p. 70).

1765: Work on vault of church (AdSS, Notary Vincenzo Labisi, 007235, 1765–67, p. 112).

1768: Painting of church (AdSS. Notary Vincenzo Labisi, 007238, 1768–69, ff. 283).

1770: Work on monastery and cleaning of stuccos of church (AdSS Notary Vincenzo Labisi, 007239, 1769–70, f. 547).

1779: Fissures in cut stone in tower and façade fixed (AdSS, Notary Vincenzo Labisi, 007249, 1779–80, f. 11).

38 D.S. III, 21a.

39 For Buontalenti's decoration see L. H. Heydenreich and W. Lotz, *Architecture in Italy, 1400–1600*, Harmondsworth, 1974, pp. 232–33. For Juvarra see R. Wittkower, *Art and Architecture in Italy*, pp. 275–82. For the decorative folk-art tradition which surfaces in Sicilian sculptural decoration see E. Calandra, *Breve storia dell'architettura in Sicilia*, Bari, 1938, pp. 125–27 and M. Accascina, *Profilo dell'architettura di Messina*, pp. 18–25; for the view that this ornament derived from Spain (possible though difficult to prove) see N. Pisani, *Barocco in Sicilia*, pp. 1–20. S. Boscarino (*Studi e rilievi* . . . pp. 26–31, 64, 68) and G. Bellafiore (*La Maniera italiana*, pp. 58–85, 92–130) effectively illustrate ties with the decorative practices of the Italian mainland rather than Spain; F. Fichera's argument for Spanish influences doesn't seem as convincing (F. Fichera, *G. B. Vaccarini* . . ., pp. 72–9). As Anthony Blunt pointed out (*Sicilian Baroque*, pp. 9–11), both Sicilian and Spanish Baroque are characterized by a similar feeling for decoration but here the similarity ends. The link between the decoration of Spain and that of Sicily has yet to be proven.

40 Documentary history of the construction of S. Chiara:

1693: Requests for funds to erect a loggia (AdSS, Notary Ignazio Buscarello, 7319, 1692–3, 17 May 1693, n.p.)

1717: Monastery in construction (Canale, 1976, p. 259).

1739: Gagliardi supervises the making of windows and the timber roof of the monastery (Di Blasi, pp. 51–52).

1746: Bells are cast for the church (Di Blasi, p. 55).

1752: Church is under construction (Di Blasi, p. 60).

1755: Stone slabs for the church are ordered (Di Blasi, p. 64).

1755: The church is being stuccoed by Onofrio Russo (D.S. III, 21a).

1758: Church consecrated. On the wall of the vestibule the dedication and consecration dates are given.

41 For the history of the monastery and church through 1935 see C. Tafaro, *Notizie* . . ., ff. 73–74. In 1949, with post-War prosperity hitting Noto full force, a number of schemes were devised, and some actually carried out in part, to attract tourists. The city engineer, Francesco La grassa, designed a plan which met the specifications of the council. The plan (which can be found in a folder in the town archives labelled 'Public Works') was to turn S. Chiara (the church and the monastery) into an incredibly hideous Art Nouveau hotel-theatre-'Circolo'-post office-telegram office. The unlikely plan was to knock the old building to ruins and build the new one *entirely* from the debris. Financial difficulties, as usual, stopped the Netinese from ruining their beautiful city and La Grassa's plan was never realized. About this time the building shifted its functions: the school took over the upper floors of the monastery and the bottom floor became the cinema 'Splendor' with all the trappings that such a name implies. In 1952 the post office now built on Via Zanadelli required that most of the eastern wing of the monastery be demolished. Eng. Muscato of Noto, who worked on the project, described the pre-demolition plan of the first floor which is indicated on the map (conversation, 1970). Today, in its decaying state, the building serves various functions (Pl. 93). In 1970, three nuns (not of the Benedictine Order, but the Order of the Sisters of Mercy) lived in the rooms just to the south of the church, but now the rooms are deserted.

42 In spite of these changes in use, Gagliardi's original plan can still be picked out with a little imaginative subtraction. Obviously the cinema stairs (I) leading to the mezzanine balcony from the first floor have to be subtracted, as do the stairs and projector box on the ground floor. Since the lowering of the street necessitated another basement story (see exterior Pl. 38), we have to subtract all steps (J). The western steps and portal (H), obviously constructed during the early nineteenth century, have to be subtracted too. The double bathroom on the west, and the southernmost rooms in back of the church (which were once trimmed in Neo-Gothic white and red) all date from the nineteenth century or later. What is left, particularly in the shape of the church and its chapels, looks very much like Gagliardi's plan. In the church, many spaces that Gagliardi had tied together are now closed off by thin divisions but his intention can still be seen in the plan; even the same stairwells are present on the west. Most of the dramatic changes have taken place in the plan of the dormitory of the monastery. The last storey of the Gagliardi plans indicates that some changes occurred even during his time. The rectangular stairwell which Gagliardi first thought to be best was replaced with the present combination of two semicircular staircases. The date over this back stairway reads 1773, obviously built after Gagliardi himself had retired. The plan of the church and dormitory, on the first floor at least, seems close to what Gagliardi indicated the arrangement was to be on his plan.

Gagliardi's plans for the monastery and church, which are illustrated in Pls 124–26, are the following:

Foundations (Pl. 124): brown ink with yellow, green, blue, painted over it (probably not intended since the wrong places are coloured in); 61 × 45 cm; watermark of three vertical crescent moons, with points facing downward, each progressively smaller than the last; labelled: Iconografia, che è la Pianta della Scena, che fa tutti li pedimenti del mon. di S. Chiara dell'Ingegnosa Città di Noto.

First floor (Pl. 125): brown ink with blue, pale ochre, green wash over it; 59.8 × 44.3 cm; no watermark visible. Labelled: Iconografia che è la pianta del diritto del primo terreno che va a regolare la scena del Promontorio, che dimostra tutte le officine necessarie. Signed: Disegnato e delineato da me Rosario Gagliardi architetto.

Second floor (Pl. 126): brown ink painted over with pink; 59.8 × 44.3 cm; crescent moon watermark. Labelled: Iconografia che è la pianta delli dormitori, e chiesa con tutte l'altre officine del sacro mon. di S. Chiara dell' Ingegnosa Città di Noto. Signed: Disegnato e delineato sopra il antico da me Rosario Gagliardi architetto.

In addition to these plans there are two others. One illustrates Bernardo Labisi's plan for the remodelling of the monastery (pen and ink with water colour wash; 60 × 45 cm; in the collection of the Biblioteca Comunale di Noto), and the other is a sectional drawing for the construction of the supports for the roof (pen and ink, with yellow water colour; 45 × 30 cm; watermark of three crescent moons; collection of the Biblioteca Comunale di Noto). The latter is interesting in light of the unusual construction of the roof.

43 AdSS, Notary Ignazio Buscarello, 7319, 1692–3, 17 May 1693.

44 A. Blunt, *Sicilian Baroque*, p. 21.

45 W. Lotz, 'Die ovalen Kirchenräume des Cinquecento,' *Römisches Jahrbuch* . . ., VII, 1955, p. 5ff.

46 For an example see A. Palladio, *The Four Books of Architecture*, New York, 1965, Book III, chap. 21, pl. 18.

47 See Lotz, 'Die ovalen Kirchenräume . . .'

48 Documentary evidence of the construction of S. Domenico:

1746: Money asked for completion of monastery; church and monastery under construction (Canale, 1976, p. 276).

1748: Gagliardi is given a salary of wine for his participation as architect of the building (D.S. III, 19).

1754: Cutting of the wood for the nave and chapels of the church ordered (Di Blasi, pp. 61–62).

1758: Stone ordered for church and cut under Gagliardi's supervision (D.S. III, 25).

1771: Gagliardi is referred to as the one who made the college (AdSS, Notary Pietro Perricone, 007472, 1769–72, f. 1).

49 Gagliardi's designs for the church of S. Giorgio at Ragusa are valuable documents of his design style and his calligraphy. The following is a description of the drawings (Pls 111–15) preserved in the sacristy of the church:

Longitudinal section (Pl. 114): pen and ink, painted with blue wash; 82 × 44 cm. Inscribed (left): Visto ed approvato da me Archidacono ed Ing.re Giovanni de Amico; (right) Visto ed approvato da me Michele Longati Ingegniere della Città di Messina; (bottom) Dissegnato [sic] delineato da Gagliardi R. e comprato dal Signor Parroco, e Cantore Don Felice Giampicciolo.

Longitudinal exterior elevation (Pl. 115): pen and ink with blue wash;

82 × 44 cm. Inscribed: (left) Visto ed approvato da me Archidicono ed Ingre, f: Giovanni de Amico; (right) Visto ed approvato da me Di Michele Longari Ingegniere della Città di Messina; (bottom) Disegnato e delineato da Gagliardi R. e comprato dal Sig. Parroco, e cianco Don Felice Giampicciolo alli 277 ore dell' anno 1744.

Ground plan of church (Pl. 113): pen and ink, coloured pink, yellow, and blue; 88 × 44 cm. Inscribed: (left) Visto ed approvato da me Archidiacono ed Ingre. D. Giovanni de Amico; (right) Visto ed approvato da me D: Michele Longari Ingegniere della Città di Messina; (bottom) Disegnato e delineato da me Rosario Gagliardi Ingre. della Città di Noto e sua valle; (below) comprato dal Parroco e cantore Don Felice Giampicciolo.

Elevation of façade (Pl. 112): pen and ink, coloured blue and brown; 44 × 57 cm. Inscribed: Disegnato ed delineato da me Rosario Gagliardi Ingre. ed Architetto della città di Noto e sua valle . . .

Also on the sacristy wall are two later drawings, not by Gagliardi, which illustrate the plan and elevation of San Giorgio's dome and the plan for one of its altars. Both seem to date from the nineteenth century.

50 As it stands now the church is a narrow version of Lorenzo Binago's S. Alessandro in Milan (1601). But it lacks S. Alessandro's wider side aisles and thus has less of the central planned quality. Nor does Gagliardi's church combine the dome over the altar and the Greek cross plan as Binago's does (see R. Wittkower, *Art and Architecture* . . ., p. 75). Derivations on the Greek cross plan (as Gagliardi's church would have been) were not prevalent in the seventeenth century but went through a revival in the eighteenth century (e.g., Francesco Gallo's Duomo S. Donato at Mondovi (1743–63); C. Corbellini's S. Geremia in Venice (1753–60)).

51 Documentary history of the church of SS. Crocifisso: 1728: Gagliardi's designs for the capitals of the new church are to be followed (D.S. III, 7). The date on the front of the church over the doorway is 1715. Above the date is an inscription of which the last line reads, 'In this city rebuilt', so the construction appears to have begun in 1715. C. Puglisi, *Cronica della città* . . ., p. 254 tells how the cupola of the church collapsed on February 13, 1880, which explains the similarity between the dome and that of S. Nicolò. The lions in front of the church are said to have come from the entrance to the old church in Noto Antica (G. Passarello, *Guida* . . ., p. 114).

52 See Chapter 7, note 12.

53 SS. Salvatore is the most enigmatic of Noto's buildings because it was built in at least two stages. The question is which of the two was built first?

On the basis of the evidence in Labisi's veduta I have reasoned that the lower portion of the monastery was definitely in existence in the mid-eighteenth century. It is possible that the upper portion of the monastery was likewise in existence, but since Labisi does not depict the tower of the upper monastery it seems unlikely. Stylistically the upper portion seems to follow the lower. Likewise, the tower of the upper portion (Pl. 36) faces east rather than west. If the upper part of the monastery had been built first, then it would seem the tower would have faced south to the Corso. In a document of 1751 (see below) Sinatra supervised the construction of grating opposite the monastery of S. Chiara, and I believe this is the grating on the lower portion of the building, some of which can still be seen. Nevertheless, problems with my argument still exist: according to Tafaro the first church of the monastery was north of the existing upper portion, which should indicate that the upper portion was erected early in the building's history. My hypothesis, based on intuition and the documents which follow, is that the temporary church and monastery were built north of the upper portion in the early eighteenth century. The second major building campaign culminating in the 1750s saw the lower portion completed. A third campaign after the 1750s began on the upper portion, with the façade on Via Dogali partially completed. A fourth campaign began on the western façade on the monastery on Via Gioberti, with the main portal of the monastery completed by Bernardo Labisi in the 1780s. When the first church was ruined (perhaps by a tremor) it was thought appropriate to build the new one in the courtyard or cloister of the lower portion , now the oldest portion of the monastery.

The slim documentary evidence for the early building is the following. The new church of SS. Salvatore built in the late eighteenth century replaced an earlier church which was up Via Gioberti toward Via Cavour (now replaced by the Home for the Disabled), described by Tafaro, *Notizie*, f. 686. He describes a church façade which may have had the same sensuous curve as the tower which overlooks the Piano of S. Francesco.

The documents from the eighteenth century are:

1701: 'frontespicio' of monastery cited in description of location of Antonia Palermi's property in Noto (Canale, 256).
1723: Water for construction contracted (Canale, p. 262).
1738: Gagliardi is to make a crypt in the church of SS. Salvatore (Di Blasi, p. 15).
1747: Contract for excavation of site and river stones for foundations (AdSS, Notary Nicolo Astuto, Bastardello, 10 April 1747).
1748: Contract for excavation of site and river stones for foundation (AdSS, Notary Nicolo Astuto, Bastardello, 30 December 1748).
1751: Sinatra, architect of the building, supervises construction of grating opposite the frontispiece of the monastery of S. Chiara (AdSS, Notary Nicolo Astuto, Bastardello, 1750–51, f. 218).
1753: 'Pietra bianca' for monastery contracted (Canale, p. 283).
1790: Ruin of old church (Canal, p. 297).

54 The documents for the Jesuit college and its church of S. Carlo:

1729: Stone for the college (Di Blasi, p. 41).
1729: Stone for the college (Di Blasi, p. 42).
1730: Stone for the college (Di Blasi, p. 43).
1730: Stone cut for cornices and pilasters of entrance to the church (Di Blasi, p. 45).
1735: Stone for the college (Di Blasi, p. 48).
1748: Foundation excavations for the new church (Di Blasi, p. 56).
1755: Church stuccoed by Francesco Sajola of Palermo according to the idea of the Reverend Saverio Bonanno, Rector of the college, and the architect (Di Blasi, p. 63).

The building, which is known as the Jesuit college in Noto today, is actually a combination of the old seminary, which faced Piazza S. Domenico, and the college itself, which faces the Corso. The seminary, judging from the awkward apertures and unarticulated façade, was constructed first, then the college. The seminary was damaged in the 1727 earthquake (Canale, p. 265). The college and the church may have been built at the same time, judging from the few documents that have been found. There are three portals to the college excluding the church entrance. The middle one bears the date 1749, the most easterly one the date 1730. The church, according to an inscribed tablet by the entrance, was inaugurated in November 1757.

The church has often been attributed to Gagliardi: N. Pisani (*Noto la città* . . ., p. 37) first attributed the building to Labisi's teacher, Francesco Sortino, and dated it 1736–46. He changed his mind in his *Barocco in Sicilia*, p. 67, attributing it to Gagliardi. Bottari, presumably following the documents unearthed by Lucia Cugno, also attributes the building to Gagliardi (*La cultura figurativa in Sicilia*, Messina-Florence, 1954, p. 79; and 'Contributi . . .,' p. 77). Many of the documents for the construction of the church list Gagliardi as a witness to the transactions but no document has been found which actually calls him the architect of the building. Canale equates the title 'ingegniero' which appears on the documents with Gagliardi who signs himself 'ingegniero' of Noto on his plans for the church of S. Giorgio in Ragusa.

Chapter 9

1 For Sicilian colonial history during the eighteenth century see D. Mack Smith, *Modern Sicily*, New York, 1968, pp. 243–331.

2 Accounts of the voyages of the eighteenth-century visitors to Sicily can be found in H. Tuzet, *La Sicile au XVIIIe siècle* . . .

3 For documents of Vincenzo Sinatra's life see D.S. IV.

4 The only evidence of Sinatra's draughtsmanship is a 1764 map of Noto's territory (see p. 73 and Pl. 23). There is no basis on which to attribute other drawings in Netinese collections to Sinatra.

5 D.S. III, 27.

6 D.S. IV, 1.

7 Di Blasi, p. 30.

8 Ibid.; also see D.S. IV, 1.

9 Ibid.; also see D.S. IV, 1.

10 Ibid., p. 44 on 31 July 1730, 'Mro. Vincentio Sinatra intagliatore' was paid 2 tarì a day.

11 See D.S. IV, 2.

12 In 1747–8, Sinatra was the assessor for the tax being imposed on Netinese buildings (Chapter 6, note 37). He signs his estimates Architetto e Capo Maestro. Perhaps the position of assessor and his work on the city hall provided the proof needed for him to be able to assume the title of architect.

13 Although construction is proceeding speedily in the 1740s the building may never have been completed, as Dufourny's observations (see below) seem to indicate. Construction work was still going on in 1757 (D.S. IV, 6).

14 F. Cassone's addition to the city hall might have been commissioned because of Noto's brief rise to provincial capital in the nineteenth century.

15 The second storey completed in the 1950s generally follows F. Cassone's nineteenth-century design.

16 F. Popelier ('Noto, ville baroque de Sicile,' *Gazette des Beaux-Arts*, No. 59, 1962, p. 92) referred to L.

Dufourny as a source for proving that the second storey was intended. She rightly noted that when Dufourny drew the façade in his sketchbook he wrote above the central portion 'cet étage n'est pas terminé'. But in Dufourny's drawing (*Notes rapportées . . .*) which is illustrated in my Plate 144 the only part of the upper storey which is drawn is in the centre of the building. Here he lightly sketched in a dome, which he though would eventually adorn the building. I therefore believe that Dufourny's note refers to the dome and not the rest of the second storey.

16a The city hall of Noto is referred to in the documents as Palazzo Senatorio, Casa Senatoria, Palazzo Comunale, Casa Comunale, Palazzo della Città, Palazzo Ducezio, and Casa Municipale.

17 V. Arezzo Prado *Cenni storici sugli avvenimenti netini*, Noto, 1862, p. 156.

18 See E. Bonnet and A. Joubin, *Montpellier au XVIIe et XVIIIe siècles*, Paris, 1912, p. 75 for illustration and discussion of Giral. Also see A. Fliche, *Montpellier*, Paris, 1935, pp. 85, 87 for information on Giral and the château. The close correspondence between Giral's façade and the façade of Villa Falconara indicates that Arezzo Prado's statement might be reliable. His contention that Paolo Labisi was the executor of the design is contradicted by evidence that Vincenzo Sinatra in fact directed the construction of the city hall. For one reason why Labisi would have been credited with the design see Chapter 8, p. 143.

19 L. Dufourny, *Notes rapportées . . .*, I, n.p.

20 J. F. Blondel, *De la distribution des maisons de plaisance*, Paris, 1737, I, p. 173. Also see E. Hempel, *Baroque Art and Architecture in Central Europe*, Baltimore, 1965, p. 270.

21 For Amalienburg see E. Hempel, ibid. p. 230. For Sanssouci see ibid., p. 270; also see G. Piltz, *Sanssouci*, Dresden, 1954. For Mon Repos, P. du Colombier, *L'architecture française en Allemagne au XVIIIe siècle*, Paris, 1956, text vol., pp. 184–5.

22 For the history of the development of the central rotunda which projects from the rest of a building to form a semicircle and is flanked by low wings, see L. Hautecour, *Histoire de l'architecture classique*, Paris, 1957, III, p. 21.

23 See Chapter 8, note 53.

24 AdSP, Rivelo 3758, ff. 4–4v, 10 April 1747, Sinatra signs contract to be assessor 1747–8.

25 N. Pisani, *Noto: barocco e opera d'arte*, Syracuse, 1958, document on p. 50 for 'Sinatra . . . Architetto' and Di Blasi, p. 52 for 'Gagliardi . . . Architetto.'

Sinatra is called the architect for the monastery of Montevergine, as is Rosario Gagliardi. Exactly which of the two architects is responsible for the building is debatable. The monastery itself was recently torn down but the church associated with it (called S. Girolamo) still remains intact. In the apse of the church single free-standing columns emphasize the curve of the wall in a formula which appears frequently in Gagliardi's work. The interior decorations of the nave likewise appear Gagliardesque. But the exterior of the church is unusual in relation to Gagliardi's work because of its stripped concave façade which has extremely austere ornament.

In a contract of 1748 (Canale, p. 277) the present façade seems to be described: There is to be a Doric order with the architrave, frieze and cornice of Vignola with his rosette in the middle of the triglyph. This kind of doric order can be found in the church. Dufourny in 1789 (*Notes rapportées . . .*) describes the church as we see it today:

> One of the nuns' churches (San Michele, I think) [sic] is preceded by a façade with a hollow tower with a tower on either side, and that ensemble looks very nice; finally upon entering by the door into a hall one can see the whole church from there, which creates a piquant effect.

Given the above description and the document of 1748 the church probably looked as it does now in the eighteenth century. But its strange dryness might also be explained by the fate which befell S. Michele, the church that Dufourny confuses with S. Girolamo. When the Corso was lowered in the nineteenth century the façade of S. Michele collapsed but was rebuilt exactly the way it looked before. The same thing could have happened to S. Girolamo.

The idea for the façade may be derived from Fischer von Erlach's Dreifaltigkeitskirche in Salzburg as Anthony Blunt suggests (A. Blunt, *Sicilian Baroque*, p. 149).

26 Sinatra's contributions to the design and execution of the oratory of S. Filippo Neri and the monastery of S. Agata cannot be identified. It seems unlikely that the church of the oratory (S. Caterina) bears any resemblance to Labisi's or Sinatra's church. The present structure is said to be the work of Antonio Mazza, who drew a design for it which can be seen in the Biblioteca Comunale of Noto. The dormitory of the oratory seems to have been constructed, or perhaps remodelled, in the later eighteenth or early nineteenth century.

27 AdSS, Notary Vincenzo Labisi, 006946, 1750–51, f. 531.

28 D.S. VI, 3, 4; Canale pp. 278, 280, 284, 293.

29 D.S. V, 6.

30 Juan Caramuel, *Architectura Civile, Recta y Obliqua*, Vegevano, 1678. I assume Labisi was inspired by Caramuel because his treatise was so well known through Europe. Dufourny noted on his drawings of the house of the Crociferi that some of the ornamental motifs in the courtyard were Caramuelesque (L. Dufourny, *Notes rapportées . . .*).

31 The little garden in the Landolina palace is screened by two piers flanking a balustrade. These piers, with Rococo capitals like those on the stairway of the house of the Crociferi fathers, were evidently built after the rest of the palace which is in a more restrained style. In fact the pilasters of the palace in the same courtyard are of a much more severe design dating from earlier in the century.

32 V. Arezzo Prado (*Cenni Storici . . .*, p. 181) writes the following account of Paolo Labisi's life:

> Paolo Labisi architetto e geometra distintissimo, ebbe precettore il d. D. Francesco Sortino dei baroni di Busulmone. In tenera età il Labisi mostrò i voli del suo genio nel disegno della casa dei rr. pp. Crociferi. Applaudito in Napoli dal sig. D. Nicolo Anito architetto della Maestà sua il re di Napoli. Molte opere celebri fece, ed i suoi disegni eseguiti ci sono anche nel Messico. Il suo nome ancor fra noi si ripete. Fu egli più volte chiamato in Messina ed Roma, ma per la sua pusillanimità se ne astenne. Ovunque si va nella nostra provincia i monumenti della atri parlano di Paolo Labisi. Morì egli di anni 78.

Of Arezzo Prado's many statements only the one concerning Labisi's executed works in Mexico seems to be a pure fabrication. The rest of the information he gives is quite plausible. Labisi was most likely trained by Francesco Sortino who was a local professor of mathematics and philosophy. Sortino translated a key mathematical treatise from Latin to Italian expressly for Labisi's use (see pp. 196–97). Labisi may well have died at 78. According to the 1748 tax records (AdSP Rivelo 3756, 1748, p. 51) Labisi was born in 1724. Unfortunately this document is contradicted by a baptismal record (D.S. V, 1) in which his date of birth is recorded as 1720. Although records of his death have not yet been uncovered we do know he worked into the 1790s. Therefore it is possible he lived until either 1798 or 1802 when he died at 78. I am indebted to Anthony Blunt for pointing out to me that Nicolo Anito was a military engineer who was offered a position in Naples but went instead to Palermo where he stayed until 1778 (see F. Strazzullo, *Architetti e ingegnieri napolitani dal' 500 al 700*, Naples, n.d., p. 35, and F. Meli 'Degli architetti del senato di Palermo nei secoli XVII e XVIII', *Archivio Storico per la Sicilia*, IV–V, 1938–9, p. 384). It would therefore not have been unusual if Anito commended Labisi's work as Arezzo Prado alleges. As to being called away to do designs in Rome, one first thinks that this is mere propaganda for Noto. But it may well have occurred since Labisi was known to several very famous and influential aristocratic families. For example, Labisi designed a villa outside of Syracuse for the Gargallo family; Tommaso Gargallo was one of the chief literary figures of eighteenth-century Sicily (see note 39 below).

33 See D.S. V, 1.

34 See D.S. V, 3.

35 See ACMdN Registro dei Battesimi, 5 April 1715.

36 Paolo Labisi cautions his readers against the ignorance of the capomaestri:

> . . . dovendo sempre reggersi con le leggi dell' Architettura non già autenticate quei abbusi introdotti e determinazioni fatti dagli inesperti Capi Maestri, senza nesun fondamento e raziocinio [here Labisi footnotes Vitruvius who also warns about the undertrained and continues] . . . e di unglati [?] come stabilimenti nelle città, dicendo cose e l'uso del Paese; come se una tal proposizione dettata da un ignorante dovesse far legge, contro quella, che Lui stesso deve osservare nel suo proprio mestiere; ch'è quella cognizione, che manca anche al Giurisconsulto med. (P. Labisi, *La Scienca . . .*, p. viii).

In another context Labisi affirms that those without a proper education cannot hope to obtain it from books:

> Se poi credono che le scienze sono facili ad apprendersi da se soli, e soltanto con una lettura delle cose, che si fa nei Libri gli si può francamente rispondere, che un tale assunto potrà essere preso o da un'Ignorante, o veramente da un Matto, che non ha cervello da poter discorrere . . . (P. Labisi, *La scienza . . .*, p. ix).

In this passage Labisi flatly negates the value of his own book which is an attempt to explain architecture to those who are not acquainted with classical and contemporary sources. Because of the emotional nature of the outburst, I believe that Labisi wasn't seriously concerned with teaching but in proving his intellectual prowess.

37 The mathematical treatise in Christian Wolff's *Elementa Matheseos Universae*. A MS copy of a volume entitled *Elementa Meteseos Universe* IV, 1746, is stored in the Biblioteca Comunale of Noto. It measures 15 × 20 cm. Ink on paper; bound.

The oval design of the frontispiece in Labisi's edition and the sequence and composition of its plates suggest that it was copied from C. Wolff, *Elementa Matheseos Universae*, Marcum-Michaelem Bousquet Socio, Geneva, 1732. On the title page a note reads: 'Per uso proprio dell'Architetto Reggio della Città di Noto Dn: Paolo Labisi.' On the following page below a description of Wolff's accomplishments in Italian another note reads: 'Tradotti dal latino dall' Illus:mo e Rev:mo Sig.r Dn Francesco Ma. Sortino Professore di Filisofia, di Matematica, e di belle Lettere della Città di Noto. L'anno 1746.' Although the two notes may not have been written into the MS. at the same time, they nevertheless prove Labisi's connection to Sortino; it seems logical to presume that Sortino was Labisi's teacher.

38 See D.S. IV, D.S.V, 4. For Labisi's work on the church of S. Caterina of the oratory of S. Filippo Neri see note 26.

39 Labisi's March 1765 design for the Gargallo villa in Priolo Gargallo near Syracuse is preserved in the collection of Casa Gargallo in Syracuse. For an illustration see F. Fichera, *G. B. Vaccarini* . . ., II, pl. 78. Only a small portion of the eastern side of the main façade of the villa was completed, and its design does not correspond exactly to Labisi's drawing. Although documents record Labisi's participation in the planning of the Chiesa Madre of Ispica the church itself looks unlike anything else he designed; therefore he probably began the church by laying the plans, but the structure was finished by someone else.

40 I believe Labisi was the Architect of the city of Noto in 1749 because he signed himself 'Architetto della Città di Noto' on the map he drew of Piazza S. Domenico. On the designs for the house of the Crociferi fathers Labisi signs himself 'Architetto della Ingegnosa Città di Noto.' For variations in the application of the term architect of the city see pp. 142–43.

41 See D.S. V, 10.

42 The actual cause for the delay is not stated in the Crociferi documents but the attempt to curb the growing monetary and political power of the monastic institutions probably explains it. See pp. 112–13.

The Crociferi fathers were also called Camilliari (after their founder S. Camillo de Lellis) or Ministre degli Inferme (*New Catholic Encyclopedia*, Washington, D.C., II, 1967, p. 1108 and *Enciclopedia Cattolica*, Rome, 1949, VIII, pp. 1040–1041.)

43 Labisi says that his designs were approved in 1752 (see D.S. V, 6) but the first page of his designs for the church bears two dates, neither of which is 1752. Don Francesco Tirrigno approved the designs for the convent in Palermo in 1751; the same designs were approved by local authorities in Noto on 24 September 1753.

The designs, previously displayed in the Museo Comunale of Noto, have been transferred to the safe of the Biblioteca Comunale after having suffered water damage. They include 13 sheets of drawings for the church and dormitory of the convent of the PP. Crociferi. Medium: ink on paper; size: *ca.* 30 × 60 cm. Originally all thirteen designs were bound in a large volume but now each is a separate sheet. According to an annotation on what was probably the first design, Antonio Bonfiglio of the order of Crociferi donated the set to the Biblioteca Comunale sometime in the nineteenth century.

44 For illustrations and discussion of Superga see A. Telluccini, *L'arte dell'architetto Filippo Juvara in Piemonte*, Turin, pp. 34–9 and R. Wittkower, *Art and Architecture in Italy* . . ., pp. 279–81.

45 S. Serlio, *Tutte l'opere dell'architettura et prospettiva*, Venice, 1619, Book III, p. 57.

46 G. Kubler, *Arquitectura de los siglos XVII y XVIII* . . ., p. 112 for illustration and discussion of Fontana's building in Spain.

47 R. Wittkower, *Art and Architecture in Italy* . . ., pp. 240–52.

48 See R. Wittkower, 'Carlo Rainaldi and the Roman Architecture of the Full Baroque', *Art Bulletin*, XIX, 1937, p. 247ff.

49 E.g. Juvarra's façade of Palazzo della Valle in Turin (see A. Telluccini, *L'arte dell'architetto Filippo Juvara* . . ., p. 32) and Fuga's Palazzo della Consulta (R. Pane, *Ferdinando Fuga*, Naples, 1956, p. 22).

50 E. Utity, *Christian Wolff*, Halle, 1929; H. Levy, *Die Religionsphilosophie Christian Wolffs*, Würzburg, 1928; *Enciclopedia Filosofica*, IV, Florence, 1967, pp. 1153–55.

51 E. Di Carlo, 'Per la storia della cultura siciliana nel Settecento,' *Il Circolo Giuridico*, Palermo, 1961, pp. 17–28; D. Scina, *Prospetto della storia letteraria di Sicilia nel secolo decimottavo*, Palermo, 1859, pp. 337–45.

52 See Note 37 for Labisi's copy of Wolff's treatise.

53 AdSS, Notary Natale Marotta, 006907, 1754–5, f. 557.

54 None of the designs is identical to any of Pozzo's in his *Perspectiva Pictorum et Architectorum*, Rome, 1717, although there are similarities. Nor can the designs be convincingly matched with those of any other architect or designer of the seventeenth or eighteenth centuries. The designs seem closer in spirit to Roman Baroque, however, than the Baroque architecture of Naples.

55 D.S. V, 6, 7.

56 The date of 1787 is inscribed over the first floor on the south side of the dormitory. The inside of the main portal on the west side of the dormitory bears the date '20 Xbre MCDDLXX' painted over the doorway. The south side of the dormitory appears to have been largely completed by the early twentieth century as early photographs in the Messina collection in Noto show. Probably the demolition of the church of S. Camillo in 1925 caused about half the façade to ruin. Today the mezzanine section above the old refectory on the south side of the complex is blocked off. The façade is extraordinarily uneven, bowing outward to the south. The north side of the building fell in even before the south; plans for the rebuilding of this part of the structure were drawn in 1904. They are preserved in the archives of the city hall in a folder labelled 'public works'.

57 C. Tafaro, *Notizie* . . ., pp. 80–81, states that the church was torn down by order of the mayor, Corrado Sallicano, because it threatened to collapse.

58 Paolo Labisi, *La scienza* . . ., IV, pp. 225ff., measuring 14.5 × 10.5 cm.

59 Paolo Labisi (*La scienza* . . .) mentions the city of Noto and its architectural practice only three times. First, in his discussion of the regulations governing a vacant site (see Chapter 2, note 58). Second, in relation to wages paid to workmen in the following passage (*La scienza* . . ., pp. 143–44):

> Si deve avere in considerazione se nel fabricarsi le case, come in q.ta città di Noto, si pagassero i Maestri operarii per le loro giornate, che gl'impiegano, com'anche la compra dei materiali, metà in denaro, e metà in frumento, raggionato secondo il prèzzo stabilito dal magistrato e consiglieri, colla metà imposta, quale metà porterà sempre il prezzo più alto di quanto giornalmente si vende dal popolo particolare, ed essendo così lo stimatore nel calcolo della totale somma del prezzo della casa, deve quindi per suo obligo, scemargli quell'imposto, che deve scemarsi dalla metà del frumento raggionato secondo il prezzo della metà, giacchè il prezzo tutto di essa casa vien pagato dal compratore in denaro, e non già metà in frumento, e metà in denaro, e ciò per la ragione di non essere conveniente nè pur anche di giusto.

Labisi again mentions Noto in the following passage about the legal possession of the ground floor of a building (*La scienza* . . ., p. 126):

> Per quello riguardo al tavolato, nel doversi vendere parte di essa casa, non deve essere considerato, e compreso nel valore della stanza di ṣopra, ma in q.lla di sotto, (Nei paesi però, che non si vende terreno come è in uso nella città di Notò) e la raggione è perchè siccome la stanza sottana ha con se il suolo del terreno senza pagare nessun grano, così lo deve avere la stanza soprana, cioè ha da avere anche il suolo, o sia l'uso del tavolato, o volta, invece del suolo del terreno . . .

60 See note 36 for Labisi's invective against *capomaestri*.

61 Labisi quoted from the following books which were in the Nicolaci (or Villadorata) collection, and which could once be found in the Biblioteca Comunale di Noto (these books are listed in *Catalogo Alfabetico della Biblioteca Comunale*, Noto, 1889, though I could find only no. 5 below):

1. G. B. De Luca, *Istituti civili*, Naples, 1741.
2. J. Cancerio, *Variae Resolutiones juris caesarei, pontificii et principatus cathalonie*, Lugduni, 1626.
3. D. Soto, *De justitia et jure*, Venice, 1594.
4. G. B. DeLuca, *Il dottor volgare*, Rome, 1673.
5. *Capitula regni Siciliae*, Palermo, 1741.
6. V. Tanara, *L'economia del cittadino in villa*, Venice, 1745.
7. C. Wolff, *Elementa Matheseos Universae*, Geneva, 1732.

Labisi also used C. Perrault, *L'architettura generale di Vitruvio ridotta in compendi dal Sig. Perrault*, Venice, 1672, which was in the collection of the Comune. It is possible, of course, that all these editions were purchased in the nineteenth century in both the case of the book owned by the Comune and those of the Villadorata collection. But this possibility seems unlikely.

62 G. V. Marvuglia, *Elementa di architectura*, MS Biblioteca Comunale, Palermo, n.d., pp. 182, 14, cites Wolff as an authority along with Cataneo and Inigo Jones. Marvuglia was a Neo-classical architect (1729–1814) considered to be one of the outstanding artists of his day; see S. Caronia Roberti, *Venanzio Marvuglia*, Palermo, n.d. But non-Sicilians used Wolff too: G. Masi, *Teoria e pratica di architettura civile per istruzione della gioventù specialmente Romana dedicata all'illustrissimo signor Gaspare Conte di Carpegna*, Rome, 1788, p. 221 cites Wolff. N. Carletti, *Istruzione di architettura civile*, Naples, 1772, set up his book with corollaries, problems, and definitions in a manner identical to Wolff's. No doubt the architect was copying Wolff's method of setting forth problems.

63 Canale, p. 295. Di Blasi p. 69.

64 See D.S. V, 9.

Chapter 10

1 See *Indagine demografica, scolastica e socio-economica svolta nel Comune di Noto*. Progetto c/4, Ufficio studi e programmazione, Provveditorito agli Studi di Siracusa, 1963.

2 Bernardo Labisi was born in 1747 (Canale, p. 288; D.S. V, 2) and rose to become an important architect and engineer in Noto (D.S. VI). For a description of the S. Chiara drawing see Chapter 8, note 42.

3 The drawing for the church was found in one of the Gagliardi volumes in the Mazza collection, Syracuse. See Chapter 8, note 20.

4 There is some confusion over the authorship of the church of SS. Salvatore. Traditionally the church has been attributed to Cantor Antonio Mazza (F. Balsamo, *Una visita . . .*, p. 20). Mazza is said to have corrected the designs first drawn by Andrea Gigante, one of which still exists in the Biblioteca Comunale (Canale, p. 186). Unfortunately, the corner where Mazza's signature is alleged to have appeared on a crucial drawing has been ripped off, leaving Mazza's contribution unproven. Canale (p. 186) does not help the problem by confusing an earlier Antonio Mazza with the one under discussion here.

5 Drawings for the reconstruction of the church, in the possession of Francesco Genovesi, Noto, look exactly like the façade that was originally constructed in the eighteenth century. The present façade looks like the church illustrated by Labisi in his veduta.

6 Drawings of the extent of the damage and various appeals for funds can be found in the Archives of the Noto city hall, under 'public works, Crociferi'.

Documents and Appendices

The documents which follow were transcribed for the most part without correction of spelling inconsistencies. Spanish notaries sometimes used accents and sometimes did not. Often the Spanish letter u is substituted for the letter v. The Spanish frequently changed the spelling of Italian place names: The city of Avola becomes Abola, Vizzini becomes Vicini. Similar discrepancies can be found in the Italian documents. Paolo Labisi's first name is variously written as Paulus, Paolus and Paolo.

Where documents have been published elsewhere citations are given. They appear here for the first time with volume and folio numbers.

SECTION I: DAMAGE, RECONSTRUCTION AND APPOINTMENTS AFTER THE 1693 EARTHQUAKE

Document 1

A report on earthquake damage:
Relacion de los considerables daños que han causado los temblores en el Reyno de Sicilia los dias 9 y 11 del mes de enero de 1693.

El día 9 a 2 horas y 3 cuartos de la noche, cuenta de Italia, fue el primero, que duró un largo Credo. Si bien en Mezina no veo daño alguno, pero el segundo, que sobrevino a los 11 del mismo a 4 horas y media, duró un cuarto de hora que causó gran lástima pues no quedó casa ni palacio que no se abriese con muchos que quedaron en tierra. Y los muertos que hasta ahora se han sabido son hasta 43, que como los ánimos están abatidos, no se ha podido descubrir más. Las procesiones y penitencias ásperas que se hacen no hay ejemplar en el mundo. Y muchas confesiones en público, y este Sn prelado predicando, por iglesias, plazas y calles a pies descalzos, con sandalias, [illegible] religiosos, y clérigos, y aunque no estén aprobados, les ha dado licencia para que confiesen y absuelvan de todos los pecados estimados reservados al Pontifice. El terreno de la marina está abierto en diferentes partes. En Terranova también con Santa Cruz en tierra y la mayor parte de sus casas, y nadie se atreve a caminar por las calles. Y por último se vive de milagro que ha obrado Su Divina Magestad a intercesión de la Virgen Santa María de la Letra. Y los temblores duran pero son muy leves y al más mínimo estruendo se antoja temblor, que a tanto llega el temor en que nos ellamos todos. En el Reyno se a sabido hasta ahora la pérdida de Carlentin, Lentin, Militelo, la Ferrula, Noto, Vicini, Sortino, Francoforte, Milili, Calatagiron, y Achi el Real, La Itriza, Mascari, Augusta, Zaragosa, Sigale, Modica, Ragusa, Abola, Spacafurno, Misterbianco, Fenicia Moncada, . . . Palermo, . . ., Torre de Grifo, Nicolosi, Borrello, Pedura, Via grande, Tres Castanas, San Antonio, la Cadena, la Catiana, Santa Lucia, y Achi, y su castillo, San Phelipo, Bonacursi, San Gregorio . . . el trapito, la Punta, Tres Misterios, Pelo Verde, y el castillo de la Brucula todas estas ciudades, villas y casales han quedado por tierra sin que parezcan aun los cimientos. La ciudad de Catania a quedado como la palma de la mano, menos las murallas que miran a la mar, habiendo soterrado sus ruínas más de 16 almas, y aseguran que asi en esta ciudad como en las demás perdidas se sienten debajo de tierra muchos clamores de personas que piden misericordia y auxilio, y que en la cathedral, hallándose dentro de ella la mayor parte del pueblo, a tiempo que el canónigo D. Josep Zeleste, y Vientemillas, le echaba la bendición con el Sanctisimo Sacramento en las manos, de improviso cayo toda la iglesia cogiendo debajo toda la gente menos el referido canónigo, que quedó intacto como así mismo quedaron en pie las dos capillas colaterales al altar mayor, donde está la Madre de Dios la Letra y la de la Gracia con coro y habitáculo donde se halla la gloriosa Santa Agata cuyo cuerpo expusieron el día siguiente del primer temblor sobre altar mayor y dicen que fue preciso acudir por tres veces a repararle porque se caía del altar y que el rostro, que siempre le tenía risueño ye alegre, le vieron entonces melancólico y ceniciento.

De Palermo avisan por cartas que los temblores derribaron en aquella ciudad muchos palacios y casas, pero que han quedado sentidos y abiertos todos los demás. También cayó Puerta Felice, el campanario de la Iglesia de los Bucheros[?], y parte de la abadia de las Virginelas con un lienzo de la vicaria, el cual cogió debajo un preso que el día antes del temblor mató un hombre malamente y allí pagó su pecado. Todos los habitadores de dicha ciudad se hallan esparcidos por las campañas y que las casas y palacios sentidos se apuntalan a toda priesa.

AGdS, Estado 3507, no. 4, 11 January 1693

Document 2

Report of the Duke of Uzeda to the King
describing his appointments to the earthquake juntas and the positions of Vicars General

. . . El Vicario Gen. Principe de Aragona aquien nombre Vicario gen. de Noto cayo enfermo dela gota con que fue precisso dejarle en el Val de Mazzara y bolver a encargar al obispo de Zaragossa cuidasse del Val de Noto. El Duque de Camastra acuio cargo pusse el Val Demone estava el dia 30 en Nicossia cercado de nieves y de aguas y siendo precisso seguir el camino a passos lentos aun que llevava la prevención de gastadores pero a esta hora le supongo en Catania donde el mismo da 30 havia llegado el Juez Dn Joseph Asmundo y siendo esta ciudad una delas que mas cuidado me davan . . .

[There are a great many dead. Prince Butera is helping in Augusta assisted by Dn Juan Mario. Francesco de Bustamente is helping too. Arriving in the fort of Augusta on January 30, Col. Don Carlos Grunemberg surveys the damage. Don Sancho de Mirando takes precautions for the defence of the island. But the Viceroy himself cannot visit the stricken areas of the island.]

Considerando que para tanto como ôcurre asì para el remedio delas ciudades Regias y Baronales como el arreglamento que se deve dar para la manutenz.n, deste Reyno es menester brevedad y menos confusión de la que ay en los Tribunales por los negocios de su Ynstituto y los que se aumentaran entre partes y el Fisco por falta de sucesión[?] delos que han perecido en este accidente y mas êxpezialmente por que he conocido en esta ôcasión que en ellos se atiende más a las utilidades proprias de Parientes of Amigos que a las particulares del Servº. de V. Mgd. y Generales del vien comun. queriendo que el erario Regio se convierta en aquellas y no en esta me ha parezido formar una Junta compuesta del Regente Dn Juo. Anto. Iopulo, del Preste, Dn Joseph Scoma, del Consr. Don Antonio Ybañez del Veedor gen, Marques de Analasta de mi S.rio, Dn. Feliz dela Cruz Haedo, del Mro Razional, Dn. Seu. Gessino del Avogado Fiscal, Dn Balthasr. del Castillo y Dn Pedro Capero como Diputado del Reyno para que en la secretaria se junten los Viernes y Martes de cada semana y se discurriran los medias que fueren del maior servicio de V Mgd vien de estos vassallos y delo que se fuere obrando hire dando quenta a V Mgd.

Siendo tantas las Parroquiales Monasterios, de Monjas de Religiosos y de Abadias Regias que se han arruinado en estos accidentos y estando desamparadas las Monjas desvandados los religiosos y sin forma de zelebrar con decencia en los Pueblos, he mandado formar otra Junta eclesiastica conpuesta del Arzovispo de Palermo Dn Ferndo. Bazan, del Juez dela Monarqa, Dn Greg.o de Solorzano del primer Inquis.or, Dn. Phelipe Ignacio De Trujillo, del Mro Fr. Alesando Conti del Duque dele Gruti como Diputado del Rey.o a fin de ir occurriendo por todas los medios posibles al reparo de quanto han desquadernado estos accidentes, ê ire dando qta, â V. Mgd. AGdS, Estado 3507, no. 10, Palermo, 5 February 1693

Document 3

Report to the King on Noto, Syracuse and Catania

Representando a V. Mg.d en Consi.ta de 13 del corr.te que se hall a en sus Reales manos.

El Marqs de Villafranca
DnAlo de Guzman
Dn Pedro Guerrero
Dn Anto Jurado
el Conde de Bornos
DnDiego Iniguez
Dn Genaro de Andrea
Respta de S. Mg
Comp parece
——————en 6 de Mayo

Senor
Continuando el Duque de Uceda las notas de los terremotos del Reyno de Sia que ultimamte participo en Carta de 19 de Feo de que el Consejo tiene dada qta a V. Mgd en Consita de 13 del corrte Dice en otra de 5 de Mayo que se vio con el Ordinario que llego antes de Ayer, haversse sentido hasta el dia 20 de febo en diferentes lugares de Valdenoto, como el Vicario Gen Duque de Camastra le aviso desde Noto cuia Capital Ciudad de aquel Valle quedo totalmte destrvida haviendola desamparado sus Moradores asi por el orror de los temblores, como por haverlo hecho toda la Nobleza sin cuidar su Senado y Ministros de Justicia en 20 dias de Residir a su Vista hasta que con el arrivo del de Camastra, se dio metodo a Su Gouno y sustento de la Gente que se iba recogiendo, teniendo por muy digno su fervor y zelo de que V. Mgd se de por servido de el alentandole con esta honra.

f. 135r
Que la Ciudad de Catanea por las disposiciones del mismo Duque de Camastra, y el Summo amor, conque los Naturales miran su Patria queda puesta en metodo y tratando de la Reedificacion con el dictamen del Ingeniero Carlos Grunemberg que les asistira por la duda que havia en si se mudaria o no su asiento.
Que en Noto havia la misma duda que remittio a disposicion del de Camastra, prohibiendoselo el que en caso de mudar de situacion no sea avecindandosse a la Mar, ni perdiendo de vista el Castillo si ha quedado capaz de Repararsse Que el pueblo de la de Lentin se dividio en Parcialidades una pte reedificar en elmismo suelo y otra por que se uniesse a Carlentin, lo qual ajusto el de Camastra, y dio terreno a menos de media Milla de que quedaron gustosos y sin el inconuete de perder una Ciudad demanial
Que Mongiuelo no havia arrojado materia alguna obseruandosse solo que desde 3 hasta 11 de Febrero ha via dado grandes Estallidos y despedido

f. 135v.
Cantidad de Cenizas embuelta en el fuego oyendosse devajo de la tierra Rumor como de viento que haze vivir con desconsuelo a aquellos naturales hasta que la Montana arroge, o los vapores se exalen cuia continua da desgracia atrasa el Reedificar como sucedia en Zaragoza y Augta aunque se iban desembarazando las fortificaces arruinadas poniendo en defensa las que quedaron ilesas montada toda la Artilleria con los ajustes que fueron de Meza preuenidas las municiones que se sacaron de los Almagacenes, que caieron, y los G..les de las Plazas con incesante desuelo executando quanto cave en la possibilidad con el Coronel Grunemberg en aquellos parages para asistir a todo lo conueniente El Consejo da quenta a V. Mgd del contenido de la carta referida del Virrey a fin que V. Mgd se halle con indiuidual noticia de lo que occurre, Remittiendosse a lo que pte estos incidentes tiene propuesto a V. Mgd en la Consta referida de 13 del este Mes.
V. Mgd mandara lo que fuere seruido. Mdo 15 de Abril de 1693.
Con senales del Consejo
AGdS, Secretarias Provinciales Libro 745, 15 April 1693

Document 4

The Duke of Uzeda reports to the King

[He begins by discussing the rebuilding of churches and monasteries and the amount of money allocated for them to pay the government. He continues . . .]
El que se comprehenda enesta contribuzion lo que el Estado eclesiastico contribuye a V. Mg.d por razon de tandas y donatibos, me pareze irrazonable, por que ademas de que Va. Mg.d por algun tiempo es preciso remita las Cantidades que por esta Razon pagan los Obispados de Catania y Zaragosa pa. que se emplean en la Reedificazion de sus Igesias cathedrales y Palacios espiscopales, y las que contribuian algunas Abadías secularizadas por haverse del todo arruinado sus Iglesias y Conventos que es porcion muy considerable estando las tandas y Donatibos aplicados para reparar las fortificaciones de las Ziudades, Castillos del Reyno, municionarlas y pagar la milicia; y hauiendo se arruinado las de Zaragosa y Augusta, los Castillos de Catania, la Brucula y otras para cuya reedificacion se nezesitaba de sumas muy considerables, no debe esta porcion divertitse a otros efectos, quando los eclesiasticos son tan interesados en la perfeccion destas Plazas, y Castillos como defensa total deste Reyno. AGdS, Estado 3507, no. 55, Palermo, 16 May 1693

Document 5

Report from Consejo de Italia to the King on earthquakes and problems of rebuilding Noto

A 27 de May de 1693
El Consejo de Italia da qta a V Mgd de carta del Duq de Uceda de 16 de Abril con auiso de la forma en que el dia 8 de aquel mes, se continuauan los terremotos en el Valdenoto, y otras partes, imposibilitando las Rehedificazes; que se quedauan formando Relaciones de la perdida de Gentes y lugares para Remittirlas en la Posta sigte

El Marq de Villafranca	Senor
Dn Alo de Guzman	El Virrey, Duque de Uzeda en carta para V. Mgd
Dn Po Guerrero	de 16 de Abril avisa que el dia 8 del mismo

D[n] Ant[o] Jurado	continuauan los temblores en el Valdenoto sintien-
El Conde de Bornos	dosse algunos con igual fuerza a los del dia 11 de
D[n] Diego Iniquez	
D[n] Genaro de Andrea	

f. 156v–157
Henero en las Vecindades del Mongiuelo, y en lo mas apartado con maior templanza, augmentando la descomodidad a los que estan en la Campaña y imposibilitando la Rehedificacion; que en Mez[a] se experimentan tambien alg.os Aunque leues; y en Palermo y su Valle ningunos; que el desembarazar las Calles de las Ruinas y sepultar los Cadaveres, que ha sido su primer cuidado parecia (segun las cartas del Duque de Camastra y otro Ministros) se hallava casi concluido menos en la Ciudad de Noto. Que por su estravagancia da mas en que entender que todo el resto de lo arruinado, por querer que q[to] hay que reparar y asistir salga de la R[l] Haz[da] de V. Mg[d] y que se les socorra para Iglesias, Casas Alimentos y mutacion al nueuo sitio donde han de Rehedificar, pero esperava con la ida de D[n] Joseph Asmundo y ex[on] de las ordenes que lleuaua, poner en buen metodo aquella Ciudad como lo estan las demas del Valle; que se quedavan formando las Relaz[es] para remitirlas el Correo sig[te] de las not[as] individuales de lo que han padecido todas las tierras del Valdenoto, y creia llegaran a 102 Personas las que murieron y a 16 los lugares Demaniales, y Varonales, que se arruinaron, aunque no todos igualmente. El Consejo da q[ta] a V. Mg[d] del contenido de esta carta para que se halle enterado de ello. M[d] a 27 de May de 1693.
Con señales del Consejo
AGdS, Secretarias Provinciales Libro 745, 27 May 1693

Document 6
Report on the state of Carlentini and Noto

f. 156v–157
Que el Comissario Gen[l] D[n] Joseph Asmundo le auisava se proseguia a la formacion de la Ciudad de Noto en el nuevo Sitio de Lemeti, hav[do] senalado a este fin los correspondientes para las Casas, Iglesias y Magazenes, Repartiendo las tablas que le iban llegando para la de las Barracas.
Que la duda de si la de Lentin havia de Fabricar se en la p[te] que determino el de Camastra, o, Unirse a Carlentin la fomentavan dos Cau[los] de aquella Ciu[d] y siendo las esempciones y Previlegios de la ultima tan antiguas, como observados, se Remittieron al mismo Camastra las inst[as] para que examinadas con publico Consejo de las dos Ciudades y de suerte que con Renuncia de Carlentin no quede lessa la R[l] Haz[da] Informarsse muy por menor para executar (con parezer de la Junta) lo que conuiniesse al bien de ambos Cuerpos y util de la Corte. Que de las Relaciones que le han embiado los Comissarios generales se ha sacado el Mapa que Remitte y que sube con esta para que se halle V. Mg[d] caualm[te] enterado de las Almas que tenia cada Pueblo la calidad de sus Ruinas, la R[ta] annual que gozaua V. Mg[d] en ellos, y el numero de los que perecieron Siendo impracticable en esta p[te] dar punto fijo, por no hauer noticia que corresponda con otra mediante la intencion o la buena o mala inteligencia de los que las subministran, pudiendosse creher prudencialm[te] que no diran . . . murieron dos faltando quatro.
AGdS, Secretarias Provinciales Libro 745, 29 May 1693

Document 7
Reports on Camastra at Noto and Syracuse's fortifications

f. 143v
Que los Jurados de Noto le escribieron que la Gente de la Ciudad padecia muchas y pestilentes enfermedades, y hauiendo ordenado al Duque de Camastra pasasse personalm[te] a averiguarlo le saco del cuidado embiandole-

f. 144
fees de Medicos de no haver muerto desde 22 de Marzo hasta 19 de Abril mas que Cinco Personas de enfermedades conocidas ratificandosse el de Camastra en la impertinencia de esta Gente, y volvio a ajustar con gran maña y quietud el pasage de la havitacion al sitio señalado de Limete dejando al cargo del Juez D[n] Joseph Asmundo la ex[on] de lo nueuam[te] establecido. Que en Lentin se havian vuelto a suscitar las dificultades en mudar aquella Poblacion al sitio señalado por el de Camastra, con que le mando volver al ajuste de esta materia y le juzgaua en aquella Ciudad. Que las Murallas que tenia Carlentin quedaron arruinadas y Reconocidas por el Coronel Grunemberg necesitavan de gran gasto para Rehedificarlas y por que q[do] se construyeron no hauia fortificac[es] en Zaragoza y Augusta le han aparecido con dictamen del mismo Coronel abaondonarlas, y applicar toda la fuerza de dinero y cuidado a Aug[ta] y Zaragoza a donde (como tiene Repres[do]) hauia embiado

f. 144v
los medios que estavan señalados al Duque de Savoya y se huviera conseguido tener en moderada defensa estas Plazas a no embarazarlo los temblores continuados, pues ya se havia empezado a fabricar, y ha sido menester suspenderlo por no perderlo otra vez, applicandosse los prov[es] (como lo tiene prevenido) a fortificarsse con faginas y Murallas en seco hasta que se aquiete la Tierra y que a Zaragoza havia embiado dos Colm[as] de Infanteria en Re[e]mplazo de la que se perdio en las Ruinas y se Vyo por el espanto, y a Aug[ta] embiaria mas gente, lo q no ha ex[do] por hallarsse con poca Infanteria para guarnezer tantas Plazas como tiene el Reyno pte los hombres que le ocupan la guarnicion de las Galeras, faltandole tambien medios para reclutas, hau[do] tenido la desgracia de que Un Capitan que el año pasado a levantar y salio con 12 hombres del Grao de Valencia el dia l[o] de Henero perecio con una Borrasca segun los Indicios que tenia.
AGdS, Secretarias Provinciales Libro 745, 10 June, 1693

Document 8
The Duke of Uzeda reports to the King

[After a report on finances, a note on the necessity of fortifications rather than religious buildings in Syracuse:]
Que este era el fruto que hauia podido sacar dela junta eclesiastica, deviendo asegurar a V. Md. que si se huviese de seguir la opinion delos mas de aquel Estado, se hallaran medios p.a reedificar combentos, e Iglesias; pero para Repara Castillos y Plazas ninguno proporcionado, pues en su rapension deve ceder esta importancia indispensable, a la obra piadosa no reparando en que los Conbentos han quedado, sin el peso de muchas monjas, y con alajas de plata, y otras preseas de que poderse valer, de mas de sus rentas, que si se han deteriorado no se han perdido del todo, lo que no sucede en las fortalezas, donde sin tener propiedad solo se adornan de Balas y Municiones y estas se han perdido.
AGdS, Estado 3597, no. 50, 14 July 1693

Document 9
Report to the King of continuing earthquakes, signs of unstable territory, and the rebuilding of Syracuse and Augusta

Señor
Se sirbe V. Mg[d] en despacho di 1 de Mayo aprovar el cuidado y desbelo con que he procurado quanto ha cavido en mi possivilidad ocurrir al alivio y Reparo de los estragos que han hecho los terremotos, y desde el Correo pasado hasta este solo ha havido en Catania uno muy leve y en Noto hasta Cinco poco sensibles, acreditandose q aquella parte por mas concaba o por mas dispuesta a los embates del mar contra las Grutas que ay en las orillas, esta mas sugeta a padezer, pero como digo tan levemente que ba inquietando menos a los naturales. Asientan todas las cartas que en la Ziudad destruida de Noto, se oye antes que llegue el temblor un Rumor como de viento debajo de tierra, y en el nuebo sitio que se ha elegido para reedificarla no se ha obserbado, discurriendose de que este es terreno igual, q.el otro es pedernal con algo de montañoso. Y sin embargo destas tenues Repeticiones y no unibersales, se suspende el fabricar en muchas partes por que estando la tierra con movimiento aunq ligero, y tan sedienta que tiene algunas aberturas Juzgan los practicos se deben suspender las reedificaziones hasta que llueba.

En Zaragoza y Augusta se continuan las obras con ferbor y en la ultima se introdugeron todo genero de municiones y armas que me pidio el Gov[or] con que a ambas plazas solo les falta el concluir las fortificaciones lo qual requiere muchos anos por q. no es Capaz de hazerse tanto como se arruino en brebe tiempo y como se pueda continuar el trabajo que pareze probable ya por q ban decayendo los temblores, se adelantara, lo que cabe por que en todo lo que da de si se ba apresurando la diligenzia de Reparar.

Sirbese V. Mg[d] en el Zitado despacho del desaprobar el medio que Resolvi a Consulta de la Junta de que se valiese el Duque de Camastra de la 1[a] 2[a] o 3[a] parte del oro, plata y otras cosas que se Recuperasen de particulares, y puedo decir a V. Mg[d] que este medio no se puso en practica por que Reboque la orden immediatamente previendo dificultad, y el desconsuelo que podia producir; y sobre la extension que V. Mg[d] ha Resuelto de que tambien los bienes Raizes y fuedos q yo Reserbe para la Corte queden a beneficio de los propios lugares q padecieron; He mandado al Tribunal del Patrimonio expida los Vandos para que sea publico a todos el grande amor y piedad con que V. Mg[d] mira y atiende a su mayor alivio.

Asi mismo he dado la orden para que de estos Vienes vacantes se haga el Anibersario por las animas de los que perezieron en las Ruinas como V. Mg[d] me previene. D. G. G. E. L. C. R. P. de V. Mg[d] como la xpo ha m. Palermo 11 de Junio 1693
AGdS, Estado 3507, no. 52, Palermo, 11 June 1693

Document 10
The Duke of Camastra's accomplishments as described in request for noble privilege, 1682

Don Pedro de Aragon
Duque de Alva
Conde de Chinchon
Duque de Albuquerque

El sargento general de Batalla, duque de Camastra, príncipe de San Estaban representa a V.M. en un memorial que se ha visto en el Consejo que ha que sirve a V.M. desde el año de 1664 de Capitán de Caballos Corazas del servicio militar del Reyno de Sicilia, Capitán del Justicia y Pleitos de la ciudad de Palermo, Diputado del dicho Reyno y que en ocasión de la rebelión de Mesina fue el primero que levantó un tercio de infantería italiana y sirvió con él en la escaleta hallándose en muchas ocasiones de aquella guerra portándose en ellas con toda aprobación de sus superiores como lo han representado a V.M. diferentes veces los Virreyes de aquel Reyno en cuya consideración, la calidad y méritos de su casa, el grande dispendio de hacienda con que él los ha continuado sirviendo, no tan solamente sin sueldo alguno, sino empenando su patrimonio en más de 809 ducados de plata en socorrer su tercio y alentar los naturales, suplica a V. M. se sirva hacerle merced de honrarle con la llave de Gentilhombre de la Cámara de V. M. para que pueda tener este honor en su casa, por única hasta hoy, de otra honorifica ni de congruencia[?]. El Consejo juzga ser estos motivos muy dignos de la Real consideración de V. M. por la calidad, celo y rara inclinacion de este caballero a la nación española para que en la forma que el Consejo puede representarlo se sirva V. M. honrarle y favorecerle.

V. M. mandara lo que mas fuera de su Real servicio.
Mandado a 3 de enero de 1682.
AGdS, Estado 3502, 3 January 1682

SECTION II: THE FOUNDATION OF AVOLA

Document 1
Early history of Avola

Relazione di quanto si è operato nella nuova città d'Avola dal giorno del Terremoto Il Gennaro 1693 . . .
Per ordine del Sr. Principe di Santa Flavia, e Sr. Consultore fu inviato a quella città il fratello Angelo Italia della Compagnia di Gesù M.ro Architetto per osservare il sito più opportuno e l'aria più salubre per la riedificazione della nuova città.
Si confinò sopra loco il suddetto Fratto Angelo, ed osservando con ogni esattezza tutto il Territorio d'Avola non trovò luogo e sito migliore che il fego dell'università d'Avola detto Mutubini nel quale si tiro la nuova città, nella forma che fu trasmessa a V.E. lontana dal mare da un miglio, e mezzo in circa, in una bellissima amena[?] e molto larga pianura che si stende da parte di ponente più di 40 miglia e da parte di levante da 30 miglia da potersi viaggiare in carrozza nel mezzo della città passa l'acqua della Fontana detta Miranda. Le mura delle case attorno la Città servono per difesa perchè tutte circondate di piccole aperture per tenere lontani l'Inimici con pochi moschetti e scopette. Furono inviati alcuni Maestri Muratori da Palermo ad Avola per dar principio alla fabrica come in fatti si diè principio alla chiesa madre, alli Magaseni di Frumento dell'Università al Fondaco, e posata ed ad altre chiese e case; Fra tanto tutti li cittadini si portarono in detto nuovo sito per fabricare le loro baracche di tavole, chi sino al presente arrivano al num.o di duemila, . . . V.E. può considerare la grossa spesa che si è fatta nel piantare le dette baracche . . .
[Stones and bells are brought from the old site of the city to the new . . .] Si sono fatte molte canne di fossi attorno al nuovo sito per difesa degl'Inimici mentre non si sono fabricate le case, ma perchè le Spiaggie d'Avola sono tutte piene di scogli, e sicchè perciò è molto difficile lo sbarco di Corsari, come infatti da più centinari d'anni, che non vi è memoria esser sbarcati corsari . . .
AdSN, Archivio Pignatelli, Scaffo IV, parte 2, LVI, no. 4050, f. 83

Document 2

The King of Spain writes a letter to his Viceroy in which he recounts the story of Avola and endorses its new site.

Ilustre duque de Uceda, Primer Gentilhombre de la Camara, mi Virrey, Lugar Teniente y Capitán General del Reyno de Sicilia; por parte del Duque de Terranova se ha presentada memoria con un papel de las razones que hay sobre mantenerse a los moradores de la tierra de Abola la nueva población que han empezado después del accidente de los terremotos, cuyo tenor de uno y otro es el que si dijo el señor el duque de Terranova y Monteleón, marqués del Valle, Gentilhombre de la Camara de Vuestra Magestad. Dijo que habiendo quedado destruída totalmente, con la desdicha del terremoto, la tierra de Abola, que era una de los principales del estado de Terranova, concurrieron los vecinos de ella a los Ministros de Vuestra Magestad en Palermo, particularmente al consultor D. Antonio Ybáñez, Administrador de todos los estados, para que diesen providencia a la conservación de aquel pueblo, y designasen sitio competente para la nueva población, respeto de ser impracticable la reedificación en la misma parte que destruyo, evidente riesgo de nueva desgracia por ser montañosa. Y el mismo consultor, precedente informe que tuvo de personas de toda satisfación, y de un religioso ingeniero enviado allá para elegir el sitio más seguro y acomodado, mandó señalarle, con acuerdo y permiso de los más Ministros de la Junta que a este fin está formada, lo llano de la marina al pie del lugar destruído, donde empazaron los pobres vecinos a eregir habitaciones de tablas, con grande aliento de labrar casas, habiendo hecho hasta ahora cerca de dos mil barracas, y grandes prevenciones de materiales para casas y edificios y algunas iglesias. Pero nuevamente, con motivo de haberse ordenado por V. M. que ningun lugar de marina, de los que padecieron, puedan labrar nueva población menos que no sea dos millas distante de la mar (cuando la referida dista sólo poco más de una milla) se ha opuesto la dicha Junta, por contradición del Fiscal, sin embargo del permiso dado, pretendiendo que se deshaga lo dispuesto y ejecutado y se señale otro sitio para la población, siendo así que sólo el que se eligió, y no otro ninguno, puede ser acomodado y de conveniencia para los pobres vasallos, por todas las razones que se expresan en el adjunto papel. Y siendo grande el desconsuelo de aquellos naturales que se haga esta novedad después de haber padecido tanto, y gastado muy considerables cantidades a V. M. suplicó que se sirva de mandar al Virrey de Sicilia que, sin embargo de la referida orden, dé la providencia necesaria para que se conserve la dicha población en el sito en que está empezada, atendiendo a tantos y tan justos motivos que corren para esto, demás de ser tan corta la diferencia de distancia de la mar, que no cabe el poder dudarse de inconveniente ninguno que en ello recibirá muchas razones que asisten a favor de los pueblos del lugar de Abola destruído para que hagan de labrar la nueva poblacion en el mismo sitio que se ha empezado.

Primero. porque la labranza en el sitio antiguo no se deja por falta de voluntad sino por precisa necesidad, así por ser la montaña toda abierta, como por lo estrecho del dicho sitio y sus calles. Y están las casas labradas en forma precipitosa, una sobre otra, de forma que al menor temblor que padezca una se tira consigo todas las demás, como se conoció en el terremoto pasado que el mayor daño fue ocasionado por la mala disposicion del dicho sitio, y de consecuencia se conoce que ninguna seguridad pudieran tener los vecinos si volvieran a labrar en la misma parte; a que se añade el ingente gasto que hubieran de hacer en reducir aquel sitio apto a nueva labranza, estando amontonadas las materiales de tantas ruínas, que no pueden ser desproveído ninguno.

Segundo: asentado por fijo (como lo es) el deberse labrar en otra parte, no podrá ser el nuevo sitio otro que el elegido y señalado donde está empezado, uno por ser casi el único del llano con saludable temple en consideración de las cuatro abundantes aguas y ríos que hay en él; segundo por ser aquel paraje feudo de la Universidad con que bien amenorarse el gasto de la labranza a los vecinos, no habiéndose de pagar censo de propiedades por el suelo de dichas casas.

Tercero: porque después de haber vivido aquellos pobres vasallos desperdidos por aquellos campos, tan miserablemente, hasta cuatro meses, todos se han vuelto a dicha nueva población con haber erigido en ella sus barracas en número de cerca de 55 y labrádo iglesias también por devoción de particulares y sepulturas, canceles, almacenes, y molinos, de forma que se ha reducido lo universal al estado primero sin que haya otra diferencia que la de estar las casas de tablas cubiertas con techos.

Cuatro: porque en dicho sitio se han transportado, a mucha costa de dichos vecinos, todas las maderas de sus casas destruídas y otros muchos materiales, para la nueva fábrica.

Quinto: por las consecuencias que pudieran seguirse de hacer apartar aquel pueblo al número de seis mil almas de tan buena disposición que ha hecho con el permiso y aprobación de los superiores y con tan buena fe y ley de atentos y obedientes vasallos, señalándose entre todos los demás lugares baronales que padecieron en grado, que cuantos han visto la nueva población han alabado al mayor grado la atención y desvelo de los vecinos.

Sesto: porque atendidas las miserias de aquellos pueblos cuya puntualidad los ha reducido hacer el último esfuerzo a muy crecida costa para ponerse debajo de cubierto y salir de los trabajos padecidos; con estar tanto tiempo como brutos en el campo han quedado tan humanos; imposibilitados a poder hacer cualquiera otra mudanza que el preceptarse las demás de ser contra la ley de piedad con un pueblo tan miserable, pudiera ocasionar los efectos que se dejan considerar de la gran prudencia de los Ministros superiores, retirandose todos a otros lugares.

Y por última razón: se representa que de labrar dicho lugar en el referido fuedo no pueden seguirse los inconvenientes que se consideran fundados en el riesgo de invasiones de enemigos y de extracciones furtivas en perjuicio de los intereses de la Regia Corte porque le playa, por relacion del ingeniero enviádose a este fin, que fue Angelo de Italia de la Compañía de Jesús, es distante dos tiros de canon de la referida población y la parte hasta donde pueden acercarse embarcaciones enemigas dista más de cuatro millas en consideración de la calidad de aquel mar todo lleno de sacas y muy bajafondo en grado que las [unreadable] que suelen ir cada año a cargar las azúcares, con ser pequeñas no pueden acercarse más que dos millas lejos de la playa, y siempre se ha estilado embarcarse allí con gana de [unreadable] horas distante del lugar de lo cual también se infiere que las furtivas extracciones se hayen muy difíciles, y por la nueva población viene a hacer menos practicables de lo que antes podía. Sucede al tiempo que estaba el pueblo en la montaña, pues se hallan a la vista todos los vecinos para observarlos si conviene. Y atendiendo a esta instancia os mando que oida la Junta destinada para estas materias, precaviendo el que no pueda resultar inconveniente alguno, deis las ordenes necesarias para ejecución de lo que más convenga. Dados en Madrid a ix de septiembre de MDCXCIII

YO EL REY

AdSN, Archivio Pignatelli, Scaffo IV, no. 3944, XXXVIII 1369–1695, ff. 129–32

SECTION III: ROSARIO GAGLIARDI IN NOTO

Private Life

1 27 April 1680
Gagliardi's Parents' Origins
'Essendo state fatte le tre solite denunciazioni more sotto In tribus diebus. Testicus Int missarui sollemnia . . . La p. a 14 d. Aprile 1680 la Ba. Dominica In dei Pasche vulureconis o.n.g. e la fa a 22 a cielem In fra Domenico Gagliardo figlio leg. et Nat.le dell. q.ta Fra.co et Elisabetta olim Iugal. di Gagliardo Naturale dello Casale di Santo Onofrio del Regno di Calabria et habbitatore di questa nostra SSma. Città di Siracusa sposo d.o una parte u Maria Ver.ge di Condi Figlia leg. et Nat.le del gda Salvatore Conde e Filippa sei essente di Cannava olim Iug. Nat.le della Città d'Augosta.'
ACMdS, Registro dei matrimoni, Vol. II, f. 302v (Di Blasi, p. 30)

2 6 February 1681
Gagliardi's Older Sister Born:
'Agata Sebastiana e Elisabetta figlia Leg.ma e nate d. Horofrio Domenico Gagliardo e Maria la condi Iug. di Gagliardo fù battezzata da me d. Nicolo Buttaforo . . . Il patrino Giuseppe Comiti di Randazzo.'
ACMdS, Indice Baptismi, Vol. VII, f. 29 (Di Blasi, p. 30)

3 4 April 1748
'Rivelo che fa Rosario Gagliardi figlio del fu Onofrio e della vivente Maria olim Ing di Gagliardi di questa Città di Noto in virtù di Bandi promulgati in questa die.

Anime
MC Rosario Gagliardi d'anni 50 capodicasa
F Maria Madre di il Revelante
F Carmela nipote
F Maria
Not.o D. Giuseppe Capodicasa nipoti de'anni 43

Beni Stabili
'Tenemento di case diece stanze vive due solerasse, e otto con terrane, portico, cisterna, sito vacuo, e qtu del Monico dell'Arco, conft. con case di Dn. Antonio Buscemi in frontis proprio del d.o mon.rio tre strade pubbliche . . .
AdSP, Rivelo 3745, 1748, f. 76

Career

4 20 March 1713
'Apoca Notar Gaspare Leone nomibus cum Magistro Rosariu Gagliardi. Gagliardi deve esser pagato 5 15 pro eius merced ut dr. d'haver fatto il disegno del d.o Monastero dell'Arco, ed haver assistito col Capo Mastro di Siracusa Ignatio Puzzo nella mesura della Fabrica di d.o Monastero . . .'
AdSS, Notary Ignazio Pintaldo, 7492, 1751–52, ff. 305–305v (Di Blasi, p. 34)

5 17 November 1721
Padre Vincenzo Maria Cappello declares that he paid Rosario Gagliardi *praefectus* and seven masters for the construction of a new mill in the *contrada di Turturone*.
Notary Natale Marotta, 7440, 1721–22, f. 231 (Di Blasi, p. 37)

6 3 November 1727
Maestro Paolo Scarrozza of Noto declares to have received 3 *onze*, 26 *tari*, and 15 *grana* from Don Bartolomeo Deodato Scammacca, Baron of Frigintini, for the repair of the vault of a magazine threatening ruin. All was done in conformity with the 'relazione fatta da Rosario Gagliardi arbitro seriam.te . . .'
AdSS, Notary Nicolo Astuto, 7515, 1727–28, f. 178 (Di Blasi, p. 39)

7 4 January 1728
Corrado Bertolo *faber murarius*, is bound by the Rectors of the church of SS. Crocifisso in Noto to '. . . farci dieci archi d'intaglio alla d. nuova Chiesa del SS.mo Crocifisso di questa suddetta città uguale disegno di detta Chiesa, e misura le darà Rosario Gagliardi Architetto, e simili di disegno fatto dal suddetto Gagliardi, come pure fare la ghirlanda all'archi suddetti, e li capitelli alli pilastri dell'istessi archi, a parim.te. tutto intaglio di liscio, che sarà dibbisogno per d.a. nuova Chiesa, e tutta la Fabbrica di calce, e d'arena corrispondente al detto disegno . . .'
AdSS, Notary Natale Marotta, 7451, 1727–28, f. 559 (Di Blasi, p. 39)

8 28 April 1728
Monastery of S. Maria dell'Arco of Noto concedes territory in the *contrade* of Commaldo, Rova, Sarculla, Marco, Lenzavacche; map in the concessions act is 'Disignati, Misurati e delineati da me Rosario Gagliardi Architetto'
AdSS, Notary Natale Marotta, 7451, 1727–28, ff. 1079–1132 (Di Blasi, pp. 39–40)

9 26 July 1730
Obbligatio between Corrado Bertolo and the Rectors of the church of S. Maria La Rotunda of Noto:
Bertolo must '. . . farci tutta quella quantità di fabrica di quantità calce ed arena, che detti Maestri Rettori vorran fatta per servizio della Nuova Chiesa sotto titolo di S. Maria La Rotunda qui sta il disegno fatto da Rosario Gagliardi Architetto . . .'
AdSS, Notary Natale Marotta, 7455, 1729–30, ff. 245–47 (Di Blasi, p. 44)

10 1 December 1730
Obligatio between the Jesuit college and M.ro Paul Sequencia *et c.bus*
Contract between Padre Ignazio Maria Roberti and several *maestri muratori* among whom is Paolo Sequencia '. . . di fare tutta quella fabrica ad opera d'intaglio di liscio cornice Base di Pilastri, Pilastri, di Porta e Cornicioni di qualsiasi larghezza, che vorrà l'Ingegniero di d.o ven.e Collegio d'una o più porte dell'infra.tta. chiesa, che vorrà il sudo. Padre Rettore fatte per il nuovo Collegio, e Chiesa di questa Città di Noto secondo il disegno dell'Ingegniero di d.o Collegio . . .'
AdSS, Notary Giuseppe Gaita, 7560, 1730–31, ff. 191–193v (Di Blasi, p. 45)

11 7 January 1731
'Apoca p. The.rio domus Refugiis c. Rosariu Gagliardo.'
Gagliardi is 'Architector Edificiis Domus Refugiis.' He receives 11 *onze* and 27 *tarì* for 'aver travagliato giorni 69: p. d.o edificio c.e architetto' for object better specified in *mandata* of 23 December 1730.
AdSS, Notary Nicolo Astuto, Bastarello, 1731 (Di Blasi, p. 45)

12 28 January 1733
'Declaratio facta per Rosariu Gagliardi, ad istantia Rev. di Cantoris D. Salvatoris Buccheri h. u. Netis . . .' Attached *Relazione* of Gagliardi:

'Rosario Gagliardi, Architetto di questa Ingegnosa Città di Noto . . . a petizione ed istanza del Cantore D. Salvatore Buccheri come commissionato dell'Ill.mo e Rev.mo Sig.r D. Matteo Trigona Vescovo di Siracusa delle spese che abbisognano nelle case del Feudo delle cave secche per ridurle abitabili come delle spese tante necessarie per acconciar le gisterne in esso ex.nti . . . e questa e la mia Relazione fatta oggi in Noto li 25 Gennajo 1733.' Rosario Gagliardi architetto . . . AdSS, 7613, Notary Giuseppe Maria Capodicasa, 1732–33, f. 251 (Di Blasi, p. 47)

13 9 July 1733
'Mag.ri Corradus Bertolo, Demenicus Errigo, Giuseppe Risino et Filippus Fancello, fabricatores, . . . sollemniter se obligaverunt et obligant magnif. Bartolomeo Deodato D.no et Baroni terre Frigintini . . . tamquam Viceportulano Oneratoriis Vindicariis uixta rela.ne facta p. Rosariu Gagliardo Architectu h. Us. Neti in officio d. Spet. Viceportulani . . .'
AdSS, Notary Giuseppe Gaita, 7562, 1732–3ff. 413–6 (Di Blasi, p. 47)

14 15 January 1737
'Obligatio Pro Rosario Gagliardi cum M.ro Joseph Fancello et c.tes . . . Giuseppe Fancello, Carmelo dell'Angeli, Gaetano, Antonino and Lucio Giachino, Natale and Antonino Zappulla, Pasquale dell' Angeli, Giovanni Trapani, Corrado Gemma and Natale Falcone,' must do all the work described in the 'Relazione fatta da me infr.tto Rosario Gagliardi Architetto di questa Ingn.sa Città di Noto sopra l'acconcio della strada del passo del fiume dell'Aranci dolci . . .'
AdSS, Notary Giuseppe Maria Capodicasa, 7619, 1736–37, f. 229 (Di Blasi, p. 50)

15 20 August 1743
'Enfiteusis Pro Ven.le Convento S. Domenico h.u. Cum Paulo Bruno.' Map of territory leased perpetually from the monastery of S. Domenico by Paulo Bruno, drawn by Rosario Gagliardi.
AdSS, Notary Giuseppe Maria Capodicasa, 7627, 1742–43, pp. 636–56v. map f. 649 (Di Blasi, p. 54)

16 16 August 1744
'Mandatu onze 86, tarì 16, grama 10 Pro Cont.u Carmeli cum d. Joseph Venia.' For the main stairway and the cornice on the southern part, a number of people are paid. Among them 'più onze due per averle pagate a Rosario Gagliardi Architetto per aver assistito alla fabrica del nuovo edificio di d.o Conto.'
AdSS, Notary Vincenzo Labisi, 7805, 1742–45, f. 444

17 8 July 1748
'Obligatio Pro Ill.re D. Rodrigo Zappata Marchione S. Flori Cum M.o Petro Turrisi . . .' The Catanese carpenter Pietro Turrisi must '. . . farci un ornamento d'arcovia su facciata di legname e d'abete, arbano e tiglio di scultura giusta la forma del disegno che è piaciuto visto, rivisto ed attalentato al detto Zappata e dal medesimo consegnato al detto fabbro di Turrisi, e ciò magistrevolmente come si conviene dovendo essere benvisto finito, che sarà all'Architetto Rosario Gagliardi, dovendo cominciare da dimani in poi d.a opera, e così successivamente finirla per tutto il mese ottobre p.v. 1748, e collocarla e sue proprie spese a suo luogo nel Palagio del d.o Ill.re Marchese . . .'
AdSS, Notary Giuseppe Maria Capodicasa, 7633, 1747–8, ff. 573–573v (Di Blasi, p. 57)

18 6 March 1752
'Obligatio Pro Ven.le Monasterio S.tae Maria de Arcu huius Urbis ac. Mag. rum Vincentium Rotondo, et c.tes'. Gagliardi asked to intervene in the construction of the vault for the new church of the monastery of S. Maria dell'Arco. The construction of the vault, the gessoing, and the tiling of the church is to be done '. . . giusta la forma del disegno fatta dal sud.o di Gagliardi Architetto . . .'
AdSS, Notary Natale Marotta, 7492, 1751–52, f. 305–305v (Di Blasi, p. 59)

19 12 April 1748
'Si fa certa e indubitata Fede a chiunque spetta osservar la pnte. per me qui sotto scritto, come Borsario de Ven.te Conv.o di San Domenico della Sudtta. Città qualm.te nelli Bastardelli annuali, e libri maestri, come d'introito, così d'esito di detto com.to si ritrovano le infratte distinte partite d'introito, ed esito annuali, e vitalissi . . . cioè . . .' The accounts of the convent follow. Among them is an annual payment to Gagliardi: 'Nel libro Magistrale della Fabrica . . . Nel libro Magistrale d'esito di vino a Tog. 72. Dona il conv.to al Sig.r Rosario Gagliardi Architetto della Fabrica ogni anno per salario ordinario salme quattro di vino, soddisfatto a complim.to. dell 'XI Inda. 1747 e 1748 . . .
AdSP, Rivelo 3757, 1948, f. 313

20 17 December 1753
'Obligatio pro Ven.le Monasterio St.a Maria de Arcu h.s Urbis ac Mag. Joseph Meli', Special order and payment from the deputies of the fabbrica of the monastery of S. Maria dell'Arco, Noto, to maestro Giuseppe Meli from Catania. He is to 'fare tutte le forme che saran necessarie per formare i dammusi di pietra e gesso al tutto della nave della nuova chiesa del sud.to Ven.le Monastero e alli tetti delli mezzi arangi di detta nuova chiesa . . . dovendo cominciare dal primo del mese di Gennaio dell'anno venturo 1754 . . .'
AdSS, Notary Natale Marotta, 7494, 1753–54, ff. 145–46 (Di Blasi, p. 61)

21a 13 March 1755
'Obligatio Pro Ven.le Monast.o Sta. Maria de Arcu hs. Us. ac Honophrium Russo.' Russo, a stuccoist from Agrigento is contracted to stucco the new church of the monastery. Gagliardi's models and designs for the capitals, pilasters, the 'tabelle' over the six chapels, the windows, the chapel and the major vault must be followed. Russo is to 'incominciare a stucchiare d.a chiesa dopo serà finita di stucchiare la da. Chiesa del Sud.o Ven.le Monastero di Santa Chiara e dopo avera cominciata a stucchiare dovrà proseguire senza desistirsi sino alla fine . . .' The 'spincioni scorniciati alle lunette' of the church of S. Maria dell'Arco are to be like those in S. Chiara. '. . . stucchiare la nuova Chiesa di detto Ven.le Monastero del modo seguente, cioè che la Chiesa sud.a dovrà stucchiarla d'ordine Jonico di Michel'Angelo Buonarota col capitello. Di più deve fare sopra la base delli pilastri tutta l'Architettura sino all'ordine bastardo per come al disegno fatto dal sud.o di Gagliardi Architetto, con dover fare quattro statue alle quattro nicchie per come le richiederanno i Rev.di P.re Priore, e Padri di d.o Ven.le Monastero.
L'Architettura delli pilastri deve farla come al detto disegno col rabisco nel mezzo alla Chiesa, e li modelli dell'architettura rilevati dall'istesso Architetto. Le tabelle sopra le sei Cappelle giusta la forma del d.o. disegno.
L'ordine bastardo scolpito, e striato giusto la forma del d.o. disegno.

Le finestre per come se gli darà il disegno, su modello delle cornici a tenore di d.o. disegno.
Il Cappellone dovrà farlo con una sfera del Blandini per come si vede in d.o. disegno.
L'arco maggiore a tenore della forma di d.o. disegno. I due archi d'immezzo si devono levare, per non restare l'architettura senza fine se gli devono fare due grastoni di fiori, per terminare l'architettura con ordine. Alle lunette gli si devono far gli spiconi scorniciati, come quelle della chiesa di Santa Chiara di questa Città, con la sola cornice liscia senza rabischi come al numero tre di d.o disegno.
Nelli due pilastri che si levano d'immezzo, gli si deve fare un quadrone secondo il disegno le farà d.o Architetto. Il mezzo arangio della porta Maggiore si deve fare giusta la forma di d.o disegno, e tutto quello servizzo di stucco dovrà farsi in detta nuova Chiesa dovrà esser benvisto al sud.o Architetto di Gagliardo . . .
. . . Di più che tutti i modelli di legname saranno necessarii per la stucchiattina di d.a Chiesa, sia tenuto, ed obbligato darle al d.o. di Russo il sud.o di Gagliardo . . . e di quelle forme che saranno dal medesimo di Gagliardo Architetto designate di patto.'
AdSS, Notary Natale Marotta, 7496, 1754–55, ff. 607–609v (Di Blasi, pp. 62–4)

21b 3 March 1756
'Obligatio Pro Venle Monasterio Sta. Maria de Arcu huius Urbis ac Franciscum Guadagna.'
Francesco Guadegna, stuccoist from the city of Piazza, is contracted to 'perfectionare' the stuccos of S. Maria dell'Arco left incomplete because of the death of Onofrio Russo. Guadegna is to complete the stuccos and the statues in the four niches of the church. The work has to be executed 'giusta il d.o disegno fatto dal sud.o di Gagliardi Architetto . . .'
AdSS, Notary Natale Marotta, 7497, 1755–56, ff. 273–78v (Di Blasi, pp. 64–65)

22 18 September 1757
'Obligatio Pro Ven.le Mon.rio S.ta Maria de Arcu huius U.s ac Mag.m Michaelem Cilardo et c.tem.' Michele Cilardo and Corrado Scarrozza, carpenters, are contracted with Gagliardi by the Priors and Deputies of the monastery of S. Maria dell'Arco to 'fabricarci la porta grande dall'Oggetto dell'Occidente, e la porta piccola dall'Oggetto della Tramontana di legname della Nuova Chiesa del su.o. Monastero, cioè, la porta grande simile a q.lla della nuova Chiesa del Ven.le Con.to di San Francesco d'Assisi, dei Minori Conventuali di questa Città a Cardenale scorniciata con due portelli con i cartaponi, cioè, li detti cartaponi due alla porta grande, e due alli portelli con il sopraporto ben visto al sud.o di Gagliardi, e la porta piccola, dovrà essere liscia ammarzapanata a Cardinale con due Cartaponi pure ben viste al sudo. di Gagliardi Architetto . . .'
AdSS, Notary Natale Marotta, 7500, 1757–8, ff. 42–3 (Di Blasi, pp. 65–6)

23 8 January 1758
'Obligatio Pro Mon.rio S.ta Maria de Arcu huius U.s ac Mag.ru Sebastianu Rubera.' Master Sebastiano Rubera, 'fabbro ferrai' of Noto, by special order and payment of the Priore and Deputies of the 'fabbrica' of the monastery of S. Maria dell'Arco of Noto must 'farci li infra.tti ferramenti per lo servigio della porta Maggiore e della porta Minore della Nuova Chiesa di d.o Ven.le Mon.rio, quali ferramenti dovranno essere li infra.tti . . ., cioè . . . Di più Franzisetti paia otto fatti a Martello in tre interrazzati uguali a quelli della porta Maggiore della nuova Chiesa del Ven.le Collegio della Compagnia di Gesù di questa Città . . .'
AdSS, Notary Natale Marotta, 7500, 1757–8, ff. 204–205v (Di Blasi, pp. 66–7)

24 3 February 1758
'Apoca Salma I frumenti Pro Monasterio S.ta Maria de Arcu huius Urbis ac Rosarium Gagliardi.' Payment in wheat as thanks to Gagliardi for his part in designing the stuccos of the church, and the models, and for supervising the stuccoists '. . . e tutti gli altri servizi come architetto di questa Città fatti a d.o Mon.ro d'anni due a questa parte . . .'
AdSS, Notary Natale Marotta, 7500, 1757–8, ff. 236–37v (Di Blasi, p. 67)

25 15 April 1758
'Oblig.o Pro Ven. Collegio Con.tus S.ti Dom.i h. U. Neti cum M.ro Xaverio Cannarella et c.bus.' Masters Saverio Cannarella, Andrea, Melchiorre and Corrado Frasca are contracted with Ludovico Sortino, Procurator of the 'fabbrica' of S. Domenico of Noto '. . . di fare l'imbalatato della d.a Ven. chiesa di longo a longo . . . dovendoci mettere li detti obligati per la loro risp.a medietà tutte le Balate di pietra d'Intaglio di San Corrado di Fuori buona e soda con che le Balate devono essere un palmo e tre quarti di quadro intagliate e grossezza devono essere un quarto di netto e metterli ed assettarli e questo bene e final.me e magistrevol.me e diligente.me secondo ricerca l'arte dovendo essere benvisto sud.o Imbalato all'Architetto Rosario Gagliardi e M.ro Antonio Mazza . . .'
AdSS, Notary Giuseppe Gaita, 7596, 1757–8, ff. 495–96 (Di Blasi, p. 67)

26 11 June 1758
'Ap.a cum subin.ta Pro D. Mario Sortino cum m.ro Paschale Mazza.' Pasquale Mazza, Netinese 'muratore' says he has been paid just amount as established by Don Paolo Labisi and Rosario Gagliardi, 'estimatori eletti', for a shop on the Piano del Collegio di S. Domenico at Noto.
AdSS, Notary Vincenzo Labisi, 7816, 1757–8, ff. 585–86

27 23 August 1762
'Vendito Domus pro Concetto Civello cum Rosario Gagliardi.' Gagliardi sells house [perhaps his own?] and accessories in the quarter of the monastery of S. Maria dell'Arco for 9 onze and 24 tarì to Don Concetto Civello. The price was judged fair by Didaco Enrigo and Antonio Mazza. At the bottom of the act, where Gagliardi's signature should be, Sinatra wrote 'Io Vincenzo Sinatra tanto per me quanto per p.te di d.o Rosario Gagliardi mio zio per esso non sapere scrivere . . .'
AdSS, Notary Francesco Randazzo, 7739, 1760–6, ff. 41–41v (Di Blasi, pp. 70–1)

SECTION IV: VINCENZO SINATRA IN NOTO

Private Life

1 15 June 1747
'Rivelo che fa Vincenzo Sinatra di questa Città di Noto, fig.o leg.i delli fu Antonino Sinatra e Paolo olim Jug.li in virtù di bando publicato sotto gli 16 Aprile 1747:

Anime

M.C. M.ro Vincenzo Sinatra d'anni 40: capodicasa
F. Alfia Sinatra d'anni 35: moglie
M. Giuseppe fig.o; d'anni 13
M. Antonio fig.o: d'anni 9 fig.o
M: Francesco di Avola d'anni 5: figlio
M: Rosario d'anno uno: fig.o
F. Maria d'anni 8: figlia
F: Anna Bacucco d'anni 13: serva

Beni Stabili

Tiene esso Revelante un tenimento di case solerate consistente in quattro stanze di sopra, e quattro sott.te esiste con gisterna in questa Città ed in contrada del Castello, confinanti colle case d'Alfio Sinatra, colle case in frontispicio di Corrado Bila, strada publica, ed altri confini . . .'
AdSP, Rivelo 3749, 1748, f. 299

Career

2 1746
Agreement among Senators to subscribe to the building of the Casa Giuratoria in Noto. After they pledge various amounts of money to the enterprise, accounts of the work appear, indicating which of them paid for the building in the past.

f. 401v
'A 28 Giugno 1742 Sig.r Gaetano Buontalente Teseo delli danari in vostro potere pervenuti per conto della fabrica della casa Senatoria pagati ad Antonino Rubino una onza e conto del prezzo della calce che si è obbig.ta fare . . . Conto della Fabrica della Casa Senatoria di tenere pagate a M.o Antonino Rubino onze vent'otto cioè onze vente p. cavalca della pietra di fiume che deve portare . . .

f. 402
Noto il 9 obre 1742: 'Sig.r B.ne di Bonfala V:S: Issma paghi a m.ro Vincenzo Sinatra onze ventisei e gr. due al suddetto d.a Sinatra c.e Architetto per la fabrica della casa Senatoria suoi travagli, e il disegno onze ventiquattro, ed al Med.mo, p. pagare nella giornata al M.ro Concetta Ingarao, Bonaventura Miranna . . .'

Between ff. 401–2
Bill dated November 1742: 'ho ricevuto Nov. 1743, Vincenzo Sinatra.'
Bill dated October 1742: written at bottom: 'per distribuirla . . . Vincenzo Sinatra'.

Between pledges ff. 407–8
Bill dated 1743; written below: 'Gennaio 1743 Vincenzo Sinatra Architetto'.
Bill dated 13 March 1743: 'Vicenzo Sinatra Architetto'.
Bill dated 24 March 1743: 'ho ricevuto Vincenzo Sinatra'.

f. 409
'Piu a M.ro Vinc.o Sinatra . . . per mezzo totale di cartone p. li modelli delle Cornici . . .

Between ff. 413–94 Sinatra is called 'Architetto' six times.
AdSS, Notary Nicolai Astuto, 006941, 1745–6, ff. 399–417.

3. 1750
'Obligatio Mon.rio SS. Salvatore cum Mg.o Felice Vaccarisi.' Vaccarisi must make iron grating for windows in the new 'frontispizio' of the monastery of SS. Salvatore. Vincenzo Sinatra, 'Architetto', supervises.
AdSS, Notary Nicolo Astuto, Bastardello, 1750–1, f. 218

4 14 November 1751
'Apocha onze 49; tarì 28: grani 11 Pro Con.tu S.M. Jesus cum m.o Jeanne Castiglia.' Castiglia is contracted to vault the convent 'inalzare la fabrica nell'oggetto della tramontana sud.a . . . di palmi cinque e mezzo, in scaricare il tetto di canali conne, bordoni, e forbici, con trasformare di med.mi bordoni e forbici d'altra idea secondo il parere dell'architetto . . .' The architect whose idea Castiglia is ordered to follow is Vincenzo Sinatra, as the account at the end of the document indicates: 'Vincenzo Sinatra architetto per aver più volte fatto visloco pello riparo il suddetto dormitorio . . .'
AdSS, Notary Vincenzo Labisi, 007221, 1751–2, f. 139

5 30 July 1753
'Obligatio Pro Ven.le Oratorio S.ti Philippo Neris cum Mag.rum Paulem Caruso . . .' Workers are contracted to 'dare e consegnare al sud.o tetto sbrigato di tutto punto, ed atto a poterei metterci l'oratorio il gesso, e coprirlo con i canali . . .' Everything must be 'ben visto all'architetto Vincenzo Sinatra . .'
AdSS, Notary Natale Marotta, 006904, 1752–3, f. 479

6 17 May 1757
'Declarat.nes Pro Domo Senatoria . . . cum Vincenti Sinatra' Expenses and money pledged for 'fabrica nova domus Senatoria . . .'
AdSS, Notary Vincenzo Labisi, 007226, 1756–7, f. 565

7 26 April 1771
'Divisio inter Antonium Sinatra et D: Antonium Valvo'. Property exchange for which Sinatra writes the following *Relazione*:
'Relazione che si dona da me qui fra s.o scritto Architetto Vincenzo Sinatra di questa Ing.sa Città di Noto, esperto comunemente eletto da Dn. Antonio Chetuti e Sinatra e Dn. Antonia ve.da del. gndo Da Felica Valvo, del prezzo del tenemento di case consistente in più corpi esistenti in questa città e nel quartiero di S. Francesco d'Assisi in frontispizio del ven.le monasterio del SS.mo Salvatore confinante con le case ed orto ove al ponte abita il Rev.do Sac.te d. Onofrio Belluardo da una parte, con due strade pubbliche dall'altra parte, con le case di M.ro Calayero Manoli, ed a late delle tre botteghe di Dn. Domenico e Dn. Bernardo Fratelli di Labisi . . .'
AdSS, Notary Vincenzo Labisi, 007240, 1770–1, ff. 519–25

8 10 February 1772
'Relatio dimensionis pro Ill.o: D. Hieronymo Landolina cum Vincentio Sinatra.' Sinatra 'Architectur' makes map.
AdSS, Notary Vincenzo Labisi, 007241, 1771–2, f. 377

9 10 September 1772
'Apoca: cum suba. pro Ill.º :D: Corradino Nicolaci cum
'Nom.o Pro Ill.º D.ne Impellizzeri cum Vincenzo Sinatra.'
architetto . . . per sua assistenza nella fabrica nelle case nello fondo di Capopassaro . . .'
AdSS, Notary Vincenzo Labisi, 007241, 1771–2, ff. 337–8

10 13 January 1774
'Nom.o Pro Ill.º D.ne Impellizzeri cum Vincenzo Sinatra.'
Sinatra does estimate of house in Feudo vulgarly called 'delli Gadeddi'.
AdSS, Notary Giuseppe Pizzi, 1772–4, f. 195

11 3 September 1776
'In Noto gli 3: Sett.re del 1776: Ill.o Sig.r Barone D. Giuseppe di Lorenzo delle somme pervenute in potere di V.S. per conto della fabbrica della casa giuratoria come depositorato dal Trib.le eletto in . . . di dispaccio sottoli 14 Novembre 1745. p.ntato ed eseguito agli atti dell'ufficio Giur: sotto li 22 novembre d'anno si sincera pagare a Vincenzo Sinatra Capomastro el Reu. Sac: fra D. Corrado Minaci lo: [so]praintendente onze 2: tarì 5: Grani 7: per tante da Loro spece . . .' Some of the expenses were for the following:
'per tre tavole per far una porta rustica'
'per quattro baroni ed un anta'
'per chiodi, carohari, ed aguti oc'
'per una fermatura'
'per Maestria della detta Porta'
'per quattro Corbelle p. nettare i fossi'
'per una loggetta per i maestri intagliatori'
'per cinque costate per detta loggia'
'per compra d'un crivotto per cernere la rina . . .'
AdSS, Notary Nicolai Astuto, 006942, 1746–7, f. 62

12 28 August 1777
'Sub emphysis pro D. Angelo Guerrier cum Xaviero Mandala.'
Sinatra estimates the prices of a piece of property: 'Relazione della stima dell'orto . . . di qu. Città di Noto e q.da. della ven.le Chiesa di S. Pietro Martire . . . fatto . . . Architetto Vincenzo Sinatra.'
AdSS, Notary Vincenzo Labisi, 007246, 1776–7, ff. 511–12

SECTION V: PAOLO LABISI IN NOTO

Private Life

1 12 October 1720
Paolo Labisi Born:
'Paulus Salvatore Franciscus et Nicolacis Filius leg.mus et nat.is Joseph Labisi et Bartolema Costenzo iug: fuit baptizatus a me Sac.to: D. Salvatore Buccheri. Patrinus fuit Paulus Rigano messanensis filius Francisci e quo Marie olim Iug:de Rigaro . . .'
ACMdN, Registro dei Battissimi, 1708–26.

2 2 October 1747
Paolo Labisi had a son
Michaelangelus Bernardus Conradus Joseph f. 1. et n. Dn. Pauli Labisi et Conradina Valvo, Patrinius fuit Illr.is Don Bernardus Trigona Marchio Cannigaroi . . .'
ACMdN Registro dei Battesimi, S. Spirito 1747–8

3 20 October 1749
'Rivelo che Frate Antonino Labisi di Noto, figlio del già Giuseppe fa in virtù il Bando 291 d'orde. della Regia monarchia . . .

Anime

MC. Frate Antonino Labisi d'an 34
M. Notario D. Vincenzo Labisi: fratello d'an. 31
M. D. Paolo Labisi: f.tto d'anni 25
M. Domenico Labisi: nipote d'an 3
F. Bartolomea Labisi: madre
F. Corradina Labisi: cognata
M. Salvatore Menta: servo d'anni 18
F. Anna Moncada. serva forata.
F. Savaeria Menta: serva

Beni Stabili

'Possiede fu Revelante un Tenimento di Case, fabbricato di Terra e pietra di sue abitazioni, posto nel quartiere di S. Franc.so d'Assisi, e nei confini delle case degli Eredi di Gius.e Griente Berrettagrande, e d'altri. Un sì fatto Tenimento contiene quattro stanze ed una cucina; una delle quali è solerata: La volta di questa, essendo di gesso, è stata diroccata da frequenti tremuoti, di cui va soggetta La città di Noto; cosicchè pensa il Revelante di gettarla e di formarne una sola stanza; ragiona questo tal Tenimento per sole tre stanze le quali per la Relaz.e gente degli Esperti ragionati a tarì 8 per cada una, . . .
AdSP, Rivelo 3756, 1748, f. 51

Career

4 25 February 1748
'Obligatio Pro Ven.le Oratorio S.ti Philippi Neris H.s Urbis cum Mag.m Paulum Caruso.' Mag.ro Paulus Caruso, 'Faber lignarius' is contracted by the Reverend Sacerdote and Padre D. Conrado Landogna to . . . 'farci tutte la forme saranno necessarie per la fabrica del Dammuso del Cappellone della Nuova Chiesa di d.o ven.le oratorio a tenore del Disegno che farà Paolo Labisi, architetto, con doverci mettere d.o obligato tutta la legname . . . chiodi come pure fare il ponte di legname, sopra il quale do ci van travagliare i maestri per fornare d.o Dammuso con doverci mettere d.o obligato tutto il legname, corde, e scale necessarie per la fattura di d.o ponte.'
AdSS, Notary Natale Marotta, 006897, 1747–8, f. 225

5 1762
'Relatio Pro D: Nuncio Burlo et q.tes cum D: Paulo Labisi.'
Labisi estimates cost of house on Piazza S. Domenico.
AdSS, Notary Vincenzo Labisi, 007232, 1762–3

6 8 June 1770
Interpellatio Pro. D. Paulo Labisi
'. . . Dn. Paulus Labisi . . . che ritrovandosi egli Regio ingegnere di q.sta ing.sa città di Noto, eletto architetto della nuova fabrica della casa, e chiesa dei RR PP Crociferi eretta in qu.ta città dal med. in virtù d'alberano firmato dal fu Rev.o P.re Andrea Clacuzzi, P: Giuseppe Spardao, e Fra.llo Sebastiano Guerrera, in qualità allora di Prefetto, P.re e fra.llo di d.o ospizio sotto li 24 Maggio 1749; coll'obligo di formarne il disegno; il quale formato, ed esaminato già, com'anche approvato dal P: Emmanuele Caruso, dal P.re Ferdinando Lombardi architetti cruciferi, e dall'architetto D. Francso Terrigno nell'anno 1751; in Palermo com'altresì approvato dai Fide comni: dell'ospizio sud.o il 4 maggio 1751 dal P.re Visitatore Prov.le: il P.re Crimibella qui in Noto in virtù di decreto scritto e sottoscritto nel disegno sud.o sia modello in carta sotto li 24 Smbre 1753; ed infine confirmata del Rev.mo. P.re Generale della Med.o Religione trovandosi in visita qui li 30 S.mbre 1765; in virtù di suo decreto scritto e sottoscritto . . .

f. 541v
Dal med.o formata in persona del sud.o architetto Labisi nella qual si vede, non solo approvato il disegno e la fabrica già eretta nell'anno 1752, ma anche l'alberano sud.o è stato nondimeno dai 30: Aprile sin oggi contro la mente dei sud.o suoi supri: maggiori indebitamente e meso capriccio dal P: Sup.re Luigi Venuta, e da uno dei fi. d'economigo D. Corradino Pizzi *arrogata la potestà d'escludere, e togliergli non solo la giurisdizione della sopraintendenza al sud.o architetto, che ha sopra la fabrica ma anche quello devono sodisfargli a tenore dell'alberano in ogni giorno p. sud.o sopraintendenza, con servirsi d'altro architetto p. nome Vincenzo Sinatra*, nulla curandosi, che la casa soffrisse dei eccessivi dispendi nel fabricare, e nello sfabricare a di loro piacere con il positivo sconcerto della fabrica medesima finchè non avere fatto ridurre in pezzetti moltissime cianche o siano pezzi accomodati, comprati dalla casa a caro prezzo, servendosene p. pietra ordinaria nella muratura, con permettere dei maggiori interessi inutilmente come sarà costare e con averne loro permesso anche la riforma del sud.o disegno in parte della Facciata e con moltiplicare le scale inutilmente . . . contro l'espresso ordine del suo Rev.mo gen.te . . .

f. 542
'Labisi viene leso non solo nell'onore p. l'alterazione della sua opera, perchè ideata d'un pensiero nobile, ma anche . . . dei tarì tre al giorno determinati comunemente in soddisfazione della sua assistenza, come, altro si ha preinteso, che pretende il sud.o di Sinatra anche spiantare l'ornamento, dei pilastri, e colonne fabricate, ed eretto nell'entrata tutta la sua altezza, si pure riformare la scala principale con tutto il suo ornamento anche eretto con voler deguastare indebitamanete una camera p mezzo della riforma di essa scala che dovrà sovrapporsi alla med.a nel dormitorio sopra; che dovrebbe ereggersi, e con tett'altro, che giornalmente va pensando disfare in pregiudizio della casa o per capriccio, o per l'ispertezza del med.o giacchè si è dichiarato di non avere sin oggi compreso il disegno . . .' sud.o è venuto a far notificare un atto protestatorio al P: Superior Luigi Venuti . . .
AdSS, Notary Vincenzo Labisi, 007239, 1769–70, ff. 541–43v

7 13 June 1770
Intimatio. Labisi's attacks are rebuffed by those he accuses: 'del Rev. Sac.e d: Corradino Pizzi tutto ciò che s'è pensato fallo p. evitare l'esorbitantissime spese, che ricercarà il disegno di Labisi uniformandosi con ciò alle disposizioni del Governo, ed anche preparare a quelle rovine, che ha minacciato la fabrica eretta in tempo del sud.o Labisi conforme tutto farci costare . . .'
AdSS, Notary Vincenzo Labisi, 007239, 1769–70, f. 543v

8 3 December 1779
'Procuratio pro D: Paulo Labisi in pna Nota D. Mariani Salvo.' Labisi to be paid for designs he drew of the church of SS. Annunciata in Ispica.
AdSS, Notary Vincenzo Labisi, 007249, 1779–80, f. 135

9 24 January 1781
Testimony to Labisi's work on S. Agata given by witnesses so he can be paid.

f. 127
Paulo Conforto attests to his work:
'Io qui infr.o Maestro Intagliatore di pietra faccio certa e giurata fede se chi spetta veder la pn.te, come qual lavoro d'intaglio bianco, fatto, e fabricato con archi, e volte nella nuova chiesa del ven.le monastero di Sant'Agata di questa città di Noto, è stato fatto fabricare da me, ed altri maestri Intagliatori, e muratori colla giornale direzione dell' architetto sigr. D: Paolo Labisi, per lo corso di mesi sei, e giorni otto, contando delli quattro marzo, sino a Settembre 1775: a tenore del Disegno da lui formato ad una nave figura Rettangolare, con Cappellone, nave, Portico, e sacrestria de'Preti, delle Religiose, ed oratorio sottano nè lati di essa chiesa, ad istanza dell'Ill.re Marchese di Cannicarao D: Bernardo Maria Trigona; riformando, e adornando nell'interiore, ed esteriore quella medesima chiesa antica, che trovavasi con averla alzata, e fatto un Parlatorio de' Secolari più grande del primo, e che per far tutto ciò ne abbiamo ricevuto in quel tempo del medesimo architetto giornalmente di modali, necessari delle cornici, e trazzi, transportando in grande tutte le parti di esso ornamento interiore ed esteriore della pianta, ed alzata come quelle del cappellone, della nave, della cappella, del portico, e della facciata, e fenestre tutte ornate con delli pilastri, e colonne che situati sono nella parte interiore ed esteriore di essa chiesa . . . a richiesta del sud.o architetto.' Signed Paolo Conforto, 25 Nov. 1780.

f. 130
Don Pasquale Vela tells of seeing Labisi's design: '. . . come ritrovandomi l'anno 1771 in Palermo, ed in casa del fu J.E. Sign.re Marchese di Cannicarao D: Gaspare Trigona, viddi per più tempo, che io dimorai con esso Sigr. collocato sopra un Boffettone della sua camera un disegno della nuova chiesa che dovea edificarsi in questo monastero di S.ta Agata formato dall'architetto d: Paolo Labisi inviato da questa città al medesimo fu Sigre. Marchese per osservarlo, ed al ritorno che io dovetti far qui l'anno 1773 un tal disegno restò in casa di esso signor marchese . . ., signed Don Pasquale Vela, 2 Jan. 1781

f. 132
Sac.to: Don Domenico Belluso tells the story of the design and construction of the church:
'. . . Io qui infra.tto Sac.to Dn. Domenico Belluso faccio certa ed indubitata fede a chi spetta veder la parte come ritrovandomi nell'anno 1770 Esattore e Procuratore del ven.le monasterio di S. Agata di s.a città di Noto, e dovendosi formare un disegno della nuova chiesa d'esso monastero con tutto lo resto dell'abitazione tutta che fu gli mancava. Fu dall' Ille. Marchese di Cannicarao di Bernardo M.a Trigona fu commissario e Procuratie Generale di esso monastero col consenso della Signa. madre Abbadessa data la ammissione all'architetto sign. d.o Paolo Labisi di formare un tal disegno quale dopo d'aversi preso le misure del sito, e Fattone il visoloco del monast., pur anche delineare nel medesimo monast.o tutte le parti che mancavano al sud.o monast.o tanto d'officine, quanto di dormitorio, ed altro, ne formò in quel tempo il totale disegno in carta che gli fu ricercato con approvazione di sud.o Sigr. . . . formato a secondo del loro volere. E perchè la sig.ra Abba.ssa, e religiose tutte volevano che s'avesse dato meno all'esecuzione, per la necessità che ne avenne, ed io alle continue instanze dei medesimi ne facea le premure al sud.o Sigr. Marchese; esso Sigr. Sinando proprio, che fosse stato con tal disegno anche osservato col fu Sigr. Marchese di lui Padre, quale trovavasi in Palermo, risolse di mandarglielo e dopo osservato fargli il permesso di metterlo in esecuzione. Fu dal Sigre. Marchese di Cannicarao Padre ricevuto per mano dal [word illegible], e fu risposto dal medesimo d'essere stato di suo piacere. Ma come che il sud.o Sigr. era applicato negl'affari importanti di casa sua, non pensò più a tal disegno, ed avendogli fatto delle replicate

volte le premure di darmi il suo permesso per metterlo in esecuzione, dopo quasi un anno rispose che piùtosto avessero pensato le moniali a terminare il monas.to che all'edificazione della chiesa . . . Quindi essendo scorsi circa ad anni quattro senza che ne avesse potuto avere una concreta risoluzione, risolse finalmente all premesse istanze della signora abbadessa e religiose tutte il sigr. marchese figlio, di far formare almeno al medesimo sigr. architetto di Labisi un altro disegno, riformando la chiesa antica, che trovavasi in detto monastero . . . Labisi presse le misure . . . nell'anno 1775. Gli formò l'altro disegno, e subitamente si pose in opera colla direzione . . .' which Labisi gave until September 1775. Signed Sac.to Domenico Belluso.
AdSS Notary Vincenzo Labisi, 007250, 1780–81, ff. 79–132

10 25 April 1789
'Apocha pro D: Paulo Labisi cum D: Franco: Fassari nom.' Labisi complains about practices of the senators of the city of Noto. He addresses his grievances to the King by way of the Royal Secretary: 'Per via di nostra Real segreteria ci arriva un ricorso del tenor seguente:'
'Dn. Paolo Labisi Reggio Ingegniere Civile della Università e città di Noto colla privativa, costretto a ricorrere alla giustizia e clemenza di V.E. per li tanti aggravii, e prepotenze soffrirsi da questi Si.ri Senatori, fa presente con ogni ossequio all' V.E. come non contanti di non aver voluto, ostinatamente eseguire, dell'anno 1760: sino al 1782: una infinità di dispacci ordinati dal Rev.mo. Tribunale di V.E.: in conferma della di loro elezione fattagli di architetto di q.ta città, e che dopo aver avuto, in risulta d'un contradittorio fatto con essi loro, il possesso, anche dopo due anni d. suo esercizio, per avergli presentato un vener.issimo Real Dispaccio dei 10 Gennio 1784 nel quale gli si confirmano tutti i sud. Dispacci Patrimoniali: Eglino coll'abuso della di loro indipendenza, che mostrano avere dai superiori magri, non solamente lo rimossero dal di lui impiego; ma anche contro l'ordine Reale Secr.to in sua vece, l'elezione di architetto della città in persona di un maestro tagliapietre, il quale esercita il mestiere di prezzatore rusticano ed agrimentatore, ed in oggi, quantunque il V.E. per l'incarico avuto dalla Maestà del Re per mezzo d'un altro suo Real Dispaccio, ottenuto ad istanza dell'Exp[to], ne avesse sotto il 28 Giugno pp. per via del suo veneriss.imo Trib.le del R.P. con suo dispaccio dimandate in forma dalli medi Senatori; Eglino ciò nondimeno con tutta l'indifferenza possibile, per non poter legittimare di loro improprio operato, si sono fatti sordi, senza che avessero pensato, sin'oggi, rispondere a quanto gli è stato da V.E. e dalla Maestà del Re ordinato che perciò prega l'oratore un'altra seconda volta di ordinare all'ill.mo Senato e suoi Deputati di subitamente in vista rispondere e dar conto di q.tto gli è stato da V.E. importa sotto una ben degna pena e se non altrim.ti ordinargli, che fra il termine, che stimerà, dovessero dare, unitam.te con di loro Deputati, indirittura e senza replica il doveroso possesso [word illegible] con tutte quelle preeminenze, che gli si appartengono, a tenore degli'ordini: ordini Reali . . . Paulo Labisi come sopra
AdSS, Vincenzo Labisi, 007257, 1788–89, ff. 273–74

11 4 July 1890
'Relationes Aestimationis pro d: Antonio Caruso et c:bus cum D: Paulo Labisi et c:bus.' 'Sn. Paolo Labisi, Ingegn.re Civile' writes 'relazione' of two shops in the Piccione house.
AdSS, Notary Vincenzo Labisi, 007257, 1788–89, ff. 173–74

SECTION VI: THE COMMITTEE ON STREETS AND WATER

Volume secondo sopra la querende a carico de' deputati de'acqua e strade della città di Noto
MS Biblioteca Comunale di Noto, 1750–95

f.3 The contract for the construction of the Hercules fountain.
23 September 1757
'Obligatio pro D: Ant.no Buscemi et Burderi cum D: Joseph Orlando.' The Catanese Orlando, and his brother are to: 'farci una fontana de marmo bianco di Carrara secondo il modello fatto di Creta dal Sud.o di Orlando, gle lo tiene il d.o di Buscemi in suo potere con metterci solamente il marmo lavorato, e la sua maestria a tenore del d.o Modello il d.o obligatio, e che la d.a fontana debba essere composta d'una statua d'Ercole con un scudo a suo lato mostrando l'insegna di q.a Città come sta formata nel d.o Modello seduta sopra quattro Masceroni che dovranno gettare acqua nelle quattro Carciole di Marmo le quali sono sostenute da quattro Tironi o siano puttini, medietà di essi nella parte soltana formate a guisa di Sirene sedute sopra quattro Teste di Delfini, che in una mano portano quattro insegne o scudi per imprimervi delle descrizioni, tutto il restante della fontana va formando scogli come nel d.o modello. La proporzione della statua col suo pedestallo debba essere d'altezza palmi tredeci cioè la statua. . . .'

f.3
'con mascheroni in cui va seduta palmi sei, ed il restante dell'altezza del piedestallo con le corciole palmi sette, che larghezza della sua base palmi sei, e mezzo, e la longhezza palmi sette, quale debba allestirla nella Città di Catania p. tutto il mese marzo 1758 e nel. d.o mese marzo debba il d.o obligato. avvisare al d.o di Buscemi affine di mandarsela a prendere a spese proprie del d.o di Buscemi per infino al luogo determinato dove dovrà erigersi ing.a Città . . .

f.4
. . . che in quanto alle spese, che ricercherà la fonte, o sia vasca, che deve ricevere l'acqua della fontana med.ma all'altezza di palmi quattro in circa con li due scalini al di sotto, ed il Zoccolo al di sotto del piedestallo della fontana che gli sarà determinata giusta. La idea dell'architetto Paulo Labisi sia obligato farle solamente il d.o di Buscemi a sue proprie spese . . .

f.5
22 December 1758
Report by Rosario Gagliardi on repairs to the Testa dell'Acqua aqueduct.
'Relazione di Rosario Gagliardi Architetto della Città di Noto.' Report on repairs made on aqueduct by masters Conradi Mauceri, Antonini Carrarra, and Sylvestri Bisansia, 'qualmente essendosi conferito detto Relatore d'ordine come sopra nella Testa dell'acqua esistente in questo Ter.rio, e nel luogo nom.to di Landavacche per vedere, ed osservarci l'acconci, e ripari necessarii fatti dalli sudetti maestri, tanto in detta Testa dell'acqua, . . .

f.44
22 December 1787
The Senate of Noto deliberates on moving the Hercules fountain from the *planitie* in front of the Chiesa Madre to the *platea* of S. Domenico.

The Senate of Noto deliberated 'elevandi a Planitie huius Ven.s Eccles. Matris Fontem Ercolis eumque pro d. orbis decore, et ornatu, populique commodo asportandi, et collocandi in majori Platea ante Ven.m Contus, et Collegii S: Dominico ut ea Transactionis Instrumento. . . .

ff.45v
Architetto Dn. Bernardo Labisi reports on the reasons for moving the fountain:
'. . . sud.o architetto Labisi essendosi conferito d'ordine e mandato di s.o Ill.mo Senato nella Fonte d'Ercole esistente nel Piano della chiesa madre per vedere ed esaminare li motivi p. li quali non può correre l'acqua in d.a Fonte e la spesa che ci bisogna per trasportarsi la medesima nella publica Piazza di S. Domenico . . .'

ff. 61–66
Bernardo Labisi ('inginiere civile') makes a report on the possibilities and advantages of lowering the Cassaro.
15 September 1787
'Avendomi portato seriamente d'ordine di suddetti Ill.ri Deputati nella *strada nominata del Cassaro e dalla cantoniera della Ven.le Par.le Chiesa di S: Michiele Arcangelo sino a quella del Ven.le con.to di S: Francesco d'Assisi* per osservarla, ed esaminarla minuta.me ad effetto di livellarla per renderla praticabile adatta a potervi commodame.te camminare con riferirne di seguito la spesa che potrà portare tanto nel ribassare che nell'empiere a seconda del livello ch'esigerà sud.a. strada. Ho trovato la med.a essere nella sua essenzione di q.258:5. E siccome in essa, oltre delli due gran piani, uno nom.to la Piazza di Sig.lo Domenico, e l'altro della Casa Senatoria Ven.le Chiesa, che v'interpongono, si sono parimente dell' imboccatura di n.lo 14: strade che l'attraversano, e queste a tenore del livello, non meno che li due tetti Piani devono portare il loro rispettivo livello coll. intersezione della sud.a strada maestra.
'Quindi avendo io dunque livellato la medesima trovo che li Piani sud.i e le sudette strade traverse han bisogno venite[?] almeno nelle imboccature riattate, giusto come si dovrà pratticare in quella maestra per la scambievole comunicazione, e dipendenza. Perciò considerando che nel fatto ciò è necessario *il ribasso in diverse parti, ed il rialzamento con fabrica, e materiale in alcune altre parti.* A quest' oggetto prima d'ogni altro con il parere di *doversi piantare nel mezzo, o sia centro della strada una catena di pezzi intagliati nella larghezza di Pal:4*: alla profondità di pal:3: circa *capace a poter resistere alli carriaggi e vetturali, la quale poi venendo piantata* a norma del livello da me tirato nelli muri dovrà servire di regola, o direzione alli maestri che anderanno et cura pianare e rassettare la cennata strada tanto col picone nel tagliare l'ammassi di pietra che sopravvanzano quanto nell' empiere con di lementi le cavità che incontrerà il livello . . . si è da me giudicato doversi fare il selciato di pietre di fiume sbattute nelle sole imboccature per ora, ed in alcune altre di esse poi farvi *l'acquedotti sotterranei e le spese per ricevere tutta quella quantità dell'acque piovane che scendono della mezza città superiore, ad oggetto di evitare il* [word illegible] *della strada maestra con sí copiose acque E perchè il suolo di essa e delli piani sudi. è molto informe riflettendo io il considerevole ribasso in alcune parti e li grandi ripieni in alcun'altre*, che devonsi fare così avendone fatto di tutto un stretto conto ragionato sopra la pianta che si è da me delineata . . .

f. 630
Report on finances and organization of the 'Deputazione della strada'. The Deputation having been created in 1757 gives an accounting of its finances from tax revenue.
June 1795

f.875
A Catalogue of Noto's Senators and Mayors, 1776–86
The catalogue illustrates how a small group of aristocratic families controlled Noto's government.

1 Anno 10. 1776–77 Il B.ne Dn. Felice Astuto Dn. Franzo Nicolaci Dn. Franco Rau Marchese della Ferla Dn. Giacchino Bongiorno	Dn. Michele Bongiorno Sindaco
2 Anno 11. 1777–78 Dn. Mariano di Lorenzo B.ne S:Marco Dn. Battaglia	Il sud.o di Bongiorno
3 Anno 13. 1778–79 Dn. Pietro Battaglia Dn. Giuseppe M.a Nicolaci B.ne del Patro	Il Sudo: Bongiorno Sindaco
4 Anno 13. 1779–80 Dn. Francesco Rau Marchese della Ferla Dn. Giuseppe Landolina	Dn. Michele Bongiorno Sindaco
5 Anno 14. 1780–81 Dn. Felici Astuto Dn. Ascenzio Battaglia	Dn. Gius.e Landolina Sindaco
6 Anno 15. 1781–82 Dn. Giuseppe M.a Nicolaci Dn. Michele Zappatas	Dn. Gius.e. Landolina Sindaco
7 Anno 1 1782–83 Dn. Mariano Nicolaci Dn. Simone Rau Marchese della Ferla	B.ne Gius.e Lorenzo Sindaco
8 Anno 2 1783–84 Dn. Giuseppe Landolina Dn. Vincenzo Astuto	Dne Gius.e Lorenzo Sindaco
9 Anno 3. 1784–85 B.ne Dn. Antonino Astuto	Meteo di Lorenzo Sindaco
10 Anno 4 1785–86 Dn. Francesco Rau Dn. Giuseppe M.a Nicolaci	Dn. Gius.e Landolina Sindaco

SECTION VII: MISCELLANEOUS DOCUMENTS

Document 1

A number of gentlemen seek the establishment of a road from the slope to the Pianazzo.

20 November 1700

i Giurati dell'anno 1693, come in tempo del nostro governo in questa città nel medesimo anno si stabilisce alla nostra presenza dover restare in questa città una strada fra mezza le case del R.d Sact.o D. Nicolò Costanzo e le case del . . . Domenico Gentile per poter salire una carrozza nel pianazzo . . .
AdSS, Registered Acts of the Università di Noto, 634 (32), 1700–1, f. 26

Document 2

Tommaso Impellizzeri reports that he owned a house in Noto Antica and wants to build in the new city. But because of the confusion over where the city would be re-erected he did not claim his site on the 'piazza', originally conceded to him.

1701

. . . Sn. Tomaso Impellizzeri e Scamanaca B.ne di Bufalu della Città di Noto diceva che avendo per la causa del terremoto dell'anno 1693 persa non solo tutta la sua roba, ma . . . la casa che possiede sudetta in detta Antica città in altra parte più distante secondo l'ordine . . . dell'detto Duca di Camastra . . . e il stabilimento di detto nuovo sito, habbe l'essa concessa la pianta in detta nova città per potervi fabricare la sua casa nella piazza di detta nova città però perchè si è stato sin l'ora con dubbio della situazione di detta . . . ciò l'esp.te non soprende la certezza se debbia restarvi in detta nova città e pure ritornarsi nella antica non ha fabricato la sua casa in detta . . . sopra concessata nella sud.a piazza di detta nuova città per potendo l'dubitare che da qualche altro suolo si pretendesse voler fabricare nel sud.o loco di detta nuova città concesso all' esp.te . . .
AdSS, Registered Acts of the Università di Noto, 634 (32), 1700–1

Document 3

Nobles and clergy ask permission to return to Noto Antica for building materials:

1700–1

'Li RR.d. Can.ci Tomao della Matrice Chiesa di q.ta pre.da c.a come della Parrochiale, e filiale Chiesa del SS.mo Crucifisso, di RRd. Capi della Ven.le Religione, maggior parte della Nobiltà, e del Clero, e quasi tutta la cittadinanza di q.ta med.ma Città espongono alle off. Ill.me che volendo [word illegible] dell' ordine di S.A. . . . in virtù della quale si concede ad ogn'uno che volesse fabricare in questo nuovo sito la facoltà di potere fare liberamente principiare, perfectionare, e finire le loro fabriche in q.to nuovo sito, hanno necessità di valersi dell'attratto[?] le pietre d'intaglio delle loro fabriche rovinate nell'antico sito . . .'
AdSS Registrum Actorum, Università di Noto, 634 (32), 1700–1701, f. 14

Document 4

Disagreement over extension of the Monastery of Montevergine is taken to the King for resolution.

20 April 1702

The Abbess of Montevergine asked that the case be considered 'per decoro monastico'. She asked that a wall be constructed around the monastery: 'recingere di muro tutto il sito di quello situato . . . al dove terminare [di] sopra [il] Pianale per non essere le monache del med.mo soggette all veduta d'tutti, necessitando per esser la parte nel scoceso del monte alluvigarsi canni sei per securità delle fabriche come per poter fare a suo tempo un belvedere per veduta delle processioni et altre funzioni . . .' Against this plan and blocking it are the Vicariate of SS. Annunziata, the Abbess of S. Agata, and the Baron of Frigintini.
AdSS, Registrum Actorum, Universita di Noto, 635 (33), 1701–2, f. 51.

Document 5

Protest by a religious house against an invasion of their privacy by a new construction.

8 November 1746

'Obligatio Pro Con.tu S.ta Maria Carmeli H.s U.s Cum Franco Mazzone . . . Siamo stati supplicati del tenor che siegue: Ecc.mo Sig.re Il Rev: P.re Priore del ven.le convento del Carmine de' PP Carmelitani della stretta osservanza della Città di Noto supplicando a V.E. umilmente espone che tenendo e possedendo Francesco Mazzone Paniere di detta città alcune case terrane a dirimpetto del d.o ven.le convento colla strada intermedia fabricate pochi anni addietro dall'istesso di Mazzone, . . . ave fatto ivi trasportare una gran quantità di materiale, ed'ave dal med.mo pre inteso che intende fa d.e case terrane fabricarci, e quelle appalazzare, e perchè Ecc.mo Sig.re: alzandosi d.e Fabriche e Facendosi dal d.o di Mazzone un altro appartamento fa de case ove ci devono fare diverse aperture tutte in Frontispicio delle celle dei religiosi di d.o con.to non solamente si viene ad occupare l'aria salutare al detto convento ma pur anche si viene ad inducere al med.mo una positiva servitù quanto che i poveri Religiosi sarebbon forzati per la loro modestia, ed osservanza regolare privarsi attatto dello lume di dette finestre d.non esser provveduti dalle finestre che dovrà fare d.o di Mazzone, e rendere inutile e diserta l'abitazione d'un intiero corridore di celle Religiose con grave danno, ed interesse di d.o povero convento ed altresì con evidente pericolo della modestia religiosa, essendo ciò proibito da tutti i Dottori Canonisti . . .' Because of this invasion of privacy the Carmelites ask the Senate of Noto to stop Mazzone from building a second storey on his house.
AdSS, Notary Vincenzo Labisi, 007217, 1745–8, f. 69

Document 6

Protest against the closing of an access road.

1770

'Protestatio ad instam Ills: D: Bernardi Ma. Trigona.' Protest against Antonio Sinatra. Trigona owns a shop 'dietro il ven.le Con.to de PP. minori conventuali sotto il titolo di S. Francesco d'Assisi e di rimpetto al ven.le Mon.ro di San Salvatore; dovrà appartenere tutto il sito vacuo di canne diciotto, e palmi sì in longhezza e di canne otto in larghezza . . . [as is recognized by

the court] Antonio Sinatra dover lasciare sempre libero lo rimanente del sito per commodo di quelli, che abitano nei lati dell'istesso sito, come da moltissimi anni è stato pratticato, avendone la di loro uscita ed entrata nel tramezzo delle sud.e botteghe . . .'
AdSS, Notary Vincenzo Labisi, 007240, 1770–71, f. 411

Document 7
A house is described which is in the area around the castle or jail where houses owned by Vincenzo Sinatra were located.

13 December 1756
Testament of Dn. Conradi Serrentino:
'Beni Stabili urbane . . .
Un tenimento di case . . . esistente in q.ta città ed in contrada del Castello confinante in prospetto delle case del Rev.o Con. Tesoriero D. Bonaventura Deodato via del mezzo in prospetto delle case dell'architetto Vincenzo Sinatra . . .'
AdSS, Notary Vincenzo Labisi, 007226, 1756–7, f. 261

SECTION VIII: ACCOUNTS OF NOTO 1871–1910

C. Puglisi, *Cronica della Città di Noto*, MS Biblioteca Comunale di Noto, 1871–1901, gives the following accounts of the improvement and lowering of the streets, as well as notices concerning sewers, new parks, markets, and civic monuments.

Jan. 1873: 'Lungo il mese si è lavorato a migliorare le condizioni della nostra Flora, facendo i condotti d'acqua per irrigazione e rinnovando molti alberi. Nuovi alberi sono stati piantati nella floretta dell'immacolata, in quella di Ercole e nella piazza dirimpetto al lavoro di conversazione, dove si reelute di e fatto il nuovo palchetto della banda musicale'.

Nov. 1873: 'Dobbiamo notare molta attività nelle opere pubbliche—appenna compiuto l'incanalamento dell'acqua nella parte superiore del paese, si è dato opera a sistemare e a livellare quasi tutte le strade del pianalta, ed è un piacere a vederle. E la prima volta che (assisto) ad un lavoro così radicale. La proprietà privata ha sofferto, ma v'ha acquistato la simmetria, e, avuto riguardo alle spese sostenute, quelli che abitano al pianazza, non hanno più ragione di lamentarsi, non avendo che individuare a quelli della parte inferiore. Si lavora anche a rifare le scale che per Via S. Agata mettono nella piazza del pubblico mercato . . . Agli antichi ciottoloni si sostituiscono lastre di pietra che si cavano alli Crociferi e di un valore uguale della pietra vulcanica detta sciara . . . Intanto a dare i mezzi di comprarsi il pane, per quanto . . . dalla strettezza delle finanze comunali, si è incominciata la sistemazione della Via Roma e . . . strade secondarie . . .'.

March 1875: 'Il notinese Francesco Cassone, ingegnere comunale, ha pubblicato per la stampa . . . "Basolamento del Corso Vittoria Emanuele". . . . il bravo giovane spiega il motivo per cui si va all'idea delle banchine, e non a quella del basolamento generale della via principale del nostro paese.'

Sept. 1876: 'E'incominciato il trasporto dei materiali per il lastricamento della banchine lungo il Corso Vittorio Emanuele . . .'.

Dec. 1876: 'Il nostro popolo mira con compiacenza i lavori che s'eseguiscono sui marciapiedi del corso. Veramente quelle basole [word illegible] colle quali si fanno le banchine, sono di un bello effetto sul bianco della scala . . .'.

March 1877: 'Lungo il corso dei mesi scorsi si è lavorato all'incanalamento delle acque nella parte inferiore del paese e ciò con denaro anticipato dal nostro sindaco . . . Ora tutte le opere pubbliche sono state lasciate in apo. Di banchine lungo il corso non si parla più. Gli esecutori del progetto, quasi tutti catanesi, [sia] tornarono alle loro case dopo aver protestato contro gli appaltatori . . .'.

April 1879: 'Si sono intrapresi i lavori per sistemare e rendere accessibili le strade della parte occidentale del nostro paese'.

May 1879: 'Orologio comunale: Nel lato orientale del monastero di Sant' Agata sono incominciati i lavori per edificarsi la torretta nella quale deve impiantarsi il nuovo orologio'.

Jan. 1880: 'La guinta municipale . . decise d'intraprendere la costruzione di una nuova strada nella parte occidentale del paese, che cominiciando dal Corso Vittorio Emanuele mettesse capo nella Via Cavour, precisamente dirimpetto alla chiesa di S. Antonio Abate . . .'.

Feb. 1880: ' – Chiesa S. Michele – Quando si impiantarono i marciapiedi, lungo il Corso Vittorio Emanuele ci fu fatto un profondo scavo destinato ad accogliere ed a condurre le acque piovane; onde, cosa alla quale allora non si badò, furono indebolite e scosse le fondamenta di creta. Poco dopo terminate le banchine, si vide che la facciata della chiesa aveva una fenditura quanto era lunga, fenditura ch'è divenuta poi più sensibile dopo le poggie cadute, e mette in apprensione non solo i vicini ma tutti gli abitanti. A causa delle pioggie minaccia rovina il campanile [sic] di S. Maria dell'Arco. "E per la stessa ragione sono crollate le mura di varie piccole case" '.

April 1880: 'Il pubblico vede con compiacenza i miglioramenti che il Principe di Villadorata ha fatto eseguire nel locale del pubblico mercato: il loggiato, le nuove banche, . . . etc.'. [What follows is essentially a description of the market opposite the site of S. Camillo on Via Pirri which can still be seen today.]

Nov. 1880: 'Sono incomiciati i lavori per livellare le due piazze laterali al palazzo municipale (casa-città) . . .'
march, 1889: 'Livellamento del fosso: i lavori di riempimento del fosso furono proseguiti con grande alacrità durante i primi quindici giorni del mese, adoperando anche materiale ottenuto ampliando la flora dal lato confinente con l'orto dei PP. ex-Cappuccini . . .'.

June 1889: 'Ultimati i lavori per livellare il fosso, gettato un po'di materiale che sopravanzava . . .'.

March 1895: 'Lungo il mese si è lavorato a sistemare il Corso Vittorio Emanuele e le principali vie del paese. Si è anche livellato il piano a sud della Flora, nel centro del quale sorgerà un palchetto in muratura per la banda musicale . . .'.

June 1896: 'Arrivati i lavori del lastricamento innanzi la porta del municipio . . .'. [Here there is a stone which can still be seen today, with the date 1896 on it. Puglisi says that the names of the officials of the city and a silver coin can be found under it.]

July 1896: 'Condotti i lavori di lastricamento nel corso sino alla cantonata S. Chiara, l'ultimo del mese i maestri hanno impreso a basolare dalla Porta Reale a salire sino al luogo nel quale interruppero i lavori . . .'.

APPENDIX 1: RELIGIOUS HOUSES IN NOTO

Religious houses are crucial to the visual appearance of Noto and its functioning as a city in the eighteenth century. In the appendix pertinent information on the names, locations, orders, and inhabitants of the religious houses is given. Since the important information on each institution differs (for example, some churches do not have both official and popular names) the format is not consistent for each entry.

The institutions listed below were functioning during the mid-eighteenth century. They comprise only the religious houses within the city, excluding those in the territory of Noto but outside the city proper. The Casa del Refugio was listed as a convent and is therefore included here. Because the seminary appears in the 1748 population tallies as one of the religious houses it too has been included.

Institution name:	**Monastery of S. Maria dell'Arco**, or Convent of S. Maria dell'Arco, or less frequently, Abbey of S. Maria dell'Arco
In Noto Antica:	yes
Order:	Cistercian monks
Church popular name:	S. Maria dell'Arco
No. Labisi veduta	8
Inhabitants in 1748:	religious members Rev. Padre Dn. Corrado Greco (Prior) Rev. Padre Dn. Pietro Sovino Rev.Padre Maestro Dn. Simone Bongiovanni Rev. Padre Giuseppe Donades El. mo Padre Dn. Antonio Ignazzurra Fra. Corrado Nisi Fra. Giovanni Grienti Fra. Nicolo Dvago man servant Giuseppe Marziana
Present use:	The church still functions. The rest of the institution has been converted into apartments.

Instituion name:	**Monastery of S. Chiara**
In Noto Antica:	Yes
Order:	Benedictine nuns
Church:	S. Maria dell'Assunta
Church popular name:	S. Chiara
No. Labisi veduta:	4
Inhabitants in 1748:	religious members S. Roas Maria Oddo (Abbess) S. Michelagnela Azzolini S. Saveria Campanella S. Giuseppa Cantone S. Ignazia Maria Landolina S. Antonia Landolina S. Palma Vittoria Landolina S. Maria Terza Lorenzo S. Pietra Angela Lorenzo deacon D. Maria Fortunati Ettore boarding-school pupils D. Perla Battaglia D. Geroloma Battaglia D. Doradea Nicolaci D. Antonia Nicolaci D. Angela Zappada servants of the monastery Domenica Leggio Severa Landolina Geronima Cardinale Sebastiana Molisanti Carmela Terzo Concetta Roveli

Present use: School, practice room for band, convent in 1970 (since abandoned). Church remains intact.

Institution name: **Casa del Refugio, Monte di Pietà.**
In Noto Antica: Yes
Popular name: Also called S. Teodoro
No. Labisi veduta 31
Inhabitants in 1748: 1 sister
42 orphan girls
Present use: Provincial jail. Exterior walls and church are still intact.

Institution name: **Monastery of S. Giuseppe**, or S. Joseph
In Noto Antica: yes
Order: Penitent Brothers of the Third Order of S. Francis
No. Labisi veduta: 10
Inhabitants in 1748: 3 sisters and 5 lay sisters
Present use: no trace survives

Institution name: **Monastery of Montevergine**
In Noto Antica: yes
Order: Bernardine nuns
Church: S. Girolamo
No. Labisi veduta: 22
Inhabitants in 1748: 6 sisters, 1 deacon, 3 boarding-school girls, 3 servants
Present use: Monastery destroyed. Church survives intact.

Institution name: **Monastery of SS. Annunziata**
Popular name: Badia Nuova
In Noto Antica: yes
Order: Benedictine nuns
Church: SS. Annunziata
No. Labisi veduta: 27
Inhabitants in 1748: 12 sisters, 2 noble deacons, 4 servants
Present use: The monastery is used as living quarters for priests, the church remains intact.

Institution name: **Monastery of S. Agata**
In Noto Antica: yes
Order: Bernardine nuns
Church: S. Agata
No. Labisi veduta: 26
Inhabitants in 1748: 12 sisters, 2 deacons, 2 noble boarding-school girls, 4 servants
Present use: Hospital for the city, Ospitale Trigona. The church remains intact.

Institution name: **Jesuit college**
In Noto Antica: yes
Order: Jesuit monks
Church: S. Carlo Borromeo
No. Labisi veduta: 17
Inhabitants in 1748: 8 fathers, 6 lay brothers
Present use: School; the college and church still survive intact.

Institution name: **Monastery of S. Tomaso Apostolo** or S. Tommaso
In Noto Antica: yes
Order: Bernardine nuns
Church: S. Maria degli Angeli
No. Labisi veduta: 32
Inhabitants in 1748: 9 sisters; 4 servants
Present use: Provincial jail. Church no longer exists

Institution name: **Monastery of SS. Salvatore**
In Noto Antica: yes
Order: Benedictine nuns
Church: SS. Salvatore
No. Labisi veduta: 3
Inhabitants in 1748: abbess, prioress, 20 sisters (among them members of the Landolina, Impellizzeri, Bongiorno, Di Lorenzo, Rau, Deodato families), 6 noble deacons (among them members of the Prado, Paredes, Deodato, and Bongiorno families), 7 servants
Present use: Gutted by fire in 1934, interior of Monastery totally rebuilt as Seminary from 1945–1955, a function it still serves. The late eighteenth century church survives. The earlier church is no longer standing.

Institution name: **Convent of S. Antonio di Padova** or S. Antonino
In Noto Antica: yes
Order: Padri Minori Osservanti Riformati
No. Labisi veduta: 25
Inhabitants in 1748: 15 fathers, 2 minor clerics, 8 lay brothers
Present use: Orphanage

Institution name: **Convent of S. Domenico**
In Noto Antica: yes
Order: Dominican, Padri Predicatori, monks
Church: SS. Annunziata
Church popular name: S. Domenico
No. Labisi veduta: 14
Inhabitants in 1748: religious members
Padre Lettore e Priore Fra Andrea Bonicontro
P. Mr.o Espo.tore Corradino Bevilacqua
P. Lettore sotto P.re Fra. Pietro Martire di Corenzo
P. Lettore Fra. Ludovico Sortino
P. Lettore Fra. Tommaso Coniglio
P. Lettore Fra. Vincenzo Boniglio
novice
Domenico Landolina
professed lay brothers
Fra. Vincenzo Cappello
Fra. Salvatore Dato
Fra. Antonino Belluado
Fra. Rosario Corso
Fra. Domenico Grande
Fra. Vincenzo Conforto
servants
Vincenzo Amato
Corrado Amato
Present use: School. Istituto Magistrale. Except for southern façade convent totally gutted and rebuilt. Church survives intact.

Institution name: **Convent of S. Maria del Monte Carmelo** called the Carmine
In Noto Antica: yes
Order: Carmelites of the New Strict Observance of Syracuse, monks
Church: S. Maria del Carmine or del Carmelo
No. Labisi veduta: 12
Inhabitants in 1748: 4 fathers, 4 lay brothers, 1 man servant
Present use: Remaining wing of convent is police station. Church remains intact.

Institution name: **Convent of S. Francesco di Paola**
In Noto Antica: yes
Order: Padri Minimi di S. Francesco di Paola, monks
Church: Apostolo S. Bartolomeo
No. Labisi veduta: 34
Inhabitants in 1748: 4 fathers, 3 lay brothers, 1 servant

Present use:	Private house; the church remains intact although closed for regular services.
Institution name:	**House of the Crociferi Fathers** or less correctly Convent of the Crociferi Fathers
In Noto Antica:	No
Order:	Ministri degli Infermi; Chierici Regoli; Padri dei Crociferi
Church:	S. Camillo
No. Labisi veduta:	15
Inhabitants in 1748:	3 people
Present use:	School: Scuola Avviamento Professionale, Offices of Justice, apartments.

Institution name:	**Oratory of S. Filippo Neri**, or less correctly Convent of S. Filippo Neri
In Noto Antica:	yes
Order:	Padri Filippini
Church:	S. Caterina
No. Labisi veduta:	21
Present use:	Offices and Caserma of the Guardia di Finanza

Institution name:	**Convent of S. Maria di Gesù**, sometimes del Gesù
In Noto Antica:	yes
Order:	Padri Minori Osservanti, monks
Church:	S. Maria di Gesù
No. Labisi veduta:	28
Inhabitants in 1748:	6 fathers, 2 lay brothers, 2 man servants
Present use:	Institute for orphaned women, Istituto Giavanti. Church remains intact.

Institution name:	**Convent of S. Francesco d'Assisi**
In Noto Antica:	yes
Order:	Franciscans, Padri Conventuali, monks
Church:	S. Francesco all'Immacolata
No. Labisi veduta:	5
Inhabitants in 1748:	6 fathers, 4 lay brothers
Present use:	School – Scuola Media; church remains intact.

Institution name:	**Seminary**
In Noto Antica:	yes
No. Labisi veduta:	16
Inhabitants in 1748:	total population of 20 males
Present use:	School; well preserved.

Institution name:	**Convent of P.P. Cappuccini**
In Noto Antica:	yes
Order:	Capuchin monks
No. Labisi veduta:	36
Inhabitants in 1748:	16 men
Present use:	Istituto dei Padri Stimatini, Cantina Sperimentale Statale, and school of Agriculture. The church has been gutted. It is now called Ecce Homo or the Pantheon of the Fallen.

Institution name:	**Hospital or Convent of S. Maria della Scala**
In Noto Antica:	yes
Order:	Carmelitani Osservanti, monks
Church:	S. Corrado
No. Labisis veduta:	29
Inhabitants in 1748:	7 fathers, 11 brothers, 3 novices, 2 servants, 2 man-servants
Present use:	Used as private dwelling.

Institution name:	**Hospital of the Convent of the Padri Benefratelli di S. Giovanni di Dio**
In Noto Antica:	yes
Order:	Frati Benefratelli di S. Giovanni di Dio, monks
No. Labisi veduta:	30
Inhabitants in 1759:	4 fathers, 1 priest
Present use:	School; church gutted.

APPENDIX 2: ARISTOCRATIC PALACES IN NOTO

Where were the aristocratic palaces in Noto? Labisi's veduta (Pl. 20 and Map 8) gives a general idea, but identification of specific buildings is difficult. The aristocratic palaces are identified on the Labisi veduta by numbers over 40. A late inscription on the upper part of the map (the ink is slightly blacker than that used in the original legend at the bottom) identifies each of the aristocratic families, and the palace(s) it occupies. The legend reads as follows:

> [word illegible] Città di Noto otra intorno Canne 1,901 cioè due miglia ed un quarto. Si rende .·. . e iosa[?] nel Regno di Sicilia per le Fal: [?]
> che ai singolar architettura e magnificenza. Oltre le qui sotto descritte si contano 20 Case di Nobili cioè Prin.pe Di Villadorata 2
> March:e di Terzana 3 Marchese di Canicara.o. 4 Ma.che di S.ta Floro 5. Marchese della Ferla: 6 Br. di San Giacomo 7. Br.e di Burello
> 8 B.ne della Burgia Maucini. 9 B.ne del Padro 10: B.ne di S: Marco ll B.ne d'Alfano [13 B.ne di San Lorenzo—written in line above S. Alfano]
> 12 B.ne di tre Filiotti: 13 B.ne di Fargione
> 14 B.ne della Pizzui 15 B.ne delle Regie Tande di Melilli 16 Dn. Emmanuele Salonia e Manente
> 17: D. Michele Buongiorno 18: D. Giuseppe Bongiorno 19 D. Gian Batta Bonanno 20 B.ne dieteceme[?] grande
> Si contano quattordicimila e più anime: Centosessanta Preti; quattordici Notari
> Dodici Legali. Cinque Parrocchie Due Collegiate di Canonici;
> cioè una nella Madre Chiesa con 17 Canonici incluse le Dignità Preposite Cianto e Tesoriere. La seconda nel SS.mo Crocifisso con
> quam: 12 Canonici incluse le Dignità di Archidiacono Ciantro e Tesoriere. Due Collegii di Studii
> In Seminario di A°. 24: Alumni ed altri Convitteri . . .

Before writing the corresponding numbers on the veduta itself the person adding this information must have realized the confusion that would result since the same numerical system had been used originally for the ecclesiastical buildings in the city. He began his numerical system with either 41 or 42 and continued it throughout the 20 noble palaces. Later, perhaps in 1783, someone drew a second set of numbers over the first, confounding the identification problem still further.

The ambiguity of the numbering system employed in the late inscription requires two different correlations, one (correlation

A) beginning with the number 41, and another (correlation B) beginning at 42. The correct correspondence between the number and the present palace of the family is indicated in the right-hand column.

Palaces (Family Name)	*A*	*B*	*Actual Location*
Principe di Villadorata (Nicolaci)	41	42	41
Marchese di Terzana [Trezzana] (Landolina)	42	43	42
Marchese di Cannicarao (Trigona)	43	44	44(b)
Marchese di S.ta Flaro (Zappata)	44	45	49
Marchese della Ferla (Rau)	45	46	46(c)
Barone di San Giacomo (Impellizzeri-Ribera)	46	47	45′
Barone di Burello (Deodato e Moncada)	47	48	
Barone della Burgia Maucini (Deodata e Moncada)	48	49	48
Barone del Padro (Nicolaci e Bellia)	49	50	
Barone di S. Marco (Di Lorenzo)	50	51	47
Barone di S. Alfano (Landolina)	51	52	42 and 52
Barone di Tre Filiotti (Prado)	52	53	near 49
Barone di San Lorenzo (Di Lorenzo e Salonia)	53	54	47
Barone di Fargione (Astuto)	53	54	45a
Barone della Pizzuti (Battaglia)	54	55	56
Barone delle Regie Tande di Melilli (Moncada)	55	56	
Dn. Emanuele Salonia e Monente	56	57	
Dn. Michel Buongiorno	57	58	48 or 51
Dn. Giuseppe Buongiorno	58	59	48 or 51
Dn. Giambattista Bonanno	59	60	

Following is an account of the remains of major Netinese palaces which can be seen in the city today with a short description and a list of dates (if any) inscribed on the building:

Nicolaci Palace (Villadorata) number 41
1737, the earliest date appearing on any Netinese palace, is inscribed over its doorway, indicating that the main façade of the palace facing via Nicolaci was built at that time. A second part of the palace facing Via Cavour is far more restrained and clumsy in style. The courtyard side of this section bears the date 1765. The 'U' plan of the palace, and its large windows and elaborate balconies, are typical of Netinese palace architecture. The particularly ornate carved balconies of the façade of the palace make it one of the most interesting in the city.

Rau Palace (Ferla) number 46c
Now partially occupied by the Banco di Sicilia and tenants and descendants of the Ferla family. The palace was entirely redecorated in the nineteenth and twentieth centuries. Its most interesting feature is the southern façade facing Via Ducezio which incorporates a central three-bay loggia.

Di Lorenzo Palace (Castelluccio) number 47
The date 1782 written over the portal of the palace seems to coincide with the Neo-classical frigidity of its façade. In the small courtyard two plaques from the seventeenth century removed from Noto Antica can be seen. The interior of the palace was remodelled in the nineteenth and twentieth centuries.

Landolina Palace (S. Alfano) number 42
Date over portal 1748? Neo-classical façade mixed with baroque elements. The courtyard of the palace shows the building was constructed in two separate campaigns. The Tuscan piers on the north side of the main block have been discontinued and a whole new programme begun. The rectangular inner courtyard also has a small private garden which was built in a third campaign. The attic on the façade of the building was added in the nineteenth century.

Trigona Palace (Cannicarao) number 44b
A two-family palace designed to appear as a single unified dwelling. 'U' plan, with projections opening up to the south. One of the most interesting buildings in Noto. Date over the entrance 1781, seems to be in keeping with its style. The site it occupies was vacant when Labisi drew his veduta. The semi-circular garden wall, and the eastern raised garden date from the nineteenth century. The north-eastern part of the façade is not identical to the rest, which might indicate that it was built at a later date. It is possible that Bernardo Labisi was the architect of this portion of the palace or of the palace as a whole. He is called the architect in a document of 1791 (Canale, p. 298). But in the same document a 'cornicione antico' is mentioned, perhaps indicating an earlier construction phase which terminated before Labisi became architect. Labisi therefore may not have been the sole architect of the building. If he was the architect he studiously reproduced a Gagliardesque ornamental treatment. The lower part of the palace façade on Via Cavour and the bottom of the entrance itself were added when the street was lowered. The original building's ornament shows signs of Gagliardi's hand, or the hand of someone copying his style.

Impellizzeri Palace (S. Giacomo) number 45[1]
Date of 1752 over doorway seems correct. Neo-classical façade. Rectangular plan. The interior has been completely remodelled.

Modica Palace number 42
Completely remodelled in nineteenth century Neo-Baroque

Battaglia Palace number 56
High Baroque eighteenth century palace on a rectangular plan. A document of 1733 specifies Rosario Gagliardi as 'architetto' (Canale, p. 276).

Astuto Palace number 45a
Like the Trigona palace this one is not present in the Labisi veduta. 'U' plan with garden in rear (north). One of the most beautiful palaces in Noto, it seems to have been the work of either Paolo Labisi or Vincenzo Sinatra.

Bibliography

Accascina, M. *Profilo dell'architettura di Messina dal 1660 al 1800.* Rome, 1964.

Agnello, G. *I Vermexio.* Florence, 1959.

'Una Pompei siciliana: Netum: Noto Antica'. *L'illustrazione Vaticana*, 1938, 823–26.

Agnello, G., and Agnello, S. *Siracusa barocca.* Caltanissetta-Rome, 1961.

Agnello, S. L. 'La rinascita edilizia a Siracusa dopo il terremoto del 1693', *Archivio Storico Siciliano*, Series III, IV, 1950–1, 449–75; and V, 1952–3, 109–38.

'Un ignorato architetto del secolo XVIII: Luciano Ali'. *Atti del VIII convegno nazionale di storia dell' architettura*, Caserta, 1953; Rome, 1956; 213–20.

Airaghi, C. *Una Pompei medievale.* Milano, 1894.

Amari, M. *Storia dei Musulmani in Sicilia.* 5 vols. Catania, 1937.

Amato, G. *Studii et Opere.* 6 vols. MS Museo Nazionale di Archeologia, Palermo, n.d.

Amato, P. *La nuova pratica di prospettiva.* 2 vols. Palermo, 1714 and 1733.

Amico, G. B. *L'architetto practico.* 2 vols. Palermo, 1726 and 1750.

Amico, V. *Dizionario topografico della Sicilia.* 2 vols. Translated by DiMarzo. Palermo, 1856.

Lexicon Topographicum Siculum. 5 vols. Palermo, 1757.

Arezzo Prado, V. *Cenni storici sugli avvenimenti netini.* Noto, 1862.

Atti e Memorie, Istituto per lo Studio e la Valorizzazione di Noto Antica, Noto, Anno I, 1970.

Atti e Memorie, Istituto per lo Studio e la Valorizzazione di Noto Antica, Noto, Anno II, 1971.

Atti e Memorie, Istituto per lo Studio e la Valorizzazione di Noto Antica, Noto, Anno III, 1972.

Auria, V. *Historia cronologica delli Signori Vicere di Sicilia (1409–1697).* Palermo, 1697.

Balsamo, F. *Una visita a Noto la città d'oro*, Noto, 1973.

Balsamo, P. *Giornale del viaggiò fatto in Sicilia e particolarmente nella Contea di Modica.* Palermo, 1809.

Sulla istoria moderna del Regno di Sicilia: memorie segrete. Palermo, 1848.

Bartells, J.-H. *Briefe über Kalabrien und Sizilien.* 3 vols. Riga, 1793.

Bellafiore, G. *La civiltà artistica della Sicilia.* Florence, 1963.

La Maniera italiana in Sicilia. Palermo, 1963.

Benevolo, L. *The Architecture of the Renaissance.* 2 vols. Boulder, Colorado, 1978.

Biagi, L. 'Giacamo Amato e la sua posizione nell'architettura palermitana'. *L'Arte*, XVII, 1939, 29–48.

Blunt, A. *Sicilian Baroque.* London, 1968.

Boëthius, A. *The Golden House of Nero.* Michigan, 1960.

Boglino, L. *I manoscritti della Biblioteca Comunale di Palermo.* Palermo, 1884–1900.

La Sicilia Sacra. Palermo, 1900.

Bonfiglio Piccone, C. *Il Santuario di S. Corrado in Noto.* Noto, 1888.

La Chiesa del Crocifisso. MS Biblioteca Comunale di Noto, n.d.

La Famiglia Sortino. MS Biblioteca Comunale di Noto, n.d.

Santa Maria della Scala. Noto, 1894.

Borch, C. de. *Lettres sur la Sicile et sur l'ile de Malte, écrites en 1777 pour servir de supplément au voyage de Mr. Brydone.* 2 vols. Turin, 1782.

Boscarino, S. *Studi e rilievi di architettura siciliana.* Messina, 1961.

Vicende urbanistiche di Catania. Catania, 1966.

Bottari, S. 'Contributi alla conoscenza dell'architettura del Settecento in Sicilia', *La Giara*, IV, 1955, 14–27; *id.*, *Palladio*, VIII, 1958, 69–77.

La cultura figurativa in Sicilia. Messina-Florence, 1954.

Boyer, F. 'Les promenades publiques en Italie du centre et du sud au XVIIIe siècle', *La Vie Urbaine*, IV, 1960, 130ff.

Brandi, C. 'Itinerari architettonici', *L'immagine*, 1948, 450–2; 1949, 165–74.

Bresc, E. 'Il casale suburbano e la sua eredità: l'esempio di Noto' in *Il problema Siciliano dei villaggi abbandonati nel Medioevo*, proceedings of the Gruppo Ricerche Archeologia Medioevale, Palermo, 1972, pp. 7–9.

Brydone, P. *A Tour through Sicily and Malta.* 2 vols. London, 1773.

Burgigny, J. de. *Histoire générale de Sicile.* The Hague, 1745.

Burgos, A. *Lettera per le notizie dei danni cagionati in Sicilia da' tremuoti a 9 e 11 gennaio 1693 con una Elegia in fine.* Palermo-Naples, 1693.

Calandra, E. *Breve storia dell'architettura in Sicilia.* Bari, 1938.

Callejo y Angulo, P. del. *Description de l'isle de Sicile, et de ses côtes maritimes, avec les plans de toutes ses forteresses, nouvellement tirés . . .* Vienna, 1734.

Canale, C. G. *Noto – La struttura continua della città tardo-barocca.* Palermo, 1976.

Capitula Regni Siciliae. Palermo, 1741.

Caracciolo, E. 'La ricostruzione della Val di Noto', *Quaderno della Facoltà di Architettura dell'Università di Palermo.* No. 6, 1964, 40–52.

Carlyle, M. *The Awakening of Southern Italy.* London, 1962.

Caronia Roberti, S. *Venanzio Marvuglia.* Palermo, n.d.

Caruso, G. B. *Memorie istoriche di quanto è accaduto in Sicilia.* Palermo, 1744.

Cassone, F. *Osservazioni intorno al basolamento del Corso Vittorio Emanuele in Noto.* Noto, 1875.

Castonius, Maria. *Horografia universalis seu scrittoricum omnium planorum horizontalium, tum verticalum, tum inclinatorum, tum portatilium, gnomonice nova metodo . . .* Palermo, 1728.

Catalogo alfabetico della Biblioteca Comunale. Noto, 1889.

Cavallari-Murat, A. *Forma urbana ed architettura nella Torino barocca.* 2 vols. Istituto di Architettura Tecnica del Politecnico di Torino. Turin, 1968.

Corboz, A. *Invention de Carouge 1772–1792.* Lausanne, 1968.

Cugno, L. 'Episodi storici e cronologici sulla ricostruzione della nuova Noto'. *Città di Noto, Bollettino del Comune*, Jan., 1955, no. 5, 5–7; Feb., 1955, no. 8, 6–7; March, 1955, no. 10, 8–9.

De la Croix, H. 'Military Architecture and the Radial City Plan in Sixteenth-Century Italy'. *Art Bulletin*, XLII, 4, 1960, 263–90.

'Palmanova, A Study in Sixteenth-Century Urbanism'. *Saggi e Memorie di Storia dell'Arte*, 5, 1966, 23–41.

'The Literature on Fortification in Renaissance Italy'. *Technology and Culture*, IV, 1, 1963, 30–50.

Denon, V. *Travels through Sicily and Malta.* Perth, 1790.

Voyage en Sicile. Paris, 1788.

De Orchi, M. 'Barocco a Noto'. *Arte Cristiana*, LI, 1963, 21–4.

Di Blasi, L., and Genovesi, F. *Rosario Gagliardi, architetto dell'ingegnosa città di Noto*. Catania, 1972.

Di Blasi e Gambacorta, G. E. *Storia civile del regno di Sicilia*. 17 vols. Palermo, 1811–21.

Storia cronologica de' Vicere, Luogotenenti e Presidenti del Regno di Sicilia, seguita da un'appendice fino al 1842. Palermo, 1842–43.

Di Carlo, E. 'Per la storia della cultura siciliana nel Settecento'. *Il Circolo Giuridico*, Palermo, 1962, 17–28.

Viaggiatori stranieri in Sicilia nei secoli XVIII e XIX. Palermo, 1964.

Dryden, J. *A Voyage to Sicily and Malta*. London, 1776.

Dufour, L., Huet, B., and Raymond, H. *Urbanistique et société baroques*. Institut d'études et de recherches en architecture et urbanisme, Paris, 1977.

Dufourny, L. *Notes rapportées d'un voyage en Sicile fait par lui en 1789*. MS Cabinet des Estampes, Bibliothèque Nationale, Paris.

Emanuele e Gaetani, F. M. *Della Sicilia Nobile*. 2 vols. Palermo, 1754–57.

Falzone, G. *Viaggiatori stranieri in Sicilia fra il '700 e l'800*. Palermo, 1963.

Fischera, F. *G.B. Vaccarini e l'architettura del Settecento in Sicilia*. 2 vols. Rome, 1934.

Fliche, A. *Montpellier*. Paris, 1935.

França, J.-A. *Lisboa pombalina e o iluminismo*. Lisbon, 1965.

Freeman, A. *History of Sicily*. 5 vols. Oxford, 1891.

Gallo, C. 'Arte e monumenti dell'Antica Noto'. *Archivio Storico Siciliano*, V, 1952–53, 7–34.

'Dall'inutile referendum del 1698 circa il sito della riedificanda città di Noto alla definitiva decisione del Cardinale Giudice'. *Archivio Storico Siciliano*, XIX, 1970, 3–111.

'Episodi di anarchia nella Noto del Cinquecento'. *Archivio Storico Siciliano*, XXI, XXII, 195–232.

'Il terremoto del 1693 e l'opera di governo del vicario generale Duca di Camastra'. *Archivio Storico Siciliano*, IV, 1975, 3–21.

'Il trasferimento del capoluogo di provincia da Noto a Siracusa nel 1848', *Archivio Storico Siciliano*, VIII, 1956.

'Noto agli albori della sua rinascita dopo il terremoto del 1693'. *Archivio Storico Siciliano*, XIII, 1964, 1–125.

'Noto dopo il terremoto del 1693, l'acquedotto di Coffitella ed il debito Starabba'. *Archivio Storico Siracusano*, XIII, 1967, 33–64.

'Opere di pubblica utilità e abbellimento in Noto Antica'. *Archivio Storico Siracusano*, XV, 1969, pp. 30–44.

'Problemi ed aspetti della ricostruzione a Noto e nella Sicilia orientale dopo il terremoto del 1693'. *Archivio Storico Siciliano*, XV, 1966, 89–190.

'Una visita pastorale di Monsignor Fortezza a Noto e lo stato della chiesa netina prima del terremoto del 1693'. *Studi in Memoria di Carmelo Sgroi, 1892–1952*. Turin, 1965, 445–476.

'Vicende della ricostruzione di Noto dopo il terremoto del 1693 (1697–1700)'. *Archivio Storico Siciliano*, XVIII, 1968, 1–47.

Gangi, G. 'Contributo alla storia d'una città: Noto'. *Il Vetro*, 1963, 949–956.

'Forma e avventura della città di Noto'. *Palladio*, XVIII, 1968, 133–143.

Il barocco nella Sicilia occidentale. Palermo, 1968.

Il barocco nella Sicilia orientale. Palermo, 1964.

Giuffrè, M. 'Utopie urbane nella Sicilia del '700'. *Quaderni dell' Istituto di Elementi di Architettura e Rilievi dei Monumenti della Facoltà di Architettura di Palermo*, nos. 8–9, December 1966, 41–75.

Miti e realtà dell'urbanistica siciliana. Palermo, 1969.

Gourbillon, M. *Travels in Sicily and to Mount Etna in 1819*. London, 1820.

Guarini, G. *Architettura Civile*. 2 vols. Turin, 1737.

Guastella, S. 'Chiese che parlano'. *Città di Noto, Bollettino della Città*, August, 1961, 28–33.

Gubernale, G. *Brevi cenni sulla città di Avola*. Modica, 1910.

Noto la ingegnosa. Milan, 1927.

Guglielmini, P. D. *Catania distrutta*. Palermo, 1695.

Guido, M. *Sicily: An Archaeological Guide*. London, 1967.

Gutkind, E. A. *Urban Development in Southern Europe: Italy and Greece. International History of City Development*, IV. London, 1969.

Hager, J. *Reise von Warschau über Wien nach der Hauptstadt Siziliens*. Vienna, 1795.

Hager, W. 'Guarinis Theatinerfassade in Messina'. *Das Werk des Künstlers*, 1960, 230–40.

Hittorff, J. J., and Zanth, L. *L'architecture moderne de la Sicile*. Paris, 1835.

Holst, H. P. *Sicilianische Novellen und Skizzen*. Leipzig, 1855.

Houel, J. *Voyage pittoresque des isles de Sicile, de Lipari et de Malte*. 4 vols. Paris, 1782–7.

Ide, J. J. 'Noto – the Perfect Baroque City'. *Journal of the Royal Institute of British Architects*, no. 66, 1958, 11–15.

Indagine demografica, scolastica e socio-economica svolta nel Comune di Noto. Progetto C/4, Ufficio studi e programmazione, Provveditorato agli Studi di Siracusa, 1963.

Labat, P. *Voyages en Espagne et en Italie*. 8 vols. Paris, 1730.

Labisi, P. *La scienza dell'architettura civile*. MS Biblioteca Comunale di Noto, 1773, IV.

LaMantia, V. *Antiche consuetudini delle città di Sicilia*. Palermo, 1900.

Lapidus, I. M. *Muslim Cities in the Later Middle Ages*. Cambridge, 1967.

Lavedan, P. *Histoire de l'Urbanisme*. 2 vols. Paris, 1959.

Leanti, A. *Lo stato presente della Sicilia*. 2 vols. Palermo, 1761.

Libro Giallo del Comune di Noto. MS Biblioteca Comunale di Noto, *ca.* 1690–1800.

Littara, V. *De Rebus Netinis*. Palermo, 1593.

Storia di Noto Antica dalle origini al 1593 (De Rebus Netinis). Translated by F. Balsamo, Rome, 1970.

Lojacono, P. 'La ricostruzione dei centri della Val di Noto dopo il terremoto del 1693'. *Palladio*, 1964, 59–74.

Lotz, W. 'Italienische Plätze des 16. Jhs.'. *Jahrbuch der Max-Planck Gesellschaft*, 1968, 41–60.

Mack Smith, D. *Medieval Sicily, A History of Sicily*. II. New York, 1968.

Modern Sicily, A History of Sicily. III. New York, 1968.

Magdaleno, R. *Secretaria de estado, reino de la dos Sicilias, siglo XVIII*. Valladolid, 1956.

Marvuglia, G. V. *Elementa di architettura*. MS Biblioteca Comunale, Palermo, n.d.

Masi, G. *Teoria e pratica di architettura civile per istruzione della gioventù specialmente romana, dedicata all'illustrissimo Signore Gaspare Conte di Carpegna*. Rome, 1788.

Meli, F. 'Degli architetti del senato di Palermo nei secoli XVII e XVIII'. *Archivio Storico per la Sicilia*, 1938–39, IV–V, 305–407.
Minissi, F. *Aspetti dell'architettura religiosa del Settecento in Sicilia*. Rome, 1958.
Mols, R. *Introduction à la démographie historique des villes d' Europe du XIVe au XVIIIe siècle*. 2 vols. Louvain, 1955.
Mongitore, A. *Biblioteca Storica e Letteraria di Sicilia*. ed. G. di Marzo, Palermo, 1871, VII.
Mori, A. 'Sulla formazione di nuovi centri abitati in Sicilia negli ultimi quattro secoli'. *Rivista Geografica Italiana*, Anno XXVII, Fasc. IX–XII, Sept.–Dec. 1920, 149–83.
Morini, M. *Atlante di storia dell'urbanistica*. Milan, 1963.
Murè Ruiz, I. and Leante, G. *In memoria di Corrado Nicolaci Principe di Villadorata*. Noto, 1902.

Napoli, T. M. *Breve ristretto dell'architettura militare e fortificazione offensiva e difensiva*. Palermo, 1723.
Notizie di alcuni privilegi del secolo decimoquinto in favore della città di Noto. MS Biblioteca Comunale di Palermo, 18th century.

Passarello, G. *Guida della città di Noto*. Noto, 1962.
La chiesa del Crocifisso. Noto, 1961.
Netum ante Christum natum. Noto, 1962.
Noto, guida della città (2nd ed.). Catania, 1970.
Personalità netine di tutti i tempi. Catania, 1969.
Santa Maria del Carmelo in Noto. Ragusa, 1961.
Pecora, A. 'Insediamento e dimora rurale nella regione degli Iblei'. *Quaderni di Geografia umana per la Sicilia e la Calabria*, IV, 1959.
Pirri, R. *Chronologia Regum penes quos Siciliae fuit imperium post exactos Saracenos*. Palermo, 1630.
Sicilia Sacra Disquisitionibus et Nobilis Illustrata. Palermo, 1733.
Pisani, N. *Barocca in Sicilia*. Syracuse, 1958.
Noto – Barocco e opera d'arte. Syracuse, 1950.
Noto la città d'oro. Syracuse, 1953.
Pitrè, G. *Palermo nel Settecento*. Palermo, n.d.
Policastro, G. *Catania nel Settecento*. Catania, 1950.
Pontieri, E. *Il tramonto del baronaggio siciliano*. Florence, 1943.
'Sulla distribuzione della popolazione in Sicilia nel secolo XVIII', *Atti del XI Congresso Geografico Italiano*, Naples, 1930, II, 299–308.
Popelier, F. 'Noto ville baroque de Sicile'. *Gazette des Beaux-Arts*, no. 59, 1962, 81–92.
Pragmaticarum Regni Siculae. 3 vols. Palermo, 1636–1700.
Pragmaticarum Regni Siculae. 2 vols. Palermo, 1773.
Privitera, F. *Dolorosa Tragedia rappresentata nel Regno di Sicilia, nella città di Catania*. Catania, 1695.
Puglisi, C. *Cronica della città di Noto*. MS Biblioteca Comunale di Noto, n.d.
MS donato alla Biblioteca di Noto. MS Biblioteca Comunale di Noto, 1871–1901.

Riedesel, J. H. *Travels through Sicily and that part of Italy formerly called Magna Graecia and a tour through Egypt*. Translated by J. B. Forster. London, 1773.
Rodolico, F. *Le pietre delle città d'Italia*. Florence, 1953.
Russo Ferruggia, S. *Storia della città di Noto*. Noto, 1838.

Saint-Non, R. de. *Voyage pittoresque ou description des royaumes de Naples et de Sicile*. 4 vols. Paris, 1781–86.
San Martino de Spucches, F. *La Storia dei feudi e de' titoli nobiliari di Sicilia*. 12 vols. Palermo, 1927.
Santocono Russo, G. 'Precisazioni sull'architettura barocca di Noto'. *Palladio*, XVIII, 1968, 145–54.
'Rosario Gagliardi e la ricostruzione di Noto', *Città di Noto*, Aug. 1964, 42–45.
Savioli, G. 'Le colonizzazioni in Sicilia nei secoli XVI e XVII'. *Vierteljahrschrift für Social und Wirtschaftsgeschichte* (Leipzig), Band I, 1903, 71–79.
Scarafoni, C. S. 'L'antico statuto dei Magistri Stratarum e altri documenti relativi a quella magistratura'. *Archivio della R. Società Romana di Storia Patria*, L, 1927, 239–308.
Scarfe, L. 'Noto and the Villas of Bagheria'. *Motif*, IX, 1962, 31–46.
Scavizza, C. P. 'Le condizioni per lo sviluppo dell'attività edilizia a Roma nel secolo XVIII: la legislazione'. *Studi Romani*, XVII, 1969, 160–70.
Schiaparelli, L. 'Alcuni documenti dei Magistri Aedificium Urbis . . .'. *Archivio della R. Società Romana di Storia Patria*, XXV, 1902, 5–60.
Schudt, L. *Italienreisen im 17. und 18. Jahrhundert, Römische Forschungen der Bibliotheca Hertziana*. XV. Vienna-Munich, 1959.
Scina, D. *Prospetto della storia litteraria di Sicilia nel secolo decimottavo*. Palermo, 1859.
Scuderi, V. *Architettura e Architetti barocchi del trapanese*. Trapani, n.d.
L'opera architetturale di Giovanni Biagio Amico, 1684–1754'. *Palladio*, XI, 1961, 56–65.
Sicilia, Guida d'Italia del Touring Club Italiano. Milan, 1968.
Singer, C. (ed.). *History of Technology*. 5 vols. Oxford, 1957.
Sitwell, O. *Discursions*. London, 1931.
Sitwell, S. *Southern Baroque Revisited*. London, 1967.
Stella, M. 'L'architetto Angelo Italia'. *Palladio*, XVIII, 1968, 155–76.
Stolberg, F. L. *Reise in Deutschland, der Schweiz, Italien, und Sizilien*. 4 vols. Koenigsburg-Leipzig, 1794.
Swinburne, A. *Travels in the Two Sicilies*. 4 vols. London, 1790.
Sylos-Labini (ed.). *Problemi dell'economia siciliana*. Milan, 1966.

Tafaro, C. *Notizie storico-religiose e civili dell'antica e moderna città di Noto*. MS Biblioteca Comunale di Noto, *ca.* 1890–*ca.* 1940.
Tafuri, M. *L'architettura del manierismo nel Cinquecento europeo*. Rome, 1966.
Tedeschi, A. *Comentari sacro-politici dell'antica ingegnosa città di Noto*. MS Biblioteca Comunale di Noto, 1780.
Testa, F. *Capitula Regni Sicilae quae ad hodiernum diem lata sunt, edita cura eiusdem regni Deputatorum*. 2 vols. Palermo, 1743.
Titone, V. *Economia e politica nella Sicilia del Sette e Ottocento*. Palermo, 1947.
La Sicilia spagnuola. Mazara, 1948.
Tobriner, S. 'Noto's Cassaro, an Eighteenth Century Sicilian Street'. *Journal of the Society of Architectural Historians*, XXXIII, No. 2, May 1974, 169.
The Architecture and Urbanism of Noto, an 18th Century Sicilian City. Ph.D. Dissertation, Harvard University, Cambridge, Mass., 1971.
Torres Balbas, L. et al. *Resumen historico del urbanismo en España*. Madrid, 1954.
Tortora, F. *Breve notizia della città di Noto prima e dopo il terremoto del 1693*. ed. C. Bonfiglio Piccione, Noto, 1891.
Breve notizia della città di Noto . . . ed. F. Balsamo, Noto, 1972.
Tuzet, H. *La Sicile au XVIIIe siècle vue par les voyageurs étrangers*. Strasbourg, 1955.

Valléry-Radot, J. *Le recueil de plans d'édifices de la Compagnie de Jésus conservé à la Bibliothèque Nationale de Paris*. Rome, 1960.

Valussi, G. *La casa rurale nella Sicilia occidentale, Ricerche sulle dimore rurali in Italia*. XXIV, Florence, 1968.
Volume secondo sopra le querende a carico de' deputati de'acqua e strade della città di Noto. MS Biblioteca Comunale di Noto, 1750–95.

Wolff, C. *Elementa Matheseos Universae*. 4 vols. Geneva, 1732.
Elemanta Meteseos Universe. MS Biblioteca Comunale di Noto, IV, 1746.

Zappulla, N. *La Cattedrale di Noto*. Noto, 1963.
Ziino, V. *Contributi allo studio dell'architettura del '700 in Sicilia*. Palermo, 1950.

Index

Acagna, Ferdinando 52
Accademia degli Trasformati 174
Agnello, G. 13, 219 (*n.* 19)
Agriculture 34–5, 42, 49, 200
Alberti, Leone Battista 206 (*n.* 18)
Alleys 74 (*fig.* 3) (*pls.* 25–6), 119, 120, 121, 206 (*n.* 21), 214 (*nn* 30, 31)
Vico Trigona 119 (*fig.* 3) (*pl.* 65)
Amalienburg 176
Amari, Michele 205 (*n.* 7)
Amico, Giovan Bagio 144, 145, 170, 197
S. Anna (Palermo) 167
Amico, Vito 40, 205 (*nn.* 4, 5, 6)
Anchorage 25
Antigua Guatemala 43, 203
Antonioni, Michelangelo 11, 205 (*n.* 3)
Apulia 125
Arcades 24, 103, 207 (*n.* 25), 215 (*n.* 83)
Architects of Noto 142–3, 218 (*n.* 1)
borrowing of designs 139–140
see also individual architects
Arezzo Prado, V. 174, 176, 181, 222 (*n.* 32)
Aristocrats in Noto 20, 51, 52, 97, 98, 99, 114, 118, 181, 203, 204
number of households 114, 205 (*n.* 8), 216 (*n.* 29)
patronage by 108, 112, 205 (*n.* 9)
Asinara River 21, 29, 33, 36 (*pl.* 10), 37, 38, 46, 56, 72, 73, 208 (*n.* 43)
Asmundo, Giuseppe 28, 39, 43, 46, 47, 48, 54, 55, 208 (*nn.* 19, 25), 209 (*nn.* 5, 8), 211 (*n.* 16), 228 (*Docs.* 6, 7)
as surveyor 57–8, 60, 61, 65
Assisi 24
Astuto family
collections of 118, 217 (*n.* 45)
palace 99, 118, 123, 139, 181, 244
Augusta 40, 50, 229 (*Doc.* 9)
Austria 172
Avola 29, 30, 33 (*pl.* 10), 72, 108, 203, 204, 209 (*n.* 65)
fortifications 40
leasing of Noto 38
plan of 40 (*pls.* 11, 12), 61, 62, 104
siting of new city 32–3, 35, 229–30 (*Docs.* 1, 2)
transferred 29 (*Map* 2), 30, 32
Aymard, Maurice 210 (*n.* 33)

Bagheria 13
Balconies 97, 118, 123, 126, 132
Baroque architecture and ornament 11, 24, 86, 89, 132, 139, 140, 144, 151, 152, 156, 161, 162, 164, 170, 172, 176, 190, 191, 202, 203, 204
(Roman) influence in Noto 89, 126, 193, 201
Bath 107
Battaglia Palace 118, 143, 184, 244
Bellofiore, Corrado (head parish priest) 50–51
Belluso, Domenico 236–7 (*Doc.* 9)
Benedictines 112, 159, 192, 206 (*n.* 19)
Bernini, Gianlorenzo 24, 79, 89, 164, 166, 179
Blondel, Jacques François 176
Blunt, Anthony 13
Boëthius, Axel 122
Boglino, L. 205 (*n.* 9)
Borromini, Francesco 24, 85, 113, 126, 131, 159, 162, 170
Boscarino, Salvatore 13
Bottari, Stefano 14
Bourbons: Naples 202
Spanish 102
Braunfels, W. 205 (*n.* 9), 206 (*n.* 18)
Bresc, E. 205 (*n.* 8)
Buccheri 121
Builders and workmen: contracts 231 (*Docs.* 7, 9, 10), 232–3 (*Docs.* 13–26 *passim*), 234 (*Docs.* 3, 4, 5), 237 (*Docs.* 3, 4, 5)
Bulding materials
concrete 202
earth 117
plaster 122, 123
rubble 119, 122, 123, 217 (*n.* 49)
sandstone 122
stone (*pietra d'intaglio*) 119, 122, 123, 202, 217 (*nn.* 54, 55)
(re-use of) 66, 122, 212 (*n.* 5), 239 (*Doc.* 3)
stucco 134, 232–3 (*Doc.* 21a)
timber 66, 212 (*n.* 4)
Buildings, Public, and Monuments (Noto Nuova)
Bishop's Office 56, 211 (*n.* 11)
Bishop's Palace 118, (*pls* 82, 83, 84), 217 (*n.* 40)
Casa del Refugio, *see* Monte di Pietà
Cavalry quarters 207
City Hall 56, 87, 125, 172, 173 (*Pl.* 141, *figs.* 7, 8), 174 (*pls.* 143, 144), 179, 221 (*nn.* 14, 15, 16), 234 (*Doc.* 2), 235 (*Doc.* 11) (origins of design) 174, 176, 177, 179
City Hospital 56, 211 (*n.* 11)
City Library 181, 201
Civic and public gardens 73, 76, 77, 214 (*n.* 40)
(Villetta Ercole) 94, 97
Fountain of Hercules 86 (*Pl.* 39), 89 (*pl.* 46), 96, 142, 215 (*n.* 61), 237 (*ff.* 3, 4, 44, 45)
Jail 71, 211 (*n.* 9)
Madonna Statue 58, 83 (*map* 5), 86
Market Place 96–7, 240
Monte di Pietà 56, 101, 112 (*pl.* 19), 124, 132 (*pl.* 55), 143, 207 (*n.* 23), 211 (*n.* 10)
schools 202
Town Clock 56, 240
Triumphal Arch of Ferdinand II 76, 79 (*pl.* 30), 80, 81, 97, 201
Buontalenti, Bernardo 159
Burgigny, J. de 205 (*n.* 2)
Buscemi 29, 31, 121
Busulmone, fuedo of 29, 36

Caltagirone 99, 143
Camastra, Giuseppe Lanza, *Duke of* 28, 29, 45, 46, 48, 49, 204 (*n.* 17)
accomplishments of 27, 229 (*Doc.* 10)
and rebuilding of Noto 28, 37, 38, 43, 55, 56, 208 (*nn.* 25, 28), 227 (*Doc.* 3), 228 (*Doc.* 7)
site decision of Noto 29, 208 (*n.* 28)
Canale, Cleofo G. 14
Cannicarao, *Marchese* 197, 236 (*Doc.* 9)
Caprarola 125
Caracciolo, E. 13
Capodicaso, Antonio 172
Caramuel, Juan 180, 222 (*n.* 30)
Carlentini, *see* Lentini
Carouge 12, 107, 203
Carriages and carriage rides 97, 98, 99
Caruso, G. B. 205 (*n.* 2)
Cataneo, Pietro 40, 63 (*Pl.* 14), 212 (*n.* 34)
Catania 13, 21, 22, 23, 29, 76, 81, 125, 192, 204, 206 (*n.* 15)
architecture of 125 (*pl.* 67), 140, 167, 204
earthquake in 25, 26, 207 (*n.* 4)
reconstruction of 28, 104, 106, 203
revolt in 27
site, refusal to abandon 30–31
Cavallari-Murat, Augusto 12–13
Charles III (Bourbon) 112, 113
Chinoiserie 134–5 (*pls.* 88–9), 204, 218 (*n.* 11)
Churches (Noto Antica)
S. Crocifisso (S.M. de Castello) 23,56, 206 (*n.* 17)
Jesuit College 24
S. Nicolò (Chiesa Madre) 23, 56, 206 (*n.* 19)
parish churches 206 (*n.* 19)
Churches, Convents, Monasteries (Noto Nuova)
Appendix 1, map 7
façades of 131–2
number of 111, (*map* 7), 216 (*n.* 5)
planning and form 113–14, 216 (*n.* 10) (*nn.* 22, 25)
S.Agata (Labisi) 51, 66, 100, 131 (*pl.* 91), 134, 143, 184, 197 (*pl.* 175), 198, 207, 236–7 (*Doc.* 9)
interior 198
S. Antonio di Padova 100, 202, 243
PP. Benefratelli di Dio 101 (*pl.* 19)
S. Calogero 143
S. Camillo, see Crociferi
Capuchin 73, 76, 243
S. Carlo Borromeo (Jesuit college) 60, 71, 91 (*pl* 45), 93, 113, 124, (*pl.* 80), 132 (*pl.* 47), 139, 143, 161, 170, (*pls.* 47, 140), 171, 204, 213 (*n.* 21), 221, (*n.* 54), 231 (*Doc.* 10)
Carmelites 97, 242
S. Caterina 184
S. Chiara (Gagliardi) 60, 66, 70, 71, 81, 83, 86, (*pl.* 38), 89 (*map* 5), 113 (*pls.* 123, 126, *figs.* 5, 6), 114, 124 (*pl.* 37), 131 (*pl.* 127), 132, 140, 143, 159–164, 166, 171, 186, 201, 213 (*n.* 19), 241
construction, history 220 (*nn.* 40–42, 232–3), (*Doc.* 21a), 232
conversions 160
dormitory 159, (*pls.* 124–126, *figs.* 5, 6)
stairs 159 (*figs.* 5, 6)
church of (S. Maria Assunta) 160–64
attic 164 (*pl.* 107)
bell tower 161 (*pl.* 127)
capitals, design 162
exterior 160, 161
façade 162 (*pl.* 129)
nave 164 (*pl.* 180)
oval ground plan 164
portal 160–61
windows 161
Chiesa Madre *see* S. Nicolò
Crociferi Fathers, House of (Labisi) 70 (*pl.* 19), 71, 95, 99, 112, 114 (*pls.* 160, 161), 125, 179 (*pls.* 162–68), 181, 184, 186 (*map* 7), 202, 204, 223 (*ns.* 42, 43, 56), 224 (*n.* 6)
collapse of part 196, 202
construction changes 180 (*pls.* 156, 157, 165, 166, 181)
plans and designing 184 (*pl.* 160), 186 (*pls.* 162–65), 193 (*pls.* 171, 172, 173,), 195–6
refectory 196
staircases, 187 (*pl.* 161)
Church of (S. Camillo) 180 (*pl.* 174), 190–91 (*pls.* 160, 167, 168)
substitute for 196 (*pl.* 174)
SS Crocifisso 54, 55, 56, 64, 65, 66, 113, 134, 140, 143, 167, 168 (*pl.* 138), 171, 206
construction, history 221 (*n.* 51), 231 (*Doc.* 7)
façade 168
plan 168
S. Domenico (Gagliardi) 113, 125 (*pl.* 48), 132 (*pl.* 52), 139 (*pl.* 131), 143, 164–67 (*pls.* 132–4, 135–7), 171, 211 (*n.* 5), 221 (*n.* 50), 232 (*Doc.* 20)
construction, history 220 (*n.* 48), 221 (*n.* 50), 232–3 (*Docs.* 15, 25)
façade 164, 166–7
plan 113, 167
tower 167
S. Filippo Neri (oratory) 99, 124 (*pl.* 76), 179, 184, 201, 222 (*n.* 26), 234 (*Doc.* 5), 235 (*Doc.* 4)
S. Francesco 66, 81, 83, 124 (*pl.* 78), 131 (*pl.* 90), 179, 243
S. Francesco di Paola 46, 55, 179, 202
S. Giovanni di Dio 131
S. Girolamo 99 (*pl.* 54a), 132, 222 (*n.* 25)
S. Isidoro 131
Jesuit college, *see* S. Carlo Borromeo
S. Maria dell'Arco (Gagliardi) 112, 131, 132, 143, 152–59 (*pls.* 117–119), 161, 172, 202
church of 154, 232 (*Doc.* 18)
construction, history 219–20 (*n.* 37), 231 (*Doc.* 8), 233 (*Docs.* 22, 23)
doors 156 (*pls.* 121–22)
façade 154 (*pls.* 119–20)
interior 156 (*pl.* 123), 179
portal 154, 156 (*pl.* 119)
stucco design 156, 159, 162, 233 (*Docs.* 21a, 216)
tower 161
S. Maria Assunto, see S. Chiara
S. Maria del Castello, see SS Crocifisso
S. Maria del Carmine 60, 69, 70, 99, 113, 125 (*pl.* 79), 132 (*pl.* 54b), 134 (*pls.* 86–7), 139, 140 (*pls.* 95–6), 143, 181, 213 (*n.* 18), 239 (*Doc.* 5), 244
S. Maria di Gesù 46, 55, 179 (*pl.* 92), 244
S. Michele 97, 202, 224 (*n.* 5)
Montevergine 51, 97, 99, 179, 222 (*n.* 251, 239 (*Doc.* 4)
S. Nicolò, (Chiesa Madre) 45, 46, 54 (*map* 4), 55, 56, 62, 69, 70, 87

(*pl.* 41), 91, 113, 132 (*pl.* 93), 139 (*pls.* 94, 96), 140, 143, 168, 179, 218 (*n.* 12), 219 (*n.* 18)
façade 169 (*pl.* 96)
plan 169
S. Pietro 99
Repentite 207
SS. Salvatore 60, 81, 86, 89, 124 (*pl.* 36), 132, 143, 179, 186, 201 (*pl.* 176), 202 (*pl.* 177), 221 (*n.* 53), 224 (*ns.* 4, 5), 234 (*Docs.* 3, 7), 242
redesign of 83, 84 (*pl.* 36), 85
tower 169 (*pl.* 139), 170
S. Tommaso Apostolo, 207
SS. Trinità 66, 113
Churriguera, José Benito 103
Cistercians 112, 153
Clergy 20, 51, 52
Colle val d'Elsa 24
Comiso 143
Corboz, André 12
Coreglia 24
Corrado, *Saint* 43
arc of 43, 54, 209 (*n.* 3), 216 (*n.* 11)
Corteranzo
Chapel of S. Luigi 145
Craig, James 107
Cugno, Lucia 14, 206 (*n.* 16), 208 (*n.* 25)
Cugno di Vasco 33
Cuvilliés, François 176

De Luca, Giovanni Battista 196
Della Porta, Giacomo 176
Denon, D. V. 77, 110, 205 (*n.* 2)
Descartes, René 192
Di Blasi, G. E. 205 (*n.* 3)
Di Blasi, Luigi 14, 144, 218 (*n.* 8), 219 (*nn.* 20, 23)
Di Lorenzo family (Marchese di Castellucio) 89, 215 (*n.* 75), 235 (*Doc.* 11)
palace 99, 118, 139, 242
Diodorus (Siculus) 205 (*n.* 5)
Dominicans 55, 112
Ducetius, *King* 21, 205 (*n.* 5)
Dufourny, Léon 72, 174, 205 (*n.* 2)
on City Hall 176
on Noto 124
Dürer, Albrecht 125

Earthquakes 11, 12, 25, 26, 27, 30, 33, 66, 195, 196, 203, 205 (*n.* 2), 213 (*nn.* 8, 10), 229 (*Doc.* 9)
and Gagliardi's designs 145, 152, 154
layouts of cities and 29–31, 49, 81
Edinburgh 107

Façades, curved 126, 164–7 *passim*, 218 (*n.* 10)
Falconara, feudo of 29, 35 (*pl.* 5), 208 (*n.* 49)
Falda, Giovanni Battista 125
Fazello, T. 205 (*n.* 4)
Ferdinand III of Sicily 172
Ferla 29
Ferla Palace 119
Ferrerio, R. 125
Finley, M. I. 205 (*n.* 5)
Florence 23, 159
Fontana, Carlo 190, 191
Formenti, Giuseppe (Engineer) 49
map by 58, 60, 102 (*map* 5), 211 (*n.* 17, *n.* 23)
Fosdinovo 24
Franco, José-Augusto 12

Frascati
Villa Aldobrandini 176
Frederick II of Prussia 176, 192
Frederick William I 192
Freeman, A. (205 (*n.* 5)
Fuga, Ferdinando 191

Gagliardi, Agata 172
Gagliardi, Rosario 14, 102, 116, 125, 126, 142–171, 172, 179, 180, 181, 184, 197, 198, 203, 204, 218 (*n.* 8)
and the Baroque 144, 151, 170
beginning of work in Noto 143
career: summary 170–1, 231–3, 237
as City Architect 142
combination of styles 159
conservatism of designs 145
domes 150 (*pls.* 105, 107)
drawings 150–1
façades 150 (*pl.* 109)
fragments of his work 168–9
influence on other architects 143
lack of master plan in Noto 152
and pentagonal design 145 (*pl.* 98), 146
and proportion 144–5
studies of churches 146 (*pls.* 100–5), 150 (*pls.* 108, 109)
treatise on architecture 144–52 *passim*, 167
title page of 144 (*pl.* 97), 219 (*n.* 24)
works in Noto and other cities 143, 152–71, 219 (*n.* 19)
Gallo, Corrado 13, 205 (*nn.* 3, 4, 11)
Gangi, G. 13
Garello, Francisco 107
Gargallo family 184
Genovesi, Francesco 9, 14, 144
Gibellina 31
S. Giovanni detto la Lardia (Hermitage) 29, 33, 38, 72
Giral, Jean 176, 222 (*n.* 18)
Giudice, Cardinal (Viceroy) 52
Giuffré, Maria 9, 13
Gonzales, Joachim 142
Grammichele 29, 31, 104
Gregorini, Domenico 166
Grunemburg, Carlos von (Engineer) 28, 208 (*n.* 20), 227 (*Doc.* 3)
Guarini, Guarino 57, 126, 145, 164, 219 (*n.* 31)
Guépière, Pierre-Louis-Philippe dela 177
Gutkind, E. A. 13

Hapsburgs (Austrian) 102
(Spanish) 27, 102
Helorus 29, 34
Hiroshima 25, 207 (*n.* 6)
Hofer, Paul 14, 214 (*n.* 43), 218 (*n.* 1)
Hospitals (Noto Nuova)
S. Maria della Consolazione 112
S. Maria della Scala 112
S. Teodoro 112
Hyblaean Mountains 21 (*pls.* 1–4), 36

Ide, John J. 11, 14, 205 (*n.* 4)
Impellizzeri family 9
Antonino (Captain of Justice) 28, 29, 43, 47, 215 (*n.* 80)
motives for dissent 48
Palace 100, 102, 123, 124 (*pl.* 77), 242
Tommaso 51, 55, 239 (*Doc.* 2)
Ispica 29, 31, 72, 184, 236 (*Doc.* 8)

Italia, Angelo (Fra) 32, 61–2, 64, 65, 212 (*n.* 33)
plan for Avola 32, 62, 64
Ittar, Stefano 140

Jesuits 112
Jesuit College, see churches, S. Carlo
Jones, Inigo 124
Juntas 32
ecclesiastical 27, 227 (*Doc.* 2)
secular 27, 226 (*Doc.* 2)
Juvarra, Filippo 145, 159, 164, 187 191

Karlsruhe 107

Labisi, Antonio 114
Labisi, Bernardo (Engineer) 142, 159, 201, 218 (*n.* 7), 224 (*n.* 2)
Labisi, Giuseppe 181
Labisi, Paolo 38, 72, 102, 114, 125, 142, 143, 172, 179, 180, 181–98, 204
as architect of Noto 184, 218 (*nn.* 2, 4), 223 (*nn.* 40, 59, 61)
on *capomaestri* 184, 222 (*n.* 36)
on the city 110, 215 (*n.* 1)
grievances of 237 (*Doc.* 10)
influence of Gagliardi 190–1 (*pl.* 169), 193 (*pl.* 170), 194
influence of Wolff 191, 192, 193
map of Noto 67 (*pl.* 53), 95 (*pl.* 53a), 96
scandals on his construction 195 (*pls.* 152–3, 162–4)
and Sinatra 179, 180, 184, 195, 236 (*Docs.* 6, 7)
summary of his work 198, 222 (*n.* 32), (*pp.* 235–8)
treatise on architecture 97, 115, 196, 197, 217 (*n.* 32)
veduta of Noto 66 (*pl.* 17), 67–72 *passim*, (*pls.* 19, 22), 73, 74 (*pl.* 19), 76, 79, 83 (*pl.* 34), 87, 95 (*pl.* 50), 102, 119, 122, 174 (*pl.* 40), 200, 213 (*nn.* 10, 11)
Labisi e Constanzo, Bartoloma 181
La Grassa, Francesco (City Engineer) 220 (*n.* 41)
Lampedusa, Giuseppe di 119
Landolina family 39, 48, 60
chapel of (S. Elia) 60, 168, 212 (*n.* 29)
Francesco Rau e Landolina 117
Giovan Battista Landolina Salonia 60–1, 212 (*n.* 30)
palace (S. Alfano) 117 (*pls.* 45, 74), 118, 128, (*pls.* 73, 74, 75), 181 (*pl.* 151), 212 (*n.* 24)
Lanza, Giuseppe, *see* Camastra, *Duke of*
Leblond, Jean Baptiste Alexandre 10, 211 (*n.* 15)
Lecce 125 (*pl.* 66), 204
Leibnitz, Gottfried Wilhelm von 192
Lentini 203, 228 (*Doc.* 6)
Lévi-Strauss, Claude 76
Lisbon 23, 203
Baixa district 107
earthquakes in 25
rebuilding of 12, 207 (*n.* 5)
Littara, Vincenzo 205 (*nn.* 4, 5)
London 203
Longhena, Baldassare 146
Longhi, Martino (the younger) 150
Louis XIV 27
Loyola 190

Madonna del Marina (plain) 29, 35, (*pls.* 6, 7)
Madrid 103
Malta, Knights of 33
Managua (Nicaragua) 25
Masuccio, Natale 24
Mazza, Antonio 142, 143, 144, 201
Mazza, Corrado 142, 201
Mazza, Giuseppe 9, 144, 219 (*n.* 20)
collections of 144, 219 (*nn.* 20–23)
Messina (city) 21, 145, 192
citadel of 28
earthquake in 25
governor of 52
rebellion in 22, 27, 48
Meti, feudo of the 29, 32, 43–52 *passim*, 208 (*n.* 56), 209 (*n.* 2)
Pianazzo on 33, 43
selected as city site 36–42 *passim*, (*map* 3)
planning on 54–65 *passim*, 66, 71, 74
Michelangelo (Buonarroti) 24, 125, 156, 159, 179, 180
S. Giovanni dei Fiorentini 146
Modica 72
Modica palace 244
Mols, Roger 206 (*n.* 14)
Monte Alveria 20, 21, 23, 38
Montevago 55 (*fig.* 2)
Montpellier 174
Château de la Masson 176
Mussolini, Benito 79

Nancy 108 (*pl.* 62), 204
Naples 108
Neo-classical architecture and decoration 140
Nicolaci family 60, 217 (*nn.* 43, 44)
church (S. Elia) 60
Giacomo, *Baron* 174, 197
library 118, 193, 197
palace 117 (pl. 70), 118, 123, 124 (*pl.* 70), 126 (*pl.* 69), 132, 174, 217 (*n.* 37), 244
Niscemi, Prince of 52
Nochistlan (Mexico) 104 (*pl.* 59a)
Noto Antica 20–42, 72, 98, 108, 113
abandonment of site 25, 31–2, 42, 52
Alagona Palace 24
appearance of 24
as commercial centre 31, 205 (*n.* 11)
convents and monasteries 206 (*nns.* 19, 23)
destruction by earthquake 11, 20, 24, 25, 226 (*Doc.* 1)
Ducetius, King 21, 205 (*nn.* 4, 5)
ecclesiastical history 205 (*n.* 4)
evacuation of old site 43
fortifications 22, 23, 40, 205 (*nn.* 3, 10)
history 205 (*n.* 4)
hospital 206 (*n.* 19)
Institute for Studies of 20, 205 (*n.* 1)
Jesuit college 24
land and water rights 22
Magistrate's Palace 23, 206 (*n.* 18)
Moslem city (comparison) 206 (*n.* 21)
Moslem rule in 205 (*n.* 3), 206 (*n.* 21)
name, origin of 22, 205 (*n.* 6)
Panorama of 24 (*pl.* 3), 206 (*n.* 23)
Patron Saint 43
Plan, overall 24, 209 (*n.* 67)

political importance 21, 205 (*n.* 3)
population 22, 23, 206 (*n.* 13)
Porta della Montagna 206 (*n.* 19)
position on Monte Alveria 21 (*pls.* 1–4)
preservation of 9
privileges 205 (*n.* 8)
products 22–3, 205 (*nns.* 8, 11)
rebuilding 11, 28, 31, 227–8 (*Doc.* 5), 228 (*Doc.* 6)
relocation, and resistance to 12, 20, 25, 36
ruins, re-use of stone 66
Sikels in 21, 205 (*n.* 5)
street pattern of 23
territory 23 (*map* 1)
views of 23 (*pl.* 2), 206 (*nn.* 16, 23)
Noto Nuova 29, 192
accounts (public) 240–1
appearance in 1750's 66–7 (*pl.* 17)
appearance today 67–8 (*pls.* 20, 21), 200–4 *passim*, 240–1
aqueduct (coffitella) 38, 45, 47, 58
(Testa dell'Acqua) 237 (*Doc.* 5)
architecture of 13–14, 126
Avola, lease by 38–9, (*pl.* 10)
axis, north-south 70
Bishop's Office 56, 153, 202
boundaries of 72–3
Camastra and Noto's future 27–8
central core of city 68–9, 70, 76, 214 (*n.* 32)
churches, *see under* churches
City Headquarters, position 27 (*pl.* 2)
Committee on Streets and Water 237–8
earthquake of 1756 195
epidemic of 1693 45, 54, 210 (*n.* 15)
exteriors of buildings 123
fire of 1693 54
fortifications (lack of) 40, 50, 71, 213 (*n.* 23)
housing, upper and middle class 114–16, 202, 240 (*Doc.* 7)
(number of rooms) 115, 123
(social status in) 122–3
(storeys) 66, 115, 116 (*pl.* 63), 122, 213 (*n.* 7)
housing, lower class 119 (*pls.* 25–27), 217 (*n.* 46)
(dating of houses) 119, 217 (*n.* 47)
(description) 119–22
(growth with needs) 122
(heating, lighting, sanitation) 79, 114, 121, 122, 217 (*nn.* 51, 52)
(lofts) 121, 217 (*n.* 51)
(storeys) 122
(and ownership, claims and use) 39, 46, 48, 51, 110, 209 (*nn.* 58–61)
map (anonymous) 67 (*pl.* 53b)
map of 1749 67 (*pl.* 53), 213 (*n.* 13)
map of 1764 66–7 (*pl.* 23), 213 (*n.* 12)
as open city 71–2
open spaces 97
patron saint (S. Corrado) 43, 44, 209 (*n.* 3)
Pianazzo site 29, 37–8, 43, 46, 50, 131 (*map* 7), 210 (*nn.* 13–15)
plan and planning 11, 30, 31, 32, 46, 54–65
(axis) 56 (*maps* 3, 4)
(east-west views) 76
(grid system) 54, 55, 56 (*maps* 3, 4), 57 58, 68, 73, 203
(Italian and European) 102–9 *passim*, 203
(overall plan, 1712) 65
(symmetry of) 104, 106 (*pls.* 60a, 60b)
(two cities division) 73–4, 75
population 11, 45, 66, 101, 205 (*n.* 1), 212 (*n.* 2), 215 (*n.* 79)
preservation and restoration 202
property confiscation 29
as provincial capital 202, 204
religious architecture in 110–14
religious houses established 58, 211 (*n.* 20), 241–3
roads to and from city 42, 51, 72, 209 (*n.* 70), 213–14 (*nn.* 25, 28), 239 (*Docs.* 1, 6)
Senate and Mayors 54–5, 142 (*List*), 238
site: choice, advantages and disadvantages 20, 25, 28, 29, 33–6 *passim*, (*map* 2), 43–52 *passim*, 210 (*nn.* 27, 28, 33)
stylistic unity of 124–40 *passim*
summit 100–2 (*pls.* 21, 25, 26), 210 (*n.* 18)
(Cozza della Fiera) 54, 210 (*n.* 1)
tax accounts and assessment 38, 115, 142, 209 (*n.* 64), 219 (*n.* 5)
tax (ecclesiastical) 47, 210 (*n.* 23)
tribunal on future of Noto 49–52 *passim*
vedute of 66 (*pl.* 17), 67–74) *passim*, 87 (*pl.* 40), 213 (*ns.* 10–11)
water, lack of 38, 45, 47, 54, 208 (*n.* 55)
Nuevo Baztán 103 (*pl.* 58)

Oratory of S. Filippo Neri, see under *Churches*
Orders of architecture 217 (*n.* 1)
composite 124
Corinthian 139, 154
Doric 124, 131, 156, 161, 162, 191, 193 (*pls.* 164, 171)
Ionic 124, 125, 135, 146, 156, 159, 191
Tuscan 124, 131
Ornament and ornamental motifs 125–30
See also Baroque, Neo-Classical, Renaissance, Rococo
Orvieto 24

Padri Conventuali 206 (*n.* 19)
Palaces (Noto Nuova) 117–19) (*map* 8), Appendix 2
decorations 118
façades 114 (*map* 8), 123
interiors 117, 123
S. Alfano, see Landolina
Villadorata 174
Villa Falconara 174, 176 (*pl.* 140)
See also under family names
Palazzolo
S. Michele 201
Palermo 13, 21, 75, 77, 98, 108, 112, 142, 192, 214 (*n.* 36)
earthquake in 25, 26
revolt in 27
S. Anna 126, 167
S.M. dei Miracoli 154
Palladio, Andrea 124, 145, 164
Paredes, Giovanni 95
Parillos, Raimondo 33
Paris 107
Palais Bourbon 176
Passalatqua, Pietro 166
Passarello, Gaetano 9, 14, 205 (*nn.* 3, 5)
Passero, Capo 23, 33, 72
Patte, Pierre 107
Philadelphia 107
Philip II, King of Spain
and city planning 103–4
Piana dei Colli 13
Piazze (Noto Antica)
Piazza Maggiore 23
S. Crocifisso Piano 23
S. Venere 23
Piazze (Noto Nuova) 54, 58, 62 (*map* 6), 213 (*n.* 14)
Calatafimi 54, 210 (*n.* 1)
S. Crocifisso Piano 58, 62, 70, 102
S. Domenico (XVI Maggio) 47 (*map* 6), 54 (*map* 3), 58 (*map* 5), 59, 64, 69, 74 (*pl.* 53), 89, 94 (*pls.* 48, 49, 51, 52), 95, 96, 97, 142, 171, 184, 211 (*n.* 22)
S. Francesco Piano 58, 59 (*map* 5), 62 (*map* 5), 62 (*map* 6), 63, 69, 81–2, 83 (*pl.* 32), 84, 85, 93, 94, 215 (*n.* 50)
main piazza 60, 64, 69, 87–9 (*pls.* 42, 43), 212 (*n.* 26)
Mazzini 102 (*pl.* 56)
Taranto 79 (*pl.* 27)
Piedmont 126, 145
Pietro da Cortona 24, 166
Pignatelli and Dukedom of Terranova 38, 208 (*n.* 57)
archives of 38
Pirri, Rocco 205 (*n.* 4), 206 (*n.* 13)
Pisani, N. 13, 218 (*n.* 8), 220 (*n.* 39)
Pitrè, G. 119
Pizzi, Corrado 195, 236 (*Doc.* 7)
Plato 197
Pombal, Sebastiano José 203
Pontieri, E. 206 (*n.* 13)
Popelier, Françoise 14, 121 (*n.* 16)
Potsdam
Sanssouci 176 (*pls.* 147, 148)
Pozzo, Andrea 193
Puzzo, Ignacio (capomaestro) 143

Ragusa 29 (Ibla), 51, (*fig.* 1), 143, 203
plan 30 (*fig.* 1)
S. Giorgio (Gagliardi) 150 (*pls.* 110–12), 167, 168, 220–21 (*n.* 49)
Raguzzini, Filippo 166, 170
Rainaldi, Carlo 146
Rau, Francesco. *See* Landolina family
Rau Palace 242
Religious houses: scandals 45, 46
Renaissance architecture and decoration 24, 62, 124, 126, 144, 156, 170
Rococo architecture and decoration 85, 132, 134, 151, 170, 172, 180, 181, 193, 198
Rome 24, 204
Baroque architecture in 126
Hospital of S. Gallicano 126, 170
Piazza Navona 89
Piazza del Popolo 91
Piazza S. Ignazio 107
Piazza of St. Peter's 89
S. Anna dei Palafrenieri 113, 164
Sapienza, S. Ivo of the 159
S. Carlo ai Catinari 113
S. Carlo alle Quattro Fontane 170
S. Croce in Gerusalemme 166
Spanish Steps 107
tabernae in 122
Viale della Conciliazione 79
SS. Vincenzo e Anastasio 150
Rosati, Rosato 113
Rumanello, Plain of 29, 36, 208 (*n.* 51)
Russo, Onofrio (stuccoist) 156, 159, 164, 232–3 (*Doc.* 21a)

Saint-Non, R. de 205 (*n.* 2)
St. Petersburg 106–7 (*pl.* 61), 203, 211 (*n.* 15)
San Antonio (Texas) 104 (*pl.* 59b)
San Francisco 25, 207 (*n.* 2)
S. Giovanni detto la Lardia Hermitage 29, 33, 38, 72
Salamanca 103
Santiago (Guatemala) 43–4
rebuilding of 43. See Antigua
Santocono-Russo, Gioacchino 13, 206 (*n.* 19)
Sardinia 172
Savoy, House of 102, 145, 172
Scamozzi, Vincenzo 40, 63
'ideal city' of 63 (*pl.* 16), 64, 107, 211 (*n.* 15), 212 (*n.* 35)
Secondo, Giuseppe 196
Serlio, Sebastiano 125, 145
pentagonal temple of 145 (*pl.* 99), 150, 190
Sicily 11, 12
agriculture in 27
Arab rule in 22, 205 (*n.* 7), 206 (*n.* 21)
architecture and urbanism 13–14
conservatism of 126
culture of 102
domes, Moslem in 24, 207 (*n.* 24)
earthquakes and cities damaged 25, 26 (*map* 1), 27, 29, 31, 207 (*n.* 13), 208 (*n.* 32)
economic conditions in 22, 206 (*n.* 12)
new cities in 42, 211 (*n.* 8)
plantation towns 104
political turmoil 172
Spanish rule ends 172
Sikel people 21, 205 (*n.* 5)
Sinatra, Vincenzo 72, 102, 114, 142, 143, 153, 172–81, 198, 204
as *capomaestro* 172
as tax assessor 117, 179, 221 (*n.* 12), 235 (*Doc.* 12)
and Labisi 179, 180, 184, 195, 196, 236 (*Docs.* 6, 7)
map of Noto 66 (*pl.* 23), 173, 234 (*Doc.* 8)
style and artistic personality 179, 180, 181
summary of work in Noto 234–5
work on City Hall 173–9, 234 (*Doc.* 2), 235 (*Doc.* 11)
Sirugo, Melchiore, *Baron* 38, 209 (*n.* 58)
Sitwell, Osbert 11, 205 (*n.* 2)
Sitwell, Sacheverell 11, 204, 205 (*n.* 2)
Sladen, Douglas 205 (*n.* 4)
Smith, D. Mack 205 (*n.* 2), 206 (*n.* 12)
Soria, G. B. 131
Sortino 29, 31
Sortino family 36
Sortino, Francesco (Professor) 184, 193, 223 (*n.* 37)
Spain
policy of 27, 40, 42
rule of 11
Stampace Tower 29, 34, 35

Streets (Noto Nuova)
Via S. Agata 240
Via Aurispa 68, 75
Via Bovio 184
Cassaro 75
Via Cavour 68, 75, 99, 240
changes of names 75, 214 (*n.* 33)
58, 79, 107, 142
Corso Vittorio Emanuele 58, 68, 69, 75, 79, 80 (*pl.* 31), 81–6 *passim* (*pl.* 37), 91–7 *passim*, 107, 142, 202, 240
Via Dogali 68, 69, 81, 84
Via Ducezio 60, 68, 69, 75, 99 (*pl.* 54b)
Via Galilei 68, 100
Via Garibaldi 101
Via Grimaldi 116 (*pl.* 64)
gutters in streets 240
lowering of streets 77, 79, 80, 83, 101, 160, 214 (*nn.* 46, 47), 238, 240
Viale Marconi 76 (*pl.* 28)
Via Mauceri 100
Via Napoli 72
Via Nicolaci 60, 99
Via Occhipinti 184, 187
pavements 240, 241
Via Rocco Pirri 60, 184, 196, 212 (*n.* 28)
Via Roma 68, 72, 99, 240
Via Ruggiero 68, 97
Via Sallicano 101
Via Sofia 100
street numbers 75
trees in streets 77, 240
Via Umberto 101
width of streets 80–1, 214 (*n.* 48)
Via Zanardelli 68, 81
Stuttgart
Ludwigsburg
Château de Mon Repos 177 (*pl.* 146)
Superga 187
Swinburne, Algernon 99
Syracuse 21, 22, 23, 40, 42, 48, 50, 72, 76, 108, 110, 143, 192, 202, 204, 205 (*n.* 3), 206 (*n.* 15), 223 (*n.* 39), 228 (*Doc.* 7), 229 (*Doc.* 9)
fortifications 228 (*Docs.* 7, 8)
rivalry with Noto 34
State Archives 9

tabernae 122
Tedeschi, Antonino 205 (*nn.* 4, 8), 206 (*n.* 23)
Termini, Asdrubale, *Bishop of Syracuse* 49, 50
Todi 24
Tokyo 25
Tortora, Filippo (*Padre*) 28, 29, 46, 207 (*n.* 7)
description of Noto 54, 205 (*nn.* 4, 5, 8), 206 (*n.* 13), 208 (*n.* 25)
Trapani 21, 167
Tribunal of the Royal Patrimony 49, 51
Trigona family 236 (*Doc.* 9)
palace 99, 118, 139 (*pls.* 84, 85), 181, 201, 242
Turin 12, 145
Palazzo Madama 159

Uzeda, Duke of (Viceroy) 27, 49, 226–7 (Doc. 2), 227 (*Doc.* 4), 228 (*Doc.* 8)

Vaccarini, Giovanni Battista 140, 146
S. Agata, Catania 146–7 (*pl.* 106), 164
S. Giuliano, Catania 167
Val Demone
Vicar General 27
Val di Noto 21 (*map* 1), 22, 31, 205 (*n.* 7)
Vicar General 27
Valladolid 103
Valussi, G. 115
Vance, J (Jnr) 12, 205 (*n.* 5)
Van Dogen, Matthias 150
Vasi, Giuseppe 170
Vauban, Sebastien le Prêtre de 40, 209 (*n.* 66)
Vendicari Tower 33
Veraguas, Duke of, *Viceroy* 49
Versoix 107
Vescovo (Bishop), see Bishop's Palace
Vicars-General 27, 208 (*n.* 16), 226 (*Doc.* 2), 227 (*Doc.* 3)
Vignola, Giacomo Barozzi da 113, 124, 125, 126, 127 (*pl.* 72), 135, 150, 151
Villalpando, J. B. 197
Vitruvius 33, 57, 145, 197, 211 (*n.* 14)
Vittone, Bernardo 126, 145
Vittoria 104
Vizzini 110

Weht, Hans 205 (*n.* 6)
Wittkower, Rudolf 13, 191
Wolff, Christian 125, 184, 191–6 *passim*
theories of 192, 196, 197, 222 (*n.* 37), 223 (*n.* 62)
Wood, John 107
Wren, Sir Christopher 203

Zappata, Marchese
palace of 117